COMMUNISM, POETRY

COMMUNISM, POETRY
COMMUNICATING VESSELS

(INSUBORDINATE WRITINGS 1999-2018)

Darko Suvin

Political Animal Press
Toronto • Chicago

Political Animal Press

www.politicalanimalpress.com

Distributed by the University of Toronto Press

Cataloguing data available from Library and Archives Canada

ISBN 978-1-895131-43-7 (paperback)

ISBN 978-1-895131-46-8 (ebook)

Typeset in Adobe Caslon, designed by Carol Twombly, Brandon Grotesque, designed by Hannes von Döhren, and Gravesend Sans, designed by Rian Hughes

Printed and bound in Canada

Le choix que je suis [The choice that is me]

Jean-Paul Sartre, *L'Être et le néant* (1943)

... [C]ontent warnings serve as advance notification of difficult material.... to enable participants to work effectively with the material. Content warnings should not serve the purpose of avoiding controversial content.

From *MLA Statement on Content Warnings* (2018)

People for the most part (99 per cent of the bourgeoisie, 98 per cent of the liquidators, about 60–70 per cent of the Bolsheviks) don't know how to *think*, they only *learn words by heart*. They've learnt the word "underground." Firmly. They can repeat it. They know it by heart. // But *how* to change *its forms* in a new situation, how to learn and think *anew* for this purpose, this we do not understand.

V.I. Lenin, "Letter to Inessa Armand," transl. A. Rothstein (1913)

Understanding the poem is not only an intellectual act, but a political act.

Frantz Fanon, *The Wretched of the Earth* (1959)

The Beginning is near!

Slogan of Occupy Wall Street people

Paul Gauguin, *D'où Venons Nous / Que Sommes Nous / Où Allons Nous* (1897) translated as *Where Do We Come From? What Are We? Where Are We Going?*

To Fred Jameson:

Almost half a century of friendship, mutual reading, learning from you

With love and solidarity

Contents

ACKNOWLEDGEMENTS & THANKS

Special thanks to my *landsmann* from ex-Yugoslavia Sezgin Boynik, a 2015 interview with whom first nudged me to explicate the image of communicating vessels between historical cognitive forms and politics; who commissioned for a book edited by him an essay that is here much changed as Essay 9; and who read various other essays in this book.

For all matters relating to ex-SFR Yugoslavia, indispensable guides were Boris Buden, Mladen Lazić, Gal Kirn, and Marko Kržan; Ozren Pupovac, together with Ivana Momčilović and Slobodan Karamanić, stimulated my thinking about about its singularities. Many more debts are detailed in my book *Splendours*.

Thanks also to the editors of all periodicals mentioned below who helped much, and especially to Victor Wallis, who improved all essays published in *Socialism and Democracy*. In such first publications, longer thanks to friends who helped with materials and suggestions may be found.

Warm thanks for comments on various stages of the Introduction go to to Boynik, Jameson, and Nenad Jovanović.

First publications of the contents were as follows: essay 1 in *Socialism and Democracy* 16.2 (2002); both parts of essay 2 in *Socialism and Democracy* 16.1 (2002), containing a long note of thanks, especially to Fred Jameson, Tom Kuhn, and Marc Silberman for all their inputs into my Brechtian considerations; essay 3 is a shortened reworking of two essays on terrorism from *Rethinking Marxism* 14.2 (2002) and *Socialism and Democracy* 19.1 (2005); essay 4 in *Critical Quarterly* 57. 2 (2015), but before that in translations into Macedonian, Croatian, and Slovene; essay 5 in www.themontrealreview.com/2009/Power-Without-Violence-A-Lesson-from-Tribal-Communism.php and a later version in Serbian translation in 2013; essay 6 in *Socialism and Democracy* 30.1 (2016), with special acknowledgement of the exchanges with the Novi Sad comrades Gordana Stojaković, Maja Solar, Andrea Jovanović, and Lazar Atanasković, as well as thanks to Eric Canepa, Mladen Lazić, Marcelline Krafchick, and Michael Stöppler; essay 7 in *International Critical Thought* 6.2 (2016); essay 8 in *Minnesota Review* no. 91 (2018), with special thanks to editor Janell Watson and the staff for corrections during my illness. Essay 9 is a radical redoing of the postface to S. Boynik ed., *Coiled Verbal Spring: Devices of Lenin's Language*, Helsinki 2018; essay 10 an even more radical rewrite of passages from an essay of mine in *Arcadia* 5.2 (2017), with thanks to Vladimir Biti, Ivana Perica, Gloria Macmillan, and to my long duration comrade and co-fighter Tom Moylan for his unpublished paper on Bloch and Postmortality.

Introduction: Here Is the Rose*

> The hell of the living is not something future; there is one, it is already present, we live it every day, we shape it together. There are two ways to avoid its suffering. One seems easy for many: to accept hell and participate in it to the point of not seeing it any more. The second is risky, it asks for continuous attention and learning: to search for and know how to recognise who and what, amidst hell, is not hell, and to make it last, and to give it space.
>
> Italo Calvino, *Le città invisibili*, 1972

> Hence arises a possible conflict between what is and what ought to be....
>
> G.W.F. Hegel, Preface to *Philosophy of Right*, 1820

1. Capitalocene and Exodus: "Something Is Missing"

1.0. This book deals with two Twos. The first is the irreconcilable antagonism between the epochal descent of our rulers and societies into savagery – superadding to the daily "normal" violence of exploiting people's labour-power also war, terrorism, and mass misery – and the indignation it sparks in anybody who needs freedom from hunger and stress. The second Two is the friendly and complementary juxtaposition of the two main forces I see as able to counteract the "capitalocene," that is, radical conceptual masters such as Marx, Brecht, Benjamin, Lenin, and Gramsci alongside poets of all ages: *communism and poetry*. In my terms (cf. Suvin "Revelation") the first is a conflict and the second a revelation.

This mutually validating alliance or alloy – to me unexpected though dimly felt as far back as my memory reaches – can also be thought of as communicating vessels of scientific and Surrealist fame: their contents either could chthonically mingle, which led to success, or communication between them broke down, which led to defeat. Both are plebeian and sensual, personal yet also collective activities. Interestingly enough, the great Hesiod traces an affinity between rulers and poet-singers, who should ideally define each other since, even though their expertise is different, both use words to influence and soothe minds of people (vv. 76-103). Within this association, Hesiod sees the rulers as favoured because they add to the gifts of the sweetly talking Muses (v. 966) also those of Zeus, who watches over justice; accepting the stress on justice, we can today no longer stress a privilege of rulers but only that of freedom. I think of freedom and justice, in the shape of a centrally associational democracy, as the indispensable political mediation, the conduit between these containers and their precious liquids.

A good entrance to our Calvinian hell is Bert Brecht's great play *Rise and Fall of the City of Mahagonny*, a 1928 "essay in epic opera." It analyzes an allegorical City of perfect and unbridled heroic individualism, where the values are sturdy eating, drinking, male companionship, sports, and leisure – including heroic prostitutes. But in all of this "something is missing," something sense-giving, meaning-bestowing, and essential for the protagonist representing (a certain view of) Humanity: *Etwas fehlt* (GKA 2: 349-50). Finally, all is swept away in a disaster. True, what was identified here is the worm at the heart of competitive capitalism's apple: how much more needs to be added to envisage the involution into the tightening and even more disastrous web of monopoly and then financial capitalism!

This volume was therefore shaped by what turned out to be an ambitious aim: to elucidate, at least initially but in some probes also more deeply, two complementary and deeply intertwined though empirically different sets of events and existents (I would like to think of this as an instance of Badiou's dialectics centered on the primacy of the Two as against the One – see his *Theory* 22, and cf. *Of an Obscure*). First, the set that is being *imposed upon* our lives, that renders it hellish, in brief: *what is the reader supposed to be against*. Second, the set that by contraries defines what we lack and indicates a really possible if most difficult way out, in brief: *what is the reader supposed to be for*. Both these sets must be understood, but the second is axiologically privileged for it approximates a Spinozist Truth that is the measure of itself and of its contrary. Their depth common denominator is "*what happens in* and so to speak *to* the production process" (Balibar 30), but I would add *what happens around and makes possible* a production process – which involves not only all material goods but also, and in decisive ways, the people who produce and are produced, the politics of production. Politics for me means – as Russo formulated it about the 1968 movement – "all endeavours that aim at deconstructing the ritual hierarchies of the social world and freeing the subjective potential of anyone in any field" (140). An example: the coming about of a worker violently "freed from" all possessions except his labour-power; or contrariwise, lineaments of worker disalienation in a system of Workers' Councils running the economy (cf. the essay "Communism Can"). Prominently, to understand both the pro and contra sets, we have to face not only the central 19th-century or Marxian theme of capital but also the central 20th-century or Leninist theme of revolution, "really obtaining socialism," and its downfall.

My thesis is that the debilitating Left melancholy, where the Freudian melancholic *does not know what he has lost* (cf. Dean "Communist" 81-82 – as opposed to the necessary but also, in all sane cases, limited mourning) and that prevents a fertile analysis of the first or "capitalism running mad" theme, largely stems from the loss of alternative horizon consequent upon the "downfall of the alternative block" theme. Any present amputating its significant past – say the American, French, October, Yugoslav or Chinese Revolution, regardless of the full success or failure of this past – has no emancipatory future. Sensing this in an initially dim way, I have in these last decades pursued a two-pronged research, analysing some salient aspects of crazed capitalism (war, including "war on terror") but also, and at greater length, just what happened in ex-SFR Yugoslavia, and then in ex-USSR, and what were Brecht's causal "events behind the events" there. The negative set may begin with the question what are the forces that got us all to such infernal dungeons from what now seem the halcyon days of Welfare State and its elixir of life, full employment (cf. Jameson). However, the positive set looking for a radical alternative must delve into the – apparently different and secondary – matter of post-revolutionary plebeian democracy and its relationship to the dominant form of the State. This is a crucial political reconsideration, without which the alternative imaginary horizon of the Left cannot be persuasively constituted, so that it will remain stymied in impotent quiescence or inconclusive anarchism. Work on politico-economic contradictions after the revolutions and on their outcomes may enable us not only to understand why and how these past revolutions failed, but primarily how to use both their strongest aspects and mistakes for moving on today.

This book is not at all a survey of poets that could be considered communist. What I present here is rather a series of epistemological probes (I much mistrust ontologising) with spirally recurring leitmotifs. "Essay" originally meant a probe or tryout, it is a major cognitive form from Bacon and Montaigne through Hazlitt, Heine, and Marx to the great efflorescence of the "long" 20th century, structured by the wish to explain historical reality and its latencies. It is an experimental form cognate to the scientific experiment, though opposed – and therefore complementary – to the "objective" form modern science chose. I found that dealing in urgent historical matters is most usefully to be presented as essays in their historical sequence. The chronology melds results with the ways they were arrived at; I have therefore supplied each unit with its date: "I stamp my writings with their history, as calves on a ranch," said Brecht.

1.1. With perhaps a quarter of this book explicitly about poetry, this volume can only have building blocks towards an initial hypothesis about it. Yet I have been delighting in and learning from poetry as long as I can remember, and had fortunately an education where much of it had to be learned by heart and recited in various languages from the age of 5 on. When I was 21, I started writing poetry. However, while penning some student texts on Laforgue, Eliot, and other contemporary Anglophone poetry, and translating from that time on a lot from half a dozen (later more) languages, I did not continue to write about poetry, but turned first to drama and theatre, where I also dealt with Brecht's verse, and then to science fiction and narrative. However, I was from the word go deeply persuaded that literature, theatre, and arts are not only most pleasurable but to boot centrally cognitive pursuits: they enable people to understand their world/s. So I was glad to find in Badiou – often my favourite person to disagree with – a fulminant encapsulation I fully share: "literature can name a real to which politics remain closed" (*Peut-on* 31); and I would add "to which philosophy remains closed," which he accepts only when philosophy gets to be impure and secondary to poetry, about 1880-1960. Philosophy's building blocks are concepts; literature's building blocks are a mixture of impure concepts and sensual spacetime topologies which can never be reduced to a conceptual paraphrase (itself useful when handled gingerly, as every sensible critic knows).

My lack of research about verse poetry was not due to loss of interest. I felt from my youth on that it was a tremendous and beauteous mystery, a siren song that might well swallow me hide and hair, and I had other fish to fry. Thus it was only by the way of renewed commitment to own verse writing and of metaphor studies 20 years later that I again approached this mystery. In the studies excerpted here, I was struck – in particular, when I adjoined Fortini to Brecht, who had always insisted on *how* to present the *what* – by the resonances between a shapely proposition in word art (or other arts) and shapely possibilities of personal life, individual and collective: that is, between communism and poetry. To begin with "the poem is an exercise in intransigence" (Badiou, *Age* 23), that is, in radically ruthless consistency and autotelic self-government – and so is communism (my C1, see "15 Theses"). Both believe, with Kant, that a thousand years of something being the case does not prove it is right.

So, although this Introduction does not delve further into poetry,[1] I take for this book a cue also from two poetic saws.

The first is the locally famous 1846 Croatian epic by Ivan Mažuranić, *Smrt Smail-age Čengića (The Death of Aga Smail of the Čengićes)*, about a Southern Slavic revolt against a Turkish feudal lord. In it there's a gnomic distich:

> Dobar pastijer jer što kaže inom
> I sam svojim potvrdjuje činom

(non-poetic translation: For the good shepherd whatever he utters/ By his action doth confirm)

I therefore thought my argument that *poetry is essential for justice and communism* should be given whatever support I could find in actual verse to be presented in this book, so that my locution, illocution, and perlocution would fit each other. I first envisaged an anthology of such verse, but this would have burst the bounds of allowed volume. Thus, being what is in Canada called "a published poet," I have interspersed this book with some poems – in two cases translations – of mine after each chapter. They are also supplied with a version of dating (with no direct relation to that of the essays, except for the poem "Zum Geleit").

The second saw is from Hegel's Preface to his *Philosophy of Right,* a fairly uninspiring document except for two places. One is in my epigraph above. The second one is where he varies the ancient adage from Aesop rendered in Latin as *hic Rhodus, hic salta* – literally "here is Rhodes island, here jump," meaning "prove your point here and now" – by adding a quibble on *rhodos*, meaning in Greek also the rose, as "Here is the rose, here dance!" (Marx cites this toward the beginning of his *18th Brumaire*).

This connects seamlessly to the famous slogan of the workers' movement "bread and roses," coined by Rose Schneiderman, a socialist feminist IWW leader of the great Lawrence MA textile workers' strike of 1912. She said: "What the woman who labors wants is the right to live, not simply exist – the right to life as the rich woman has the right to life, and the sun and music and art.... The worker must have bread, but she must have roses, too." (see Schneiderman) Poetry is for me about bread and roses: sustenance and beauty facing death, as the immigrant women of 40 ethnic groups faced the bayonets of Massachusetts militiamen. I regret I haven't developed my essayistic prose sufficiently to dare calling this book "Bread and Roses."

1.2. Both revolutionary democracy and communism, the two great attempts at collective power "of the people by the people and for the people," have led to some violent catastrophes (cf. Rancière). This was not at all expected by their heralds, partisans, and martyrs: quite the contrary, these breaks were dreamt of in stark opposition to and emancipation from servitude, humiliation, and lesion.[2] I believe the catastrophic turn came about because full political decision-making in the community by all citizens (democracy) and full economic decision-making within the production by all workers (communism) were sundered instead of fused. If and when fused, they remain the *only* way out of the present anti-utopian and counterrevolutionary horizons. Thus we need to discuss the lessons of the past for the future, and look at why and how the fusion should and could have come about, and why it did not.

"Socialist" or properly speaking communist revolutions against capital have in their first historical round, Hobsbawm's "short twentieth century" of 1917–89, failed to reach their own horizons, which also entails they have pragmatically failed. There were heaven-storming hopes, even great and memorable successes alongside mountains of dead, but the revolutions finally did not overcome the formidable internal and external obstacles which we can in one word call *the capital* – outside and inside the countries of revolution. How can we begin summarising the lessons of that failure? In three ways, I believe: by reconsidering the political economics of the supposed "transition period" between the revolution and its goal of a fully just communist society, following the cruces of accumulation and planning; by reconsidering our epistemology, which also means our methodology – that is, how to understand a multiply contradictory history; and by reconsidering the indispensable nexus between communism and democracy suggested above. To all of this, the delightful lessons of poetry are to be added, and well stirred in.

As to method, I believe verbal indicatives are indispensable but insufficient unless accompanied with suggestions or projects of inherent alternative possibilities as optative conjunctives of desire. There is no critical stance without the foil of utopia as eutopia, the good place – and at that, without Bloch's concrete utopia, in constant feedback with reality as opposed to a myth of imaginary achievement. A strategic use of polarising oppositions is indicated, while avoiding black and white religiosity.

2. Disalienation of Labour as Self-determination

2.0. I consider integral *self-government from below* in all human affairs, meshing workers' control of the workplace and civic associational politics outside the workplace, our only hope to oppose financial turbocapitalism as well as its turn towards neo-fascism. I have approached this thoroughly radical democracy or democratic communism in writings about utopianism and political epistemology (collected in *Defined, Darko,* and *In Leviathan's*) and tried out its yield in two case studies, the lengthy *Splendour* and the compact overview of *Lessons*. In this vein are here the theoretical overview of "15 Theses," arrived at when discussing SFR Yugoslavia by opposing the "really existing" post-Leninist rule to the emancipatory project of the young Marx, and a revisitation with provisional summing up in "Communism Can."

A kindred matter of more general scope is *power-cum-violence*, omnipresent in this book but not articulated as a separate argument except by contraries, as in the essay on "Power without Violence" and whenever freedom or emancipation are discussed (see also note 1).

From many matters I could not consider here, two mega-devices of disciplining radical plebeian discontent that come urgently to mind are capitalist technology – also a huge multiplier of violence and domination – and identity politics; I address both briefly in the "Capitalism" essay. Here I wish to mention the aspect of extensive and relatively long-duration *planning*, without which technology – whether as alienating force or wrenched around by communism toward emancipation of both worker and consumer – cannot exist. All the mass media heavy drum-fire against planning for the last century is merely a smoke-screen for leaving planning to the large corporations and their carving up of the market as well as to governments controlled by them and spending taxpayers' money. Best proof: US government spending rose from 8.2% of GNP in 1913 to 38.1% in 1977, while during World War II it peaked at nearly 50% (see Best and Connolly 32–40, 207); immediately after the 2008 shock, "military keynesianism" reached a peacetime peak – for now – in 2009-10 at 42.5% (https://tradingeconomics.com/united-states/government-spending-to-gdp). A communist political programme would have to plan a much more responsible use of technology and simultaneously how to reshape it to its own needs, ferrying it towards disalienation inside each workplace and towards eco-sustainability outside of it. To the contrary, "real socialist" use of technology, from the USSR to present-day China as a rule did not do so. Lenin necessarily took his cue for economic organising and industrialising from the central planning introduced in all major capitalist States during World War I, especially the German one whose efficiency he much admired, and "the war economy remained the basic model of the Soviet planned economy" (Hobsbawm 9). This super-productivist economism determining politics for a time beat not yet fully integrated capitalism at its own game, but it had the downside of being totally unfit for industrial and civic democracy.

2.1. I proceed from the Archimedean fulcrum of Marx's anthropology of labour and alienation in societal life. He did not work out a theory of political disalienation of labour beyond some precious and central theses about revolution and proletarian power (see Feenberg, especially 51–60). Still, in Marxian doctrine disalienation would be based on what might be called the organisation of use-value politics within people's self-government:

> In fact, however, when the limited bourgeois form is stripped away, what is wealth other than the universality of individual needs, capacities, pleasures, productive forces, etc., created through universal exchange? . . . The absolute working-out of [man's] creative potentialities, with no presupposition other than the previous historic development, which makes this totality of development, i.e., the development of all human powers as such the end in itself, not as measured on a predetermined yardstick? Where he does not reproduce himself in one specificity, but produces his totality? Strives not to remain something he has become, but is in the absolute movement of becoming? (Marx, *Grundrisse* 488)

Thus, Marx's key category of "productive forces" ought to be looked at, as against economism, as "the term designating the sum-total of the resources for liberation available to a given society" (Marcuse, *From Luther* 213) – and the most important "machine [or] instrument of production [is] the working class itself" (Gramsci, *Ordine* 134, reprinted in Horvat et al. eds. 232). In that vein, "the creative transformation of nature (labor) and the collective self-regulation of society (politics)" are firmly linked, so that the disjuncture of production and politics is counterproductive (Burawoy 83; cf. Wood 19 and passim). Their separation is a quintessentially capitalist move, a new thing under the sun of history stemming from the desire to evade any and all societal regulation in order to ensure their sectarian quest for profits. This was taken over by "really obtaining socialist" economism and productivism, which at best reduces socialism to the labour process and relations within it, isolated from the democratic control of society from below.

After his early writings, Marx focused on the analysis of labour-power and capital as the strategic way of understanding emancipation, and refused politics as a ploy of exploiters. Yet in so doing he assumed that associational democracy would be consubstantial with an emancipated labour process. We have learned that politico-ideological emancipation is just as necessary within and for the process of overcoming class society, and that it must proceed as a parallel, mass self-education process if the reorganisation of production is to come fully about. Unfortunately, the practice of the endangered and then ossified USSR belied the strongly emancipative aspect of Lenin's theory and abandoned politics exclusively to the domain of Party/State rule. Inside the European left this stance was countered only by the "council communism" of Pannekoek and Korsch, most useful as developed by Gramsci's uniting it with post-Lenin political struggle. Even Lukács's reappropriation of Marx for the analysis of production as reification (in *Geschichte*) shared the messianic illusion, as he later phrased it, that the revolution in power will automatically abolish societal alienation. "Western Marxism" then stressed the reification, having learned from experience that messianic confidence in the revolution, the Party or even the industrial proletariat is by itself insufficient and can turn pernicious. As Bloch once phrased it, behind the *citoyen* came the bourgeois: God help us, who is coming behind the comrade?

The most tenable hypothesis is, in late Althusser's language – following on Lenin, Mao, and Gramsci – that <u>*the relationships of production*</u>, focused by and on class struggles, <u>*have strategic precedence over productive forces*</u> (Althusser 56 and 240–45). The "relations of production" are simultaneously an essential factor within material productive forces and a hinge to the class and political factors outside material production: these two factors participate, in different ways, in what we categorise as economics and politics, and to call either only economic or only political leads to grievous error. This is true though occulted in capitalism, which is shamelessly based on tyrannical government in the workplace, which "moulds the hierarchies that govern the entire collective life" (Russo 141). It was foregrounded in "socialist" societies where "[a] defining feature... is the fusion of the apparatuses of the workplace with those of the State" (Burawoy 113).

Within such a fusion, self-management poses central questions for a radical democracy. First of all, can the relation between economic enterprises and the State be rethought around disalienating self-government? Clearly, ***self-determination*** (Marcuse, *One* 251–52) is broader than the somewhat bureaucratic term of self-management that does not clearly connote the radical liberatory aims and horizon of collective emancipation for one and all. This centrally needs an integral civic democracy, "economic" and "political," intertwining with self-management in the workplace like a double helix, but encompassing both the traditional negative and positive freedoms, in the manner of F.D. Roosevelt's "four freedoms" (see Passerin d'Entrèves, 282–305, especially 292–93). The negative freedoms protect individuals, the positive ones constitute popular sovereignty. This fusion constitutes a radical plebeian democracy, as the institutional form of what I mean here by communist politics.

I use as shorthand for people whose interests and practice are opposed to the exploiters and power-holders the term "plebeian," as Brecht did (also Babeuf and Bakhtin, and now Garcìa Linera). I could also have used – just as metaphorically – Marx's term "proletarian."[3] However, it seemed to me that the first designation was not only less abused in history and less tied to the industrial workers of the 19th-century type, but that it also stressed the element of civic opposition to the State power of a ruling class rather than the equally important position within the production process of goods. In a wider sense, I would mean by either of these terms a congeries of social classes and/or fractions – in propitious cases a historical block – defined as working for their subsistence and not having had political power: the working people (called that in S.F.R. Yugoslavia: *radni narod*). The most important groups composing this plebs would be women (except those from the ruling class), working peasants, intellectual labourers, the old manual working class, and the hugely growing fractions oscillating between precarious and outcast on the margins of capitalist social space (cf. Žižek's "How," 226). The plebeians are the only societal segment whose interests demand a thoroughgoing and radical democracy.

3. Introductory on Communism

3.1. What are we talking about when we say communism, how can we begin making sense of it? First of all, we have to unpack the term. The chthonic roots of communism are, no doubt, in the cry of suffering and of indignation that accompanies class society as its dark twin, in the deepest desires for the reversal and subversion when we must live in an "inverted world" of injustice. In that sense communism is as immortal as that society; when repressed, it flows as a subterranean Karst river. However, the water becomes analysable only when it begins to spring out above earth, when the cry is articulated into an organised movement. Organised or articulated communism can be ***a locus***, ***an orientation*** *for a movement*, and *a horizon* (cf. Suvin "Locus"). Puzzlingly but richly, each of these implies and needs the other two: a consubstantial trinity, each of whose members may yet be approached and used independently for some purposes and in some situations.

Communism as *horizon* is the future Earthly Paradise of a classless society, a society of equals: possessing equal right to define and participate in common collective projects for well-being and happiness. In it oppositions will not be dealt with antagonistically, through murder and hunger: not by pistol but by pencil, as Brecht says in the nearest approximation to it he allowed himself to pen, the Prologue to the *Caucasian Chalk Circle* – which also sketches the ideal role of the intellectual as keeper of collective historical memory for crucial present discussions in Arkadi Cheidze, the Singer-presenter of the play. As all horizons, it is orienting, often inspiring, and always unattainable, for it moves with the viewer and pursuer oriented toward it. As long as there is such a pursuer, the horizon cannot be extinguished.

Communism as *locus* is any real society proposing to be largely or even asymptotically utopian or non-antagonistic (harmonious, as the Chinese "communist party" hypocrites today say) – that is, radically reducing exploitation and ignorance, developing satisfactory work, equality of rights, education, health services, and just opportunities for all. It could be, as all classical socialists and communists believed, a first absolutely necessary step towards a disalienated life of people in a community. However, this holds IF and only if it, a/ is not stifled by poverty and aggression, and b/ does not pretend to be the oxymoron of a finally reached horizon, an illusion that also necessarily grows into a religion and a lie (Nietzsche can be useful here). This locus existed in partial and always endangered ways in the first phase after the Soviet, the Yugoslav, the Chinese, and probably the Vietnamese Revolutions; I believe it still exists, in a most threatened way, in Cuba. Yet most unfortunately, as a rule it soon became a façade for struggles between a new class formation, an oligarchy developing from the elite Party reaches and some fringes, and the working people. Since the imperfect attempts of Trotsky and (better) of Mao to "fire on the headquarters" failed, the communist locus was finally destroyed by a combination of relentless outside capitalist pressure and inner hollowing out or corruption.

Today, bereft of locus, we still might have – if we don't lose the faith – the *orientation*, a vector leading out of our quite anti-utopian and catastrophic locus of capitalist descent into violent oppression towards the horizon of a critical eutopia. Orientation means, etymologically, turning toward the Orient of the rising Sun, the source of light and warmth, indeed of all life. Within Brecht's central category of bearing or stance (*Haltung*), the orientation toward a communist horizon as a "determinate negation of capitalism and its concrete forms" needs to be fused with determinate ways of cognition to have a chance for the movement for justice, militant and triumphant, to succeed (Toscano 203-04). Among these ways of cognising a privileged one would also be the scientific one, if purged from "objectivist" scientism.[4] However, in this volume I focus on artistic or poetic cognising, including essayistic forms: on *a close alliance of – and mutual learning between – communism and poetry*.

The orientation towards Bloch's "concrete utopia" is today our minimum requirement, without which all talk of communism should cease. But for a proper collective orientation, that is, a *movement* with this orientation, we need what Lenin urged: a cultural revolution. This means many things, but to begin with at least two: a rebuilding on the basis of an updated Marx for a Post-Fordist age and amid a most dangerously rotting capitalism; as well as a clear idea how to organise, that is, what to take from Lenin and what not. Anarchism, noble as it is in many ways in people like Kropotkin, and with which we should practice fraternal solidarity in its radical refusal of any oppression, will get us nowhere: as we have seen in these last 20 years from Seattle and Genua on.

This orientation reaches for the self-preservation of humanity and its close interaction with nature, to be reached through radical self-determination on all levels, by means of peace and disalienated labour. To be or not to be, that is the question.

As to what to keep from Marx and what not, I argue in this book that we cannot do without, at least, the cognitive notions of: social relationships of production; classes and the unquenchable contradictions arising from capital's expropriation of labour-power; and the necessity, necessary for the naked survival of our species and planet, of swerwing toward a radically new society rid of antagonistic classes. However, following Brecht's proposal in one of the little "Mr Keuner" stories that "we" – Marxists, communists – should compile, "in the interests of propaganda, a list of problems we consider quite unsolved" (GKA 18: 451), I would propose that the cognitions of and in Marxism be divided into three groups:

- what Marxism claims to know (with reasonable certainty, sufficient as guide for action until revised);
- what Marxism doesn't know (whether the bulk of its practitioners is conscious of that or not);
- what Marxism is not interested in knowing (in this epoch; and for the cases that might become of interest in the blue distances of future, this may no longer be Marxism but some sublating successor).

As long as something like this is not heeded, any Marxist or communist group remains a Church or sect.

3.2. The plagues of capitalism were for a long time mainly hidden in the slums of the "North" (meaning North America, western Europe, Oceania, Japan, and the Asian "Little Tigers") and in the far-off South of the world. True, poets and thinkers whom existence had brought into contact with the exploited masses have always warned us, in the words of Césaire, that this is a decaying civilisation which cannot cope either with the metropolitan or with the colonial dispossessed or proletariat. These ills and dangers are now growing obvious and all-pervasive: nobody – not the middle class, already reduced to utter dependency, not the youth, reduced to precarious begging for crumbs, not even middle management and the majority of scientists – will be spared. Capitalism has greatly furthered the destruction of all qualities, the capillary savaging and alienation of all areas of daily life, including science and the arts; and quantitatively, a reduction of life-span or outright killing of millions through immiseration, wars, and attendant evitable illnesses. On the horizon are further dirty wars, with unchecked use of uranium and phosphorus weapons, possibly nuclear ones too, and a world war against China is on the drawing board. Quite certainly, an ecological collapse is a matter of a few decades, its symptoms are already present. These ills are not only horrendous, worse than anything even the degenerate loci of "real socialism" brought about, but also systemic: they flow out of the central and all-consuming urge of capitalism for vampiric maximisation of profit. They cannot be reformed.

But why not call the alternative "socialism"? As Saussure taught us, all designations are sociohistorically arbitrary: but some are less arbitrary than others. The historical corruption of partly and potentially communist loci after, say, 1917 means that the terms of socialism and communism both became a cover-up for increasing repression of impulses from the people and for inefficiency, and are by now sullied by horrendous abuse. Indeed, socialism might seem to have an advantage, as it could be associated with clearly beneficent changes in the Scandinavian societies or post-1945 Britain. But these have not only been equally wiped out, but also turned out to be cover-ups for imperialist dominion and warmongering, exporting killings out of sight. So to my mind, as far as historical record and opprobrium goes, there is nothing to choose between these two terms. I prefer communism as the name for our final horizon because of the greater potential fertility of the term, based on its greater philosophical and historical depth. Communism is the only radical – that is, systemic – alternative to, the only counter-system able to face up to capitalism: "the communist combination of emancipation and egalitarianism is unique" (Dean, "Communist" 92). Socialism means either a halfway house or a wishy-washy compromise with no lasting consequence in order to prevent radical revolution.

However, what the movements and eventually liberated areas on the road to a communist horizon will call themselves seems to me best left to the concrete contingencies.

Works Cited in Introduction

See in *Works Cited in this Book* the following titles, by Author surname plus (when the author has several titles) first "headword" or identifying syntagm in the title:

Part 1

Badiou, *The Age, Of an Obscure, Peut-on, Theory;* Balibar; Brecht; Dean, "Communist Desire"; Hesiod, *Theogonia*; Jameson, "Utopia"; Lukács, *Geschichte;* Rancière, "Interview"; Russo; Schneiderman.

Parts 2-4

See also Brecht, Dean, and Russo from Part 1.

Althusser; Badiou, "The Communist Idea"; Best & Connolly; Burawoy; Feenberg; Fineschi; Hegel, Preface; Hobsbawm; Horvat et al eds.; Lukács, *Geschichte;* Marcuse *From Luther, One-Dimensional;* Marx, *Grundrisse;* Passerin; Suvin, "An Approach," *Darko*, "Death," *Defined,* "Epistemological," "On the Horizons," *In Leviathan's,* "Locus," "Revelation," *Splendour,* "Two"; Toscano; Wood; Žižek "How."

POEMS 0

I seem insane to you. I'm not sorry.
But tell me your reasons. "Because you go on
About justice, because you were always bewitched
By the Great Goddess." Indeed i do, indeed
I was, i am. This folly, all ye godheads
& sea-nymphs, may it never leave me!

14109

Drummer, drum on & have no fear
& kiss the bare-breast Liberty!
This is the whole of science & art
The sum of all philosophy.

Drum & inveigle the drowsy people
Send the snake's hiss & roar of lions,
One step in front, ready to die,
This is the sum of art & science.

This is old Karl's dialectics
Of all philosophy it is the Summa.
I've understood it because i was endangered
& saw the Revolution one Summer.

700

MEHR LICHT

So go now *canzonetta mia*, into
This cruel world where you lack common
Sense, be non-profit but profitable, non-sentimental
Always sympathetic to the suffering & exploited
Courageously try to bring some more light
Air for smogless breathing, food
For starving stomachs & ganglia.
                                        Be
Common, communist, for the commons, sensual,
Be of the part of writers & readers, the bombed &
The starved, the Four Whales that hold up
The world: women, workers, lovers, liberators.
Your dress may be tattered but smile upon them
Ironically & cheerfully   announcing & denouncing
Exclaiming & proclaiming WHOA:
        We have
        Our alternative.

281018

Glossary: canzonetta mia = my little song, Dante's phrase
Mehr licht = more light, reputed dying words of Goethe

1

Capitalism Means/Needs War (1998-2001)*

When, when, Peace, will you, Peace? ...
That piecemeal peace is poor peace. What pure peace allows
Alarms of wars, the daunting wars, the death of it?

G.M. Hopkins, "Peace," 1879

War is distinguishable from murder and massacre only when restrictions are established on the reach of battle.

Michael Walzer, 1977

mékhris téo katákeisthe...
...en eirénei dè dokeîte
êsthai, atàr pólemos gaîan hápasan ékhei
(How long will you go on being inert?... In peaceful sloth
You are lying down, while war keeps command of the whole land.)

Kallinos, after 700 B.C.E.

Counter-revolution by the center against the periphery
Blood on stone   blood & stones
Thou shalt not get out from under world banks   fish mouth silently
This is Moses & the prophets.

D. Suvin, "Le Ceneri di Tito," 1999

0. Introductory: War?

0. Amid systematic obfuscation, I wish to recall Dorothy Dinnerstein's great confession of faith:

> … we must try to understand what is threatening to kill us off as fully and clearly as we can.… And… to fight what seems about to destroy everything earthly that you love – to fight it… intelligently, armed with your central resource, which is passionate curiosity – is for me the human way to live until you die. (viii)

I shall be unable here to go, as she did, into the murky psychic depths of what drives the lust to power, profit, and killing. These are initial soundings, to limn what is afoot.

The overriding question for today is: What may be workable, embodied answers to the present stunted rationality of wars, of a capitalism unable to survive in peacetime? How are we to delineate the new collective body, the new sensorium humanity needs for survival? For if we don't at least guess at the alternatives, approximate them, try to forecast them, pave the way for them, help – however initially – to make the alternatives possible or maybe bring them about, capitalism may well destroy all that humanity has achieved in the last 1000 years or longer. A radical change in reasoning is needed for us to use Marx's great insight that no theory or method can be understood without the practice of social groups to which it corresponds.

We have to find our answers in action. Vico argued that whatever we cannot intervene into, we cannot understand: in a more elastic way, I would argue that *what we can imagine intervening into, we can begin understanding*. In other words: for action we need a clear horizon and possible vectors toward it. The horizon for our opposition seems clear: only use-values can stand up to capitalist unequal exchange. Ancient designations for the life-furthering use-values were compassion, indignation, and love: they are today gathered up into communism and poetry. We need also to realise that there is no poetry without communism, and no communism without poetry. All poets know this is their encompassing horizon, often in fantastic metamorphoses; few communists apart from Marx, Morris, Brecht, Césaire or Neruda have allowed their suspicion to flower. When sundered, what we get are caricatures which compromise the potential horizon of either.

My initial question on how to at least begin understanding the spreading blight of warfare in all of its forms, literal and metaphoric, may today be only answered fragmentarily, since it is one aspect of a consubstantial unholy trinity: mass murders, mass prostitution, mass drugging. For it is the case that by mass prostitution one could mean not only that of the sexual services – in majority female – but also, as Balzac did, the prostitution of the mind – of intellectuals, in majority male – making death-bringing commodities seem sexy. It is also the case that drugging is the inflecting of the mind to momentary euphoria bringing death, so that one can include in it identical effects wrought without pharmaceutical substances, such as most PR and the prevailing Disneyfication of consumer virtues. And finally, by mass murder could be meant all the victims of starvation and poverty-induced illnesses, as well as of the drugs. I have tried to indicate their inextricable links in previous writings (cf. "On Cognition as Art and Politics" and other essays in my *Defined*); here I concentrate on war only.

To begin with, I shall cull from my readings on war a provisional, operative definition: *war is a coherent sequence of conflicts, involving physical combats between large organised groups of people that include the armed forces of at least one state, which aim to exercise political and economic control over a given territory*. One or more fights or skirmishes, even between groups of people, do not qualify. The aim of war was originally the forcible expropriation in favour of a given social class (sometimes tribal or ethnic group[1]) of booty, land (or other productive forces), and/or labour-power from the vanquished: "A simple definition of a warrior might be a person who survives by taking what others have or have produced" (Love and Shanklin 283). However, in developed class societies war has also always been *ultima ratio regum*, a means to evade inner revolutionary tension by outer conquest, while in a multi-State system other indirect and intermediary (but crucial) aims may be added, such as securing advantages for coming tensions and conflicts – e.g. dominion over sea lanes or oil resources – and the destruction of commodities and people.

It ought to be noted that the demarcation line to mafioso gang clashes, indicated by my "*that include*..." clause, grows increasingly thin as unchecked private wealth balloons and the moral legitimacy of many States converges toward zero: practically all wage undeclared wars using civilian killings; all States are today "rogue States" to different degrees, most clearly in the undeclared US wars on Vietnam and Serbia bombing them back into the Stone Age; terror killings cannot be differentiated morally but only by scale (cf. Virilio and Lotringer 25-27, Lens). The ratio of military to civilian casualties in wars has in the course of 20th century "progressed" from 8:1 to 1:8 (eight civilians killed for each combatant), while the fighting units diversified from regular armies into paramilitary groups, police forces, mercenaries, local warlords and "pure" criminal gangs (Kaldor, *New* 8). It is by now received Western media wisdom to treat the ex-Yugoslavia civil wars or the Russo-Chechen war as conflicts between exploitative gangs in power, but the same could be said for both Gulf Oil Wars and for the NATO-Serbia War. This means that Clausewitz's restriction of war to the politics of State-like entities reflects only the historical rise of capitalist nation-States which arrogated to themselves the monopoly of organised violence through their armed forces in exchange for "civil" pacification through police (cf. Weber). The monopoly was always threatened by gang and revolutionary violence, and there are indications this "State dominance period" may have been limited to 1600-1990. The privatisation of violence, a logical result of the corporate enforcing of economic privatisation at the expense of State authority, also means that the line between the "policing operations" of the army and a technoscientifically beefed-up police (and then private militias and illegal gangs) grows almost indistinguishable. Nonetheless most major armed conflicts – defined ad hoc as "battle-related deaths of at least 1000 people" (SIPRI 1998: 17) – are still conducted by State or aspiring proto-State entities.

1. War and Classes

In the 20th century probably more people have been murdered in mass killings than in all of world history up to 1900. Around one hundred million people have been slaughtered by bomb and bayonet, and probably billions by imposed starvation and maladies of poverty – the class war of the few ever more rich against the many ever more poor. Tuberculosis, the malady testifying to misery, is back in force, and even the plague has returned in India. The excuse that, *proportionately* to the number of people alive, the century is no worse than any other may or may not be statistically correct, but it is irrelevant. If we have the knowhow to ensure the survival of more people beyond their twelfth month, then we surely must use it to ensure their survival to their (our) natural end. Each person is a body in hope and pain, in theological terms in direct one-to-one relation to divinity. No proportions apply.

The first materialist rule in societal affairs is to ask of major events and trends in whose interest do they happen, *cui bono*? I believe there is an iron rule according to which those societal classes in whose interest these events did happen have in fact brought them about – in however direct or indirect, unicausal or overdetermined ways. In the Malthusian world of keeping poverty safe for the rulers, war presents many advantages for them and for the State they rule, but at a minimum it always has at least three systematic and consubstantial objectives. The first one is huge new profits, buttressing an always endangered economy; the second one, mass destruction of commodities, to match the mass production that cannot be disposed of in a pauperised world and to enforce development of new technologies able to kill more people and dispense with more people as workers. A few more words might be useful to discuss the third objective, keeping population – and especially the poor, humiliated, and marginalised, the threatening masses – down.

Summarising immemorial ruling-class practice, Adam Smith had coolly observed that "The demand for men, like that for any other commodity, necessarily regulates the production of men" (80); and Marx supplied the decisive understanding why this demand leads within the capitalist mode of production to waves of (for capitalists) surplus population through periodical waves of higher salaries, which population is then in the next – our present

– wave redundant (cf. *Kapital. MEW* 25: chap. 13 and 14, esp. 228-33, and *Theorien* 2: 569-72). War is a prime technology of *population control*, and – if we have forgotten the lessons of the World Wars – the last 20 years teach us that its role in modern class struggles should be accorded much more attention. For obviously, the present Post-Fordist social system does not need even approximately as many producers as Welfare State Fordism did. To the contrary: since the rise of living standards caused by Leninism plus the Keynesian response to it has led to overproduction of people, they have to be over-destroyed (cf. the splendid book by George). Consumers are still needed, but the poorer ones – non-"Whites," most women, the very old and very young – don't count for much: "Nearly two-thirds of the world's population is basically written off as far as foreign investment is concerned" (Tabb 22)! One average North American citizen consumes 13 times more energy than one Chinese and 1300 times more than a Bangladeshi: in direct proportion, the US media count carefully their own body-bags but not the dead of its bombing and starving out.[2] All statistics we have are inadequate because the indirect effects of wars will kill people in Vietnam or Iraq – and in the USA – for generations to come. But even inadequate, the statistics are revealing: in Vietnam, ca. 60,000 US soldiers vs. over 3,000.000 Vietnamese killed; in the first Iraq War, a few dozen NATO soldiers vs. 1,200,000 to 1,500.000 Iraqi dead of bombing or the subsequent embargo. In the vein of Swift's *Modest Proposal*, I can propose that for the rulers of our globe, the corporate-military complex, major demographic bloodletting among the poor is most welcome (more than a touch of racism may be found here). At the very least, there is no reason to spend serious money on preventing it – in wars (Angola, Rwanda, Bosnia, and more to come), epidemics, terminal drugging, or endemic famines. About (organised!) starvation alone, cautious international sources speak of some 40 million people dying from its immediate consequences each year, while "about 500 million are chronically malnourished," that is, on the way to dying soon, and a further 800+ million in "absolute poverty," that is, bordering on famine and dying a bit more slowly (Drèze-Sen 35, *Human...1996* 20, idem *1998*). War, with its attendant politico-ecological catastrophes, such as hundreds of thousands of refugees as well as delayed killings by toxic ingredients of the explosives used and by not yet exploded mines and bombs, much accelerates such "population control" (see Thompson, and cf. the satirically sharpened but serious arguments in *Report* 72-75).

The cannon fodder or mortified meat in wars, prostitution, and drugging, the mass casualties, are as a rule people marginal to "White" patriarchal capitalism: the poor, the "colored," women. "Lower" class, race as well as gender, are expendable, though spoken of with nauseatingly sentimental hypocrisy: and especially when these categories overlap in, say, Black volunteers for the US armed forces or prostitutes displaced into big cities (cf. A. Davis). "Colored, sexed, and laboring persons" are denied epistemological visibility and thus political agency (Haraway 32, and cf. 26-30), they have traditionally not been

Cartesian and Lockean "individuals" – who were, before the onset of counterrevolutionary hypocrisy in the 19th century, forthrightly defined as those who have possessions. The blended out – the unemployed, the "criminal," and the female people – bear the full weight of the enforcement of super-profits, the degradation, and the legal persecution that were formerly focussed on the dangerously organised male White industrial workers and on intellectuals, who now advance to privileged bearers of social-democratic reformism (cf. Marcuse 134 and passim, Haug 190 and passim). However, Post-Fordism and the US New World Order has also especially targeted the middle classes and "middle" nations that threatened to rise, such as Russia, Yugoslavia, and Iraq. Indeed, it seems that the social basis of the al-Qaeda cadres are the middle classes of Egypt and Saudi Arabia (cf. Minolfi 19). Beyond outright killing in wars and enforced misery, all such colonial and semi-colonial vanquished swell the ranks of the super-exploited today in all our cities under mafioso debt slavery as they did in times of chattel slavery[3]. Both the social-democratic and the communist movements catastrophically undervalued the significance of this change in exploitation modalities toward a kind of sub-proletariat (though the Bolsheviks were, at their revolutionary beginning, the first to indicate it).

2. War as a Dominant in Necrophilic Capitalism

When I was arguing (in "On Cognition") that war, drugs and brainwashing were the present dispensation's riders of the Apocalypse, I found out that war is the *lead* rider – the determining spring of life under capitalism. Before I get to some empirical data, it has to be stressed that deep forces are at work here. The heartbeat of capitalism is antagonistic competition regardless of human lives: for one small example, there were more dead and maimed per year in US car crashes than US casualties at the height of the Vietnam War. Any sane society, unwilling to sanction killing for the sake of profits to a few, would have tightly regulated highway traffic of the kind known in the USA; instead, the US model has conquered the world. Considering both the emotional mainspring and the brute result in humans killed, the capitalist way of people cohabiting is Hobbes's "time of war, where every man is enemy of every man"; extrapolating from the English Civil War after 1640, he realised this was centrally a permanent civil war. Two centuries later, the best European codification noted that war is properly likened "to business competition," and even more to "State policy, which... may be looked upon as a kind of business competition on a great scale" (Clausewitz 1: 121). While "competition... does not establish [the laws of bourgeois economy]," it is its "essential locomotive force": "competition is generally the mode in which capital secures the victory of its mode of production" (Marx, *Grundrisse* 552 and 730). *War is therefore more than a metaphor for bourgeois human relationships, it is perhaps their allegorical essence.* This was always understood in the workers' and socialist movement: Jean Jaurès phrased it as "le capitalisme porte la guerre comme la nuée porte l'orage" (capitalism brings war as the cloud brings the tempest). Much before Lenin, who did something about it, the socialists' slogan was "war upon war" (cf. Angenot *Antimilitarisme*).

As soon as classical primitive accumulation of capital – pushing down the cost of labour-power, dispossessing the peasants – is no longer possible, capitalism is threatened by "global crises and led, inexorably, to the kinds of primitive accumulation and devaluation [that is, physical destruction of both capital and labour] jointly wrought through... wars" (Harvey 443). Furthermore, the effect of wars is not spread equally over the globalised globe; on the contrary, the destruction is unevenly distributed to benefit the victors, as a rule the strongest capitalist countries. But this unnatural state of affairs generates so much misery that drugs and brainwashing have to be resorted to, in the finally vain endeavour to find a breathing space, to shut out Death. Fidel Castro in his speech at the "Summit of the South" (G-77, Havana, April 2000) summarised the only partially available, undervalued data from *Human...1998* as: "800 billion dollars are spent yearly for arms and armies...; at least 400 billion for drugs [not including alcohol and tobacco], and a further 100 billion for commercial propaganda which obfuscates reason just like drugs."

Even when we limit ourselves only to warfare in the narrower sense defined above, that is, involving one or more entire States, continuous warfare has *never* ceased under capitalism. In that respect capitalist States do not centrally differ from preceding social formations in which the main government departments were, as Marx observed, "that of Finance, or plunder of one's own people; that of War, or plunder of other peoples" (Marx, "Die britische" 129; cf. Avineri 239). There are strong claims that the economic basis for the triumph of capitalism was colonial warfare-plunder from the 15th to the 18th and 19th centuries (Headrick, Parker), prepared by Venice in the eastern Mediterranean as well as by the "internal colonies" of England's "Celtic fringe" and France's Languedoc. At the same time it provided the major impetus for mass production for a standardised "population," pioneered by the famous arsenal of Venice. Armies strongly influenced the process of industrialisation with its "reserve armies" of workers, and as Marx noted, they were important for division of labour within one branch and had since Antiquity the first developed wage system (Marx-Engels 529-30). War financing – which constituted throughout the 18th century three quarters of State budgets in Europe – resulted in the setting up of modern bureaucracy and central national banks (Anderson 31-33, Kaldor, *New* 18). A temporary lull in European wars ensued after 1871, when the metropolitan powers had divided the world and the British navy was policing this division; this was accompanied by mass colonial and semi-colonial murderings of more than 60 million peasants and tribals (Watts 125, and cf. M. Davis).

Yet the warfare returned from brutal domination of Asian, African and Latin American labour-power to the North at the latest by 1911 – date of the major carving up of a precapitalist European empire, the Ottoman one, and the first major world revolution, the Mexican one – in a permanent chain of war carnages, which show no signs of abating. The Oslo Peace Research Institute PRIO counted 66 wars in the year 1992 and a German peace research consortium 34 in 1999. Definitions of war differ, but around 160 wars seem to have raged between 1945 and 1993, of which about three quarters were civil wars, and in them more people were killed than in World War 2; the frantic search of the US corporate-military class for enemies that might justify further hundreds of billions out of the pockets of taxpayers shows the USA-USSR competition was only a welcome excuse for "a permanent war economy" (phrase by Wilson, chairman of General Electric in 1944 – in Lens 14). Summing up, we are already within the most terrible (almost) Hundred Years' War in human history. Is this an accident? No. Just as capitalism came about in plunder wars, there is no evidence it could climb out of economic depressions without huge military spending, a "war mega-dividend" (best examples: the 1930s and the 1990s – cf. Amin 48). I return to this in Section 3.

The strictly political fall-out of militarisation, which is not the focus of this essay, is the spread of military rule that subordinates all other aspects of civil society to its barbarity not only during wars but in times of official "peace" (cf. Pannekoek 183-85). Dictatorships enforced by bayonet and gun muzzle were the rule in all imperial possessions; in the 20th century they are more common in nominally independent States than at any time since the rise of the bourgeoisie, marking well its degeneration. This is technically facilitated by the enormous elaboration of armaments, accessible only to large economic systems, and it is underpinned by the spread of both organisational complexity (cf. Andreski 69-72, 87-88 and passim) and of the brainwashing industries such as cinema and TV. It should never be forgotten that the armies' sabers, bullets, and bombardments – first by the feudal landowners' armies and then by those of the centralised State – were always the upper class's final answer to any uprisings for justice from below. All these factors were behind Foucault's question: "[I]sn't power simply a form of warlike domination... a sort of generalised war which assumes at particular moments the forms of peace and State?" (123) I am uneasy at politico-economically unanchored generalisations such as "power." But they may be useful if historicised into actual mediations, focussed not on the question why the ruling classes need and wage war, but rather on how come that they're as a rule able to find plenty of lower class cannon-fodder. Bourgeois power under capitalism is thus in feedback with and exercised through strong institutionalisations and ideologies disciplining huge masses: besides outright military dictatorships whenever necessary, I can only refer here to technoscience and identity politics (chauvinisms and ethnic exclusivisms). One could call these the two faces of bribing the middle and lower classes: by finance and by ideology.

Technoscience: Modern technology and technoscience has since the Industrial Revolution, if not earlier, been largely and increasingly shaped by the needs of capitalism and warfare. "[B]y and large, technoscience is part of a war machine and should be studied as such," concluded Latour, looking at data which in 1986 showed that ca. 80% of the US federal budget for research and development was devoted to "defense" (171 and 172); half of all US scientists and engineers work today for military priorities (C.H. Gray 231, cf. Tirman ed.). At the very least, "value-free" technoscience is the central means for – and thus intimately shaped by use for – war, literal and metaphorical: mass production in capitalism needs mass destruction for the cycle to go on (cf. C.H. Gray; also Toffler 42, 64ff, Virilio 11-12, Virilio & Lotringer 20).

This means that, to begin with, for the worker technology is the mode of capitalist domination and the tool enforcing heightened exploitation and disempowerment:

> As wage labour ... is totally alien from the aims of production (producing use-value for the satisfaction of consumers' needs), technology is for the proletarian a set of prescriptions regulating his or her behaviour while working for a wage.... But it is imposed in an obligatory fashion upon the worker; this is institutional coercion shaping the worker's time and steering his or her activity. There is no escaping it, hence it is not true that it is uncoerced. It is an obligation, thus it is political. (Tamás 123)

As to the citizen, modern technoscience leaves him naked to his rulers: he is now worldwide the surveillance object either of an open or for the moment still fortunately hypocritical Police State. This is a subtle form of introducing almost unnoticeably – except in their hugely alienating and anti-democratic results – components of what I call (in "To Explain") Fascism 2.0, most visible in the dictatorship of the point-like present (just look at the people glued materially and morally to their iPods and iPads[4]). Not only lessons from past experience but also the very imagining of a radically different future are strongly precluded here.

Identity politics: Among the most efficient brainwashings that have developed since the collapse of credibility of socialism and rampant immiseration is mega-group exclusivism, usually named after its psychological motivation "identity politics." Any means of helping downtrodden and impoverished groups, such as most women or "racially" oppressed people, to fight for justice are welcome, and identity-based awareness may become such a means for a while. But its perversion into resentful exclusivisms "triggers violence [and] diminishes solidarity with the victims of that violence" (George 93; cf. Angenot *Idéologies*). The perversion may be pinpointed as coming about when justice is demanded only for one's own group, regardless of whether this might lead to injustice or even crass humiliation and exploitation, up to genocide, of those defined as enemy Others. It is unavoidable that the hundreds of millions of unemployed people rejected to the margins of society, with third-rate or no social services in Post-Fordism, should fall prey to "isolation, shame, depression and violence" ("Éditorial" 19). But it is not unavoidable, unless orchestrated from above, that this should lead to hatred of other, usually equally downtrodden "identities," ethnic cleansings, and civil war; however, this worst case is a clear possibility. It is practically always keyed to a sudden rise of misery and disorientation. A PRIO study of 98 wars in 1990-96 concludes that "a particularly strong correlation exists between high external debt and the incidence of civil war" – especially "crucial" are the IMF conditions imposed on the country! – and between "falling export income from primary commodities [and] the *outbreak* of the civil war" (cited verbatim in George 95, PRIO's emphasis; cf. Smith). The three civil wars in ex-Yugoslavia – in Croatia, Bosnia, and Kosovo – are a prime example that "the economy, stupid!" is an absolutely necessary, though not sufficient, cause for such wars (cf. at least Woodward). The increasingly direct entry of major European nations and then the USA into such wars fits well into their swap of internal welfare (for all people) for external warfare (profiting only capitalists and to a minor degree employees of armament industries), as the capitalist ruling classes seek by all possible means to stabilise military expenditures and profits at the very high Cold War level (see also section 4. below).

3. Weapons Commodities as Extra-Profit and System Pillar

In the "metropolitan" sites of mature capitalism (that is, the countries of the Trilateral: North America, Western Europe, Japan and a few other places), the appropriation of surplus value is carried on "democratically" through economic instruments, that is, primarily by means of brainwashing, with the police visible but the army only called out in emergencies. In very rarefied liberal societal theory, abstracting from the existence of States and of all other factors of uneven development, as well as from the internal inexorable limits to capital (cf. Harvey), this might be taken to mean that war could be dispensed with. As usually presented by bourgeois common sense, overt military coercion was the rule for pre-capitalist societies but seems to be a thing apart from capitalist economic production. And it has in fact today, from the global point of view, shifted either into (so to speak) non-metropolitan politics inside one State or between two States, or into threatening but not fully ripened intercontinental rivalries: the US does not today need war to dominate in North America, nor does Germany need it in Europe. However, armament production is, as Kaldor noted ("Warfare" 262), not only an object of consumption – finally though not always immediately needing wars – but also an object of production bringing profits. I'd add that its enormous size and central position (the world war industry was calculated as 10% of the world GNP in the 1960s; it is surely more than that today, and disproportionately more in major powers such as the USA) bring also system stability.

True, the money value of the huge international armament trade – oscillating between 20 and over 30 billion US$ yearly in the last 30 years according to the SIPRI yearbooks – dropped abruptly after the collapse of the USSR because the burgeoning conflicts did not as a rule need superbombers and heavy tanks but infantry gear and helicopters, which could also increasingly be local products or bought cheap either from the huge stockpiles in the black market belt between Cambodia and Russia or direct from the major pestiferous trader of retail arms, the hundreds of legal US producers. But armament outlays have not only been again steadily climbing from the mid-90s on, with a noticeable spurt in the USA as of 1998, so that its military budget was at the end of the 90s again 95% of the Cold War one; *armament production has remained at the heart of this epoch's financial capitalism*. Furthermore, in the 90s the trend toward global business alliances has reached the arms commodity, which is also increasingly incorporating advanced non-military technoscience, such as electronics (Keller x). I can best indicate it by a summary from McMurtry:

> The capital-intensive market systematically favours armaments commodities for production because of:
>
> (1) their uniquely high value-added price... (for example $26 billion for the first five years of the US "Star Wars" programme...);
>
> (2) their specially rapid rate of obsolescence and turnover...;
>
> (3) the monopoly or semi-monopoly position of armaments manufacturers which flows from: (a) the designation of military production... as state secrets; (b) the high capital costs of armaments technology and manufacture; and (c) the privileged linkages of established military producers with government defense and procurement agencies;
>
> (4) the large-scale and secure capital financing of military research, production, and cost additions... ensured by... public taxation, [and]... available to no other system of commodity production. (*Cancer* 170)

No moralistic wailings about the madness of this almost unimaginably enormous institution will matter a whit unless we zero in relentlessly on this fact: from the inception of the modern State and market, wars have always been "the greatest and the most profitable of investments" (Lefebvre, *Production* 275). By the time of the Gulf War, a conservative estimate of spending for military purposes was nearly a trillion – one million millions – US$ annually (the Tofflers 14), or between 2 and 2.5 billion dollars daily. Of this, the armament-commodity production accounted for ca. 200 billion US$ annually, or for about one fifth (SIPRI 1999: 9), of which half was located in the USA. Its imperial outlay dwarfs its British predecessor: the US spends on armaments as much as the next 12 strongest States combined, whereas the Royal Navy only wanted to be greater than the next two combined. For one huge example: of the 18 US nuclear submarines, "each one carrying the equivalent in injuring power to 4,000 Hiroshima bombs [...or enough] to destroy the peoples of an entire continent,... eight have been made... since the opening of the Berlin Wall" (Scarry 28). The USA also accounts for more than half of the world armament exports (Keller 12). A huge part of these trillions goes to the superprofits of Northern corporations, and a smaller but appreciable part for the maintenance of practically all the ruling mafias and classes of the world. Last but not least, "[t]he new wars could be viewed as a form of military waste-disposal – a way of using up unwanted surplus arms generated by the Cold War, the biggest military build-up in history" (Kaldor, *New* 96). Disposal of surplus commodities that simultaneously disposes of surplus people: what a neat trick!

In particular, as is well known to all specialists though obscured by media blather, the military-industrial establishments of corporate capitalism, led by the US one, both produce "life-killing commodities" as the most profitable part of global trade (cf. McMurtry *Understanding*) and are the strongest factor of organised international violence. However, only a few critics have begun to show that these establishments are simultaneously – marvellous synergy! – possibly the strongest factor enforcing a world cultural revolution for the total colonisation of human life-worlds and eco-systems by commodity economy. This was pointed out by Rosa Luxemburg even before the huge acceleration organised through World Wars (see her chapters 27-30) and other globalisations. She concluded that capital cannot accumulate without the productive forces and the consumption markets of more primitive societies (her examples are India, Algeria, and China), whose economies it eventually turns inside out: "Violence [*Gewalt*] is the only solution open to capital: the accumulation of capital employs violence as a permanent weapon, not only at its genesis, but further on down to the present day" (371). This was invariably accompanied by militarism, and by the eradication of rural industries in favour of a sharp rural-urban divide usually called industrialisation (her example is the dispossession of farmers in post-Civil-War USA).

Marx had already made of "State power, the organised and concentrated violence (*Gewalt*) of society" a lynchpin of his theory of primitive accumulation, which was however still strongly endogenous to his example of England (but also of Scotland and Ireland)." Yet the "genesis of the industrial capitalist" proceed also for him largely from colonial conquest: "The treasures captured outside Europe by straightforward looting, enslavement, and murder (*Raub-*

mord) flowed back to the mother-country and were turned into capital there" (*Kapital, MEW* 23: 779, 777, and 781). Thus, Luxemburg could extrapolate this to a thesis that "Accumulation is... primarily a relationship between capital and a non-capitalist environment" (417), which is in the imperialist phase characterised by: "foreign loans, railroad constructions, revolutions, and wars" (419 & ff.). Militarism is "the executor of [such an] accumulation of capital" (439) under State compulsion. Along with the normal metropolitan commodity market, the accumulation of capital needs "colonial policy, an international loan system... and war. Violence, fraud, oppression, looting are openly displayed [here].... In reality, political power is nothing but the vehicle for the economic process. The conditions for the reproduction of capital provide the organic link between these two aspects of the accumulation of capital." (452) Replace direct colonisation with nominally independent native elites, and you have the present system.

Thus, what does it matter that the production of armament commodities contributes little to improving any economy's productivity, since the output is used neither for the growth of means of production nor for consumption? What does it matter that, if the US economy sanely spent as much to make the buildings in that country airtight as was spent by the US military in *one year* of the mid-80s (before the Gulf Oil war) on the forces meant to ensure the West Asian oilfields, no imports of oil from that region would be necessary (the Lovinses 27)? What does it matter that the recurring pork-barrelling and misinformation about the cost of new weapons systems lead in 90% of cases to doubling – or multiplying up to seven times – the original cost estimate (Weisberg 81), which is surely not a rational or economic way of organising production? And finally, what does it matter that the cost of one war casualty has risen from 29,000 DMark in WW1 to 34,500 in WW2 and to 338,000 in the Korean War (Heinig 25 – the 1962 exchange rate to US$ was 4:1, so the cost of one war casualty in the Korean War was US$84.500)? For, from a profit point of view, all of these aspects in the development, trade, and turnover of armament commodities are supremely rational. The tens of millions of dead in World Wars brought about tens of trillions of profitable investments in the huge new opportunities of reconstructing the destroyed homes and industries – a million dollars or more per dead body. And today, from the point of view of the US military-technoscientific bloc – and of analogous, though not quite so central, blocs in a few other major powers (Germany, France, the UK...) – armament maintains the national military-industrial base; for the ruling establishments, dominated by big corporations, its use abroad is equally rational. So are all the death-bringing improvements from chemistry, atomic physics or electronics; so is selling not only the commodities but increasingly also their means of production, the underlying technologies of mega-destruction, to anybody with ready cash. In Marcuse's words, "The union of growing productivity and growing destruction; the brinkmanship of annihilation; the surrender of thought, hope, and fear to the decisions of powers that be; the preservation of misery in the face of unprecedented wealth constitute the most impartial indictment [of this society]" (*One-Dimensional* xiii; cf also Mailer).

What is irrational is the final cause of all these increasingly destructive flows: the profit principle itself. No capitalism without increasingly destructive weapons and wars: and today wars destroy the world. "It is estimated that the single greatest source of environmental destruction in the US is the military-industrial complex, and that one-quarter of the public monies which are expended on weapons commodities across the world would eradicate poverty, homelessness, and illiteracy, as well as pay for the cleanup of all our major environmental pollution at the same time" (McMurtry, *Cancer* 174). This is most apparent in nuclear weaponry and the civilian uses that developed out of it, including not only Chernobyl and Three Mile Island but the regular US government dumping of nuclear waste into the oceans (cf. Weisberg 83). However, ABC (atomic, bacteriological and chemical) weaponry is now being joined by further super-technoscience with incalculable effects. Just one example of a planned new generation of US weaponry was HAARP (High-Frequency Active Aural Research Program) for "weather warfare."[5] It proposed to use powerful radiowave beams that heat and then sweep away areas of ionosphere, allowing huge amounts of energy to bounce back to Earth in order – as a US air force scenario put it – to "own the weather" either by pinpointed local modifications of weather patterns (say in a "rogue nation") or by global weather disruption. This would not only disrupt communications but it could be combined with a spacelab to deliver amounts of energy comparable to a nuclear bomb anywhere on Earth, via laser and particle beams. Besides climate manipulation, the returning waves could also affect human brains, and earthquake effects were being envisaged. Nobody knows how many similarly destructive projects were or are now being pursued by the most powerful military forces. The dirty megaweapons of today – such as the US uranium-encased bombs and shells in Iraq as well as in ex-Yugoslavia and the Adriatic Sea, cf. Chossudovsky "Low" – and even more of tomorrow threaten the survival of a "sustainable" vertebrate biosphere (cockroaches may survive). Clearly, there can be no sane ecology or even survival without going against the profit principle and unlimited growth: beginning with wars, armament industries, and technoscientific military research.

A crucial factor in the unprecedented post-1940 rise of production was the "permanent military reflation" through World War 2, the Korean War, and the Cold War up to today (Went 76). The military cluster of industries, with a locked-in permanent market and assured high profits, seems to be the key sector of the US economy, propping up the national and then the world economic structure. The decisive question may well be whether capitalism could economically and psychically survive without warfare and mega-armaments. Baran and Sweezy made a strong argument that it could not have done so in the 1930s-40s, and the evidence of the first small reduction in new procurements after the fall of the USSR, which resulted in a deep depression in a dozen or more major US states, speaks as strongly in favour of this black argument today. As Benjamin had intuited, capitalism is a permanent "martial law": the bourgeois welfare State – welfare first for the upper class, and then, reacting to the threat of Leninism, for the middle and parts of the working classes – is also a warfare State. Threats "against the 'national interest' are usually created or accelerated to meet the changing needs of the war system" (*Report* 30). In that respect, even the fully degenerate "State socialism" of the USSR was better: it did not need war, it was bankrupted by the armaments race forced on it. True, US armament-commodity procurements jumpstarted startling new technologies – aerospace, semiconductors, medical technology, etc. – out of the trillions given by taxpayers (US$1.5 trillion 1950-75), at the time that 40% worldwide of both research and its financing were devoted to military R&D. But by the same token the high-tech commodities for killing took 40% of world research and material resources *away* from more economical, certainly less destructive, purposes (Tirman ed. 11-16, 46, 148, 216-21 & passim, Brenner 56n).

Finally, the deflection of so much financial and brain-power, so much human labour, into profitable commodities for killing makes a sham of democratic control and decision-making. As Wallerstein has repeatedly argued, ideological and economic liberalism is incompatible with democracy. The war economy palpably marks the divorce between capitalism and civic responsibility for other people and for the planet. But the stakes are even higher: if "the enduring, primary symbiosis between capitalism and war" (Kolko 474) means that wars are indeed necessary for the survival of this social formation, then the capitalist social formation is truly, as McMurtry argues, a cancer in the body politic, and the only way we and this planet can survive is to get rid of it once and for all. As Pannekoek remarked in his remarkable chapter on war already in 1947:

> When we say that war is inseparable from capitalism, that war can only disappear with capitalism itself, this does not mean that war against war is of no use.... It means that the fight against war is inseparable from fight against capitalism.[6]

4. Wars of Reterritorialisation

4.1. As mentioned at the beginning, the totalisation of war in the 20th century leads to "whole populations com[ing] to be more and more regarded as legitimate objects of annihilation" (J.G. Gray 132). This can only be done if wars are waged in the spirit of quasi-theological "emotion-drenched... abstract hatred," compounded of repugnance and fear (ibidem 132-34), "the enemy" being an incarnation of total evil. An early culmination of such an *odium theologicum* was the insane US and NATO doctrine of nuclear warfare.

The *genus* war had (not counting fights between tribal groups) up to the 20th century a few recognised species: a/ war between States or quasi-State entities; b/ civil war within a State; c/ partizan warfare in an occupied State. All of them were defined, among other matters, by a circumscribed territory of warfare, be this Caesar's Gallia, a frontline, or the quarter-worlds of the World War 2 "theatres of war" (European and Pacific). This territorial limitation begins to waver and fade with the advent, first, of military air power, and second, of instant global communication, primarily on TV, which brings a "war for the hearts and minds" to the nations and the people involved. Leaving "war on terrorism" for a separate discussion later, now we have to face two new species in a dual military world: the exogenous war exported by the North, usually the USA, into the "global slums" of the poorer South, and pursued by high-altitude bombing plus internal subversion (which I cannot examine here); and the supposedly – but in reality only partly – endogenous species of "armed turmoil" in the South. This is concatenated with the dual economic world, where 90% of world investment and trade are already contained within the "North" (meaning North America, western Europe, Oceania, Japan, and the Asian "Little Tigers"),

The war pitting one State-government-army against another was a recent invention codified in 1648 by what Arrighi would call Europe's "unique fusion of State and capitalism" (1). There have been some early warnings about a shift of warfare modes away from this species, notably in van Creveld's astringent and stimulating book programmatically called *The Transformation of War* (cognate considerations are in Gantzel, Gibbs, C. H. Gray, Schreiber, and Woodward). Though van Creveld says very little about the crucial nexus of economics with wars, he noted that in the age of telecommunications and modern means of transport, controlled by ca. 25 states, such Clausewitzian war is becoming outdated. Thus for him "battles will be replaced by skirmishes, bombing, and massacres" (207). In such sporadic small scale-war, regular forces easily degenerate into police or mere armed gangs, while on a global scale there develops a "security business."

The most detailed hypothesis about this latter species, the one manifested primarily or "purely" in African or Yugoslav civil wars, is Kaldor's *New and Old Wars* (further as K with page number; cf. also her "Warfare and Capitalism"); I shall proceed to critically interpret it for my purposes. Her approach is rather phenomenological, so that it to my mind suffers from one major failing and one perhaps minor one. The major gap in the diagnosis is a minimisation of the external pressures, support, and enablement making for both the outbreak and the continuation of these wars. This is the more regrettable as it is well known in the literature on separatism that "international factors are clearly decisive. Whereas the emergence of separatist movements is determined largely by internal factors, their success is contingent on obtaining a level of external support that is in fact seldom available." (Zolberg et al. 243) In particular for the conflict in Bosnia-Herzegovina, on which much of Kaldor's investigation is concentrated, it is well known that German ruling interests – alongside US Right-wing groups and probably the Vatican – favoured and financed the Croat side, that the much weaker Russian ones backed the Serb side, while the Clinton administration after 1992 supported the Bosnian "Muslim" side, favouring its arming by Iran and Saudi Arabia and the arrival of thousands of Islamist Mujahideen fighters (cf. from among a huge welter of titles Conert 5-13, Gibbs, Halberstam, Hofbauer, International, Wiebes, and Woodward). There is probably little or no purely endogenous "armed turmoil."

Kaldor's other limitation is signalled by her empiricistic and inelegant name of "new war/s," a term limiting our understanding. I propose they should be provisionally called "reterritorialising wars," that is: wars conducted to control a limited territory and its goods by an elite claiming to act in the name of an ethnic group (however invented).

Nonetheless, while Kaldor's prescriptions therefore remain insufficient, her description is indispensable.

4.2. The ostensible *goal* of the new wars is not universal ideologies, such as the no longer fashionable socialist or "national liberation" ones, but "identity politics": ethnic or tribal exclusivism "for the purpose of claiming State power" (K 76) in a new State or for making a new group dominant in an old State. The identities usually are invented traditions no older than the 19th- or 20th-century arrival of market economies into those colonial territories and the need of the incipient local bourgeoisie to control its own market. They are culturally constructed communities claiming a "blood" basis which is threatened by impure admixtures. Their fiercely mini-collectivist ideologies have a sweeping disregard for personal rights, often directly inherited from their Fascist or Stalinist roots and re-actualised by their oligopolistic corporate backers. Behind the chauvinisms, however, other interests hide. First, "a politics fostered from above" (K 78) by an ethnic elite that covets State power and enrichment, and enlists for that purpose a part (often quite small) of its poorer co-ethnics promising them immediate plunder of neighbours, careers, and glory. Second, interests of multinational companies over valuable resources (oil, ores) in the disputed territory. Third – overlapping with second – interests of major military powers over its strategic position in relation to other territories.

The necessary precondition for any such "identity" crystallisation is a major *economic crisis*, in a world where structural impoverishment of the South is imposed by the global capitalist order: the ratio of real income per head between the richest and the poorest countries was 3:1 in 1800, 10:1 in 1900, and is 60:1 in 2000 (cf. Dummett). This crisis may be partly due to and exacerbated by internal difficulties or errors by the original State's ruling classes but it is always ignited by corporate interests: Shell in Ogoniland-Nigeria, but usually the World Bank and IMF (for Yugoslavia cf. Chossudovsky *Globalization* 243-63 and "Low," International, and Woodward). It results in staggeringly massive unemployment and immiseration plus a grab for major possessions starting at the power-top and spreading downwards. Legal norms are necessarily forsaken in such straits, and livelihood comes to depend on Kaldor's "parallel economy" – "networks of corruption, black marketeers, arms and drug traffickers, etc." (K 83), often linked to previous financial support by the CIA through the diaspora and to international illegal circuits of drug smuggling (as in the "Kosovar Liberation Army") and arms smuggling. Such a total existential crisis sometimes re-actualises but often reinvents factional, "ethnic" or pseudo-religious, conflicts. It fosters ruthless warlord or gang hegemony making for spiralling "violence markets" (cf. Elwert) against the Other, and leading to redistribution of riches without new production – a primitive accumulation for the new separatist ruling class, usually in a vassal or comprador function to foreign powers (the US or NATO, France and Belgium in Africa, some Islamic-expansion States).

Kaldor's account of what happens *once the war starts* is magisterial. It is "heavily dependent on local predation and external support. Battles are rare, most violence is directed against civilians, and cooperation between warring factions is common" (K 90). The warring units "finance themselves through plunder and the black market or through external assistance." The latter can be remittances from the diaspora, illegal trade in arms, drugs or valuable commodities such as oil or diamonds, and – crucially – financing from outside the war territory: either covertly by a major power and/or a neighbour or through plunder "taxation" of humanitarian and other international assistance. "All of these sources can only be sustained through continued violence so that a war logic is built into the functioning of the economy" (K 9 and 102). I don't know whether the following excerpt would apply to all such wars but, regardless of some shaky terminology, it is dead on for the Yugoslav civil wars:

> Because the various warring parties share the aim of sowing "fear and hatred," they operate in a way that is mutually reinforcing, helping each other to create a climate of insecurity and suspicion.... Often, among the first civilians to be targeted are those who... try to maintain inclusive social relations and some sense of public morality. Thus... [the new wars] can be understood as wars between exclusivism and cosmopolitanism. (K 9)

The main *lever of control* is neither front-line occupation of more territory nor the battle for the people's hearts and minds as in revolutionary guerrilla warfare; rather, it is "population displacement." This new warfare adapts US counterinsurgency techniques from Mozambique, Nicaragua, and Afghanistan: "poisoning the sea" in which Mao's guerrilla swims like a fish. This considerably raises the level of inhumanity:

> Instead of creating a favourable environment for the guerrilla, the new warfare aims to create an unfavourable environment

> for all those people it cannot control. Control... depends on continuing fear and insecurity and on the perpetuation of hatred of the other. Hence the importance of extreme and conspicuous atrocity and of involving as many people as possible in these crimes so as to establish a shared complicity... and to deepen divisions. (K 98-99)

Kaldor discusses at length the techniques of population displacement: by systematic murders of people categorised as the guilty Other; by ethnic cleansing in the narrower sense, that is, forcible population expulsion (see on this concept and its history Rosière); and by rendering an area uninhabitable through land mines, shelling civilians or enforced famines, powerfully aided "by instilling unbearable memories of what was once home, by desecrating whatever has social meaning," for example by destruction of religious and other historical monuments – say the famous medieval bridge in Mostar – or by systematic rape and sexual abuse (K 99-100).

Such reterritorialising wars are thus characterised by the breakdown of the "distinctions between the political and the economic, the public and the private, the military and the civil" (K 106): they are exemplary Post-Modernist cultural constructions, and should possibly be called neo-Fascist.

4.3. Lest the richer and apparently pacified West grow too smug about its presumed civility, I take Kaldor's warning about budding analogous conflicts in those climes, which only await an economic crisis to erupt, as very significant:

> The characteristics of the new wars I have described are to be found in North America and Western Europe as well. The right-wing militia groups in the US are not so very different from the paramilitary groups in Eastern Europe or Africa... [nor] is the salience of identity politics.... The violence in the inner cities of Western Europe and North America can, in some senses, be described as new wars. (K 11)

In fact, "The new war economy could be represented as a continuum, starting with the combination of criminality and racism to be found in the inner cities of Europe and North America and reaching its most acute manifestation in the [war violence] areas" (K 110).

The inner logic of these new wars is that they are the anti-successor to the vanished Welfare State, a brutal do-it-yourself welfare for small comprador elites, and the inescapable application of capitalist economico-political globalisation of plunder. As to the former, the first major German post-1945 venture into military affairs in ex-Yugoslavia coincided with the major dismantling of German social welfare (Rousseau knew it all!). As to the latter, in the new dispensation everything is permitted. Takeovers, dispossession, marginalisation, reserve armies of the miserable: What is good for General Motors is good for the Rwanda warlord.

Finally, it should be noted that these wars unfold within the overwhelming context of capitalist deterritorialisation of production and consumption (not of control, still firmly in metropolitan hands). They are a reaction to it by the local ruling classes, employing the most retrograde rhetoric of once perhaps progressive bourgeois nationalism, together with outside financial support for heavy armaments, to enlist a sometimes small fraction of a territory's lower classes to slaughter or in other ways "cleanse" other groups (in the main also lower classes). Although in Bosnia all three warring groups managed between them to enlist only ca. 6% of the population, that is, a maximum of 3% perhaps among the Serbs or Croats, this was enough to chain the whole thus constructed ethnic group ineluctably to "their" ethnic upper classes' interest and destiny.[7]

5. Against War: How?

In sum, capitalist civilisation reposes on the insoluble contradiction between a boundless increase of productive forces and boundless economic and psychic immiseration of people, because the forces of labour-power, including technoscience, are used for exploitation of a huge powerless majority of toilers and for colossal profit and power for a tiny capitalist minority. The product that subsumes and overshadows all other multifarious products of this civilisation is the production of destructive novelties, "undermining of the springs of all wealth: the earth and the worker," as Marx already told us (*Kapital, MEW* 23: 530). Capital practices "systematic robbery of the preconditions for life..., of space, air, light...," said he (ibidem 449-50), and today we could add water, silence, health in general, etc. – in fact, life liberty and the pursuit of happiness. Post-Fordist condemnation of two thirds of the adult population globally – and one third in the "rich" countries – to unemployment or piecework is a further robbery of vitality during people's youth, to be paid for in their middle and late years by defencelessness against disease and early dying. The marvellous capitalist technoscientific progress has led to one nuclear submarine carrying the destructive power of all explosives used in World War 2 (Virilio 161); as mentioned in Section 3, this is enough to destroy the peoples of an entire continent, and yet eight new US nuclear submarines have been made since the fall of the USSR!

Thus death grows into this civilisation's final horizon. This is not the easeful death each of us has a right to: it threatens the collective death of humanity. Benjamin's "Arcades project" exemplarily argued, on the traces of Baudelaire and Balzac, that the structural logic of gambling, excitement, novelty – of the ever more frenzied commodity customer's experience and time horizon – demands that its final end be Death (for example *GS* I.2: 668). Death is the end of raping the planet by economic exploitation and ecocide, where war is not only an illusory economic and psychological solution.

Whence such myopic folly, differing from past dying empires only in its speed-of-light propagation? Probably it is intrinsic to the class thirst for power or mastery which breeds also the everlasting fear of falling behind, the ever stronger post-Welfare-State dread of not having security. When Freud speculated amid World War 1 that "the impulse of cruelty arises from the instinct of mastery" (59), we might wish to reject obfuscating terms such as instinct yet see that he put his finger on a centrally sore point. (He also rightly saw as the counter-pole an "instinct for knowledge or research" – 60.) This age-old impulse has never been so powerful, unnecessary, and necrophilic as in capitalism, driven by the unending "fix" of profits: and especially, in the perfectly sinful Post-Fordist age of wars, prostitution, and drugging (literal and metaphoric). It testifies to the terrible blindness of all hegemonic social theories that they have failed to factor in such lessons of war as a dominant of capitalism (cf. Kolko 464-82).

When I concluded in Section 3 that there can be no survival for humanity without strongly muzzling the profit principle and unlimited technological and financial growth, this also meant that at the latest since the mass bombings of civilians – from the Nazis to the British and US airforce in World War 2 – and since the advent of nuclear bombs, Clausewitz's famous dictum that war is the continuation of political traffic by other means must be superseded. Politics which daily use mass violence against people and have become an alternate way of economic gain and living must be stopped by self-defence for survival. Wars, armament industries, and technoscientific military research are the clearest case of such totally destructive activity.

What are we, who should still call ourselves the Left, and whose conscious core should perhaps think again about assuming communism as its poetry and prose, then to do? Vaguely and negatively put: strive to understand, and then look for articulated and organised ways to minimise and counteract the ruling-class blight of war, old and new. As a Left-wing Christian has reminded us, our horizon should be a politics that *consecrates* life (Virilio, in idem and Lotringer 144). I can supply one basic pragmatic pointer: since all major blights such as war, brainwashing, and prostitution are now semiotically and materially interwoven, the only possible response to any of them is one that does not hinder a response to any other. Counteracting war can only be done by also counteracting the IMF impositions, drugging, the procurement and spreading of arms commodities, identity politics, etc. Beside the need of achieving oppositional critical mass, in the form of Gramsci's "historical bloc," – which would by itself be enough, this is what makes it necessary to shun sectarian politics like the plague – even by such potentially large groups as super-exploited women. Separatisms – the defunct *ouvrierisme* (reliance on industrial workers only, today noticeably diminished by the wane of mass factories, for example through automation) and rural "Maoism"; macho, feminist, and generational separatism;

etc. – are the worst internal enemy of radical politics. Rainbow politics could be a good name if it is understood that while the colours are separate, so that organising around issues limited to a given "identity" may be locally useful as a first step, the rainbow is one.

Finally (the snake bites its tail): the political equivalent of this whole endeavour of mine is the fact that a segment of the "professional-managerial" class is today – as Ernst Bloch argued in 1938 for the intelligentsia in the industrialised states (343) – the one indispensable ally in any historical bloc, say with the working classes and women, which would have a chance to get off the ground. An ally is NOT a servant: it is somebody with whom one can disagree but has strategic interests in common, a community of destiny against the terrorism of capital (cf. Lefebvre, *Cybernanthrope* 56-57), which may supply criteria for resolving disagreement. And the criteria have to be built up with contributions by each. We "professionals" are professionally trained to formulate such criteria – if we can shake off capitalist corruption and listen to political experiences from practice. For, "any erroneous understanding of truth is simultaneously an erroneous understanding of freedom" (Marcuse 147).

P.S. April 2002:

It is mandatory to update our thinking after the murderous attack on civilians of September 2001 in the New York City Twin Towers, and the even more murderous attack on civilians ensuing by the US bombing in Afghanistan (best sources speak of ca. 4,000 civilians killed as of March 2002, and the count is rising), and in other attacks to follow whenever and wherever the US administration so pleases. I can here only address two questions, perhaps two sides of the same question: a) Would the essay as it now reads have to be changed in some central formulations? b) What should be added to its formulations?

As to a), having lived with these formulations and their framework now for almost four years, I would hope such initial approach could be supplemented in many ways, to my mind primarily by clarifying what are the US class fractions whose interest leads to the present militarisation and killings. We need a new Marx to write *The 11th September of George W. Bush;* I hope one can be found. As to b), the best supplement to this essay would be to analyze the present discourse on "terrorism" and of course actions justified by such discourse. This effort needs further writing (now essay 3 of this book), in order to decide whether this armed struggle is a war or not, and if not then what. Here a few preliminary though for me central points:

I believe terrorism is most usefully defined as a strategy which consists in pursuing political power by striking dread into the *civilian population* through exemplary *killings* among them. We need to focus fiercely on the two elements underlined. If they are correct, then there is both *State terrorism* and *group terrorism* (by religious or political groups). Politically, and even corporeally or phenomenologically, there are two main ways of carrying out terror/ism or being terrorists: terror-bombing, and all other terror killings. States – such as all colonial powers in the past, and Iraq, the USA and its NATO allies or Israel in the present – can use terror-bombings (and shelling by heavy artillery), including chemical warfare; the others don't have such means – yet. That's why the Sept. 11 terrorists had to improvise flying mega-bombs by re-categorising passenger airplanes as such.

If war is a strategy which consists in pursuing political power by "a coherent sequence of conflicts, involving physical combats between large organised groups of people, that include the armed forces of at least one State, which aim to exercise political and economic control over a given territory" (definition in my essay), then the difference between terrorism and war is that the former: a) can but doesn't have to involve large groups of people, such as the armed forces of at least one State; b) doesn't aim immediately at territorial control but at changing enemy policy so as to create preconditions for later territorial control. One should add: c) terrorism has never been, even on paper, brought under some code of conduct such as the Geneva or Hague conventions on war (which forbid killing civilians).

War kills as a rule both armed and unarmed people, terrorism as a rule only the unarmed. This may make terrorism morally more hateful. But inter-State or "civil" wars compensate by their sheer scale: not to mention the two World Wars, even the victims of subsequent inter-State and/or related "civil" wars often amount to hundreds of thousands or indeed millions. This does not make the al-Qaeda "airliner rammings" any better. Neither the ground nor the air terrorists blasting civilians have any justification except political calculation of the most cynical kind. When civilians are killed in wars, this is accepted as *war crimes*. The "collateral damage" excuse wears thin very quickly: as Herman and O'Sullivan concluded about Vietnam: "Killings are not 'inadvertent' [or 'collateral' – note DS] if they are a systematic and inevitable result of calculated military policy" (51). Vietnam was then a war accompanied by massive war crimes; so were the proxy wars in southern Africa. But Indonesia, Sudan, Kampuchea or Guatemala (and others from Chile to Colombia and Mexico) were terrorist interventions by the State against its subjects. The Nazis exemplarily straddled both.

What is new in the post-September 11 world is that *the frontier between war and terrorism is being erased* – from the side of political or religious groups because they don't have airplanes or heavy artillery, but also from the side of the States (primarily the USA) adopting the methods of terrorist groups. Wars are no longer either declared or ended, prisoners are not treated under international conventions. Where Randolph Bourne famously said in 1918, "War is the health of the State," we would have to add that, more and more, "Terror/ism is the health of the State." In this sense, Hitler has won.

Works Cited in Essay 1

See in *Works Cited in this Book* the following titles, by Author surname plus (when the author has several titles) first "headword" or identifying syntagm in the title:

Amin; Anderson; Andreski; Angenot, all three titles; Arrighi; Avineri; Baran & Sweezy; Bloch, „Der Intellektuelle"; Bourne; Brenner; Buck-Morss; Caputo; Castro; Chossudovsky, all three titles; Clausewitz; Conert; Creveld; Davis Angela; Davis Mike, *Late;* Dinnerstein; Drèze & Sen; Dummett; «Éditorial»; Elwert; Foucault; Freud, *Three;* Fried et al. eds.; Gantzel; George Susan; Gibbs; Gibson; Gray Chris; Gray J. Glenn; Halberstam; Haraway; Harvey, *Limits;* Haug, *Politisch;* Headrick; Heinig; Herman & O'Sullivan; Hofbauer; *Human... 1996* and *1998;* International; Kaldor, both titles; Keller; Kolko; Latour; Lefebvre, both titles; Lens; Levidow & Robbins eds.; Lewin; Love & Shanklin; Lovins & Lovins; Luxemburg; Mailer; Mann; Marcuse, *Feindesanalysen* and *One-Dimensional;* Marx „Die britische," *Grundrisse, Kapital* 1 and 3, *Selected, Theorien;* McMurtry, both titles; Melman; Merlo; Minolfi; Pannekoek; Parker; *Report;* Rosen; Rosière; Scarry, "Beauty"; Schreiber; Smith Adam; Smith Dan; Stockholm International Peace Research Institute, both titles; Suret-Canale; Suvin, *Defined;* Tabb; Tamás; Thompson; Tirman ed.; Toffler & Toffler; Virilio; Virilio & Lotringer; Watts; Weber, *From Max;* Weisberg; Went; Wiebes; Woodward, *Balkan;* Zolberg et al.

POEMS 1

EX: FUDÔ 2000

To Predrag Matvejević, chanter of ex

HEADNOTE: Fudô = esoteric Buddhist godhead of wrath, irate aspect of Enlightenment: blue-black face appearing amid flames, sword in one hand & rope in other hand to cut off & bind evil passions. – Please observe the deviant stresses on the <i’>s.

What poems, mind of mine, may you now sing
When corrupt desire rules the ex-communìsts
When massy murder brainwash & whoring enlists –
Few are saved – their lust for easeful things?

What hopes may now be found to grow new wings?
We in our youth, emerged from bloody mists,
Saw Fudō's sword in hands of antìfascìsts
& the people's rule a real thing,

Wrathful & kind.
Now i let my country go,
Murderously after false gods a-whore.
When surgical verse cuts deep it is to know,
To find at understanding's furthest shore
Why poison invades the brain's every pore.
Yet every poem encodes: I loved you so!

30500

2

Brecht's "Manifesto" Today (2002)

Bertolt Brecht: THE MANIFESTO

Translated by Darko R. Suvin

In memory of Jochen Bunge, who first smuggled this text out to me in the 1960s, and of my father, who first gave me to read the *Communist Manifesto*, printed by a Croatoserbian partizan brigade, in 1945.

> If we then in a poem now & here consider the nature
> Of people, as the great Lucretius considered the nature
> of things,
> It's because we too are only vouchsafed a dim break of
> day...
>
> Brecht, *On the Poem for Learning*

Wars are destroying the world, & the ruins are visibly haunted
By an enormous spectre, not simply born of war.
In peace it could already be sighted, terror to the rulers
But friend to the children of slums. In scanty kitchens
Often it peeps, horrified, angry, into the half-empty pots.
Often it waits for the exhausted in front of shipyards & mines;
It visits friends in jails, passing without passport.
Even in offices it may be seen & in lecture-rooms
Heard. At times it dons a hat of steel, enters
Huge tanks & flies with deadly bombers. It speaks in many
Tongues, in all of them. And in many it holds its tongue.
It sits as a guest of honour in hovels, a headache of villas,
It has come to change all things & stay forever, its name is
Communism.

You've heard much untruth about it from enemies, from friends
Much untruth also. This is what the classics say:
History books speak of great individuals, how
Their stars wax & wane; how their armies roam;
And further how empires resplend & fall. But the doubting great
Teachers examine the old writings for other lore
& they teach: history is mostly the story of how CLASSES STRUGGLE:
For they see all peoples split into classes struggling among
Themselves. Slaves & plebeians once, patricians & knights;
Artisans, peasants, nobility; burgesses then
& proletarians, processing the enormous economy,
Stand at daggers drawn in enormous contentions of power.
In daring subversion the partisan masters thus added
The story of ruled classes to the story of classes that rule.

Yet the ruling classes behave differently at different times,
Rome's patricians act other than Spanish grandees,
Burghers of early cities than the later cities' bourgeois:
Here, a class cleverly uses the hulking despot,
There, the despotic plurality of their own Houses;
One opts rather for bloody wars, another for slyness,
As their specific position allows, but always to strengthen
The rulers' rule, & always struggling against the ruled.
When peoples leap in slaughter on peoples, behind their battles
Other battles are raging, not so loud, steering the former.
The armies of Rome storm into the far-off icy Pontus
While back at home, in Rome, plebeians & patricians fight.
Germans are warring on Frenchmen, yet German cities, allies to
The Emperor of Germans, also wage war on German lords.
When a truce unites inimical classes to counter the external
Enemy, in true danger or artificial entrapment,
Both win the fight but only one the victory:
That class returns victorious, the other rings the bells,
Cooks the victory banquet & builds the triumphal column.
For deeper & longer lasting than the wars our primers render
Are the wars of classes, open or secret, not for enemy
Cities but for their own, ending only in revolution
Or in a joint downfall of the fighters, rulers & ruled.

Thus came about the age, which now is ending, of the bourgeois:
A fleeing serf, he became a burgher of the market town,
Then of the city, & behind its secure walls the guilds
Flourish. Cloth keeps crossing the walls, & commerce awakens
The dreaming country. Seaports build ships that sail to new shores,

Busily round Africa & set courageous sights
On American gold. Opening Chinese & East Indian
Markets, the New World, the accumulation of wares & moneys
Give wings to manufacture, & powerful there appears
From feudal relations a new societal ruler, the burgher.

Industry overtakes crafts. Long will endure the distaff,
But the master crosses the market with less resounding footsteps
& work once divided by guilds is now by the factory owner
Divided within one, bigger workshop. & still the markets
Insatiably grow. Even manufacture can no longer fill
The new demands, & lo! machines & steam overturn
All again, & manufacturer gives way to captain
Of industry, commander of workers & financier –
Our bourgeois. The Teachers show us in detail how large
Machine-based industry created a worldwide market
& the market in turn helped to concentrate industry
Till the bourgeoisie had fought its way to eminent rule:
State power attends to the business of the bourgeoisie now
Clothed in pomp & purple raiment, a willing executive board.

& this class has proved a hard & most impatient mistress.
With brazen cheek & iron heel it stamped out the rotten
Patriarchally still idyll, tore up the feudal old
Motley ties that bound protector & protégé,
Permitting no nexus but naked self-interest between people,
Payment in cash. The chivalric masters & loyal servants,
Love of native soil, honest craftsmanship, serving
A cause or inner calling, it has drowned in the icy jet
Of calculation, & brutally sold off dignity of persons
As small change. In place of the numberless chartered freedoms
It set up the sole Freedom of Trade. No doubt, those ties were
A natural, pious exploitation; now it is naked
& shamelessly wielded.

Physician & priest & judge & poet & researcher, in the past
Still met with pious awe, it hires as workers for wage,
Sends to a doctor the ailing as paying customers, & he sells
His recipe, & the priest sells his consolation.
Justice may now be purchased from the watchman of property, the judge.
Whatever ploughs its inventor imagined, its dealer sells
For swords. Hungrily the artist glorifies, with quick
Nobilitating brush-stroke, the bourgeoisie's visage,
Versed in the artifices of art he massages for money the lady's

Languid emotions. Smirking, the bourgeois turns the poets
& thinkers into paid lackeys. The temple of knowledge becomes
A stock-exchange, & even the family's holy abode
Hustling he stamps with the seal of unholy haggling.

Indeed, what are to us the aqueducts of Rome, the pyramids,
What a Crusade, & what even the Great Migration of Peoples,
To us who have seen the titanic buildings & expeditions
Made by this all-upsetting class, that always & wherever
It breathless reaches replaces what it created, living
On upset? Without pausing it alters machines & all products.
Formerly unimagined forces it hauls from air & water,
Creates new materials, never seen on this planet:
Thrice in one generation it changes the cloth of one's clothes,
The hold of knife & fork frequently alters its feel
In the hand, & the eye is always faced with new formations.
So too are people changed, peasants are into factories
Driven, craftsmen driven in droves to new savage shores.
Villages shoot up & cities where this class digs for ore,
Dead & unpeopled in a flash when it moves away. So quick
A boom was never seen before, nor so quick a bust.

Retaining unaltered the way of production was always the first
Business of the classes that rule – this class is the first that erects
Upsetting as the sine qua non of society. Building its buildings
On permanently quaking soil, fearing nothing
So badly as rusting & moss, it enforces daily change
On the force of existing relations, all that was stable habit.
The steady & solid is pulled down, the sacred desecrated,
& people stand unsafe, the Earth rolling beneath their feet,
Finally forced to examine their living with sober sight.

& all of this happens not in one country or two
For an unquenchable urge to sell off the bulging commodities
Ceaselessly drives the bourgeois class across the whole
Worldwide expanse of the Earth. It must everywhere look around,
Build upon, settle in, everywhere tie the sticky threads.
It makes consumption & production cosmopolitan.
It is at home everywhere & nowhere. It destroys the rich
Crafts & indigenous arts, & fetches its raw materials
From furthest-off places. Its factories service fashions & needs
Brought forth by the most diverse climates. High amid
Clouds the feverish commodities climb up the mountain pass.
They trample on rotting toll-bars that have stood for a thousand years.

Their password is CHEAP! & who are the white-bearded geezers there,
Priests come to curse the blasphemers? Not a chance, they are buyers.
& those walls there, never conquered? – The agents smile
& with bales of lightest calico batter soundlessly down
The Chinese walls. Mountains make way, islands regroup,
Peoples start needing each other. Spiritual wealth too becomes
A commonwealth of spirit. The Roman scholar avidly reads
A formula from Poland, lines penned by an English hand are completed
By a Japanese hand, & together scholars all over the world
Design an image of the world. Literatures of various peoples
Become the world's literature.

Panting, the coolie hauls from entrails of foreign vessels
Products never before beheld, & sweating behind them
The great new begetter itself, the machine. Thus the bourgeois
Civilises the barbarians by turning them into further bourgeois.
Like joins to like & produces more likeness, the bourgeoisie
Produces a world after its own image & likeness.

Thus cities lord it over the country, & they grow gigantic
Constantly tearing people from the doldrums of rural duration.
& as cities over country, so the bourgeois nations lord it over
The peasant henceforth; the civilised rein in barbarians
& semi-barbarians, the East becomes dependent on the West.

Machinery & property & people, up to now scattered about
Coalesce into huge formations. Faster & faster,
Implements pile up in prodigious workshops, masses of people
Agglomerate into abundantly producing centers, & the swelling
Property piles up in the hands of a few proprietors.
New political fields are created: loosely bound regions
Separately ruled, with separate laws & separate tariffs,
Are pressed together into one nation, with one single
National interest of the class that rules over all.

Never before did such a creative ecstasy happen
As was set ablaze by the bourgeoisie at the time of its triumph.
It created power out of steam & electricity. In few years
It cleared up, as by magic, the wildest continents of the world,
Pumped petrol out of the ground & propelled ships with it & cars,
Extracted coal & amassed it into heaping useful mountains,
Dug up iron untouched by a thousand generations
& forged steel into flexible bridges & heavy turbines
Milking the rivers & lakes to light up villages & towns.

It changed forests into weightless paper. Into distant prairies
The daily paper is flung by trains, good news & bad.
In five decades, as if humans wanted simultaneously
To live in all places of the planet, the ether became a carrier
Of messages. And now the first people rise up in steerable aircraft
Above the earth. No dream had ever shown to humanity
That such forces slumbered in its formative womb nor such liberations.

This gigantic creation of goods was confined & fettered
By aristocracy's mortmain & its State of absolute kings:
Wrathfully the bourgeoisie exploded its fetters.

Like unto hurricanes arise the creative forces & shatter
Ancient power, supposed eternal. Other classes,
Yesterday servile, tear up the property deeds, codes
Of law & ledgers of debtors, laughing at senile rights.

Ruling opinions were always the opinions of rulers, they follow
The rulers' downward path, for the flight of thinking must follow
Such tempests: they force the thoughts of people down to the ground
Or wheel them forcibly round to other flight paths.
Right is no longer right, wisdom not wise, all is other.
The temples had seen & defied a thousand seasons' change
When they tumbled down into dust, shaken by the victors' step.
But in those left standing, the gods' countenance changes:
La! the Old Ones wondrously look like the rulers today!
Huge are the changes occasioned by new creative forces.

But liberty equality fraternity, what happened to it?
Freedom for the bourgeois to exploit people, say the classics, equality
Before the law for the rich & poor to buy palaces
Or to be permitted to sleep under the bridge arches.

Born out of tempests that bore it to power, the bourgeoisie
Beholds the deadly tempests violent gather against it.
For now that this class, with its new property deeds & rights,
Had conjured forth forces never hereto imagined
It seemed a conjurer who has lost control of the underground
Forces he has brought up. As rain quickens crops, but unceasing
Completely washes them out, so the rising creative forces
Multiply fortunes & powers of the class that rules, but rising
Still further, they endanger that selfsame rule.

From now on the story of commerce & mass production tells

How the forces that create the goods engage in rebellion against
The bourgeois ownership & bourgeois ways to create goods.

Colossal crises, recurring in cycles, similar to huge
& blindly groping hands that grip & throttle commerce,
Convulse in speechless rage companies, markets & homes.
Immemorial hunger had plagued the world when granaries emptied:
Now, nobody knows why, we're hungry when they're too full.
Mothers find nothing in the bare pantry to fill the small mouths
While sky-high mountains of grain rot behind walls.
And while bales upon bales of cloth are warehoused, the ragged family,
Overnight kicked out of its rented home, wanders freezing
Through emptied city quarters. He who cursed exploiters
Now cannot find exploiters. Ceaseless was his work,
Ceaseless is now his search for work. But the gate is locked.

Alas, even hell functions no longer. Where now? The giant
Edifice of civil society, built with so much exertion
By so many sacrificed generations sinks back into barbarism.
Not the TOO LITTLE is threatening, the TOO MUCH makes it totter.
The house does not exist for dwelling, the cloth for dressing
Nor the bread for stilling hunger: they must bring Profit.
If the product however is only used, but not also bought
Since the producer's pay is too small – were the salary raised
It wouldn't pay to produce the commodity – why then
Hire the hands? For they must produce at the workbench more
Than a reproduction of worker & family if there's to be
Profit! Yet what then with the commodities? In good logic therefore:
Woolens & grain, coffee & fruits & fish & pork
All are consumed by fire, to warm the God of Profit!
Heaps of machines, tools for entire armies of workers,
Blast furnace, shipyard & mine & iron & textile mill
All sacrificed, cut up to appease the God of Profit!

Yet their God of Profit is smitten with blindness. He never sees
The victims. He's ignorant. While he counsels believers he mumbles
Formulas nobody grasps. The laws of economics
Are revealed as the law of gravity at the time the house collapses
Crashing on our heads. In panic torment the bourgeoisie
Starts cutting to pieces its goods & wildly runs with the remains
Around the globe, searching for newer & larger markets
(The plague-stricken thus flees but only carries the plague
Along & infects the places of shelter!). In new & larger
Crises it wakes up staggered. But upon the impoverished people –

Whose multitudes the bourgeoisie is whirling around
In planless plans, now thrown into saunas now onto icy
Streets again – it dawns that the springtime of the bourgeois class
Is over: its constricting world can't grasp the riches created.

Against the bourgeoisie the weapons are raised that once
It death-dealing swung to shatter the feudal world, for it has
In its turn brought forth a class which swings the death-dealing weapons
Against it. Together with it from the very beginnings there grew
In huge masses its inseparable servant, the proletariat,
That only lives by work but only picks up work
If it quick & abundant adds to the bourgeois' capital.

As the capitalist is selling commodities so the worker
Sells his commodity, labour-power, & is forced to compete
& to share the ups & downs of the capitalists' market.
Appendage to the machine, he sells his manipulation
& gets his subsistence & what it costs to propagate
& rear his useful kind, for the price of labour-power,
As of other wares, conforms to the cost of its coming about.
These workers cohabit no more in the patriarchal workshop
Of a master of their craft. Drilled in long columns, foot-soldiers
Of machine trades, they stand in the wide factory halls,
Slaves of the bourgeois class, daily & hourly enslaved.

Work is divided. The workers perform their monotonous part.
The hours run on killing the mind & exhausting the muscle.
What the journeyman of the crafts saw, the product of his hands,
They see no more, no shoe or plough which they would have made.
The machine is ingenious, the worker grows dull, for the grips are
simple:
But the effort put in is still huge, the wheels revolve quicker.
No doubt, anybody can do it. Sweating women & children
Surround the workbench, gender & age count no longer.
All they are now is mere tools & living levers, producing
Commodities whose end it is to create Profit.

When they've given their exploiter more than they cost, when
th' exhausted slumping
Hands finally clutch the scanty pay envelope,
At factory gates new robber bands await them: landlord,
Usurer, shopkeeper, physician, all stage their raids.

No doubt, soon enough such "middle classes" as traders, peasants,

& craftsmen fall into the proletariat, because the small profit
Is not enough to buy new machines, or because factory
Production devalues their specialised skill – all are kicked out
From shop or workshop or tenant farm to the army of workers .

And the proletariat climbs up step by step in the war
That rages between the owners of hands & the owners of tools,
A war that came to be as soon as these classes came to be.

Single workers to begin with, then workers of a single plant
Fought their bourgeois owner. They began by fighting the ways
& not the whole system of bourgeois production of goods. They trashed
Foreign commodities & machines, & burned factories down
To rid themselves of this new, more profound enslavement, to get
Back to the feudal enslavement, to arrest, despairing & tired,
The iron hand on the world clock, by themselves forged.

Still scattered all over the country, the proletarians remain
Long disunited, divided by deadly competition
For work, & the divided workers fight first the enemy of their
Enemy, absolute monarchs & landowners, guildsmen
& clerics; for still the flag of progress flutters over
The bourgeoisie, & it's able to incorporate all victories.
But any victory strengthens also the class it needed
For winning. The growing large industries concentrate proletarians
Into ever huger masses. Workers grow alike:
Who may find a wave in the turbulent torrent? Past differences,
Industriousness or skill, are cancelled working the machine.
Wages are equalised too. They fluctuate & sink in crises
Or totally cease whenever no work is to be had. All of this
Torments all at the same time. Coalitions of workers appear
Seeking to protect their wages. Open collisions begin.

Here & there, briefly, workers may win. More often they lose
The local battle for which they united. But the union stuck
& transcended localities. Trains & then phones connect places.
All over the country scattered skirmishes grow to struggles
Of classes. As a class the workers now fight the political fight.
& the class, oft sundered through competition among its needy members,
Always united anew through new fights fought in common,
Reaches for the letter of bourgeois law & forces the employer
To come a cropper here & there, it manages to pinch
A fleeting little hour or so off the long working day.

But it knows, & when it forgets blows will bring it back:
It has to seize hold of the law & finally break its letter.

The rising class gains much from the old classes' dissension
And constant infighting. Still the bourgeoisie has to fight
Aristocrats in army & civil service, then within
Itself as the deadly roller of progress rolls over some of it,
& above all & always it fights the bourgeoisie of other
Countries. All these require fellow-fighters from lower
Strata, so it drags the proletariat to political struggles
As helper, & arms its own enemy in the arena.

The proletariat learned how to learn. Painstakingly
Exploited at workbench, drill & construction crane, it needed
Education & was forced into schools. Meagre the knowledge
It got & mostly falsified, but knowledge still of the power
Of knowledge & awareness about their thirst for their own
knowledge.

Angry abuse would a Haroon al-Rashid hear on the market
Against the bourgeoisie. The failing corner-store keepers,
Owners of petty businesses as well as rentiers & farmers
Fight tooth & nail to keep their minuscule property intact.
The carpenter luridly curses furniture factories, the farmer
Big agribusiness, & all deplore our moral decline.
These good people don't want to subvert the societal structure, its lone
Good side they are attacking & accusing, the great production
Of goods, shaking their shattered fists in vain.

The rotting mob of our cities, formed from putrefaction
Of the old society's lowest strata, is also oft
Pulled by revolution into proletarian ranks but it is
Only a victim, not an enemy of bourgeois rule, & easily bought
As a bestial servant to batter the proletarians down.

The only class finally that may vanquish the bourgeoisie
& shatter its fettering State is the proletariat. It has
The proper stature & position. What ensured life in the old
Society has long since been swept away & wholly destroyed
In the being of the worker. Without property, to wife & child
Neither family head nor bread-winner, discernible
Barely by nation & race, since identical servitude bound
To identical bench & machine endow him with the same
Identity from the Ruhr to Canton, the proletarian

Sees in religion & morals mere fata-morganas,
Prejudices to him behind which hides the robbing grab.

Other classes, having come to power, protect what they got
While dictating to everybody else the novel way of getting.
This class conquers the goods-producing works by wholly repealing
The way they are got. This class has nothing to safeguard for itself.
Conversely, all individual safeguards it must destroy.

Mountains of machinery behind fences & walls & hidden even better
By laws, & on this side millions upon millions of willing workers
Terribly torn away from the means of working by fences & walls
& the State's laws, each a singleton that may be hired
By the hour to set in motion the machines, hired like water-power
Or electricity, for the cost of production, but only if that
Blind God of Profit, the crazy one, nods, the gambler.

The rulers' rule was always founded on the fact that the ruled
Could somehow live from the toil: their exploitation was sure.
But now the bourgeoisie can manage no more to ensure
A servile life to their serfs. Instead of feeding off
Its proletarians, now it must feed them. It needs to employ them
But has no employment for them & yet lets their numbers swell.
And dehumanisation wins, marking the victims
& victimisers, chaos results from the bourgeoisie's
Plans, the more plans more chaos, & lack is born from production
Wherever it rules, death-dealing to the vast majority.
No longer can society live under its rule. The new class
It raised, the proletariat, will bring it down: it raised
Itself the giant hands that dig its grave.

The vast majority is in this movement, & when it rules
This is no longer ruling but suppression of rule. Only
Oppression shall here be oppressed: the proletarians, lowest
Level of society, must, in order to rise, smash
Into pieces the whole social structure with all its upper levels.
How may the workers break their own class chains?
Only by breaking everybody's chains.

ON BRECHT'S "THE MANIFESTO": COMMENTS FOR READERS IN ENGLISH*

> Dal principio alla fine
> è conveniente seguire ogni giustizia.
>
> Giampiero Neri, *L'aspetto occidentale del vestito*
>
> [From beginning to end/ it is proper to follow all justice.
>
> G.N., "The Western Aspect of Clothing," ca. 1960]

> This most rich poet scattered into all he created seeds of thought destined to spring into full life only later. He was persuaded that any living work grows and works on by immanent force, that it changes with each listener and reader reached. His poems are based on this presupposition, and only the future shall make visible the full width and plenitude of his work.
>
> Lion Feuchtwanger, "Bertolt Brecht" [1957]

1. Some Pertinent History (as Teacher of Life)

In early 1945, most probably already in January, Brecht started working on what he at some point called a "versification of the [Communist] Manifesto" (GKA 27: 219) but at other points also thought of as part of a vaster project, a *Lehrgedicht* (poem for learning) parallel to Lucretius's *On the Nature of Things;* the title of that "Didactic Poem" or "Poem for Learning" was not yet fixed but could have been something like *On the Nature of People* or, more precisely, *On the Unnatural Character of Bourgeois Relationships*. The time slot for this venture of Brecht's in Santa Monica was found by a hiatus in co-translating his play *Life of Galileo* with Charles Laughton: Laughton had to play in the pirate movie *Captain Kidd* in order to redeem time for that translation-cum-adaptation, which eventually resulted in his playing Galileo in Los Angeles. But the deeper impulse for Brecht was the overwhelming approach of an end to World War 2 that put on the agenda the future of Germany; for émigrés of Brecht's stripe this meant: will it be socialist or not (cf. Hartinger 34-38)? During his intense concentration on what turned out to be not only a versification but also a reworking of Marx's *Manifesto* – hereinafter CM – Brecht noted in his diary on March 10, 1945: "Between the 'Didactic Poem' and the terrible newspaper reports from Germany. Ruins and no sign of life from the workers." (GKA 27: 221) Pondering on how to rediscover for German workers the obviously forgotten teachings of Marxism, Brecht concluded that "it seems to me possible to renew the propagandistic efficacy [of CM] today, one hundred years later, and to lend it new, fortified (*bewaffnet*) authority, by sublating its pamphlet character" (GKA 27: 219-20).

This was wholly in line with Brecht's central strategy, perhaps best formulated in his magisterial 1934 essay *Five Difficulties in Writing the Truth,* where the last but not at all least quality that a writer who wishes to combat lying and ignorance must acquire was *slyness*: "slyness in disseminating the truth to many people" (GKA 22.1: 81). The subject-matter of the rise and fall of the "unnatural character" – the original German *Unnatur* is something like "mis-nature" – of bourgeois rule was forced on Brecht's attention in the last years of the Weimar Republic and hugely intensified by the coming to power of Nazism. In the "Conclusion" to the *Five Difficulties*, surely one of the great essays of the 20th century, he wrote:

> The great truth of our epoch (which is not enough, but without which no other pertinent truth can be found) is that our continent is sinking into barbarism because violence is used to cling to the existing relations of property over the means of production.... We cannot search out the truth about the barbaric conditions without thinking about those who suffer under them, and while we, continually sloughing off temptations of cowardice, search for the true relationships because of those who are ready to use such cognitions, we have at the same time to think about presenting the truth in such a way that it could be a weapon in their hands, and also so slyly that this presentation may not be found out and cut off by the enemy. (GKA 22.1: 88-89)

But there was a further and deeper, or at least less moment-bound, reason to use the classical model of epic verse (which, for Brecht, meant the Latin hexameter) as a pedagogical royal road to the listener's understanding. In a memo perhaps to be titled "From Whom Have I Learned," written after the June 1953 rebellion of Berlin workers when Brecht was once again intensely meditating how to renew the efficacy of Marxian tradition for the German workers, he concluded from his experiences:

> There are at least two linked reasons why it's worthwhile to study the two great didactic poems of the Romans, Virgil's *Georgica* and Lucretius's *Of the Nature of Things*. For one thing they are models how to describe in verse the cultivation of nature and an understanding of the universe; and for another, we have in the beautiful translations of Voss and of Knebel

> marvellous elucidations about our language. The hexameter is a verse line which forces the German language to the most fertile exertions. It presents itself as clearly "manipulated," which makes learning much easier. Like Virgil, the translator must teach versification together with agriculture...; in brief, the great artistry of the Ancients is developed by treating great contents. (GKA 23: 269-70)

Today we might wish to say either that there is a feedback between a given form and a given content which determines not only the momentary success of artful writing in its time but also its efficacy and survival for following generations – that is, its becoming and enduring as a classic. Or we might wish to say that the vocabulary of form vs. content is helpful only to a limited degree, and that the how is always consubstantial with the what – most obviously so in poetry. But Brecht's optimistic conclusion might serve as a first reason to inquire further into the uses of what eventually became his unfinished poem *Das Manifest (The Manifesto)*. Discouraged by his best friends such as Eisler and Feuchtwanger, engaged in many other pressing writings, and above all unsure of who would be the poem's readers, Brecht broke off its composition in the second half (probably in September) of 1945. He cherished the project until the end of his life.

The following commentary is divided into a "technical" section and a "substantive" section. The former speaks briefly of the tradition of hexameter in English and my guidelines for translating the somewhat messy variants of Brecht's not finally revised attempt into it. It might perhaps be skipped by readers not interested in it, but they might also find that a full, understanding enjoyment would be helped by not skipping it. The longer "substantive" section focusses on relationships between poetry and history, including doctrine, memory, and associated matters. A reader skipping it might find that supposedly technical decisions – how the translation actually reads – will not be persuasive. There have been benevolent liberal attempts to "save" Brecht by sundering the poetry and the politics in his political poetry or poetical politics. This degrades both, my two sections do not fully follow this divide, and I warn the reader against it.

2. A Commentary for Technical Readers

A hexameter is a verse line with six stresses. Hexameters are in English relatively rather rare, especially longer poems in it. There are some longer English poems in hexameter, such as Tennyson's "Locksley Hall," Swinburne's "Hymn to Proserpine" or Kipling's "Danny Deever," but then they clearly lean on – often elaborate – rhyming. G.M. Hopkins wrote, I think, only one of the "terrible sonnets" ("Carrion Comfort") in hexameter, again rhymed. Unrhymed hexameters, on the Greek and Latin mould – however this mould was misread – are very rare, except for splendid single lines:

> What seas what shores what granite islands towards my timbers
>
> (T.S. Eliot, "Marina")

When hexameters are used, often it's only in conjunction with another, so to say redeeming metre, and again usually outfitted with rhyme, such as this representative first stanza of Hardy's "Afterwards," in which the final line subsides into the more normal pentameter (5 stresses):

> When the Present has latched its postern behind my tremulous stay,
> And the May month flaps its glad green leaves like wings,
> Delicate-filmed as new-spun silk, will the neighbours say,
> 'He was a man who used to notice such things'? (159)

Or, perhaps more cognate to Brecht's epic intentions, the ecological protest plus technical attention to work of Hardy's "Throwing a Tree":

> The two executioners stalk along over the knolls,
> Bearing two axes with heavy heads shining and wide,
> And a long limp two-handled saw toothed for cutting great boles... (204)

– but here too at the end of each stanza a new meter (the heptameter, 7 stresses) breaks any fears of monotony or awkwardness, not quite absent from the first-line spondee, the two stresses in the same metric unit or foot that can be noted as [nérs stálk], which I'd have never dared to use as a translator. But then Hardy's later poems are notorious for bending stress schemes to his communicative needs, see the hexameters – if they can still be called such – of "The Second Visit":

> Clack, clack, clack, went the mill-wheel as I came... (208)

****

When I decided to translate Brecht's *The Manifesto,* I found a messy manuscript situation. In the Berlin Brecht Archive, much helped by the kindness of its director Dr. Erdmut Wizisla and its staff, I found there were 10 folders pertaining to it. But the materials in those folders are partly mingled with scantier materials for that larger plan to write a "Didactic Poem on the Nature of Man," in which *The Manifesto* as it at present stands would have been one out of four parts. The latest and biggest Brecht edition, the Grosse Kommentierte Berliner und Frankfurter Ausgabe 1988-2000, prints *three variant versions* of it plus a handful of fragments not contained in any version (in volume 15, edited by Jan Knopf and Brigitte Bergheim with three more collaborators, pp. 120-57). The notes on pp. 386-407, which follow Bunge's path-breaking overview, claim there are four "stages" (*Bearbeitungsstufen*) dating from 1945 of Brecht's versification of chapter 1 of Marx's *Communist Manifesto*, plus one more "stage" consisting of only 10 verse in 1950. The three variants printed are stages 2-4.

To my mind, however, Brecht's copious rewritings as presented in GKA fall into *two* groups of variants. The first comprises of the GKA editors' stages 1 plus 2 (of which they rightly print only one, and I shall here call it draft or variant 1), and it is obviously poetically less polished. The second comprises the "stages" 3 plus 4 (printed variants 2 and 3), which are better and differ mainly in fine-tuning and in the fact that "stage" 4 is shorter – that is, its corrections were abandoned before the end.

I used as my main text the printed variant 2 (German pp. 135-48), adding however to it the ending which exists only in variant 1 (German pp. 134-35, in my translation ll. 371 on). But I took the liberty of using some formulations which I thought of as better from variant 3, more rarely from variant 1. I interpolated one fragment from German p. 157 as my ll. 203-06 ("But liberty equality fraternity...").

For my purposes of a narrative, indeed doctrinally expository, poem, I adopted Brecht's adaptation of Lucretius's hexameter, which takes for its model Knebel's 1821 German hexameter translation of Lucretius[1]; and furthermore I adopted Brecht's solution to use a loose "stress" hexameter. Eisler claimed it was a "jazzed-up" hexameter, which may be a bit exaggerated unless he rightly implied that it uses syncopation (which is anyway usual in some poetic traditions, such as the English one). However, this Brechtian hexameter is at the antipodes of – say – the stately and formal six-beat French Alexandrine in which some of the most splendid Racine tragedies are written. In "stress verse" (rather than syllable-stress verse) the number of syllables can vary. Brecht wrote the poem to be read aloud, and I much hope this could also apply to my translation. "Loose" therefore also means here that I adopted several guiding principles, all based on the wish to have lines that could be read without too much violation of usual verse rhythms: that is, without either too much stopping or too much slurring over, except for specially intended and rare purposes. My first principle was that my hexameter can go up to but not beyond 18 syllables, that is, in the Classicistic parlance I didn't want to have stress units (feet) longer than 3 syllables – with the well-recognised exception of the final foot in any line. The second was that at the end of each of Brecht's division into sections (which follow Marx's paragraphs in CM) I allowed myself a final line – a dying fall, so to say – of anything between 2 and 6 stresses, though I tried to keep them as near to 5 as possible. Also, I shunned wherever I could feet composed of a single stressed syllable (catalectic iamb) and even more so a foot of two stressed syllables (spondee). The third was that there should be generally rising rhythms – iambs and anapests – though amphibrachs (3 syllables with stress in the middle) were allowed; of course, as in all English rising-rhythm verse, the first foot plus one or even two more feet could be "falling" – trochees or dactyls – since this would not put in doubt the general rhythm, but I tried to keep away, with rare exceptions, from lines with a predominantly falling rhythm (more than 3 feet of trochees or dactyls).

As to syntactic choice: I chose to have a mildly Teutonic syntax. I found a fully colloquial English syntax of 2001 (or 1945) both impossible to attain with Marx's-cum-Brecht's vocabulary and aims, as well as unsuited to the matter at hand: the reader is goddam well supposed to invest as much energy into it as into a dozen pages of physics or political economy. On the other extreme, I hope I've avoided the awful translationese of – as an unkind friend put it – the "flowers did I for you pick" kind. A kinder friend said my halfway house made for a mild estrangement (*Verfremdung*): my heart leapt when I read him, for that's exactly what I'm aiming at. The reader should understand that this was written in German two thirds of a century and one historical epoch ago. It is a piece of history. It is in my opinion more than indifferently useful for today, otherwise I wouldn't have buckled down to translating it. Thus, the reader is not supposed to gobble but to enjoy while understanding (or vice versa), to pause when she feels like it (see "What and How" and "Using Negativities" in this book), and come back to ponder the poem's voice and meanings; ideally, this would be done as a collective effort after reading aloud parts or the whole of the poem. It is the voice of a near and dear but by now old-fashioned grand-uncle. But fashions have not only changed, they can change again: "O change of times, thou hope of the people!" (Brecht). So we who were "born after" (Brecht again) have to invest mental energy into finding out what we can learn from this buoyant, overconfident, wise, irritating, sly, doctrinaire, flexible and above all stimulating voice.

In sum: How much, and just where and how, in what parts or aspects, is this poem applicable to the present day? How much can its various passages as well as its overall tone and stance be of use in vitally needed present-day debates? A public discussion of these central points is the aim of this translation. I shall attempt to start it in Section 3.

A final principle of mine imitated (even if by eversion) the mythical constitution of the Anarchist Federation of Catalonia:

1. There are no obligatory rules.
2. The foregoing paragraph is not obligatory.

In practice this meant that any of the above rules could be violated if my ear and/or my responsibility to Brecht-cum-Marx's sense told me so and I found no other way to follow its telling. I tried not to have too many of such violations.

3. A Commentary for Substantial Readers

Most of Section 2 above might hold for any translation of a long hexameter poem into English. There are of course especially complex problems in Brecht's poem, as in any so-called didactic and/or propagandistic verse (I shall try to unpack this banal designation later). I shall first focus on *the relationship of poetry to doctrine*. One can imagine extreme ideal-types, not encountered in practice, where either is a means completely in service of the other: either verse as a flat rhythmical and mnemonic ploy to sweeten the doctrinal pill, or doctrine as overall, often far-off armature to organise the poet's different – compatible but richer – concerns. The best example that comes to mind of nearness to the second extreme is Dante's *Commedia*, or at least its first two parts. But in Brecht's case the danger is rather the first extreme, the use of verse for the overriding or even sole purpose of enunciating a cognitive theory, a use for which already Aristotle had in the first section of his *Poetics* banished Empedocles from poetry to physics. I found a wonderful example for it in a poem that was T.S. Eliot's now almost totally forgotten contribution to World War 2 propaganda in 1942. He seems to have attempted to show how the type of "universal" poetry he was writing then could express Britain's struggle in 1941-42, but the result is prose arbitrarily hacked into lines:

> The enduring is no substitute for the transient
> Neither one for the other. But the abstract conception
> Of private experience at its greatest intensity
> Becoming universal, which we call "poetry,"
> May be affirmed in verse.
>
> (in Harding 78)

To the contrary, a valid poem – that is, one which should have a good reason to exist beside a prose employing the same doctrinal (philosophical, religious, political, etc.) notions and argumentation – would be somewhere in the middle between the above extremes, in a semantic creative space where ends and means, sense and sensuality, doctrine and poetry remain in a more or less fruitful tension, from the Left of much Mayakovsky and Neruda or Brecht's *Manifesto* to the Right of Eliot's contemporary *Four Quartets* or some of Pound's *Pisan Cantos* (the "Liberal" bourgeois center, being in saddle, has no passionate reason to compose didactic poetry, which seems, since the Romantics, born of dissatisfaction).

In the 1920s Brecht famously remarked that gasoline doesn't fit into, and therefore disallows, the five-act "dramatic tension" form; and he subsequently elaborated – together with many other dramatists and theatre people – his "epic" or dialectical dramaturgy. Analogously, the language of the CM doesn't fit the dominant forms of the English individualist lyric, which have 5 stresses or less. However, it would have less trouble with the popular ballad form, which often had 7 stresses, for example in Brecht's beloved *Sir Patrick Spens* or his equally beloved urban *Moritat* (street ballad) *Das Seemanslos [The Sailor's Destiny]*, though they are usually printed as two lines of 4+3 stresses; and some ballads have even 6 stresses. Thus I believe Brecht's instinct to use the hexameter was sound even apart from the wonderful example of Lucretius.[2] Brecht inventively varied and enriched this language in his attempt to find a halfway house between doctrinal generalisation and concrete experience, to which I'll return; but his goal was to retain the power of Marx's generalisations that construct a cognitive edifice held together by terminological rigour. Therefore *The Manifesto* frequently uses words coined for such doctrinal precision rather than for euphony (sound) or prosody (rhythm). Examples of such repeatedly found terms might have two stresses, as "commodity," which at least has the right pair of rising stresses [-'-'], or as the more difficult, but fortunately rare in Brecht, "capitalism"['- -']. Almost as difficult is "bourgeoisie" (phonetically: boor-zhoo-ah-zee, similar to the French pronunciation, ['- -']), since – with the quite normal elision of its second syllable and stress – it will have 3 syllables (phonetically: boor-zhwa-zee) with a principal stress on the first and a subsidiary but often used stress on the third syllable ['-'].[3] Most difficult proved to me (this says maybe something about my political unconscious?) "proletarian" and "proletariat" which are quite unmanageable in the full 5-syllable form and must usually be, with some difficulty, elided into 4 syllables and two (falling) stresses (proh-leh-teh-ryat, ['-'-]) – on the example of Pope's "con-gen-yal." These difficulties exist also in German (Feuchtwanger took the impossibility of fitting words such as "Proletariat" into verse as excuse to cease collaborating on the project after six weeks in 1945, see his "Bertolt Brecht" 105-06 and Bunge), but given the different rhythms they seem to me smaller there.

Brecht's *Manifesto* participates in the modern (even the most modern, if you wish post-post-modern) tendencies of much in the best poetry of our age to use an "antipoetic" – or more precisely, anti-Idealist – language recuperating exact scientific or philosophical terms. This language was wonderfully defined by the Italian poet Gozzano already around 1908 as: "lo stile d'uno scolare/ corretto un pò da una serva" – "the style of a scholar/ Somewhat corrected by a charwoman" (in his poem "L'altro" ["The Other"], cited in Marcheschi 13-14). This style of poetry dovetails neatly with Brecht's constant attempt at melding plebeian demystification from below with precise intellectual critique. Its informing horizon is that of *verse narration as cognition*, not confined to but not at all shunning conceptual cognition in feedback with behavioural information about stances or bearings (cf. Suvin, both entries on "Haltung"). Poetry is here not only in strong opposition to the stifling superficial babbling of the reigning, totally ideologised *doxa* of the capitalist media or brainwashed common sense, but its main reason for existing is to be a "stumbling block" for the hegemonic babble (cf. Marcheschi 16 and Suvin "Parables") – one which forces the reader-stumbler to stop and look at what is really happening at his feet. This type of poetry remains playful but it is a serious play, the young lions exercising sudden jumps upon each other. It is necessarily fixated on the necessary complicitous reader, at the antipodes and at the expense of the narcissistic navel-gazing of most Post-Modernism. It is much concerned, as Brecht noted in his great programmatic poem "To the Danish Worker-Actors," with precise, technical, verifiable, and repeatable observation of recurring, key, and typical events and relationships. Such materialist poetry, while remaining different from the prose of precise observation, is yet also related to it by an umbilical cord – that is, the verse is in fruitful tension both with the precise observing and, as noted earlier, with the doctrinal obsessive clarity.

The poetry is therefore articulated as a rational discourse "without any inferiority or superiority complex toward natural sciences or history" (Marcheschi 17), yet never sundered from possibly discreet or hardboiled but always strong emotion. Paradoxically, it can be verified in Brecht's *Manifesto* how, at its extreme, such apparent objectivity touches upon and fuses with a functional and gnomic, almost ceremonious, ritualisation, using frequent repetitions, syntactic inversion, *enjambement* (syntactic carry-over into the next line), and a marked rhythm. Characteristically, a rhetorical figure called "adnomination" is used, which repeats noun root in verb root or vice versa (for example "passing without passport" or "Slaves of the bourgeois class, daily and hourly enslaved"). This is in my opinion emblematic for Brecht's attempt to create additional verisimilitude for Marx's concepts by replunging them into the collective activity of human working classes from which they presumably sprang. This figure may serve as a good example how cognition is to be found hidden in sensual tricks of alliteration, assonance, and echo, just as in Dante's initially obscure "Amor, che a nullo amato amar perdona" which will be found, upon reflection, to carry a serious point beneath, through, and by means of the virtuosity.[4] The poetic cognitive movement is in Brecht's usage spiral, for it is both determined, in some ways even predetermined by the nature of things, and also open to human passion and struggling endeavour (in the above examples, against prisons and slavery): nature can only work for us through human nature, and Marx's socioeconomic laws through classes of embodied people. The movement of verse enacts – with the participation of the reader – a ceremony of the struggle against overweening social injustice, in which words and things are given allegorical faces and figures, again turned toward each other; and its Great Ancestor is, indeed, Lucretius *On the Nature of Things*.

Brecht's acumen is nowhere more apparent than in his full consciousness of this ancestry. His unfinished poem had the ambition to be to Marx what Lucretius was to Epicure (himself an object of Marx's doctoral dissertation).[5] Epicure's teachings survived only in some fragments – and in Lucretius's verse (Book 5: 55), where he is repeatedly praised as the great and glorious liberator of mankind from superstition and fear of death, whose footsteps the poet wishes to follow. The premonition that the oblivion could happen to Marx too (practically if not literally) was never absent from Brecht – see his poems on the great exiled poets, among whom Lucretius is, anachronistically, also found, "Die Auswanderung der Dichter" ("The Poets' Emigration") and "Besuch bei den verbannten Dichtern" ("Visiting the Exiled Poets"), GKA 14: 256 and 12: 35. Recent history gave Brecht reason to insist on his fears.

Today, such a form of cognitive poetry is one of the best ways to carry across the roaring oceans of incessantly battering brainwashing the indispensable *memories* how great hopes flourished in the 20th century. It offers a good chance to bring about that necessary piety which entails both a repristination of familiarity with the forgotten teachings and simultaneously their "pitiless critique" (Marx). To use Brecht without criticising him, observed pithily Heiner Müller, means to betray him. In our age this holds, of course, for every cognitive endeavour, and in particular for Marx and the whole Marxian and Leftwing tradition. The poetry is a watchman: "Watchman, what of the night?" The night is deep and dark, but not unsurmountable: "it goes on for twelve hours, then comes the day" (Brecht, *Schweyk in the Second World War*). But orientations in the thick clouds of words and tear gas, or bomb bursts, are badly needed. They have to be supplied from wherever one can get them.

4. What is, then, the *relation of poetry to history*? Surely, charity begins at home: poetry cannot exist without a relation to its own history. The poet – and the translator – must be cognisant of it, but not necessarily the synchronic reader who has to fry today's potatoes today. For her, the relation is basically one of poetry to what Marx and Engels called the only science they knew – the history of relationships among people, in different social formations, in the struggles of classes differently shaping each formation. There should be no special problems here for a poet as narrating *histor*, a teller of (hi)stories committed to an understanding that functions equally as his ethics and his esthetics: for each of us has debts contracted in time toward the living and especially the dead, and the poet pays those debts. The most deeply personal economy is here at one with the sciences studying human and natural economy and with the Marxist understanding of history – those commitments to truth and memory.

However, given that readers are the central reason for the poem's existence, the overriding question for a Marxist or communist – which includes, no doubt in complex ways, a Marxist or communist poet – is the relation of the poems he is writing to the synchronic history, ongoing in the flesh of these readers. (One then also hopes for the poem's long duration, its reaching future readers too, but it doesn't do to think too much about that while writing.) What has changed in that history between 1848 and 1945, and what has not? As Braudel would put it, what are its short-duration and what the long-duration elements and aspects? A brief investigation of the relation between Marx's CM and Brecht's *The Manifesto* might provide a useful link between the relation of a poem to its own textual models and antecedents and to its ongoing historical situation.

In his diary note for February 1945, mentioned at the beginning of these Comments, Brecht continued: "The [Communist] Manifesto is as pamphlet itself a work of art," but continued by postulating that its efficacy could be "today" renewed and strengthened "by sublating its pamphlet character" (GKA 27: 219-20). This implies two main points. First, that in spite of its eminent political and artistic status, CM has been in the practice of both the Second and the Third International movements – that is, of the social democratic and the communist parties – so automatised and ossified that it no longer strikes a potentially interested and approachable reader with the freshness required for joyous perception and efficacy: as the Formalists would have said, it has to be de-automatised, or in Brecht's own coinage, estranged (*verfremdet*). Later in Berlin, he would confide to an assistant, Käthe Rülicke: "This was conceived so slyly. I thought that if the great form is found beautiful, then the content has to be accepted together with it.... Brecht laughed a lot remembering it." (Wizisla ed. 40) And of course we should not forget that the rigidity on the official Left was in great part a defense mechanism against sharp and huge physical and ideological repression. But a second point that follows from Brecht's proceeding is that the change in literary genre, from prose pamphlet to narrative poem in hexameter, was supposed to decisively intervene in this de-automatisation and new perceptibility, in the renewed and – in comparison to the dogmatic idolising – strengthened efficacy of Marx's diagnosis in actual political life. Such changes may be useful to discuss, at least partly and initially, to sharpen the reader's understanding of Brecht's ways of working and intention.

My thesis is that what unites the Marxian political pamphlet and the Brechtian poem for learning is that they both aspire (and largely accede) to a cognitive status. If we are still to bother about them, it is because at least some of their key insights are still valid as guides for action, and others are instructive as to where, why, and how they were (are) wrong. What the social-science people could and should learn from philology is that *the what is never to be separated from the how*: they are consubstantial. Therefore, this cognitive dusting off melds two modes of new understanding: it means not only a notional updating but also a rephrasing in the idiom and for the imagination of the new readers. And rephrasing is never innocent, since the how intervenes in the what. This is what differentiates CM and *The Manifesto*.

The long duration, what has been retained here from the "classical" Marxist tradition, is, first, Hegelian metamorphic forces of constant change, reinterpreted as Marx's chthonic forces at work from the magmatic depths of society; I shall return to the strengthening of the dynamic element in the poem. The "testimonial tenacity" (Marcheschi 27) of Brecht's is in dialogue with a view how Marx's cognitions about forces of history-as-political-economy operate in the flesh of working people. Second, CM is updated with some later insights of Marx's, of which I shall mention only the cyclical theory of crises and the hidden fetishism of commodity economy which are reworked as the magnificent double passage about the Ogres of Crises (translation lines 219ff.) and about the blind Moloch-God of Profit (lines 242ff.). (As usual in Brecht, there are many Biblical echoes.) Brecht participates in the style of the most effective poems discussed earlier – by Neri, for example – posited "to appear as 'marginal notes' of readings in science" (Marcheschi 17), and indeed readings in human sciences, according to Marianne Moore's statement in "Poetry":

> ...nor is it valid
> to discriminate against "business documents and
> schoolbooks"....

Brecht always treated with contempt the antagonism of two forms of understanding and learning, the scientific and the artistic one, while insisting that they cannot be confused. However, his *Manifesto* is more ambitious (and therefore longer): for *it constitutes an updating of CM for the age in which the bourgeoisie reaches for world wars in response to economic crises of its system*.

Thus, the de-automatisation of CM implies, first of all, its *desacralisation* – that is, its critical updating and modification for the 1945 situation in Germany and the world. In March 1945 Brecht wrote to Karl Korsch, the heretic Marxist theoretician whom he, for all their disagreements, revered as one of his few teachers, and who was also the most prominent among his friends to enthusiastically encourage Brecht's project and to praise it as a masterpiece (Korsch 54): "I have modified, as cautiously as I could, some matters in CM, I put instead of the immiseration theory the insecurity caused by structural unemployment, etc. Do you think this is correct?" And further about the never fulfilled plans: "I'm now getting to the second chapter of CM. In it [in Brecht's plan to adapt there Engels's *Principles of Communism*, a small "catechism" in question-and-answer form – note DS], the classics will answer questions. Should I smuggle in new questions? Which ones?" (GKA 29: 349)

Second, Brecht's estrangement entails the *historicisation* of CM. Even the title, *The Manifesto*, indicates it is a citation, a second-order reference to a classic: "CM was the report of its authors to the party they were founding. Brecht's hexameters are the report of a report." (Mayer 65). Brecht's usage relates the past to the present, entangling and disentangling them. The poem is a dialectics of history, both rooted in the past and going on. Therefore, Brecht very often substitutes for Marx's past tenses, which he uses in a few beginning lines, the present tense, which makes his report more dramatically immediate and more vivid, though no less historically sweeping: I shall underline in the two examples below (translation lines 15ff. and 51ff.) the explicit switch from past to present:

> You've heard much untruth about it from enemies, from friends
> Much untruth also. This is what the classics *say*:

or:

> Thus came about the age, which now is ending, of the bourgeois:

A fleeing serf, he became a burgher of the market town,
Then of the city, & behind its secure walls the guilds
Flourish. Cloth keeps crossing the walls...

The present tense presents both the validity of insights from CM and yet modifies it with new ways of seeing and the immediacy of direct witnessing. Paradoxically, in terms of German literary theory (derived from Schiller), where the epic is characterised by turning to the past and the drama by turning to the present, Marx is more epical while Brecht is epico-dramatic.

Third, as is proper of poetry, the already vivid but largely analytical argumentation of CM is much more strongly *dramatised*. This is achieved by various means: syntactic parallelism instead of Marx's logical subordination; further use of personification, most prominent of which is the bourgeoisie, but which encompasses also the Ogre Crises or the God of Profit, and thus builds on the strong fantastic imagery already there in Marx (see Suvin-Angenot for a lengthy discussion); and dynamic action, for example by the much more articulated and active Spectre of Communism. The main sections of CM begin with a general thesis, which is then discussed and validated in lengthy analytical passages, and leads to a general programmatic upshot. Brecht uses much of this, but always subsumed under a dramatic story of workers as representatives of a humanity subjected to an increasing whirlpool of violence, predicated on mysterious deities of Profit, and of a possible remedy to the terrible threat.

Much more could be said, for example about his vocabulary or his rhetorical figures such as the hyperbole (cf. Schober 145-65), but I shall close by noting that there is an overriding unnamed figure in the poem: the narrating voice, the poet-narrator. He is an anthropologist, advancing into the jungle of factories and cities with "a hot heart in a cold person" (Brecht, GKA 26: 207); and his rigour arises out of the blood, sweat and tears of millions through centuries. Here is an example for the foregoing discussions, the first lines of the poem:

Wars are destroying the world, and the ruins are visibly haunted
By an enormous spectre, not simply born of war.
In peace it could already be sighted, terror to the rulers
But friend to the children of slums. In scanty kitchens
Often it peeps, horrified, angry, into the half-empty pots.
Often it waits for the exhausted in front of shipyards and mines;
It visits friends in jails, passing without passport.
Even in offices it may be seen and in lecture-rooms
Heard. At times it dons a hat of steel, enters
Huge tanks and flies with deadly bombers. It speaks in many
Tongues, in all of them. And in many it holds its tongue.

The discourse has shifted into 1945, that is, out of Marx's early 19th-century situation of the Holy Alliance in Europe. We are in the modern world of world-wide wars, of tanks, bombers, and ruins, of many languages and repression in most of them; and yet still a world recognisable to Marx, with mines, shipyards, offices, and lecture halls, but – most important – with half-empty pots, exhausted workers, slums, and jails. In other passages, the most massive addition to Marx's CM is his own crisis theory, actualised through the vivid experiences of the post-1929 crash. This fits into the poem's heroic attempt to create a productive feedback between Marx's formulations (the haunting spectre, the grave-digging, etc.) and Brecht's return to the original magma of the daily experience of millions which also lay at the distant basis of those formulations. In philosophical language, Brecht's verse actualises this feedback between deduction and induction, between a framework pre-existing the matter of the poem (*ante rem*) and a verification plus modification within the matter (*in re*). The modification can best be seen in this breathtakingly daring opening, in the best epic tradition of beginning with a bang *in medias res*, in the thick of things: "*Wars* are destroying the world." The class struggle will re-emerge with a vengeance in the latter part of the poem, but to begin with it is here to arrest not simply millennial social injustice but also the by now possible smashing up (*zerschmettern*, a wonderful expression that I failed to fit into the poem's rhythm) of the world. It is my strong conviction that the wars – both the two World Wars and the over 200 "local" wars since 1945 – are an essential and indispensable tool of capitalism, without which the bourgeoisie couldn't survive (see the first essay in this book), so that the singular paucity of sustained Leftwing theorising about war borders on death-wish. Perhaps we're just beginning to climb out of this largely self-dug pit after the Gulf and Serbian wars. Brecht can here too serve as our Great Ancestor, who prophetically indicated the way.

5. Here we could then reopen the question of *didactic or propagandistic poems.* These terms are more than a little misleading, for to my mind all poetry teaches attitudes or bearings by pregnant example: say, Petrarch's about yearning for the ideal woman, Dante's about the political ethics of his time validated by and as cosmology, Baudelaire's about the beauty proper to the evil megalopolises of the bourgeoisie. This is almost genetically encoded into poetry, which began either as direct accompaniment to collective work (work songs) or as a moment of pause before or after the collective enterprise (hunt, cultivation, war, athletic competition) where the song with music and most often rhythmic movement (dance) was an organising tool: it rehearsed the reasons and modalities of action or commented on its outcome. Homer's type of epic is halfway from an oral tribal encyclopedia to a single poet writing for civic group recitals: it is still collective poetry, though by now of the aristocratic class. It takes for its scope a knowable totality: all the techniques, including those of war, of religion, of shipping, and of political oratory, the games, the geographical and cosmic knowledge, the education, the jurisprudence, etc. Its narrative agents are therefore necessarily types, positive or negative behaviour models: Penelope of the constant wife, Achilles of courage, Thersites of the hateful plebeian... Later non-choral, class-society

verse was then shaped by a type of occasion in which the single person of the poet was led to reveal his own aspirations and experiences – which however remained exemplary, pretending to collective validity. It remained valid even in the great change when the poetry came to register alienation, as in the lyrics of Catullus or Baudelaire, or in Hesiod's epic about our iron age:

> Eut'an ep'emporien trepsas aesifrona thumon
> bouleai de khrea te profugein kai limon aterpea,
> deixo de toi metra polufloisboio thalasses
> (If then you set your imprudent mind to commerce,
> Wishing to flee penury and woeful hunger,
> I'll show you what is proper to the much-roaring sea...
>
> *Erga kai hemerai/ Works and Days*, vv. 646-48)

The teaching versifiers were indifferently what Aristotle and his pre-romantic readers would call poets or scientists (or indeed political leaders, such as Isaiah or Solon or Mao). This held in spades for the hexameter tradition running from Homer and Hesiod to Lucretius and Virgil. Contravening this immemorial foundation, the bourgeois critical hegemony decided, at some point of etiolated Romanticism and fearful border-settings, that the teaching of politics was not the proper pursuit of unreliable verse, and identified all didactics with such disallowed "propaganda": "Politisch Lied, ein garstig Lied" – "political poem, a nasty poem," said the great philistine Goethe (in a political poem).

Yet in all significant cases, as in the names just mentioned, such versifiers or poets were never simply followers of a doctrine, rather they were its shapers or reshapers (which is poetically speaking the same). They were the opposite of facile moralisers: creators who went in for a vision of the essence of matters, cognisers. Brecht's voice is one of a teacher, no doubt, but a peculiar one: a Socratic pedagogic facilitator, whose overriding maxim was that the learner is more important than the lesson. In other words: the Law is here for Humanity, not vice versa; the lesson is not only to be incarnated into but also modified by the Brechtian "worker-readers," just as the versifying voice has transubstantiated and modified the original CM. This is the voice of a critical intellectual, in a Gramscian sense organic to the plebeian movement; in Brechtian terms we could call this poem the voice of an "intellectual-reader" who has found some answers reading Marx, and repeats them faithfully, that is: reworking them for the situation of mid-20th century.

In his "poetics" *Ad Pisones*, Horace discusses whether the tragic poets who take their plots from Homer are really poets, that is, creative writers. His answer is that the epic events of Homer will be transmogrified into the tragic effects of a good tragedian if he refrains from idle paraphrase and instead of being a servile imitator be a true "translator," who takes the Homeric characters and supplies them with new speeches and actions. In Book 3 of his *Scienza nuova*, Vico comments on this passage that such excellent tragedians "will be new poets in the style of Homer" (320). Vico argues elsewhere that "all ancient Roman law was a serious poem" or *carmen* (390), a binding social incantation. Thus Brecht can be called a new serious poet, penning a social incantation in the style of Marx.

For analytical convenience, we can separate his reworking into two aspects: as to the *what*, lessons that have intervened between 1848 and 1945, and in particular Marx's later work on capitalist economics and some lessons of Leninism, born and reborn out of the World Wars; as to the *how*, the new cognitive tool of Lucretian narrative poetry. (Of course, I have been arguing that how and what are in any corporeal reality, including very much the corporeal reality of practicing poetry and poetic practice, consubstantial.) From various other works of Brecht, it can be inferred he considered this tool to be at least equivalent, and possibly superior, to systematic philosophical discourse, which may be a good weapon but is prone to doctrinal congealment – Brecht likened it to a condensed snowball, which shouldn't be kept in one's pocket too long. Paul Valéry observed in his discussion of poetry that when a lion digests mutton it turns into lion-flesh. Unfortunately, he hasn't given us a metaphor as to what happens when a lion cannibalises another lion from long ago. At any rate, Marx's substance is transmuted in Brecht, as Brecht's ought to be in the reader-lamb facing any new situation – keeping however unchanged and constant the central and determining horizon of class emancipation, and the vector of desire toward it.

Brecht's poem was not finished, but it happens to end – rephrasing the end of Part 1 of CM – with what I see as a sufficient ending. It answers the initial, catalyzing violence of the bourgeois world wars of each against each with a healing levelling of the violent class structure:

> ...the proletarians, lowest
> Level of society must, in order to rise, smash
> Into pieces the whole social structure with all its upper levels.
> The workers may break their own class chains
> Only by breaking everybody's chains.

While today we may have to redefine what we mean by the proletariat (as I attempt elsewhere), the 21st century, amid still worse wars already upon us, still has to absorb – and no doubt transmute – this end.

Works Cited in Essay 2

See in *Works Cited in this Book* the following titles, by Author surname plus (when the author has several titles) first "headword" or identifying syntagm in the title. This list does not give an overview of the secondary literature on Brecht's *Das Manifest*. A number of pioneering works from 1962 to 1976 have for the purposes of my subject-matter been superseded by later research.

Brecht; Bunge & Eisler; Feuchtwanger, both titles; Harding; Hartinger; Hesiod, *Works*; Knopf; Korsch; Marcheschi; Mayer; Mittenzwei; Schober; Serres; Suvin „Haltung," „Haltung (Bearing)," „Parables"; Suvin with Angenot; Vico; Wizisla; Wormell.

POEMS 2

ZUM GELEIT: DAS MANIFEST

Interrupted by frantic faxes to banks in Europe & phone
Calls to safely steer his savings into a small piece of real
Estate, an apartment in a warmer climate that would permit him
To pass the remainder of his days with his wife & little indignity,
Slipping thru at least the most constricting capitalist meshes
– The translator laboured on this piece of antique subversive hope
In hope to gain for himself & some others usable glimpses
Of what a philosopher-poet of old had to transmit as insight,
As counsel for us professionals, subversives from the bourgeois
Class turning against this rotten class, *verjagt mit gutem*
Grund, how to face the undreamt of global degradation,
The barbarisation foreseen but bet against by old Bert,
Where we are condemned to pass our days, before the waves
Of the Red Sea close on those who disbelieved the prophets.

8-1000

<u>*Glossary*</u>: Zum Geleit (Ger.) = as escort
verjagt mit gutem grund (Ger.) = kicked out for good reasons, title of an autobiographic poem of Brecht's

3

Explorations of Terror, Terrorism, Anti-Terrorism*

PART 1: ACCESS TO AN IDENTIFICATION OF "TERRORISM": WORDS AND ACTIONS (2001)

> …neque hi… ueritatem querunt, sed pugnam.
> [Neither are they after truth but after a fight.]
>
> Petrus Abaelardus, *Theologia "summi boni"*

> [As in Orwell's 1984, the] "war on terrorism" is terrorism.
>
> John Pilger, *The New Rulers of the World*

0. While millions of words, bytes, and airwave hours talk about terrorism, and the powerful are acting in the name of repressing it, it is a word and concept used almost universally to whip up polluted emotions in order to spread polluted reasoning. Nonetheless, it is not possible to simply deny this term, tempting as this may be. It is not only practically unavoidable but my hypothesis is that there is a useful kernel to it.

Amid systematic obfuscation, I wish to adopt Dorothy Dinnerstein's great confession of faith:

> ...we must try to understand what is threatening to kill us off as fully and clearly as we can.... And... to fight what seems about to destroy everything earthly that you love – to fight it... intelligently, armed with your central resource, which is passionate curiosity – is for me the human way to live until you die. (viii)

I shall be unable here to go, as she did, into the murky psychic depths of what drives the lust to power, profit, and killing.

1.1. What Is Terror?

The English word comes from the Latin verbal root *terrēre*, meaning "to frighten," and the nominal root *terror* (probably mediated through French, thence the early spelling "terrour"). Its meanings are glossed in the OED as: 1. intense fear, fright or dread; with an adjective, or in the form "a terror" or "terrors," it was used for an instance thereof; 2. "The action or quality of causing [such] dread"; "terribleness"; and "a thing or person that excites terror."

Earlier divine and supernal, terror grew with the waning of religious feeling lay and as it were democratic, potentially lurking everywhere. Already in Juvenal's railings against popular religion, one can find a Stoic refusal of death's terrors ("mortis terrore carentem," *Satire* X: 357). Toward the end of 18th century, terribleness and induction of extreme dread becomes the staple of a whole range of prose fiction, called tales of terror, well represented by the *OED* quote from Godwin's *Caleb Williams* (1794): "The terrors with which I was seized... were extreme." Arguably it is such novels, with their insistence on death as lustful carnage and rape of the body, that prepared a double conversion of the divine and supernatural connotation of "terror": first, into an inimical and evil connotation, laicised but suffused with a satanic numinosity; second, into an action that was no longer the exclusive property of the superiors (divinities, rulers, generals – see *Dictionnaire...* 1835) but could be exercised by marginal individuals too. Thus, already in 1788 Gibbon could write: "The ferocious Bedoweens, the terror of the desert." It is quite characteristic that this first negative use was applied to warlike non-European barbarians within a discussion of the "Decline and Fall of the Roman Empire"!

The British "Gothic novels" – but their fashion spread throughout Europe – thus gave their safe readers a homeopathic dose of the evil connotation of "terror," usually located in feudal Catholic venues far off in space and/or time. This delicious fright ceased when it was transferred to the political arch-bugbears of conservative England, the Jacobins in the French Revolution whose 18 months in power (ca. March 1793 to July 1794) were dubbed "the Reign of Terror," "the Terror" or "the Red Terror," and later popularised by a whole range of melodramatic fiction, from Dickens to D'Orczy (the "White Terror" of the Royalists against the revolutionaries in 1794-96 was not popularised). Thence the term of (capitalised) Terror, as a rule provided with an adjective identifying the evil enemy, was applied to all armed suppression of internal enemies in a revolution, especially one with anti-bourgeois leanings, such as the Red Terror and the White Terror in the Paris Commune of 1871. This became a staple argument and then cliché of newspaper and other propaganda in the UK and

USA at the time of the Bolshevik revolution of 1917 and the ensuing civil war in Russia, including the White Terror after the putdown of revolutions and uprisings in Berlin, Bavaria or Hungary at the same time. It can be seen in the primly shrill *OED* definition of the Jacobin Terror as "the period... when the ruling faction remorselessly shed the blood of persons of both sexes and of all ages and conditions whom they regarded as obnoxious."

The derived word "terrorism" comes from the French. It was a neologism of the 1790s, alongside of *terroriste* and *terroriser (Dictionnaire... 1798*, Partridge 708), but it was immediately picked up in England as indicating the policy of systematic intimidation by the government of revolutionary France. This became seamlessly transferable to any policy intended to strike the victims with terror or strong dread. Two remarkable arguments from such debates, the questions about the reasons for and the indiscriminate governmental abuse of the term "terrorism," echo down to our days. The favourite English charge of terrorism, after French Jacobins, was for Irish insurgencies; from the Irish side, the following was recorded by the writer Brendan Behan: "He said it was the fault of the British boss class that the Irish were forced always into terrorism to get their demands" (*Borstal Boy* 1958). And applied to Mandela's ANC movement: "The Minister [of the South African apartheid government] cannot expect journalists to do violence to the English language by describing guerrilla warfare as terrorism at all times and in all circumstances" (the *Cape Times* of 1977).

The lexeme "terror" was then applied in different combinations, of which perhaps the most frequent is "terror-stricken," but the two most interesting ones relate to abuses by jailors and to bombing. Already in 1897 convicts "sweat terror-drops beneath their blankets" (at night), and in 1970 this is sardonically explained in G. Jackson's letter from a US jail, which runs in part: "...our cells were being invaded by the goon squad: you wake up, take your licks, get skin-searched.... Rehabilitational terror." (*Soledad Brother*)

"Terror-bombing" is documented in print in 1941 for Hitler's use against Rotterdam, but it was probably used also to describe the Luftwaffe bombing of Guernica in the Spanish Civil War and its subsequent "lightning strikes" against Warsaw, England, Belgrade, etc. The *OED* definition is "intensive and indiscriminate bombing designed to frighten a country into surrender," and from 1940 on, terror-bombing of German cities was deliberate British – and then US – military policy, estimated to have killed over half a million people (Walzer 255-62). It had its roots in Italian, Spanish, French, and British imperial repressions of colonial uprisings before 1940 in Libya, Morocco, Iraq, Somalia, and Ethiopia (see Lindqvist and Davis 15-22). It has gone on in spades in subsequent US ventures, from Dresden and Hamburg, then Tokyo and Hiroshima, to Hanoi, the Gulf Wars, Serbia, and our days, in its allies and clients, as well as in emulators such as Russia or Turkey, as a technoscientific form of mass murder. In that sense, I argue in my first essay, Hitler has won. Internationally, we live in a Hitlerite world.

1.2. Who Is a Terrorist?

The Conservative English historian and politician Harold Nicolson confided to his diary for 1968: "When people rise against foreign oppression, they are hailed as patriots and heroes; but the Greeks whom we are shooting and hanging on Cyprus are dismissed as terrorists. What cant!" (*OED* s.v. "terrorist"). Today the (non-)definition according to the US government and all the consensual NATO media is very simple, if circular: as Uri Avnery notes, terrorists are all the armed enemies of the US-led coalition against bin Laden and his (not further delimited) "terrorists." Notoriously, the official US literature on terrorism for the last 30 years or so "evades definition.... [It doesn't] define terrorism because definitions involve a commitment to analysis, comprehension, and adherence to some norms of consistency." (Ahmad) It can never be repeated too often that bin Laden's network was allowed to develop and – among other proxies all around the globe – used for guerrilla warfare, including terrorism, by the USA and its allies, so that it would not have existed but for the murderous cynicism of the morally and materially responsible States; Ronald Reagan called a delegation of Afghani anti-Soviet fighters in 1985 "the moral equivalent of America's founding fathers," and spent four billion US dollars to train and arm their zealots. And even today, as Chomsky put it, "there is plenty of bin Ladens" (as well as murdered civilians) on both sides of the conflict that burst into the world headlines with the Twin Towers attack (*9-11* 34).

The US is not alone in self-interested dodging of a definition of terrorism: its clarification makes all strong States uneasy. For an example, this was dropped from the jurisdiction of the proposed International Criminal Court in 1998 precisely because of the deadlock in defining, which seems to stem from the powerful being unwilling to accord any – even totally negative – precise and legal status to that notion. For on its heels would come the possibility of recalling the term's original meaning, which pertains to governmental actions. Avnery's own, only semi-ironical definition is: "The difference between freedom-fighters and terrorists is that the freedom-fighters are on my side and the terrorists are on the other side." After Clinton bombed Sudan and Afghanistan, Solomon mimicked the official nonsense more fully: "When they put bombs into cars and kill people, they're uncivilized killers. When we put bombs on missiles and kill people, we're upholding civilized values. – When they kill, they're terrorists. When we kill, we're striking against terror."

This type of defining is easy, for it rests on an argument by authority and ostension reducible to: "terrorism is what I point to when I say that word"; this can be thoughtlessly reproduced on the basis of one or a very few visible and televisable instances of undoubted terror attacks. Such is the case with the crashing of planes into the WTC towers. (It is interesting to note that pictures of the damaged Pentagon disappeared from all TV screens and other media follow-ups. The reasons may include army sensitivity plus smaller spectacularity, but I'd think another factor is that it was of dubious efficiency as thought-suppressing propaganda, since it raised the argument whether all those working in the Pentagon are to be considered soldiers or not. If yes, this would be an act of aggression and killing in an undeclared war – such as there have been plenty in these last years – but an act of terror/ism only insofar as the plane passengers were concerned. And propaganda cannot face arguments.) Terrorists are then "people I say have committed the act I'm pointing to (trust me, I know)."

Nonetheless, defining-by-fiat-and-pointing transgresses so offensively against elementary rules of reasoning and understanding that it eventually runs up against grave disadvantages. The well-known US columnist Michael Kinsley noted that the disadvantages were already felt in the 1980s when defining terrorism was (inconclusively) a major industry in Washington because "a definition was badly needed to explain why [the US government was] supporting a guerrilla movement against the government of Nicaragua and doing the opposite in El Salvador" – and in very many other places. He also reported that "Reuters has banned the word in reference to Sept. 11 and CNN officially discourages it." This dilemma has, for a small example, led to at least one European newspaper, quite supportive of the US war but still grasping for some elementary logic, calling its daily rubric "War against bin Laden."

An important ingredient of the Bush rhetoric is the systematic slippage between, and finally equation of, "terror" as a quality or action and as an overarching category, possibly an allegorical personification of this quality and/or action; this personification was in the *OED* examples above also called "terror" but the US Government Newspeak has settled on "terrorism." The reason for this, I suspect, is that "-isms" are by unargued assumption foreign, ideological, and non- or un-American (except for patriotism to the "Homeland," another Newspeak coinage unfortunately similar to the Nazi Germans' "Heimatsfront"). Even "terror" in the sense that implies political killings of civilians is a semantic import from Britain aimed at aliens: it is always something "they" do and "we" do not. And such a terrorism is a transcendental, evil or satanic quality, rather than a group of people. "Terrorists" are therefore not people who have such-and-such views for such-and-such reasons – both of which might be totally wrong, but one would have had to argue it clearly and convincingly. Rather, "terrorists" are people who participate in the evil totemic essence of "terrorism."

Although we are by now in an unholy alloy of heretic theology, mythomorphic ritual, and Machiavellian pragmatics, I'd agree with Kinsley that Bush's slogan of "war against terror"[1] has the obvious political advantage of rallying the citizens of USA and other nations to whatever armed actions may be proclaimed as being anti-terrorist. The undefined status of the target, the satanic ubiquity of the evil (a mutated or cloned successor to Reagan's Evil Empire), means that this can be extended at will to whatever State or group a huge propaganda campaign can successfully present as terrorists. The authority for this is derived not primarily from law but from a theological pretence at global omniscience (see Ahmad for a small list of instances where US knowledge was insufficient or wrong, but the career of bin Laden is proof enough). Thus the US government, while semantically incoherent, has at any point in time had clear practical or pragmatic delimitations as to who was and who was not a terrorist, in order to decide who is to be respectively helped, neglected, or attacked. The delimitation was based on *use of armed force against US government and corporation interests*, and will be discussed further in 1.3.

However, Kinsley rightly points out an equally obvious disadvantage: "a war against terrorism cannot be won. Terrorism is like a chronic disease that can be controlled and suppressed, but not cured [by war]." In Avnery's example, the Nov. 2001 "blockade against Palestinian villages by the Israeli army, which... denied them water and food, does not isolate the 'terrorists,' but on the contrary turns them into national heroes. The devastation caused by the Russians in Chechnya did not break – indeed, it strengthened – the opposing guerrilla forces." Thus, Avnery is right to say that "Since terrorism is always a political instrument, the right way to combat it is always political. Solve the problem that breeds terrorism and you get rid of terrorism." It can only be durably cured by removing its root causes, psychological, political, and finally economical (humiliation, poverty, and hunger). If the Talebans are to be lastingly defeated, which would be in the interest primarily of the Afghani people, this people will have to do it – with a lot of mainly economic help from outside. Otherwise, some analog to the Talebans, in or out of Afghanistan, will recur.

The question arises what will happen if the Taleban armed forces go underground, into guerrilla warfare or into abeyance, but the terror attacks do not cease. How will the war be continued? Proxies, similar to the terrorist Contras in Latin America or the murderous Northern Alliance in Afghanistan, can easily be found and paid. A little bombing here and there, as has been going on against Iraq now for ten or so years, can easily be arranged. But would this suffice for US government psychological warfare at home and abroad or for US corporations' profits (which finally subtend the government actions)?

Clearly, the temptation is huge to fabricate another "rogue State" for full-scale bombing (Iraq again? – or a number of other possibilities between Libya and the Philippines). In that case we would be quite beyond a believable link to terrorism. Other demands, such as giving up ABC weapons, would have to be adjoined. But then one wonders what would be either the legal or the moral case for keeping them by US, Russia, and other powers?

Kinsley also notes that the definition of terrorism is a problem for civil liberties. The problem was brought about by President Bush and the US government defining its response as "a war against 'terrorism,' not just against the perpetrators of the particular crime of Sept. 11." What liberals like Kinsley pretend not to see, however, is that the "'war on terrorism' ... is the long-sought-after replacement for the 'red scare', justifying a permanent war footing and paranoia, and construction of the greatest military machine ever: ...the 'full spectrum dominance' of the world" (Pilger 10). If the "war against terrorism" will be, as it seems intended, an ongoing affair of years or even entire generations, and if – given the lack of definition – anybody who opposes or even hampers "the war effort" may in a broad or elastic sense be identified as a terrorist, or helper and associate of terrorists, this practically assures a militarised Fortress North America, and a docilely following Fortress (West-Central) Europe. Since continent-sized impermeable fortresses are not possible, a patchwork of smaller "gated" security areas for the rich has already been appearing long enough for J.G. Ballard to have written several canny (or is it uncanny?) sarcastic novels about it. As it becomes clear this war cannot be won or finished once and for all but may go on to include other strikes against resurgent or even threatening evil, a constantly strengthened Police State, including private mercenaries, will be required. It is already well under way.

That this huge threat to civil liberties is real was confirmed by Bush's executive order of Nov. 13, 2001, allowing the unlimited detention of foreign suspects and the setting up of military tribunals to judge people accused of terrorism, and moreover demanding the right for those tribunals to judge anybody anywhere in the world. The whole world may increasingly look like a bloated, racially over-determined version of rich suburbs vs. sprawling slums for the poor. In such a context, imposing martial law at will is a move toward a global Iron Heel: the slogan "no to globalisation" suddenly acquires new dimensions.

Thus, since US citizens are not the only people in the world, the definition of terrorism should, to my mind, be as precise as possible: narrow as concerns civil liberties in the USA and its allies, broad as concerns preventing killings of civilians abroad.

1.3. Exemplary Killing of Civilians for Political Purposes

What then may reasonably be called terrorism, without reducing this word to an empty noise of brainless condemnation and blind self-congratulation? As Kinsley asked:

> So what distinguishes terrorism? Is it the scope of the harm? Most terrorist actions are fairly small-scale compared with the death and destruction committed by nation-states acting in their official capacities. Even Sept. 11 killed fewer people than, say, the bomb on Hiroshima – an act that many Americans find easy to defend. So can terrorism mean acts of violence in support of political goals except when committed by a government?

(This would mean, I add, that George Washington was a terrorist but Adolf Hitler was not.) What about "State-sponsored terrorism"? This too does not distinguish the "rebel groups that [USA is] flooding with help from other groups that [USA is] trying to destroy." The Hiroshima and other World War bombings of civilians may seem both far away and responses to an urgent danger – they are in fact neither – against clearly terrorist Nazi Germany and Imperial Japan. But what about US-sponsored murders and tortures of tens of thousands of civilians in Central America, or in Chile beginning on Sept. 11, 1973? Has any administration after Kissinger disavowed them or asked forgiveness from the Latin American peoples? Do the people of USA know that the World Court condemned their State for mining Nicaraguan harbours in 1986?

In that sense, where Kinsley, as a good liberal, finally throws up his hands in facetious despair, I think Avnery is right but incomplete when he defines terrorism as "a method of attaining political goals by frightening the civilian population." As he argues, bombing or otherwise killing soldiers is never called terrorism. On the other hand, the policy of Mandela's ANC did not preclude terrorism, the Maccabees killing Hellenised Jews were clearly terrorists, early ethnic cleansers, and so were the Israeli Irgun faction insurgents – says Avnery, who was himself an Irgun member – throwing bombs in 1938 into Arab bazaars in Palestine or shooting up a bus full of Arab civilians. Being a dissident Israeli patriot, Avnery points out that

> Israel has used this method [terrorism] from the day of its inception. In the early 50s the IDF [Israeli army] committed "retaliation raids" designed to frighten the villagers beyond the border in order to induce then to put pressure on the Jordanian and Egyptian governments to prevent the infiltration of Palestinians into Israel.... In the 1996 "Grapes of Wrath" operation, Prime Minister Shimon Peres terrorized half a million inhabitants of South Lebanon by aerial bombardments into fleeing North in order to pressurize the Beirut government into stopping the Shiite guerillas from attacking the Israeli occupation force and its mercenaries.

However, Avnery's definition lacks the element of *exemplary* killings in order to cow the rest of civilians *for a political objective*. Without this, we'd get to the unhelpful conclusion that, say, gangster/mafioso killings aiming for advantages such as turf domination, or sociopathological individual killers, both of which lack an agenda of full political domination, would also be terrorist. While there are grey zones here, my provisional definition would therefore run: terrorism is a strategy which consists in pursuing political power by striking dread into the civilian population through exemplary killings among them.[2]

It follows that terrorism is a matter of influencing through huge bodily harm the collective imagination by transfer contagion: an exasperated form of psychophysical warfare grafted upon techniques of economic and political propaganda in the media and spectacle age.

As to differentiations within terrorism, Webster's *Collegiate Dictionary* put it nicely: terrorism is "the use of terrorizing methods of governing or resisting a government" (cited in Ahmad). Any sane typology of terrorist entities should begin by *differentiating between State terrorism and group terrorism*[3] – though the types at times overlap, as when States use paramilitary or gangster vigilante groups for murders. This differentiation is reinforced by the additional, nowadays indispensable, criterion of the politico-technoscientific ways of carrying out terror/ism or being terrorists: States can use terror-bombings (and shelling by heavy artillery), the others don't have such means – yet. That's why the Sept. 11 terrorists had to improvise flying mega-bombs by recategorising passenger airplanes as such.

Politically, and even corporeally, there are two main technoscientific ways of carrying out terror/ism or being terrorists: terror-bombing at a distance, and all other terror killings. Insofar as the US/NATO bombings of Serbia and Iraq were not pointed at their armed forces but against the infrastructure of daily life – power stations, bridges, non-military factories, etc. – for the purpose of getting the civilian population to turn against a government obnoxious to the bombers (which succeeded in Serbia but failed in a fully dictatorial Iraq), they were terror-bombings and their perpetrators terrorists. This leaves open the vexed question of intent, that is: can "collateral" killings of civilians, when unintended, be exempt of the charge of terrorism? To my mind, in this field of systematic muddying of waters and PR spin-doctors, proclamations of intent count for very little: it is a matter of reasonably weighing both political evidence and number of victims. Bombing from high altitudes looks rather like "substituting Afghan [or Arab or Serbian – note DS] civilian for US military casualties" (Milward 164).

By far the largest number of victims of terrorism is due to State activities backed by territorial control and/or heavy weaponry: I shall discuss this at greater length in Part 2. The non-airborne terror of the political groups – we might call it lamely "ground terrorism" – is often a weapon of the weak (a Palestinian is quoted by Avnery as saying: "Give me tanks and airplanes, and I shall stop sending suicide-bombers into Israel") or simply diplomatically and strategically convenient, such as the Contras as imperial proxies in Latin America or the Serbian snipers killing Sarajevo citizens. This does not make it better. Neither the ground nor the air terrorists blasting civilians have any justification, only political calculation of the most cynical kind.

1.4. Parting Considerations

The overriding criterion that emerges is preventing killing: in the particular case of terrorism (killing civilians for purposes of political domination), which is by a ratio of about 100,000:1 or more the most prevalent one for murders from the 20th century on, I would strongly argue for extending this criterion to include the only slightly, if at all, less horrible cases of maiming, wounding, and indeed – drawing on my personal experiences as a child – of psychic terrorising by horrible fear of being killed which always accompanies and often precedes bodily injury. I believe we should reject the Al Qaeda justification that the Sept. 11 victims are a minimal vengeance for the thousands, or hundreds of thousands, of dead in Iraq, Palestine, and so on, because any "an eye for an eye" logic increases rather than diminishes killing. But then we should equally reject the undercurrent of such logic in the "Western" justifications.

This leads to rejecting both horns of the definition dilemma. First, the view according to which nothing definite can be said about terrorism: this only shows up the final sterility of fully free-floating cultural relativism (as in a briefly famous piece by Baudrillard). Second, the attempt by powerful States to define terrorism in such a way that only their enemies but not themselves would be doing it: this simply shows the arrogance of power where might is right. In both cases, terrorism cannot be persuasively delimited – or fought. What I'm arguing for is a post-Enlightenment attempt to reduce the scope of killings allowable under any name. That religious fanatics should refuse such distinctions (for example between military and civilians) is understandable: they are at least sincere and above-board. But when governments whose constitution comes out of the Enlightenment obfuscate those distinctions – so as to be, because of their power, even more murderous – they too return to pre-Enlightenment absolutism, a kind of State religion. A strong doubt then arises whether they either know or mean what they say. Therefore, we have to call with Fidel and the French Confédération Paysanne (and Pope John Paul II) for "No to terrorism, no to war."

In order to do this with any consistency and therefore chance of success, we need to focus first of all on the *causes* of terrorism; or to begin with, on the motivations of terrorist groups. The State groups do not need much debating, only a popularisation of their evident reasons: furthering the power of the State and its objectives of domination. The non-State groups' motivations are complex and different in any particular case, especially as between those who invoke religion and those who do not. But their common denominators might include (I'm trying to systematise Ahmad's splendid discussion here): a/ the experience of physical violence, hunger, and humiliation, a "mix of anger and helplessness [which] produces an urge to strike out.... to wreak retributive justice"; b/ the identification of an external enemy responsible for this, which can politicise gang or ghetto violence; after the waning of class politics, the rich and powerful humiliators are identified as ethnic and/or religious foreigners, primarily as Americans and their helpers; c/ a chance that retributive terrorism could have some noticeable effect; and d/ the absence of a horizon for revolutionary seizure of State power.

The above initial considerations do not "solve" or even enter into many other questions. Terrorism is a rare case where both moral and political criteria bring into sharp focus its inadmissibility. Even then, who are civilians? Policemen are not, to my mind, but further discussions would be necessary, for example in the case of high government officials (in the Tsarist Empire they overtly had rankings equivalent to military ones – cf. Walzer 200-01). But most glaringly, what about other forms of today's mass killings? I may be too optimistic, but straightforward genocide – as of Armenians or European Jews – seems to have left so many scars on public opinion that it is difficult to return to it, unless we get into another world conflict. Terrorism obviously borders on guerrilla warfare, which I consider admissible whenever not accompanied by terrorism, while politically one would have to judge it case by case – the old labels of revolutionary vs. counter-revolutionary are by now too simple (for example in Iran or Kosovo). Drug peddling is a constant Siamese twin of terrorism, from Latin America through Asia to Kosovo, its results are morally killings, and it is to my mind also unambiguously inadmissible (but then, what is a drug? alcohol or tobacco, anyone?)[4]. How are we to approach the equally murderous undeclared wars between States and the potentially much more murderous ABC weapons, further huge setbacks for civilisation and victories for Hitler? War crimes kill far more people than terrorist ones.

Crucially, these lines don't go into a depth discussion of the economic and psychological necessities of war for the ruling classes in today's capitalism: by the time of the First Gulf War, a conservative estimate of global spending for military purposes was between 2 and 2.5 billion – thousand millions – dollars daily (see my first essay)... This would probably be decisive to clear up my own oscillation between Marxism and pacifism in the age of modern annihilation weaponry. Even historically, terror has always been a twin of aggressive warfare: the Jacobins were sublated – overcome but also continued – by Napoleon.

Works Cited in Essay 3, Part 1

See in *Works Cited in this Book* the following titles, by Author surname plus (when the author has several titles) first "headword" or identifying syntagm in the title.

Abellard; Ahmad; Avnery; Brown; Chomsky *9-11, Culture, Necessary, Pirates;* Davis Mike, *Cronache; Dictionnaire* 1798; *Dictionnaire* 1835; Dinnerstein; George Alexander ed.; Herman, *Real;* Herman and O'Sullivan; Kinsley; Lindqvist; Milward; *Le Monde; OED;* Partridge; Pilger, *The New;* Solomon; Stohl; Suvin, *Defined;* Tigar; Türcke; Walzer.

PART 2. ASPECTS OF "TERROR/ISM": NUMINOSITY, KILLINGS, HORIZONS (2004)

> ...after a minute Humpty Dumpty began again. '...Impenetrability! That's what *I* say!'
>
> 'Would you tell me, please,' said Alice, 'what that means?'
>
> 'Now you talk like a reasonable child,' said Humpty Dumpty, looking very much pleased. 'I meant by "impenetrability" that we've had enough of that subject, and it would be just as well if you'd mention what you mean to do next, as I suppose you don't mean to stop here all the rest of your life.'
>
> 'That's a great deal to make one word mean,' Alice said in a thoughtful tone.
>
> 'When I make a word do a lot of work like that,' said Humpty Dumpty, 'I always pay it extra.'...
>
> (Alice didn't venture to ask what he paid them [the words] with; and so you see I can't tell you.)
>
> *Alice in Wonderland*, chap. 6

> ...kikhánei d'ex aelptíes fóbos.
> (From unexpected directions there comes terror.)
>
> Archilochos of Paros, 7th century B.C.E.

2.1. The Numinous (Sacred/Demonic) Dimension of "Terror" and Capitalism Today

> [The "war on terrorism" is] the bombing of an abstract noun.
>
> Terry Jones (member of *Monty Python*)

I wish to follow up on the discussion of what was "terror" in Part 1, where I started from the *OED* meanings of, first, *intense fear, fright or dread*; with an adjective, or in the form "a terror" or "terrors," it was used for an instance thereof. *Psalms* lv.4 was in the *Geneva Bible* of 1560 translated as "The terrors of death are fallen upon me," marking a vicinity to the aura of portentous, supernatural events such as the death of Christ or the irruption of Pan. The second main meaning was "*The action or quality of causing [such] dread"; "terribleness"; and "a thing or person that excites terror*," as in Addison's "The Messiah appears cloathed with so much terrour and majesty" (in 1712).

There is a depth dimension of time to which such fossil remnants in English point, and which seems to me to underlie in a semi-conscious way its present uses. Namely, there is a strong argument that at the basis of religions there lies what the Old Testament (*Tanakh*) calls *emat Jahveh*, the uncanny "God-dread" or "terror consubstantial with God," and the Greek tradition calls *deîma panikón*, "panic terror," or the "terrible gods," *deinoì theoí*, Sleep and Death in Hesiod's *Theogony* (v. 759).

Already Epicure slyly remarked that if pleasurable things liberate deviants from mental terror (*fóbous tês dianoías*) caused by celestial portents – such as comets or eclipses – or by death and pain, we should have no reason to blame such people (maxim X). In other words: religious faith begins with a strong admixture and participation of terror, while conversely philosophical (and then scientific and artistic) inquiry is sparked by wonder, *without terror*. Epicure's great poetic interpreter Lucretius explained religion as stemming from dread of death and other anxieties, in verses that have been scarcely bettered since:

> hunc igitur terrorem animi tenebrasque necessest
> non radii solis neque lucida tela diei
> discutiant, sed naturae species ratioque.
> (Prosaic translation:
> Therefore, this mental terror and these dark recesses have to be routed
> Not by the Sun's rays nor by the shining arrows of day
> But by an examination of nature and its causes.)

Rudolf Otto, who dug up the religious tradition of "the totally Other" centering on numinous horror, glosses it as a combination of unutterable terror with ensnaring fascination, a numbing and paralyzing surprise that simultaneously also attracts. That terrible force engenders in people attempts at propitiating and domesticating it by means of either magical participation or of religious devotion, conjuration, and consecration (Otto 13-16, 32, 42-43, and see the comment in Türcke 135-37). However, such a force can also be found in non-religious events of both wide and profound impact, and apart from natural catastrophes these are usually, since the French Revolution, political events. Thus, Yeats calls the 1916 Irish insurrection and attempt at revolution "a terrible beauty." As in that poem, *Easter 1916*, "All, all is changed utterly": such events, whose political quality is grounded in – though usually not confined to – Christian salvationism of Easter resurrection, portend an utter annihilation of all known orientations, akin to Death, the king of terrors (as in the 1611 *Bible*: "His confidence... shall bring him to the king of terrours" – *Job* lviii.14). The force of the term "terror" waned, then, together with classical religious feeling. This is palpable, for example, in the 1660s' "Ode to the Royal Society" by Abraham Cowley, which praises Francis Bacon for breaking the "Monstrous God" Authority that made children and superstitious men afraid with "Ridiculous and senceless Terrors!" (Heath-Stubbs & Salman 107).

Yet the tradition was then reinvented within the sphere of supposedly rational politics, where the concept of terror grew lay and democratic, potentially lurking everywhere: it was applicable first by the divine right of the Powers that Be, then by revolutions, and finally by smaller groups from below. Historically, the breakthrough of the laicised concept and word of "terror" came about in the Jacobin State at the time of Robespierre (cf. my Part 1), and it was aimed at the "evil" States. Group terror/ism, which followed in the 19th century with Russian Narodniks and European anarchists for a long time (even with the 1930s' IRA) strictly targeted only military and higher State officials against which it claimed to be retaliating.

Thus, the exclusive focus on non-State terror/ism is a blatant invention of contemporary State propaganda. It seems that "terrorism in the strict sense, the random murder of innocent people, emerged as a strategy of revolutionary struggle only in the period after World War II, ... *after it had become a feature of conventional war*" (Walzer 198, emphasis DS) – in other words, after the new "[t]otal war" had grown to be "the combination of unlimited use of highly destructive weapons for unlimited war aims" (Liddell Hart, cited in Kunz 40). Walzer overlooks some cases between the two World Wars, but those would not change his main point: that the globalisation (that is, blowback to Europe) and "democratisation" of wars in the age of capitalist imperialism was a return to pre-Enlightenment colonial and religious wars. Before this, both professional officers and professional revolutionaries cultivated "a kind of warrior honour" which impeded random killing of civilians – with the tacit exception of the colonies whose "savages" were arrogantly deemed to be outside civilised norms. Thus, when such revolutionary assassins are called terrorists, this is "a... victory for the [State] champions of order" (Walzer 197), and such officially force-fed semantics becomes an important component of politically and psychologically repressing the reality of killing civilians. In order to represent that reality, my Part 1 defined terrorism as *a strategy which consists in pursuing political power by striking dread into the civilian population through exemplary killings among them* (Walzer advocated much the same in the 1990s). In this context, it is a historical fact that *terrorism by non-State groups is a reaction to mass State oppression and State terrorism*; I shall focus on this in 2.2.

But first I want to query: why did a lay or secularised world, proclaiming rational politics increasingly supposed to represent the will of (the) people, use terror? The only answer I can see is that the economico-political situation in secularised societies was radically at odds with their proclamations of equality and fraternity, so that there were in fact no rational politics in the age of mass exploitation and warfare.[5] While classical religions became factually and in many cases even officially divorced from sociopolitical life, the sources of religious feeling – of intense fear and fascination – did not dry up but were fed anew by reaction to humiliating and murderous disenchantment, and diverted into new channels, virulently seething out of semi-conscious repression. Destiny did not pass into the hands of (the) people but re-established itself as the World Market, whose commanding godhead was Profit and executive agent the State. Arguably, it also retained or re-established traits of male gender and age domination (patriarchy) akin to feudalism and slavery. While "capitalist rationalization," which considerably advanced human domination over nature, is officially desacralising, in it "demystification was joined by depoeticization and disenchantment" (Merleau-Ponty 36). Modern capitalism weaves together two only seemingly contradictory strands: on the one hand, it *represses* the "metaphysical" questions of a sense for human life; on the other hand, modern capitalism *resacralises* in new, hidden, and unsuspected – therefore also less controllable – quasi-myths. As Hobbes was perhaps the first modern theoretician to tattle out, fear is what holds together social order. The absolute market domination turns the selection mechanisms for its many called and very few chosen into "a new variant of destiny, which sometimes absolves or damns in ways as inscrutable as that of the Calvinist God" (Türcke 9).

All students of ancient religions know that Otto's "numinous" is not simply positive, that the Old Hebrew *qados* or Greek *hagios* meant a phenomenon that makes the perceiver shudder or shake in fright and awe, it is a *mysterium tremendum*, the ambiguously dreadful mystery not conceivable without terror. Equally, the Latin poet's tag *auri sacra fames* did not mean "the holy hunger" but "the tremendous or horrifying hunger after gold." Capitalist society was reworking, with increasing high-tech speed, such archaic myths and structures of feeling. The Nazis' open adoption of such feelings and myths – say, their deep fascination with the Wagnerian "gold of the Nibelungs" – was only the consistent totalisation of these bourgeois tendencies. Their novelty seems to consist in excluding astonishment and reverence from the classical "numinous" in favour of direct terrorising intimidation by political power and violence (Brinkmann).

This involution should surprize no-one who has taken seriously Marx's great chapter on *commodity fetishism*, the first and the most stimulating discovery of a central mainspring of this resacralisation. A further important turn of the screw toward fetishism arising from the commodity was the extension and huge multiplication of industrialised audiovisual shocks spreading from the mega-cities of capitalist industrialisation. The shocks against the human nervous system and sensorium did not grow smaller in their use of mass technologies and introduction of leisure time. On the contrary, as Benjamin well learned from the poets of Paris beginning with Baudelaire – and we should add the poets of all other tremendous mega-cities, from Blake's London to Brecht's Berlin, Garcia Lorca's New York, and on – they became more frequent, and therefore had to get ever more intense in order to pass the heightening threshold of perceptive attention. The only defence against existing fear and terror of everyday life was to be found in further, prophylactic and homeopathic, administration of fear and terror. This has been best analyzed for the mass press and then for the new media, from movies through radio to TV.

A fundamental difference was introduced by the *dynamism* of the new fetish. The old monotheistic godheads were monolithic, while commodity has both use-value and exchange value at the same time. On the one hand, insofar as the market, based on exchange-value and the engine of profit, is the ultimate instance of Destiny, the instance of salvation or damnation, commodity is literally a fetish, it manifests divinity. On the other hand, simultaneously and to the contrary, insofar as the market is finally a monstrously perverted instance of conveying use-values (corn, cloth or informed knowledge) to people, commodity functions merely as a surrogate taking the place of divinity or of a supreme survival value (isotopic to it) – like Godot instead of God, if not like Lucifer. An ontological oscillation comes about[6] differing both at different times and at different ends of the market – say the stock-market vs. the super-market: the new godhead is powerful but occulted and intermittent. This is why it can successfully hide itself within the temples of official economics and politics: if you look at it with the naked eye, it is not there (you could not see capitalism in a photo of the Krupp factories but only by analyzing how they function, remarked Brecht – whereas you can see religion inside Saint Peter's cathedral or the Suleymaniye mosque). This is also why saying that capitalism is a new religion does not quite hit the target unless its newness is duly articulated and stressed, for capitalism simultaneously *is* and *is not* what we knew as religions heretofore (you need dialectics). The strong ritual cults and quasi-myths of capitalism are not simply nostalgic metaphors, nor are they its be-all and end-all. Into the amplitude of these oscillations the audiovisual shocks of mass media insert themselves and exasperate them.

A similar discourse should, to my mind, be developed about the second main fetish within capitalism, *labour-power* as the alienation of Marx's living labour. Unfortunately we don't have much on this by either Marx or Benjamin, but it clearly partakes of the Janus nature of commodity (and underlies it). Labour-power is both sold as a commodity and yet not fully separable from the body's living labour. In particular, Guy Debord's spectacle as a key to present-day class hegemony reposes on reified presentations of the body in erotics, warfare, and so on, which induce an even more intimate ontological oscillation. The need to alienate and freeze labour into disembodied machines on the one hand and invisible outsourcing on the other can clearly be seen in modern warfare (a labour of destruction, true, but labour nonetheless) with its helicopter shelling and high-altitude bombing. This may serve to characterise analogous developments in the clearly antagonistic and daily mini-warfare within production relationships in general.

Markets were always associated with spectacle: clowns, jugglers, magicians, conjurers; the masses that gathered needed relaxation after transacting affairs and had money to pay for it. Indeed, spectacle came in even before and as a part of transacting business, for goods were praised by criers, they were arranged and doctored, etc. The name of stock-market comes, so the US legend goes, from stock (cattle) led to fairs in old New York and watered by the way to make them seem fatter. Initially circumscribed in time and place, markets grew from local fairs on a given saint's day into a permanent marketing, infinite in space and time – like the Bushist war. The basis was laid for what Debord discusses as the society of spectacle: a society where *spectacle* (seeing extraordinary matters) has become a dominant on the level of ostensible daily phenomena.

Capitalism notoriously despises and fears independent esthetics: art. But capitalism has since its inception used spectacular "commodity esthetics" (Haug) to make wares circulate. One could even say (cf. Türcke 9-11) it has always incorporated a kind of totally pragmatic sub-esthetics, which is not a cloak it could shed but a skin, its protective appearance without which it would die. In that respect, fairs were always competitors to temples for using and incorporating spectacles and spectacularity, fascination with judicious admixtures of fear/terror. Both pretended to reveal the mysteries of destiny, and both sometimes obliquely managed to convey it (say in the tremendous stock-market crashes as the 1929 one). The fetish of commodity differs from old wooden fetishes of local godheads primarily by being consubstantial to the *usable* commodity and not standing outside it to be independently adored (though the difference grows thin in today's speculative future markets). But it also differs by being constantly challenged and alerted by competition between sub-species of fetishes, something unknown to static or "cold" societies before capitalism and leading to irresistible heightening of sensational spectacle. (The Late Roman Empire, when Mithra, Isis, and Christ competed with the Pantheon and local godlings, confirms the rule and throws an interesting light on today's Late American Empire.) Not only theology but also political economy and even neurophysiology – the way spectacle changes people's sensorium and perceptive capacity – is now needed to cope with the global mega-fetish and its ramifying variants.

Fascinating as all this may be, haven't we gotten too far from terror? Not if we can return to it with an appreciable gain in understanding. I would claim the gain was implicit in all the talk about the potentially tremendous mysteries, the dread and fascination brought by the fetishes of spectacularised commodity and spectacularised labour-power body. But to put it explicitly: in my defining of terrorism as a strategy which consists in pursuing political power by striking dread into the civilian population through exemplary killings, the psychological and neurophysiological element is "striking dread" or *intimidation*. It is well known also to theology, salesmanship, and war planning: "The problem of revolution, as of war, is to destroy the will of the enemy and to force him to capitulate.... War, like revolution, is founded upon intimidation... killing single persons to intimidate thousands." (Trotsky 66 and 70) Terrorism, the practice of inflicting terror, is thus – among other things but to my mind decisively – a stance, the expectation of political gain by killing civilians (this last element is *not* involved in Trotsky's use of the term). I concluded in my first part that terrorism is a matter of using huge bodily harm to influence the collective imagination by transfer contagion: an exasperated form of psychophysical warfare grafted upon techniques of economic and political propaganda in the warfare-cum-media age. I should now add two further aspects. First, that this transfer contagion has dreadful intimidation as political *end* and exemplary killings of civilians as consubstantial *means*. Both sides have, not without reason, explained the actions of and reactions to al Qaeda – itself a reaction to US domination – as holy warfare of the monotheistic, Good against Evil kind: In God We Trust vs. The Great Satan. Marx concluded the commodity cannot be understood without returning to some uses of theology; the same can be said for its bastard offspring with war-as-spectacle, terror/ism. Second, it seems to me that terrorism simultaneously publicises its murderous object-lessons and yet in a subtle way plays on the fear of the yet-unseen, the subsequent strikes that may affect any viewer of the lesson anytime anywhere. For intimidation it is essential that the image of killings should be both seen and yet projected into an unseen magnified by anxious imagination. Both State and group terrorism necessarily go in for unlimited holy killings.

Debord has argued that the spectacle ruling our social imagination has a tautological character in that its means are at the same time its ends. In a way, means and ends in terrorism can only be sundered for a retrospective analysis, for immediately they coincide. What I have called group terrorism is not only spectacular, it is parasitic upon the existence of mass media as a mass spectacle of "infotainment." Many media critics immediately noted this after September 11, best perhaps Umberto Eco: "Bin Laden's purpose in striking at the Twin Towers was to create 'the greatest spectacle in the world', never imagined even in catastrophe movies.... He was not waging a war, in which the number of eliminated enemies counts: he was precisely sending a terrorist message, and what counted was the image." The stab of dread seen at the epistemic remove of a TV screen is, as in horror movies, overlaid by the situational awareness of the safe living room – a dreadful entertainment. Without global media, there would have in all probability been no strikes at the Twin Towers. Beyond the number of victims (about which see part 2 following), what is a major difference between such group terrorism and the State terrorism that likewise kills civilians and likewise sends a media message of intimidation to potential enemies? It is that US State terrorism masquerades as war for noble humanitarian reasons and therefore evades global awareness of its killings wherever it can, in order to present them as surgical strikes in justly measured retaliation or at worst as collateral errors, which are then never counted in the media. This is again effected by controlling media through patriotic intimidation but where need be also through killings (as in the US bombing of the Belgrade TV station or its tank shelling of the newspapermen's hotel in Baghdad).

Of course, we should be careful to use terms derived from theology as Marx did: as tools taken from a repository of human methodologies – surprisingly fitting for modern capitalism but coded in an absolutist religious age and way – rather than as our final horizons. Benjamin put it well, with characteristically pithy extremism: "My thinking relates to theology as the blotting paper to ink. It is entirely imbued with it. Yet if the blotting paper had its way, nothing that was written would remain." (GS I.3: 1235) This centrally means recognising the sea-change between the religious or absolutist type of numinous horror, using fear to cause as much distress as possible, and its subsumption into humane creativeness, where ensnaring fascination sheds its paralyzing aspect and turns into cognitive wonder – as Epicure and Lucretius implied. Freud differentiates the uncanny from what is purely gruesome (14: 364), but this has been best debated apropos of art. I know no better encapsulation than Baudelaire's dictum: "C'est un des privilèges prodigieux de l'Art que l'horrible, artistement exprimé, devienne beauté, et que la *douleur* rhythmée et cadencée remplisse l'esprit d'une *joie* calme." (It is one of the marvellous privileges of art that the horrible, when expressed artfully, becomes beauty, and that rhythmical and cadenced *pain* fills the mind with tranquil *joy* – 466).

2.2. Focus on Killing: Some Hard Proportions and Consequences

> We sincerely believe that terrorism is a negative weapon, that it in no way produces the wished-for results, that it can push a people to oppose a given revolutionary movement, and that it leads to loss of life among its practitioners much higher than the advantages derived from it.
>
> Che Guevara, *The Guerrilla War*

It is needful therefore to ground our discussion by returning as far as possible to the data about killings of civilians by States as compared to those by non-State groups. I gave some examples in the first essay ("Capitalism"), but they need to be updated from whatever approximate gleanings I was able to find. To situate the data, however, some delimitations have to be recalled and re-examined.

First, the killings in "civil wars" with little direct foreign armed intervention – for example, in South Africa, Colombia, ex-Yugoslavia, Sri Lanka, central Africa, and possibly the Chinese "cultural revolution" – are not only difficult to evaluate numerically (though they are often horrendous, for example ca. 3 millions in Nigeria 1966-67, ca. 1 million each in Afghanistan between the USSR and USA interventions, and also perhaps in Algeria); they are also very difficult to allot to State or insurrectionary group intervention. These mass political killings will therefore not be discussed, though I would often view them as terrorist on one or both sides.[7]

For the rest, I propose to focus sharply on my underlined definition of terrorism as targeted killing of civilians. There follows from it, as the second step essential for any proper understanding, that we must insist upon the existence of and distinction between *State and non-State or group terrorism*[8] – the French term *groupuscule*, small group, often comes to mind here. (Of course, these two originators may overlap when States finance, protect, and often organise paramilitary or gangster groups for murders they don't want to be seen as committing – as happened after World War 2 not only in Latin America and Africa but certainly in Greece and probably in Italy, Northern Ireland, and indeed the USA. Furthermore, if we are humanists and not nationalists, we might well wish to count a good part of the casualties by invading State armed forces – say, the US soldiers – as victims both of the State that brought them there and the group that killed them.) However, the argument developed in 2.1 leads me to doubt the secondary distinction I too earlier accepted between religious and political group terrorism. True, I did point out that, after the collapse of the communist and then the national liberation projects, religion served often as the ideological self-identification of a community aspiring to political power or sovereignty, as well as that apparently purely political terrorists have since the Russian Narodniki exercised a lay absolutism that is a hidden religion. The shift in the last 160 years or so from non-State group violence in the name of social classes to that in the name of ethnic groups and finally religions is certainly worth understanding (cf. Juergensmeyer); however, whether the Oklahoma City bombing was the expression of a Christian fundamentalist or a "Sons of Gestapo" hate of the US State seems to me far down on the scale of cognitive relevance in any general politico-epistemological approach. Here too, the hegemonic common sense of the media and think-tanks proves fallacious.

Since World War 2 the overwhelmingly major source of State terrorism directly and indirectly is the US State, that is, key ruling-class fractions in its military-corporate establishment. Though censored from all the media, this has been pointed out many times by Blum, Chomsky, Herman, Herman-O'Sullivan, George, Slater-Stohl, Sluka ed. (see Works Cited), and other critics. The USA was up to the advent of Bush Jr.'s escalation officially committed to the doctrine of "low intensity warfare" (cf. Klare-Kornbluh) which was – like its predecessor "counterinsurgency" – as a rule indistinguishable from terrorism: as Chomsky points out (in *9-11* 90), all of them go back to the Nazi counter-resistance model. Counterinsurgency already went more than halfway toward undeclared warfare (in which killing civilians should be counted as war crimes), prefiguring thus the Bushist adventures. It was applied in Cuba, Kampuchea, Laos, Lebanon, Libya, Nicaragua, and almost all the rest of Latin America – and going further back, in the Philippines.

It would be unfair not to point out that others manfully participated in State terrorism. These were often US client-States, such as Chile and Greece under military rule, Indonesia, Guatemala, El Salvador or Colombia, but sometimes they were merely encouraged by the US – and secondarily by the Russian Stalinist – example: Turkey, Argentina under the military, Kampuchea under the Khmer Rouge, Russia in the Chechnyan secession war, various Central African governments. A special case, that often pioneered proceedings later taken over by the USA, were Israel's interventions in Lebanon and the Palestinian territories. In all, Rummel calculates that in 1900-80 *between 180 and 360 million unarmed civilians were killed by their own governments*.

I shall subsume Herman and O'Sullivan's Table 3.1 (from A. George ed. 41-42) and all other information found in works cited at the end and in newspaper articles in the following twofold, comparative table confined to some main examples. A caveat: all data are estimates, subject to much error (usually upward correction would be needed), but they should be correct indications of the order of magnitude, and thus usable as qualitative indications and for comparative purposes:

CIVILIANS KILLED BY STATE TERRORISM (MAIN INSTANCES IN LAST 40 YEARS):

- During US intervention in Vietnam: ca. 2,000,000
- US-inspired Indonesian army pogrom of "Communists," 1965-66: 500,000-over 1,000,000
- Intervention by South African, French, and US proxies in Angola and Mozambique: over 500,000
- During US bombing in Kampuchea: at least 200-400,000
- By the Pol Pot regime in Kampuchea: ca. 200-400,000[9]
- US bombings and proxies in Laos: ca. 350,000
- By the Indonesian army in East Timor: up to 300,000
- US-organised army repression in Guatemala 1962-96: 200,000
- By the Indonesian army in western Irian (New Guinea): 80,000
- US-organised army repression in El Salvador 1978 on: 70,000
- By the Russian army in the Chechnyan secession war: perhaps 40-65,000
- By the Turkish army against Kurds 1984 on: several tens of thousands (number not found)
- Argentinian "disappeared" & others killed 1976-83: perhaps 45,000 or more
- Israeli and US excursions into Lebanon, 1985-96: ca. 38,000
- US bombings of Iraqis in 1991 Gulf War: perhaps 20,000 or more

Counted as "smaller fry," but think about each of these zeroes being a body in pain and terror: US-organised Contras in Nicaragua: 7,000; Iraqi poison gassing of Kurds 1988, ca. 5,000; US-organised army repression in Chile: at least 3,000; Israeli military killings of Palestinians, several thousands (number not found) up to 1993 – including the first Intifada – and at least 2,000 from 2000 on; US invasion of Panama 1989, 2-3,000; US and NATO bombings of Serbia, 2,000.

A special case is the killings of civilians by the US army, mercenaries, and allies in the two wars ongoing as I write, not only because they are open-ended, but also because they arguably should be called war crimes. However, since no war was declared and since the Bush Jr.'s administration's does not apply the Geneva Conventions on war prisoners and similar, more mileage might be got by treating these one-sided wars as State terrorism:

—US and allies' intervention in Afghanistan 2002: 4,000 (and counting)

—US and UK army and allies during Iraq invasion from 2003 on: 10,000 or much more (and counting).[10]

CIVILIANS KILLED BY GROUP TERRORISM (MAIN INSTANCES IN LAST 40 YEARS):

- Italy (by "Red Brigades" and neo-fascists) 1968-82: 334
- Palestinian killings of Israelis 1968-81: 282
- Germany (by RAF and others) 1970-79: 31

GLOBAL TOTAL 1969-80 (CIA estimate): *[3.368]*

Other estimates 1980-2000:

- Oklahoma City bombing 1995: ca. 150
- Palestinian killings of Israelis during first Intifada: ca. 700
- Killings in Bangla Desh (mainly by "Islamists") 1996-2003: ca. 100
- "Islamists" based in Chechnya, 1999 on: over 1,000
- Palestinian killings of Israelis during second Intifada, 2000 on: up to 900
- Al Qaeda attack against USA, Sept. 2001: ca. 3,000
- Killings in India (mainly by "Islamists") 2001-2004: ca. 200
- Bali nightclub explosions by "Islamists," Oct. 2002: over 200
- Al Qaeda attack on Madrid commuters, 2004: ca. 200

Comments:

- *State terrorism overtakes group terrorism killing by a factor of between 500 and 1,000:1* (but see more a bit down). While we might dispute definitions and terminology, the fact remains that under any name the media of rich countries, the "North," do not devote even one hundredth of space spent on anti-North terrorism to noting – never mind analyzing – the horrendously huge killings going on in the South (see the classical Herman *Real* and Chomsky, also Rummel, and for Latin America up to the 1980s also Cockburn). This is not only an offence against reason but shows also a clearly racist bias: some lives are held to be worth 1,000 times less than others. Even the accurate accounting of the "White" victims as against the difficulty of knowing the exact number of thousands killed in the "coloured" parts of the world points to this. The Nazis' shooting 100 "lower race" hostages for one German has had a goodly progeny.

• This does not mean that the terrorist groups, whether claiming to be Left-wing, Arab/ Islamic, Irish (Ulster) Catholic and Protestant, or whatever, are as a rule morally any superior to the State killers. A radical Left-wing commentator speaks of the Italian "red" groups' practices as using mafia tactics, "assassination of prisoners, a mysticism of violence, cynicism, arrogance, and disregard for others' lives even independent of their role in the enemy machine" (Massari 421), which much likens them to the US, Israeli, and other State terrorists – besides, the "red" groups' infiltration by State apparatus is still being debated. Most terrorist groups (with exceptions among those composed largely of intellectuals) have a macho mentality, and the religious groups seem to be entirely male, though they sometimes use women for suicide missions.

• The above tables not only *do not count* the wounded, they also don't count the indirect but very real and often huge numbers of dead from other consequences of those killings. A good summary is presented by Marc Herold in a chart about ramifications of bombings. Beyond military deaths (entailing widows and orphans, and demographic imbalance) and the direct civilian deaths and injuries, it lists environmental costs, health costs, refugees, and the huge economic and psychological burdens which all these – together with destroyed infrastructure and remaining unexploded ordnance – puts on everybody surviving, leading to premature death and other loss of life for decades ahead. For Afghanistan only, Herold notes that besides ca. 4,000 (by now) civilians killed, there are 4-7,000 civilians injured, many often badly maimed and requiring prostheses, a minimum of 3-4,000 refugees dead of hunger, disease, and cold, ca. 50,000 unexploded cluster bomblets, long-term health menaces – probably carcinogenic – from uranium, cyclonite, and perchlorate detritus from ordnance, etc. (in Malik ed. 217-19).

• In general, *all the data about people killed by States should as a rule (except in civil wars) be multiplied by at least three to get the number of short-term victims only*, while the group killings, with less efficient technologies, seem to entail a smaller proportion of non-lethal victims. Counting not only the killed but all serious bodily lesions would most probably up the proportion of *State vs. group terrorism victims somewhere around 2,000:1*.

Let me take only three further examples. The first is the al-Shifa pharmaceutical plant in Sudan which Clinton's government bombed, mistaking it /?/ for a chemical weapons' plant. It thus destroyed 90% of Sudan's capacity to produce affordable medicine for malaria, tuberculosis, parasites, and other preventable diseases. The German ambassador to Sudan estimated that several tens of thousands of Sudanese have died as a result (Chomsky, *9-11* 48-49).

Second, the carefully avoided matter of *uranium* (wrongly called "depleted uranium") used in US and NATO ordnance. Vast areas of Iraq-cum-Arabia, of Afghanistan, and of ex-Yugoslavia and the Adriatic Sea remain poisoned by this highly toxic-cum-radiating material, possibly mixed with plutonium – a weapon of long-term mass destruction indeed. It seems by now clear its use was a cause of the misnamed "Gulf War Syndrome," of which 11,000 US soldiers from the First Gulf War have died while 325,000 (56% of those who were in the Gulf) are on permanent medical disability (see Moret, and cf. Chossudovsky). The British Atomic Energy Authority calculated for the First Gulf War of 1991 that 500,000 potential long-range deaths may be involved in that area alone (Pilger, *New* 51-52 and 95). However, as compared to the 400-500 tons of uranium then used, in the 2003 war between 1.100 and 2.200 tons were used, so that the potential deaths might be between 1.5 and 2.75 million people (Zucchetti ed., *Guerra* 112 and 229, Baracca 155, and cf. on radiation statistics Bertell and Pona). *This would be worse than Hiroshima plus Nagasaki*.

The best documented case are the dead from the total consequences of that war in *Iraq 1991-2002*, which killed more people than all the Mass Destruction Weapons in history, hypocritically invoked by the US government even though it is so far the only user of atom bombs and the main user of chemical weapons (the Muellers, cited in Pilger, *New* 8). UNICEF estimated in 1998 that ca. 7,500 people were dying each month in Iraq due to the devastations of its infrastructure in 1991 (bombing of food warehouses, flour mills, water-treatment facilities, etc. – cf. *Needless*) and to the embargo: *a Twin Towers' outrage each 12 days for 11 years*. In all, the best estimate of the rise of mortality attributes 1.2 to 1.5 million indirect Iraqi deaths to the effects of the 1991 war, the majority of them small children. As the *New England Journal of Medicine* editorial of Apr. 24, 1997, put it: "The Cuban and Iraqi instances make it abundantly clear that economic sanctions are, at their core, a war against public health" (Malik ed. 367-69). So is any State violence against civilians conducted by bombing (US) and heavy artillery (Israeli). So are the tens or hundreds of thousands of mines, cluster bombs, and uranium-encased shells lying about in Serbia, Iraq, and Afghanistan – the mines are to be found in every zone of the 100+ wars of recent decades – continuing to explode, poison, and kill every day as we write and read this.

This introduces the age-old weapon of killings without weaponry. If we go further, beyond either State or group terrorism, is it possible not to at least mention, and propose for further consideration, what I would call *eco-killings* (slow or sudden destruction of the eco-sphere)? Again, I shall take only one example, out of very many possible ones – the 16,000 people killed in the Bhopal explosion and poisoning. In 1984 poisonous fumes escaping from the plant of Union Carbide covered 20 square kilometres of territory in the densely populated city of Bhopal (where the US company located its plant to avail itself of underpaid labour and generous tax incentives by the Indian government, and to avoid the modest demands of US labour unions and tax authorities). 8,000 Indians died almost immediately, and about 500,000 were poisoned, of whom 8,000 more have died of the poisoning up to now, with countless illnesses continuing and incessantly adding to the number of the dead. On the night of the poisoning, the local management of Union Carbide sounded no alarm, it even turned off the plant siren "to avoid unnecessary panic." Thus, when three thousand New York employees and workers were outrageously killed in 2001, all the world TV and press media rightly reminded us of it daily and for months on end. The Bhopal killings – morally and physically just as outrageous, even if due to criminal negligence rather than criminal intent, to criminally bad planning rather than criminally good planning – were news for a few days, and have since been rarely, if ever, followed up by Western mass media. Instead, Union Carbide entered into lengthy litigation with Indian authorities, which finally accepted $470 million as a (quite inadequate) compensation for the poisoning that incides also on the present newborn (cf. the victims' site www.bhopal).

It would be inhuman to blame people for commemorating and analyzing either the Twin Towers or the Bhopal mass killing by itself. But it is equally inhuman to isolate one and forget the other: both these kinds of exemplary slaughtering are to be taken into account. We live in one world, united if not by sympathy then by mass migrations, imposed WTO trade rules, imposed IMF financial rules, military satellites, unending warfare, and news media (also by protests against all these). Responsibility for the 16,000 Bhopal killings lies with capitalist business people whose supreme value is greatest possible profits in the shortest possible time; responsibility for the 3,000 Manhattan killings lies with "Islamist" people whose supreme value is the return to the slower, pre-profit times of direct patriarchal and slave-owning exploitation, without a world trade centered in the USA. The disregard for lives of people is equal. It is the callous stance of killers, or more precisely mass murderers.[11]

Regarding these two types of killer organisations we must unyieldingly adopt what I would like to dub *the Mercutio principle*: "A plague on both of your houses!" (*Romeo and Juliet*).

2.3. Beyond This Horizon

> From the point 20th-century revolt gets separated from its roots and deprived of any concrete morality, Sade or dictatorship, individual terrorism or State terrorism become the alternatives.
>
> Albert Camus, *L'Homme révolté*

I wish to broach in an unsystematic way some prolonged consequences entailed by my whole discussion up to now. They have to do, at a first remove, with more general questions behind terrorism, that is, its root causes and the attitudes a radical Left may be expected to take up toward it. At a second remove, they have to do with the general sociohistorical horizons of the present period.

3.1. Though talking about how to understand various terrorisms, especially the "blowback" group terrorisms responding to the pressures of empires, and then how to position ourselves as against them, would require a book shuttling between political economics and depth psychology, at least two central points – again often made on the Left but never present in the media – ought to be recalled for orientation sake.

First, it is counter-productive, indeed productive of blowbacks, that "the Western right-wing and most of the [official 'terrorism industry'] establishment furiously oppose any focus on 'root causes' of terrorism" (Chomsky, in George ed. 71). Even liberals have plaintively pointed out that a purely military war against terrorism cannot be won, that terrorism entails a struggle for the "hearts and minds" of millions of people who can be up to a significant point controlled and suppressed, but finally not persuaded by bombs and shells. Already in 1989 ex-President Carter reflected:

> We sent Marines into Lebanon and you only have to go to Lebanon, to Syria or to Jordan to witness first-hand the intense hatred among many people for the United States because we bombed and shelled and unmercifully killed totally innocent villagers – women and children and farmers and housewives – in those villages around Beirut.... That is... what has precipitated some of the terrorist attacks – which were totally unjustified and criminal. (*New York Times*, March 26, 1989, p. 16, cited from Malik ed. 78)

It must be noted that, as in all liberal approaches, their end forgets their beginning.

In Avnery's example, the 2001 blockade against Palestinian villages by the Israeli army, which denied them water and food, does not isolate the "terrorists," but on the contrary turns them into national heroes. This holds in spades for all subsequent killings and destructions regardless of consequences for the civilian population. Thus, Avnery is right to conclude that "Since terrorism is always a political instrument, the right way to combat it is always political. Solve the problem that breeds terrorism and you get rid of terrorism." It can only be durably cured by removing its root causes, psychological, political, and finally economical. In sum, *group terrorism is the direct offspring of State terrorism and its predecessors in hunger, fear, and exploitation*. What we know about the al Qaeda cadres indicates they come from the upwardly mobile middle class of Arab nations – mainly Saudi Arabia and Egypt, the two principal US clients – that is blocked from independence, frustrated, and revolted by racism and torture (cf. Ali 293-94 and passim, Bishara, Klein, and Minolfi). It does not need much foresight to see that such terrorist groups will become a real threat if they get mass recruits from globalisation's new "informal proletariat," counting by now two fifths of active population in the "South" (Davis 26 and passim). Such a reservoir between one and two billion people will be fed by further military devastations and economico-political blockages. In that sense, the wars in Afghanistan and Iraq are the ideal recruiting and training grounds for group terrorism.

I cannot enter here upon the huge, though not too recondite, question of how terrorism is properly to be met (a simple answer: with justice). As Chomsky pithily put it, "Drain the swamp and there will be no more mosquitoes" ("Drain"). I shall mention here only the factor of *fear*. In his final *Comments*, Debord prophetically noted how the autocracy of market autonomy and its new techniques of governing masquerade as "a perfect democracy [which] constructs its own inconceivable foe, terrorism. Its wish is to be judged by its enemies, rather than by its results... [for] compared with terrorism, everything else must be acceptable" (24). If the US and European societies succumb to the fear so zealously propagated not only by the terrorists but also by practically all of its governments and obedient media, a vicious circle of escalation will be established. It will result in a destruction of the US social texture by adding –as of now, and at least – $885 billion to federal deficits in favour of militarised involution: "A society bingeing on fear makes itself vulnerable to far more profound forms of destruction than terror attacks. The 'terrorism war'... is using these popular fears to advance a different agenda – the re-engineering of American life through permanent mobilisation. The transformation is well under way. The consequences, if left unchallenged, will be very difficult to reverse." (Greider) As Franklin Roosevelt rightly said in an analogous crisis, the only thing to fear is fear itself.

Second, nobody on the Left can afford to neglect its long tradition of debates about terrorism (cf. Massari). Revolutionary movements have historically discouraged terrorism, though most of them probably also allowed its use at rare occasions of arguable – and often furiously debated – necessity. Marxists have always maintained that the liberation of working people is a matter of self-organisation by those masses (with further important debates as to who are crucial mediators and catalyzers for this process). This wing has therefore always had a twofold attitude toward terrorism. On the one hand, it refused terrorism as a strategy, because such a choice both stemmed from and strengthened disbelief into the central task of mass politics: the subverting of existing class relationships. It held that terrorism is a desperate choice of those who have lost faith that these relationships *can* be reversed; furthermore, acts of terrorism as a rule strengthen the bourgeois State's hold on the orientations of working people. But on the other hand, holding that revolutionary violence is often a necessary and indispensable self-defence against the dictatorial horizons of the ruling class whenever threatened – as shown in blatant clarity by fascism –

Marxists have as a rule refused ethical condemnations of most terrorist actions. Out of a long tradition perhaps it is enough here to cite the emblematic position of Gramsci commenting in 1921 on an anarchist dynamite attack against a police chief, which had been rerouted and had exploded in a crowded theatre:

> This murderous attack (*attentato*)... is another episode of the period of chaos and barbarism into which Italy has been thrown by the economic and social crisis born of the imperialist war... Before we absolve or condemn, we need to understand in the spirit of humanity.... (Massari 138)

In other words, the mendacious bourgeois outcry against violence and sentimentality about innocent victims – at a time of worldwide imperialist wars still continuing down to us and reaping millions of such victims – ought to give place to political analysis precisely in order to lessen such victimisation. With very few exceptions, this analysis meant refusing terrorism.

But today, given the escalation of State terrorism by means of new weapons portending destruction of not only thousands but if need be millions, an escalation which is politically helped by what I have called group terrorism replying to the State one, I think we must be one whole notch sharper than the Marx-to-Gramsci-and-Guevara tradition. It should be said that the few exceptions allowed by this tradition should practically mean *no exception to the rule of not killing civilians*. As the Palestinian poet Mahmoud Darwish concluded, "Nothing, nothing justifies terrorism" (*Gush-shalom*). It would remain to be discussed who are what Walzer calls "politically innocent" (200) civilians, as I attempted to suggest in Part 1. As this thoughtful and honourable liberal – as he was at the time – put it:

> Hatred, fear, and the lust for domination are the marks of oppressed and oppressor alike.... The mark of a revolutionary struggle against oppression, however, is not this incapacitating rage and random violence, but restraint and self-control. The revolutionary reveals his freedom in the same way as he earns it, by directly confronting his enemies and refraining from attacks on anyone else. (Walzer 205)

That does not necessarily mean forgetting, as Brecht said at the end of *Saint Joan of the Slaughterhouses*, that sometimes only force or violence (*Gewalt*) helps where force or violence reigns, as self-defence against absolute oppression. But it does mean avoiding the fatal confusion of tongues where force or violence is equated with terror, a term making sense only when tied to killing civilians as an example. As Engels exemplarily formulated it, "No communist has the idea of vengeance against individuals." To the contrary, while he acknowledged the unavoidable necessity of self-defence against precise enemies, in his *Condition of the English Working Class* he went on to argue that communism recognises the necessity of proletarian bitterness against its oppressors but transcends it because it is an affair of the whole mankind and not only of the workers, and optimistically concluded: "The more the English workers take up socialist ideas, the more will their present bitterness lose in savagery and crudeness" (298, cf. also 144-49).

3.2. Finally, I wish to open up these reflections onto the most general socio-historical horizons, and ask two more questions, even if in a quite preliminary way. First, are we witnessing the beginning of the end of capitalism by violent murder and suicide? Second, are there widespread popular material interests in the "North" (North America, western and central Europe, and the outlying dominions in Oceania) which make it probable that widespread popular support would be found for a fascist involution of capitalism? My tentative answer to both questions would be yes, with the rider that this should not necessarily make us merry.

David Harvey has persuasively argued in a number of places that for innermost, so to speak technical reasons of capital dynamics, "capitalism is always bound to be highly unstable unless it is held down by some coercive force (such as US hegemony backed by powerful central institutions like the World Bank and the IMF)" (xxvi). We can measure the distance travelled by capitalism since his diagnosis, dating originally back barely a decade, by the fact that the WTO-WB-IMF trefoil by now doesn't suffice to ensure the stability of capitalism, whose leading force, the USA, have therefore embarked upon permanent preventive warfare in the South – and more and more martial laws inside the North or metropolis – as that final argument of the rulers, brute force. We are therefore cycling back, in vastly inflated terms of space and time, to the situation of the First Industrial Revolution which reposed on a 12-hour working day, children's and women's labour, high mortality of popular classes, mass drugging, and other attendant desertifications of corporeal and mental values: from its very beginnings, capitalism tended to a destruction of its natural basis, land and labour-power (today also of water, air, climate, species extinction, etc.). At that earlier point, fearing the breakdown of the whole system, the British State intervened with a set of work laws that paved the way to a sustainable exploitation of the workers. The breakdowns today happen further away, in South Asia, Latin America or Africa as well as in the "sunken" third of the "Northern" and Chinese population, and are better masked by the more powerful and more cynical media of mass persuasion, so that there is an illusion they can go on forever, or at least "to the last Chinese." This also means there is less chance of a return to non-warfare Keynesianism, which was the second wave of staunching the hemorrhages of capital. There are no more true liberal reformists as a political force, not even in the so-called social-democracy.

This does not mean chances for fighting back do not exist, only that we cannot expect them to arise from within the existing power system of political parties and trade unions in the North (except for fringes). The so-called Right wing is gladly drifting toward fascist militarism, the so-called Left is barely a milder Right, and the admirable gut-feelings of the "movement of movements" still have to find their political horizon and organisational crystallisation, the "yes" in the name of which it says "no." Probabilities – surely to be fought against – speak therefore for an Iron Heel trampling legal niceties and using increasing police violence inside and army violence outside the metropolis. This is today helped by most group terrorism, in an unholy feedback of mutual ideological legitimation of oppressions with State terrorism. Wallerstein's or Chomsky's (*9-11*, 19 and 35) opinions that a Police State is unlikely repose on illusions of the Keynesian period, I fear. I hope my readers may find good arguments against what I'm about to pose, but a central part of the US – and then west European – working classes live their uncertain lives off the super-exploitation of the real proletarians or plebeians (most women, jobless, immigrants, and most of the South, immigrants being the "internal South" within the metropolis), and they would economically sink to totally proletarianised status if they did not live off it. Chances are that when it comes to the crunch their material interests will turn many of them to the Right, if need be a fascist Right, rather than the Left. The record of US popular support for governmental militarisation expenditures and policies clearly speaks for this, though occasional opposition – as the one that ended the Vietnam War – cannot be discounted if such policies come home in the form of dead youth rather than investments (cf. Hoffman). Capitalism will never share enough wealth to bribe the pauperised proletarians of the world: but it can bribe as well as intimidate maybe one third of its population in one sixth of the world. The outlook for civil liberties seems to me rather dim, when the question is which social group is the next one to go under. If needed, White Supremacist groups and the swarming groups of private mercenaries can easily be co-opted into an arm of State repression, as we saw in the German SA or today (say) in Colombia or Iraq.

Thus, when capitalism as we have known it collapses, what kind of successor formation will then be coming about? The age of individualism and free market is over, the present is already highly collectivised, and demographics as well as insecurity will make the future even more so: the only alternative is between the models of the oligarchic (that is, centrally fascist) war-camp and open plebeian-democratic commune. The dominant current of capitalist economico-political power has clearly embarked upon the constitution of a militarised Fortress Amerika and – less overtly, still centered mainly on police – Fortress Europa. Demented ventures such as the invasion of Iraq induce further group terrorism; if not stopped by focussed popular protest, they would grow into a permanent mutual legitimation of group and State terrorism. As Alberto Moravia concluded in the best early essay on terrorism I know, "While terrorism takes as its justification the desperation, reprisals take as their justification the terrorism" (Fossati 139).

Works Cited in Essay 3, Part 2

See in *Works Cited in this Book* the following titles, by Author surname plus (when the author has several titles) first "headword" or identifying syntagm in the title:

Ali; Avnery; Baracca; Baudelaire; Benjamin; Bertell; Bhopal; Bishara; Blum; Brinkmann; Chomsky, all four titles; Chossudovsky, "Low"; Cockburn; Davis Mike, "Planet"; Debord, *Comments;* Deutschmann; Drèze & Sen; Eco, "Gli alleati"; En; Engels, *Die Lage; Epicuro;* Fossati; Freud, *The Pelican;* George Alexander ed.; Greider; Gush; Harvey, *The Limits;* Heath-Stubbs & Salman; Henderson; Herman, "Pol," *Real*; Herman & Chomsky; Herman & O'Sullivan, Hesiod, *Theogonia;* Hildebrand & Porter; Hoffman; *Human … 1998;* Juergensmeyer; Klare & Kornbluh eds.; Klein; Kunz; Malik ed.; Marx & Engels. *Die heilige;* Massari; Merleau-Ponty; Minolfi; Moravia; More; Moret; Mueller & Mueller; *Needless;* „Noam Chomsky"; OED; Otto; Pilger, both titles; Pona; Robin; Rummel; Slater & Stohl eds.; Sluka, both titles; Trotsky *Terrorism;* Türcke; Walzer; Zucchetti, both titles.

POEMS 3

Red-eyed bloody business weather!
One-eyed profit-ordered town!
How i wonder when – not whether –
Earthquakes rise to break you down.

6-700

READING CECCO'S *S'i' fosse...*

To Kasia

If i had the power of fire, i'd blow up explosives
If that of water, I'd drown the makers of sorrow,
If the high one of wind, from people's brains
Blow cobwebs away – open your eyes, fools,

You can't take it with you, why strut & fret?
Omnipotent, maybe destroy this stupid
Species, for a cleaner to come from fireflies,
Electric eels or hexapods divisible

In two & three. As i'm but Darko, unreconciled
I praise women, learners, lovers, workers,
The insurgent four whales that bear the world,
With robust love may turn it upside down.

1-281019

4

15 Theses About Communism and Yugoslavia, or the Two-Headed Janus of Emancipation Through the State (Metamorphoses and Anamorphoses of "On the Jewish Question" by Marx) (2010-11)

– To the memory of my *Praxis* colleagues at the Faculty of Philosophy, Zagreb: Rudi Supek, Gajo Petrović, Branko Bošnjak, Predrag Vranicki, Veljko Cvjetičanin, Milan Kangrga

– For Boris Buden, their student, who fights for truth and justice

The State everywhere presupposes that reason has been realised. But in this very way it everywhere comes into contradiction between its ideal mission and its real preconditions.

Marx, 1844

PART 1. INTRODUCTORY[1]

1.1. The Basis of Theses

I have taken over the basic epistemological approach to people, the State, and emancipation from the first part of *On the Jewish Question (Zur Judenfrage*, MEW 1: 352-61) by Karl Marx. In the terms of his age, which at times do not correspond to today's historical semantics, he counterposes political and legal emancipation to complete emancipation. His approach uses Feuerbach's term "species-being" (*Gattungswesen*, that is, the natural possibilities of the genus Homo sapiens), to which I shall return. This way to speak about human potentials rather than about privatised individuals has however much deeper roots, theoretically in Spinoza's discovery that human freedom is primarily threatened by a belief in a predetermined, holy teleology, consubstantial to power and rule, and practically in the French Revolution. I take that this approach transcends Marx's epoch, and that at its core would in today's semantics be: what is the relationship of special political (primarily State-building) alienation to general social alienation as well as to "species-specific" de-alienation or disalienation – comporting the individuals' emancipation within the horizon of classless freedom. I believe that the relationship between emancipation and alienation remains a constant horizon for Marx. True, he still lacks here the key field between theory and practice: the economy, where commodity reification and fetishism will appear as the antagonists of freedom. But this is no Althusserian *coupure épistemologique*, as the new terminology will be a more precise reformulation of the old one from which it evolved.

The very important lack, however, means for my theses that they do not address economic relationships. Their conclusions would have to be supplemented (and perhaps significantly reshaped again) with further considerations, starting primarily from Marx's rich considerations about alienation and exploitation of living labour, about which reached some first conclusions in my essay "Living Labour." But the State and politics must be dealt with first.

This my attempt does not deal in Marxology, although I take it into account in Part 1.2. It is a *reworking*, a genre of its own. It is a quintessentially Marxian stance: he starts with reworking Hegel, and then continually and gluttonously reworks himself and other partial and incomplete cognitions (for example, Adam Smith or the experience of the Paris Commune). Since Marx's argument in the 1840s is literally inapplicable today – who cares about the State of king Frederick William IV? – I am violently tearing out, assembling, and re-functioning some passages by Marx for today's purposes. I start from a dozen passages that I completely or incompletely metamorphosise, and the resulting metamorphic text then demands to be supplemented with other considerations. This makes the whole of my essay anamorphic in relation to that of Marx: rotated into the dimension of Post-Fordism, the new Leviathan. The text is therefore mine, written considering the experience of Yugoslavia after the 1941-45 revolution, and uses Marx as an indispensable stimulus and catalyser – because his style is consubstantial to some fundamental methodological insights into philosophical anthropology that I would like, *mutatis mutandis*, to preserve.

In the 1840s' situation of the Prussian State and Europe, Marx's essay asks this question in form of emancipation from the fiction of "the religious State." My hypothesis is that – regardless of great differences between the Europe of early capitalism in 1844 on one hand, and on the other the world of full imperialist capitalism after the first anti-capitalist revolutions and after 1945 – I can usefully apply the following basic operator to Yugoslavia after the communist revolution (here briefly called SFRY): replacing Marx's official "religion" with "communism (official)" everywhere and seeing what comes out of this. Of course, I do not claim that communism is simply a religion – although it is an annunciation of *this-worldly salvation* (see Suvin "Inside") and its organised professional avant-garde easily translates into a partial analogue of the Church. But it is a sufficiently robust analogy, the basis of which is the existence of an explicit and articulated doctrine that contains all central values for the orientation of humanity in the present historical moment. The justification for its use can only be its fruits.

For the analogy to work, subsidiary metamorphic operators are also used: replacing "religious" with "ideological," and "political" (in Marx's lay meaning of opposition to the religious State and government) with "social": through society or the social, humanisation or disalienation is achieved. The reigning alienation is not to be understood, looking backward, as a Fall from Earthly Paradise (neither Eve and Adam's nor the Noble Savage's) but looking forward to the natural possibilities of the human generic being – the disalienation draws its poetry, as Marx will say, from the future. (Today we could formulate the alienation as three interlocking alienations: that of labour, that of language, and finally that of freedom and sense of life – but this transcends the brief of the present Theses.) However, an important limit of my two analogies should also be considered, which is marked by using the image and concept of the two-headed Janus.

Contextual tact and flexibility should also be applied. First, in selecting only some passages, which are not just crucial, but also roughly applicable to SFRY. And then in translating between epochs and contexts: for example, Marx's early chiasmic rhetoric (if A: B then NonB : NonA), which is nice but not always efficient as real – not only rhetorical – proof, should be used in supple ways and cautiously. I quote the passages according to the English translation, available in Spring 2011 on www.marxists.org/archive/marx/works/1844/jewish-question: this translation is (unavoidably) a half-step towards a reworking of Marx's speculative historiosophy into English empiricism, and thus useful for my epistemological purpose. In the following multiple translating, before metamorphosing it into my own text, I often corrected the English text using the German original which has been identified after each passage (I debated whether to quote the German text too, but since it can be readily found, I preferred not to overload the apparatus). Through the discussion of these passages, the method and argument will gradually crystallise.

Just as Marx distinguished between earthly and heavenly reality of religion, I start with "communism" in the earthbound sense of official, "State" communism in SFRY as a belief, as an ideological vulgate on and of the State. The obverse of "religion," Marx's "atheism," for him the true orientation towards complete human emancipation as opposed to illusory religion, is true emancipatory communism – to which Marx will explicitly arrive immediately after the *Jewish Question*. One should take care here to discern whether this denotes theory, practice or both (to Marx this was not a problem since he hadn't got that far yet).

I was thinking about naming this little tractate "Sing Me a Song of Translation." It involves not only shuttling between three languages – German, English, and the original Croatoserbian – but also among three time epochs, translating Marx's discourse from the time of the already tottering Sacred Alliance into our own discourse of looking backwards from 2011 to SFRY from 1945 to the mid-1970s. The possibility for subsequent degeneration is based on the considerations that follow; they are not dealt with explicitly here but can be found in my *Splendour*.

1.2. An Excursus on Marx and His Evolution

Though the following theses are not an exegesis, they presuppose an exegesis of some essential parameters of Marx and his evolution, and therefore of the specific weights and significance (*Stellenwert*) of the short text used here, the first part *On the Jewish Question*. The Theses develop the basic dichotomy and opposition of *bürgerliche Gesellschaft* against *Staat* from early Marx.

1.21. "Bürgerliche Gesellschaft"

Marx started with this opposition in his 1843 *Critique of Hegel's Philosophy of Right* in: "The general law is[:] the *bürgerliche* society and State are divided. Therefore the *Staatsbürger* as well as the *Bürger*, member of the *bürgerliche Gesellschaft*, is divided." (MEW 1: 281) I am here faced with the fundamental and already metamorphic problem in the form of a well-known dilemma: how to translate *bürgerlich*. The central denotation is "civil," the adjective derived from *civis*, citizen, but does this aim at „the citizen as a subject, that is, member of the State," or „the citizen as a member of the bourgeoisie or the middle class"? As in the above quote, Marx occasionally uses the term *Staatsbürger*, which is the first denotation, but he also has to add in apposition the "member of the *bürgerliche* society." While by this we might today mean the whole of the people minus the State apparatus, this second term also participates in and oscillates between both poles of the translator's dilemma: is it something like "civil society" or like "bourgeois/ middle class society"? The terminology here expresses Marx's persistent probing around the not yet completely clear joints of reality. A few months later, precisely in *On the Jewish Question*, Hegel's undeveloped opposition between the *citoyen* and the ambiguous and limited *bourgeois* (cf. Rehmann 5-6 and passim) will have become Marx's brilliant and deeply significant, though again not fully developed, dichotomy between the *citoyen* as bearer of the French Revolution and the *bourgeois* as bearer of every political counterrevolution from 1794 to 1848 as well as of anti-feudal capitalistic development of production and the corresponding miserable human relationships. Since Marx's texts were at the time only beginning to push toward clarity on this convoluted but also crucial issue, each individual instance of *bürgerlich* should be examined to see which of the two above translations, or of their contaminations, may be more correct (Rehmann 6-7 maintains that the sense of „civil society," which Marx uses when writing in French, is predominant). In English and Italian, *bürgerliche Gesellschaft* is unambiguously translated as *civil society, società civile*, perhaps also because in the Hegel of 1821 it was a translation of *civil society* by 18th-century liberals such as Adam Ferguson and Adam Smith – as Marx explained in the *Preface to A Contribution to the Critique of Political Economy*. I unfortunately have no French translation, but the very "orthodox" Labica-Bensussan dictionary explains that *société civile* is Hegel's term, *société bourgeoise* being Marx's (see 182 and 414), which is insufficient and misleading.

Each of the above solutions has significant flaws. Those associated with the use of "citizen" I have suggested above. "Civil society" does not have those flaws, but has two other major ones. First, in the major European languages, *civil* means civilian (as opposed to military, and in English "civil law" as opposed also to criminal), then committed to public interest (as in French *civisme*), and finally civilised, cultured, with a connotation of a narcissistic national, even class-related self-praise. Second, "civil society" has been taken over from English around the 1980s as a propagandistic term used by advocates of parliamentary – hence bourgeois – democracy to denote lack of freedom in officially "communist" countries of the Soviet bloc or Yugoslavia, with the purpose of wringing from the regime a return of opposition parties and the restoration of private ownership over central means of production. However, no matter how abhorrent some of us might find this one-sided and highly ideologised abuse of both Hegel's and Marx's perspectives, which are richer and deeper (if often mutually contradictory), a plebeian and associational concept of civil society seems to me utterly indispensable in a discourse about what was missing in "really obtaining socialism." We therefore cannot leave this category in the hands of its kidnappers but must use it, cleared of abuse and properly articulated, within Marx's radical perspectives of direct democracy. Binoculars do allow a better view of artillery or sniper fire at, let's say, Sarajevo, but I doubt this is reason enough to discard binoculars.

I would therefore propose to use in English "civil" for Marx's *bürgerliche* in most cases.

1.22. Marx 1843-75: Political Emancipation and the State

Thus, in the *Critique of Hegel's Philosophy of Right* Marx uses Hegel's terms in order to identify – contrary to Hegel – the opposition between the "holy" State apparatus interests of governance, coercion, and ideology, and the profane social and economic interests of the rest of society. The latter are ruled by bourgeois individualism and egotism (as in Hegel), yet they are opposed to the State as real life versus abstract universalism. Further, Marx was an avid reader of Rousseau and the Jacobins as well as "the modern Frenchmen" (MEW 1: 232 — meaning utopians and communists such as Babeuf and Buonarroti, Saint-Simon and his school, Fourier, Proudhon, and Cabet) and supporters of radical popular sovereignty; therefore, Marx diametrically opposes Hegel's allotting of priority, rationality, and absolute importance to the State. Hegel's topology of *bürgerliche Gesellschaft* is in Marx first overturned, becoming a precondition for the State; and then this antithesis as a whole has to be transcended by a total politicisation of civil society which would abolish both itself and the separate State (compare MEW 1: 326-27 and passim).

On the Jewish Question is a big step forward because it introduces *the theme of „false holiness,"* which was to culminate in the theory of commodity fetishism in *Capital:* false, but extremely important as it dominates the mind of the masses. On both sides of Hegel's dichotomy of social life between State and civil society, man is a "plaything of alien powers," under "the rule of inhuman elements and relationships" (MEW 1: 355 and 360), human "species-being" is alienated; in particular, "civil society" is Hobbes's war of all against all (MEW 1: 356). Marx's reading of Feuerbach and the *Gattungswesen* terminology about the species or generic essence of man resonates here, but he reaped the maximum benefit out of this single-minded focus on human sensuality (MEW 1: 345). First, Feuerbach's anthropology, although applied to religion only, was and remains revolutionary in its view *from the bottom up*, that is, basing and centring the creation and understanding of social beliefs and relationships in material and sensuous *humans*. His stance was a useful topological device of separation and rupture, opposed to Hegel's view downward from the height of the Absolute reconciliation (here the State) – so that Engels's later comments on Feuerbach are not sufficient. Marx aspired to such a radical anthropology even before he read Feuerbach, and it remained his absolute and fixed guiding star throughout, including his work on *Capital*. Furthermore, the epistemological limitations of Feuerbach's humanism have been largely evaded in the last quotation from Marx in this essay (see MEW 1: 370) which stresses power in society: he transfers the notion of species to politics, where instead of reposing upon the intersubjectivity of sexual love, it reposes on the Hegelian "life of the people" (cf. Kouvelakis 289). The limits are fully transcended a year later, in the essay on "Alienated Labour" from *Economic and Philosophical Manuscripts of 1844,* with the laconic formula "*Gattungsleben* [the species or generic life of man] is productive life": the direct usefulness of Feuerbach for transition to the critique of political economy comes here into view (MEW Ergänzungsband 516 — see Zolo 122, and a bibliography on the relationship Marx-Feuerbach ibidem 90). In *On the Jewish Question* the civil society stands for all economic and ideological aspects under the political State's and the ruling class's structure of power (see also "Thesis 10 on Feuerbach," MEW 3: 7). And I shall further suggest that this focus on the emancipation of people and their productivity – in the widest sense of all creativity – is not only constant in Marx's thought, but also very pertinent to later contradictions, after the proletarian revolution, between that emancipation and the "socialist" State.

I shall here briefly deal only with the perhaps most important stages in his development of this emancipatory or libertarian opposition. In the important *German Ideology*, within the "civil society" in *all* social formations there is an ongoing conflict of classes, which depends on material production relationships; still, the "civil society" itself remains the "true hearth and arena of all history"! Here this society is resolutely liberated from the narrow context of the bourgeoisie and Hobbes – although it is from the bourgeoisie that both the term for and the first full form of such a society come: "civil society [*bürgerliche Gesellschaft]* comprises the whole material traffic [that is, relationships – note DS] of individuals within a given developmental stage of the relationships of production" (all MEW 3:36). Moreover it is here, I think, that Marx for the first time proposes the thesis according to which the precondition for a free development of personalities is their rule over contingency and reified relationships, namely, a communist organisation of society (MEW 3: 424-25, and cf. 69-70).

Similar positions are to be found in the *Communist Manifesto*, with the important addition of discussing class economic interests protected by the State. But in *The 18th Brumaire* further developments can be found in the analysis of Bonapartism and its complete subordination of legislative to executive power. The deep structure is that of the youthful critique from the 1840s, with the State as the antagonist and negation of the civil society, but now also as an apparatus for regulating the economic class conflict. Marx induces from historical experience that, in a stalemate between classes, the executive can appear completely autonomous in relation to civil society (MEW 8: 197); after a further historical experience of 150 years I would add that in our "hot" society this is inherently unstable and may last no longer than one generation. This horizon is clarified and developed in two other vital writings: Marx's admiring 1871 analysis of the Paris Commune, and his 1875 critique of the German Social Democratic Party. In *The Civil War in France*, written in English, Marx rejects the earlier assumption that the proletariat should form a non-bureaucratic State centralism after the fall of the bourgeois State apparatus, and most resolutely advocates a federation of communes, therefore decentralisation, the reason being that – as in *On the Jewish Question*! – the quasi-religious sacralisation of the State, which has replaced medieval Heaven and Church, must be smashed. In the note "The Character of the Commune" (WMAW/1871/civil-war-france/drafts/ch01.htm#D1s1), Marx dismisses the State, "this supernaturalist abortion of society," and its "Holy State Power," and praises the Paris Commune counter-project of "the reabsorption of the State power by society as its own living forces instead of as forces controlling and subduing it." As Zolo's research has cogently argued, Marx's analysis of revolutionary changes in the Paris Commune opposes the economic and social element to the political and bureaucratic one: this historical overview "matches the opposed pair 'civil society'-'political State' that Marx has ever since the *Critique of Hegel's Philosophy of Right* used to express, even though with partly diverse and tentative semantic values, the basic contradiction within that formation" (176-77). This stance is the presupposition for Marx's focus on the organisation of associated labour in the Commune and the organisation of the entire nation on the basis of self-government (which is exactly what this essay of mine also wants to be).

Finally, in the *Critique of the Gotha Program* (*Randglossen zur Programm der deutschen Arbeiterpartei*) from 1875 it can be seen, by contraries, how important it was for Marx to resolve his youthful dichotomy of State vs. civil society through communism, as the only possible way out and horizon. In this perspective the State is no longer simply power over society, but – contrary to the anarchists – it becomes after the proletarian revolution the executive organ of universal social functions. Such a project can be approached, he avers, only in a scholarly way, which suggests his conclusions from *Capital* about gradually but resolutely abolishing "the commodity form" and abstract labour producing commodities for the market. The goal or *telos* of the process is to make it possible, "after the enslaving subordination of the individual to the division of labour … has vanished," that "the narrow horizon of bourgeois right be entirely transcended and [that] society inscribe on its banners: From each according to his ability, to each according to his needs!" (WMAW/works/1875/gotha/ch01.htm)

I conclude that the term "civil society," in opposition to the State as apparatus, recurs in Marx's political thought. After the *Critique of Hegel's Philosophy of Right*, it was gradually but surely liberating itself from its Hegelian matrix, where civil society meant the corrupt egotism of private interests, and approaching the meaning of interaction between politics and the sphere of social and economic relationships, the relationships which ultimately co-determine production. Civil society becomes co-extensive with those activities where social decision-making is not incorporated into the State as apparatus. The central oscillation remaining in Marx is then whether civil society is necessarily also co-extensive with class struggles, as is clearly the case in both absolutism and capitalism. His notions such as proletariat and communism as abolition of class society do not fit into the opposition between civil society and State but represent its utopian and scientific supersession (*Aufhebung*). Let me add that I would today doubt this "annulment of politics" aspect of Marx's oscillation, which was then exclusively developed by Lenin in *The State and Revolution* (see "Communism Can Only" and "What and How" in this book).

PART 2. THE THESES DEVELOPED

—ENGLISH TRANSLATION OF MARX, PASSAGE I (MEW 1: 352):): "The question of the relation of political emancipation to religion becomes for us the question of the relation of political emancipation to human emancipation."

—COMMENT: Since politics has become a substitute of religion as self-awareness by the government, Marx's relationship *lay politics : religion* should be metamorphosed into our relationship *social : officially political*. But a further complication arises: social or complete human emancipation – soon to centrally include for Marx economic emancipation from misery and exploitation – is identical to Marx's vision of communism, which I shall awkwardly, but I hope clearly, call "true communism" here. To my mind, this is a horizon of total social justice and disalienation, politically implemented through free self-determination of every person in independent working and territorial communities with no State. This means that the relationship of such complete human social emancipation to the official political emancipation is also a relationship of true communism, or of the original Marxian project (we may call it C1), to official Party and State communism (we may call it C2). True plebeian communism with direct democracy relates to, but is very different from, actually existing Party and State communism. Here then is the beginning of my reworking of Marx for the spacetime of SFR Yugoslavia.

—DS METAMORPHICALLY:

Thesis 1. The problem of the relation of complete social emancipation of people to official (and partly real) State and political emancipation is the problem of the relation of real plebeian, directly democratic communism, that liberates and empowers people, to official State and Party communism, emancipatory only to a degree.

Gloss to 1: It follows that the problems of emancipation in Yugoslavia were a version of constant conflict and permeation between two currents within the socialist and communist tradition from the Industrial Revolution on: should sovereign democracy, and even organisation, flow from bottom upward or from top down? On the first extreme of the spectrum are both Marx and the anarchists, on the other Stalin, while Lenin, perforce, moved from the first pole in his theory up to 1917 toward the other one in his extremely endangered application after 1918. This dilemma is explicated in Mao's harsh initial slogan of the first Cultural Revolution in a communist State: "Bombard the headquarters [with criticism]."

****

—ENGLISH TRANSLATION OF MARX, PASSAGE 2 (MEW 1: 353): "The limits of political emancipation are evident at once from the fact that the State can free itself from a restriction without man being really free from this restriction, that the State can be a free State [pun on word *Freistaat*, which also means republic] without man being a free man.... It follows from this that man frees himself through the medium of the State, that he frees himself politically from a limitation when, in contradiction with himself, he raises himself above this limitation in an abstract, limited, and partial way."

—DS METAMORPHICALLY:

Thesis 2. The limits of social emancipation are evident at once from the fact that the State can free itself from a restriction without people being really free from this restriction, that the State can be politically free or a parliamentary republic without people being free. It follows that when people free themselves *through the medium of the State*, they free themselves only in a limited way.

It follows also that when the State freed itself from the restrictions of capitalist class rule while preserving, in Marx's encompassing anthropological sense, a capitalist organisation of production and distribution and bourgeois law, the working people or plebeians were not really freed from the restriction of the "capital-relationship," that is, the exploitation of labour-power and all particular egotisms that arise from it on the side of the exploiters and the exploited. This is accompanied by other class alienation factors: the legacy of patriarchal despotism, different gender roles, city vs. country, intellectual vs. manual labour (readers can supply additional factors).

Gloss to 2: But in this entire essay it is very important, and not to be disregarded, that the actual spacetime of Yugoslavia was doubly philosophically "impure" in comparison to Marx's level of abstraction. It was first impure in general, as any praxis in comparison to theory, since it involves concrete politics with all the necessary compromises, anachronisms, etc. It was also impure, second and especially, since it involves a "transitional period" from capitalism to communism like the one that Marx – only initially, but fundamentally – characterised much later, in the *Critique of the Gotha Program*. Consequently, we are not dealing with a largely closed and stable historical spacetime, such as the early 1840s, but with tempestuous ebb and flow on a much more complex terrain. An example: the revolutionary enthusiasm and plebeian tradition of the Yugoslav People's Liberation War 1941-45 were in the beginning able to completely neutralise the capital-relationship (note for example the economically ridiculous radicalism of nationalisation of small family-owned stores and taverns after 1946/47). Contrariwise: this initial enthusiasm abated naturally somewhere around 1960, for biopsychological reasons of the revolutionary generation's wear and tear, and it was not being continually reinvigorated by a permanent revolutionising of human relationships, both in production – because of a ghettoisation of self-government at company level while blocking its ascent to the summits of power – and in public life or civil society (in the sense of citizen, *citoyen*, participation).

****

—ENGLISH TRANSLATION OF MARX, PASSAGE 3 (MEW 1: 353): "It follows, finally, that man, even if he proclaims himself an atheist through the medium of the State – that is, if he proclaims the State to be atheist – still remains in the grip of religion, precisely because he acknowledges himself only by a roundabout route, only through an *intermediary*. Religion is precisely the recognition of man in a roundabout way, through an intermediary. The State is the intermediary between man and man's freedom. Just as Christ is the intermediary to whom man transfers the burden of all his divinity, all his *religious constraint*, so the State is the intermediary to whom man transfers all his non-divinity and all his *human unconstraint*."

—DS METAMORPHICALLY (I use an additional operator: Marx's „atheist" = today „true communist"):

Thesis 3. **It also follows that people, when they proclaim themselves socialist/communist through the medium of the State – that is, when they proclaim the State to be socialist/communist – still remain non-communist, because they acknowledge themselves only by a roundabout route, only through an intermediary. Non-communism is precisely the recognition of people through an intermediary, by an indirect, and not by direct route. The State is the intermediary between people and people 's freedom, just as religion (a Christian would say Christ) is the intermediary to whom the working people transfer all their communism and all their unconstraint.**

It further follows that belief in the State is in a sincere – not Stalinist and counter-revolutionary – communist government a homologue of religion in Marx's Prussia and the like: it replaces further communist emancipation of the working people by a supernaturalist principle of emancipation.

It finally follows that a sincere – not Stalinist and counter-revolutionary – *communist party* is to be understood as a key attempt at neutralising the deleterious effects of this etatist intermediary after the revolution. However, for this purpose it needs to change from an instrument primarily of violence to an instrument primarily of learning and education (including educating the educators) for the most complex task of permanent revolutionising.

Gloss to 3: This mediation is not, and cannot be, seriously undermined by a *representative* (parliamentary, essentially class) democracy, but only by *associative plus direct* democracy. I shall worry at this in some following essays (see "Communism Can Only" in this book)..

****

—ENGLISH TRANSLATION OF MARX, PASSAGE 4 (MEW 1: 355): "Political emancipation is, of course, a big step forward. True, it is not the final form of human emancipation in general, but it is the final form of human emancipation within the hitherto existing world order. It goes without saying that we are speaking here of real, practical emancipation."

—DS METAMORPHICALLY ("political" vs. "human emancipation" is State vs. human emancipation here):

Thesis 4. Political and legal emancipation through the State is, of course, a big step forward. It is the final step of human emancipation possible in the hitherto existing world-order and macro-framework of States and classes.

****

—REFLECTIONS ON THE FIRST FOUR THESES METAMORPHOSISED FROM MARX

Thesis 5. What are the *limits of applicability* of this entire metamorphic transfer of Marx from the 1840s to Yugoslavia after 1945? Two clusters of arguments indicate that these limits exist.

5.1. The first cluster is that after all there are limits to the analogy religion = communism (Marx's "politics" is consequently "society" for us, and what is called politics in our spacetime is not affected by this since it is the zone of tension between the State and the rest of society – or the civil society). Other lengthy but secondary distinctions would be needed here, which I shall avoid simply by using scissors: by dealing only with those passages from Marx that I need; for, this brilliant text of his is anyway just a crucial incentive, catalyst, and indispensable base for a reworking.

Gloss to 5.1: A large-scale forgetfulness of one's object would be a very questionable practice, but since this is not a text about Marx but through him, I would vigorously defend this method.

5.2. The other cluster is that, in a largely differing historical reality, similarities to Marx's spacetime walk hand in hand with significant differences. The knot of Yugoslavia and the world in the time of multilateral revolutionary dynamics in productive forces and production relationships is much more convoluted that the static Prussian-European one when Marx wrote his diatribe. Neither the economy nor the government nor ideology were in the 1940s what they used to be in the 1840s.

Thesis 6. The reflections so far lead to a thesis fundamental for a cognitive understanding of SFRY: *the Party/State government was a two-headed Janus* (at least in 1945-68). Diametrically opposed to Marx's State in the 1840s, the Party/State government of Yugoslavia was not only a factor of alienation, but *concurrently* also the initiator and lever of real liberation – up to a certain important limit (the liberation is important and the limit is important!).

Liberation: excision of Fascist occupiers and their collaborators – capitalists, bureaucrats, and mercenaries – hence the independence of the country (Tito) as a prerequisite for all other moves toward self-government; nationalisation and creation of a unified planned economy (Kidrič); realisation of a bourgeois revolution in a patriarchal-comprador and despotic country. Such liberation included equality for all before the law including women and the young; mass rise of young peasants (to power during the revolution, to urban employment after the revolution); mass creation of industry and the working class as well as the intelligentsia; realisation of even a Welfare State with social security (employment, education, health care, electrification, a serious although inadequate attempt to build housing and urban infrastructures, etc.). It opened the doors to full freedom or disalienation, its emblem was *policy* (to adapt Rancière). It was a road to C1.

Limit: at the same time, the Party/State government was an intermediary, custodian, and protector of a liberation that, with numerous zigzags, increasingly turned towards oppression; that is, the oligarchy became a class *in statu nascendi**. It closed the doors to the freedom of Marx's "final human emancipation," its emblem was the *police* (to adapt Rancière). C2 was fossilising and fencing in C1.[2]

6.1. These two principles, horizons, and currents clashed within the leadership of the Yugoslav Communist Party and the State: so far so good. But their potential dialectics was suffocated by a "bureaucratic" tradition (in Marx's sense) of monolithism and non-transparency, here of Stalinist origin. Add the economic, as well as ideological, pressures of capitalism from outside, and then increasingly from inside as well (as per the immensely popular song

"Tata, kupi mi auto" – "Daddy, Buy Me a Car"), stir and shake well in a closed vessel, and there's the SFR Yugoslavia for you.

****

—ENGLISH TRANSLATION OF MARX, PASSAGE 5 (MEW 1: 359-60): "Criticism is, therefore, fully justified in forcing the State that relies on the Bible into a mental derangement [*Verrücktheit*, pun on craziness vs. displacement, – note DS] in which it no longer knows whether it is an illusion or a reality, and in which the infamy of its secular aims, for which religion serves as a cloak, comes into insoluble conflict with the sincerity of its religious consciousness, for which religion appears as the aim of the world. This State can only save itself from its inner torment if it becomes the police agent of the Catholic Church. In relation to the church, which declares the secular power to be its servant, the State is powerless, the secular power which claims to be the rule of the religious spirit is powerless.

It is, indeed, alienation which matters in the so-called Christian State, but not man. The only man who counts, the king, is a being specifically different from other men, and is, moreover, a religious being, directly linked with heaven, with God. The relationships which prevail here are still relationships dependent of faith. The religious spirit, therefore, is still not really secularised.

But, furthermore, the religious spirit cannot be really secularised, for what is it in itself but the non-secular form of a stage in the development of the human spirit? The religious spirit can only be secularised insofar as the stage of development of the human mind of which it is the religious expression makes its appearance and becomes constituted in its secular form. This takes place in the democratic State. Not Christianity, but the human basis of Christianity is the basis of this State. Religion remains the ideal, non-secular consciousness of its members, because religion is the ideal form of the stage of human development achieved in this State."

—DS METAMORPHICALLY (taking Thesis 6 into account!):

Thesis 7. Criticism is, therefore, fully justified in forcing the State that relies on Holy Writ to understand it is in a deranged and crazy position in which it no longer knows whether it is a fiction or a reality, and in which the dubiousness of its *empirical* aims, for which ideology (C2) serves as a cloak, comes into insoluble conflict with the sincerity of its *communist* (C1) consciousness, for which communism appears as the purpose of the world. This State can only save itself from its inner torment if it becomes the *police agent* of the institutionalised Party.

Gloss to 7: In the two-headed Janus perspective from Thesis 6 above, the idea of the State as the police for the Party is true only for one completely negative – monolithic and despotic – face of government in SFRY: this was completely and "purely" striven for by the Party conservatives, who are therefore non-Stalinist Stalinists. But with this reservation and to that extent (which is yet to be determined) – it is true. The only alternative: the State should — gradually but steadily — wither.

7.1. For the etatised, oligarchic, police face of the so-called communist State, what counts (*gilt*) is *alienation*, and not *people*. The only people who count are those of "a special mould" (Stalin), moreover directly linked with ideology (with Heaven). The relationships that prevail here are still relationships of *faith*. The religious horizon of official communism is, therefore, still not secularised or laicised.

But the "State-communist" (C2) horizon cannot be *really* secularised, for what is it in itself but the *alienated* form of a transitional stage in the potential development of human emancipation from millenary State power, patriarchal violence, and class exploitation? These alienations *demand* a schism between the earthly and the heavenly horizon, operative also in the period of potential transition from class society to communism. The State-communist stance can be realised and abolished (*aufgehoben*) only insofar as the stage of human emancipation of which it is the ideologically alienated expression makes its appearance and becomes constituted in a this-worldly, *disalienated* spirit. This may take place in such a socialist society where direct plebeian self-government would prevail over etatism and other alienations. The basis of this State would then not be State communism but the human basis of communism (C1).

****

—ENGLISH TRANSLATION OF MARX, PASSAGE 6 (MEW 1: 360-61):): "Political democracy is Christian since in it man, not merely one man but everyman, ranks as *sovereign*, as the highest being, but it is man in his uncivilised, unsocial form, man in his fortuitous existence, man just as he is, man as he has been corrupted by the whole organisation of our society, who has lost himself, been alienated, and handed over to the rule of inhuman conditions and elements.... That which is a creation of fantasy, a dream, a postulate of Christianity, *that is,* the sovereignty of man – but man as an alien being different from the real man – becomes, in democracy, tangible reality, present existence, and secular principle."

—DS VERY METAMORPHICALLY (but within Marx's vocabulary):

Thesis 8. Real and integral political democracy is communist (C1): it restrains and humanises the necessary State. State communism (C2), however, empir-

ically knows man in his uncivilised, unsocial form, man in his fortuitous existence, man as he has been corrupted (*verdorben*) by the whole organisation of our patriarchal and capitalist society, alienated, handed over to the rule of inhuman conditions and elements. Official communism (C2) may dream of and postulate the sovereignty of man as the highest being, but that is an alien being, different from the "really existing" man. In real communism (C1) this creation of fantasy and dream would however be tangible reality, present existence, material principle — carrier of self-determination and self-awareness. Marx's "transitional period" is the growth of people from C2 to C1. This is the criterion for any measure and institution in it.

****

—ENGLISH TRANSLATION OF MARX, PASSAGE 7 (MEW 1: 354-55): "Where the political State has attained its true development, man – not only in thought, in consciousness, but in reality, in life – leads a twofold life, a heavenly and an earthly life: life in the political community, in which he considers himself a communal being, and life in civil society, in which he acts as a private individual, regards other men as a means, degrades himself into a means, and becomes the plaything of alien powers."

—DS METAMORPHICALLY (this alienation is not transferrable to SFRY *tel quel*, at least not before ca. 1968):

<u>Thesis 9</u> (alternatively to Thesis 8). Where the communist State government has developed into a closed ruling elite or politocracy, people lead — not only in thought, in consciousness, but in reality, in life — a twofold life, ideal and real (heavenly and earthly). They live in the State community in which they consider themselves communal beings, and also live in the civil or bourgeois society in which they consider themselves private individuals, regardless of all other individuals that are being treated as a means, and in which they become degraded and playthings of alien powers.

****

—ENGLISH TRANSLATION OF MARX, PASSAGE 8 (MEW 1: 357-58): "The so-called Christian State is the Christian negation of the State, but by no means the political realisation of Christianity. The State which still professes Christianity in the form of religion, does not yet profess it in the form appropriate to the State, for it still has a religious attitude towards religion – that is to say, it is not the true implementation of the human basis of religion, because it still relies on the unreal, imaginary form of this human core. The so-called Christian State is the imperfect State, and the Christian religion is regarded by it as the supplementation and sanctification of its imperfection. For the Christian State, therefore, religion necessarily becomes a means; hence, it is a hypocritical State. It makes a great difference whether the complete State, because of the defect inherent in the general nature of the State, counts religion among its presuppositions, or whether the incomplete State, because of the defect inherent in its particular existence as a defective State, declares that religion is its basis. In the latter case, religion becomes imperfect politics. In the former case, the imperfection even of consummate politics becomes evident in religion. The so-called Christian State needs the Christian religion in order to complete itself as a State."

—DS METAMORPHICALLY (with a supplement):

Thesis 10. Similarly to a State which professes religion, the so-called communist State is the communist negation of State, but by no means the social realisation of communism. The so-called communist State is the imperfect State, and communism is regarded by it as the *supplementation* and *sanctification* of its imperfection, so that communism necessarily becomes a *means*, and the State – a *hypocritical* State. The so-called communist State needs communism in order to complete itself *as a State*.

Gloss to 10: In that case, the official Party-State communism (C2, although the official interpretation in Yugoslavia avoided the term "communism"!) becomes an ideology in the negative sense of an alienated view of reality. Since it still invokes the original communism (C1) of Marx and of Lenin at their best, C2 becomes hypocrisy as well, like to the Christian Pope preaching evangelic love for fellow-man (to stay with Marx's parallel) from the magnificent St Peter's Cathedral and the State enclave of the Vatican to masses gazing at the wonderful colonnade. The closing of doors to Marx's integral emancipation – lineaments of which were becoming visible as self-determination in economics and politics – transforms even the very real contributions of the first Janus head increasingly into hypocrisy. Yet that hypocrisy remains "a tribute which vice pays to virtue" (La Rochefoucauld).

C2, the "religion" of government, is in comparison to C1 always a partial – and eventually becomes a fake – achievement. It is within this discrepancy that the Zagreb magazine *Praxis* appears, as an example of the conscience of communism (C1) – which itself is also one-sided, being oppositional and militant instead of sovereign and triumphant, etc.

Thesis 11. In (important!) contrast to other-worldly religion, this-worldly communism understands the second sentence of Thesis 10 as a *temporary postponement* of perfection – until the productive forces of a people are developed and outside threats eliminated (which practically means *sine die* or, so

far as we can see in the ever worsening capitalism, when hell freezes over). I suppose that this aporetic gap gives rise to important strategic modifications for the future to Marx's political horizon itself, which are to be based on his philosophical anthropology and very costly experiences. Centrally, the necessary orientation towards the disalienating component of self-management within economic production and consumption remains pivotal, but needs to be supplemented with the disalienating component of democratic power outside direct production.

Gloss to 11: In fact, communism has no sense whatsoever unless it preserves the horizon of a radical this-worldly salvation, namely mass production of a qualitatively better life, and not only social-democratic reformism. But how? C1 is *politically* a matter of developing, within communism and as the essence of communism, efficient and intertwined forms of both associative and direct democracy, in the interaction of State and the rest of society, and *economically* a matter of developing efficient and intertwined forms of many-sided and pyramidal planning on the basis of critical feedback from such a democracy. *Philosophically*, it is a matter of resisting all pretences to the One Final Truth, and all attendant corollaries of Oneness from top down; these are best seen in Stalin's monolithism and his ubiquitous vertical chain of the "single command" system [*odinonachalie*], but are well and thriving in all Churches and capitalist corporations.

Religion (monotheistic) is beyond repair; Marxism and communism (C1) are not.

Thesis 12. *Communism cannot abolish politics*, that is, oppositions within the civil society between citizens of a State or other community. Marx gave to politics the exclusive sense of antagonistic collisions, in the final instance based on class interests; this strand runs from the passages discussed earlier to, for example, *The Misery of Philosophy*, and culminates in the *Communist Manifesto* conclusion that "Political power, properly so called, is merely the organised power of one class for oppressing another." (Tucker ed. 353) After the 20th-century revolutions, however, we know also of "non-antagonistic contradictions within the people" (Mao). Without civil-society politics to resolve them, only the State remains for that job – a necessary, but very one-sided politics from above. This became the major fault of Leninism, growing out of a backward patriarchal reality.

Today we may redefine politics as existing outside class antagonisms too – that is, in the relations of production – so that its germs could well be present in and intertwine with class politics (what else is C1 in the "transitional period"?). The State cannot really be abolished until its necessary functions were taken over by associations of producers as well as associations of citizens – civil society – in manifold institutions of direct democracy from below.

Gloss to 12: We are talking here about *the self-determination and self-awareness* of individuals interacting within the social totality (according to Hegel at his best). These terms are derived from individuals, as active and reflexive aspects of their sovereign being, and they can be understood as *self-government* of oneself and of human collective affairs against the horizon of mortality.

If self-government is understood solely as a translation of these terms into the language of mass administration (self-*management*, as in Kardelj), this remains a necessary but not a sufficient step.

****

—ENGLISH TRANSLATION OF MARX, PASSAGE 9 (MEW 1: 357): "In periods when the political State as such is born violently out of civil society, when political liberation is the form in which men strive to achieve their liberation, the State can and must go as far as the abolition of religion, the destruction of religion. But it can do so only in the same way that it proceeds to the abolition of private property, to the maximum, to confiscation, to progressive taxation, just as it goes as far as the abolition of life, the guillotine. At times of special self-confidence, political life seeks to suppress its prerequisite, civil society and the elements composing this society, and to constitute itself as the real species-life of man, devoid of contradictions. But, it can achieve this only by coming into violent contradiction with its own conditions of life, only by declaring the revolution to be permanent, and, therefore, the political drama necessarily ends with the re-establishment of religion, private property, and all elements of civil society, just as war ends with peace."

—DS METAMORPHICALLY (and, in the end, totally different but within Marx's vocabulary):

Thesis 13. In periods when the State government is born violently out of society, when liberation through the State is the form in which people strive towards their liberation, in this time of special self-confidence, the State seeks to suppress its prerequisite, the society of citizens, and to constitute itself as the real fullness of man, devoid of contradictions. But the State can achieve this only by coming into violent contradiction with its own conditions of life, only by declaring the revolution to be *permanent*, and the drama necessarily ends with a change in the character of the State or a change in the character of the society.

Gloss to 13: I think this corresponds to the ongoing dilemma of SFRY. Extraordinary: although Marx cannot be literally applied to it, he formulated the dilemma of its government as coercive power brilliantly! As we know, the drama ended with a change in the character of the State (in the worst possible version of the Yugoslav Secession Wars between feuding mini-classes and captive peoples), *because* no change had come about in the character of the citizens' society (no full direct and associative democracy) in order to empower a full vertical association of producers.

****

I have two conclusions, one based on Marx and the other on experiences from the October Revolution onwards:

—ENGLISH TRANSLATION OF MARX, PASSAGE 10 (MEW 1: 370): "Only when the real, individual man re-absorbs in himself the abstract citizen, and as an individual human being has become a *species-being* in his everyday life, in his particular work, and in his particular situation, only when man has recognised and organised his >own powers< [Rousseau, *Contrat social*] as *social* powers, and, consequently, no longer separates social power from himself in the shape of *political* power, only then will human emancipation have been accomplished."

—DS METAMORPHICALLY:

Thesis 14. Only when real, individual people re-absorb in themselves the abstract citizen of the State (*Staatsbürger*) and when individual human beings have become in their empiric day-to-day life, work, and relationships integrally human beings, only when people have recognised and organised their "own powers" (Rousseau) as *social* powers, and, consequently, no longer separate social power from themselves in the shape of *State* power, only then will human emancipation have been accomplished.

—AFTER MARX, WE TODAY:

Thesis 15. However, whenever C2 suppresses C1 (Stalinism, today PR China), we arrive to a counter-revolution that annuls the beginnings of disalienation (Enlightenment, Welfare State, attempts at self-government). The metamorphosis of Luxemburg's slogan "socialism or barbarism" in conditions of hegemonic world capitalism is: "Communism (C1) or counter-revolution into fascist savagery."

Glossary:

coupure épistemologique: epistemological break
mutatis mutandis: having changed what needs to be changed
in statu nascendi: just being born
tel quel: as is
sine die: without defined or any deadline, irony for "never"

Works Cited in Essay 4

See in *Works Cited in this Book* the following titles, by Author surname plus (when the author has several titles) first "headword" or identifying syntagm in the title:

Bobbio; Kouvelakis; Labica & Bensussan eds.; Marx, *The Civil;* Marx & Engels, *Briefe, The Marx-Engels Reader, Werke;* Rehmann; Suvin, "Inside," "Living," *Splendour;* Zolo.

POEMS 4

LE CENERI DI TITO (BERLIN DAY, END OF C20)

German winter   elder ladies with mink coats
Peroxide hair   too much makeup
Lines slashing from both mouth corners down & out
I burrow into sleep quietly on morning islands
At the bottom of the ocean schools of fish
Soft murmur of weary voices
They are bombing Beograd & Novi Sad
No more theatre festivals in springtime
Blood silting up all rivers.

Whispering of fish   jealousy of fish
If sharks were men
Big gangsters eat little gangsters
Peasants are burned out of their villages
City people bombed out of their homes
Thousands of Munch faces screaming
Humans   from their womb humanity forcibly ripped
By progressive technology & humanism
Demanding oceans of blood

Western brainwashed in uniform shoot at Balkan brainwashed
The center doesn't tolerate too much periphery
Top dollar American mercenaries bomb scared Serbian draftees
Bristly bearded gangsters from Beograd clean Albanians out of
    medieval monasteries
They are madly in love with the Serbian destiny to suffer
Smooth shaven gangsters from Washington upgrade armament
    technology
They are madly in love with the profits of arms industries
Booms in Balkan skies   booms on the stockmarkets
Communicating slaughterhouse vessels
Oceans of blood   oceans of profit
Who is king of the world jungle must be made quite clear
Sharks are not so clever   except in fable

Now you can touch what we lost with Tito's brotherhood & unity
Now you see how a people's revolution is eradicated
One million dead in the partizan war
A ton of TNT to wipe out every dead partizan
These dead are dangerous   they must be killed again by
    bombs & lies
Counter-revolution by the center against the periphery
Blood on stone   blood & stones
Thou shalt not get out from under world banks   fish mouth
    silently

This is Moses & the prophets

700-251200

Glossary: Le ceneri di Tito = The Ashes of Tito, a riff on Pasolini's Le ceneri di Gramsci
If sharks were men = a fulminant short story by Brecht, ought to be read

5

Power Without Violence: A Lesson From Tribal Communism (2009–13)*

> The dissolution of society bids fair to become the termination of a career of which property is the end and aim; because such a career contains the elements of self-destruction. Democracy in government, brotherhood in society, equality in rights and privileges, and universal education, foreshadow the next higher plane of society to which experience, intelligence and knowledge are steadily tending. It will be a revival, in a higher form, of the liberty, equality and fraternity of the ancient gentes.
>
> Lewis Henry Morgan, 1877

1. The Prophetic Dance-Song of Lack and Need

As dawn arises in the Mbya tribe, one of the last remnants of the once large group of the Tupi-Guarani Amerindians, in the jungle of large trees inside what is now Paraguay, very often a *pa'i*, a prophet-singer, rises. He turns east, toward the sun, the messenger of the highest god Ñamandu, with a lamentation and exhortation. The Mbya have steadfastly refused missionary efforts, from the 18th century Jesuits until today, to convert them to Christianity, and keep a community of faith as the obsessive guarantee of their tribe's unity, counteracting the shame and pain of their dwindling numbers and unhappiness. The prophet's dance-song speaks of the tribe's utterly sick Being, their *tekoachy*, in what the great anthropologist Pierre Clastres — from whose *La société,* 137-51, I take my data about them and many beautiful formulations — called "the sphere of distress to which the silence of the gods has abandoned them" (142). They live in the land of evil, *ywy mba'ë megua*, a corrupt and rotten land, the realm of death; they speak of themselves as the Last Men. Yet they hope that they shall receive from the gods favourable signs for a road to their passage over the horrible sea and towards the Land without Evil, *ywy mara eÿ*. To their doubts and anxiety the evocation of their ancestors is opposed, to whom the gods did once speak, to whom it was given to reach the state of perfection, *aguyje*, and thus to pass over the metaphoric sea.

The fact that the sun again rises is proof that the supreme god consents to let them live on. But life "is not simply waking to the neutrality of things" (142). The Mbya live on earth as in a space of *absence*, of questioning for its reason and a way out of it. The *pa'i* proclaims this to be the absence of the beautiful original words, *ñe'ë porä tenonde*, of the divine language wherein is to be found the humans' salvation. Their inhabitation of the present land is a wearisome interval at the threshold of their true abode. Let then the gods speak, let them recognise the humans' efforts, their fasting, their dancing, their praying! Thus arises the prayer-song-dance of their *pa'i* (I somewhat abbreviate Clastres's no doubt necessarily stylised French translation):

> My father! Ñamandu! You cause me to arise again!
> Equally you cause all the ritually adorned males to arise again,
> And all the ritually adorned females to arise again,
> And those not ritually adorned, you cause them too all to arise again.
> See then: concerning those ritually adorned, concerning those not ritually adorned, concerning all of them, I ask.
>
> And yet, concerning all of this, you do not pronounce the words:
> neither for me nor for your children destined for the indestructible country, the eternal country which no pettiness mars.
> You do not pronounce the words in which dwell the future rules of our force, the future rules of our fervour.
>
> For, in truth,
> I exist imperfectly.
> My blood is of an imperfect nature,
> my flesh is of an imperfect nature,
> it is horrible, it is deprived of all excellence.
> Things being thus,
> in order that my blood of an imperfect nature
> in order that my flesh of an imperfect nature
> be jolted and reject far away their imperfection:
> with bent knees, I bow down,[1] looking for a valorous heart,
> which is the force, which is the fervour.
> And yet, here we are: you do not pronounce the words.
>
> - - - - - - - - - -

Nothing within the entirety of things transmits a value to my heart.
Nothing points me toward the future rules of my existence.

And the sea, the baleful sea,
you didn't make me cross it, me.
It is because of this, in truth, it is because of this
that there remain only a few, my brothers,
that there remain only a few, my sisters.

- - - - - - - - - -

You cause their words to arise,
you inspire their questioning,
you cause a huge lamentation to arise from all of them.

But see: I rise in my effort,
and yet you do not pronounce the words, no, truly, you do not pronounce the words.

Therefore, here is what I'm led to say,
O god Karai Ru Ete, O Karai Chy Ete:
those who were not in a small number,
those destined for the indestructible country, the eternal country which no pettiness mars,
all those, in truth, you caused to question, once upon a time, concerning the future rules of their existence.
And certainly they knew them in their perfection, once upon a time.

And if, concerning myself, my nature be delivered from its customary imperfection,
and the blood be delivered from its customary imperfection of yore:
then, certainly, this comes from my blood of an imperfect nature,
from my flesh of an imperfect nature,
being jolted and rejecting far away their imperfection.

It is because of this that you shall pronounce abundantly the words,
the words of a great soul,
for those whose face is not divided by any sign [that is, who aren't Christianised].
You shall pronounce abundantly the words,
O god Karai Ru Ete, and you Karai Chy Ete,
for all those destined for the indestructible country, the eternal country which no pettiness mars.
Thou. You all!

I am not competent to enter into any full exegesis of what Clastres rightly calls "this language of remarkable poetic richness" (141 — anyway there is no video of the dance), except to note it proceeds by means of a repeated counterpoint between absence of existential value and request for salvation, which culminates in the latter's magical certainty. This is the poetry of a deeply wounded tribal communism: its gods have absconded[2] but the song-dance wants to enact their return. It proceeds from the anxious need for a fleshly salvation of the community, "concerning all of them," to poetically incantatory oratory, pleading for their destiny.

In another place, Clastres speaks of a legend about their god Tupan. He made this imperfect world, but left the Guarani this counsel: "If one of these knowledges resides in your ears, you shall know my traces.... Only thus shall you find the term or destination which you have been pointed toward.... I am going far, far away, you won't see me. Therefore, my words, do not lose them." (151)[3] And in Clastres' final essay drawing together the theoretical fall-out from his work, to which I shall return, his "political anthropology" characterises the virulent prophetic language of such Guarani prophets, "who in the 15th–16th centuries led thousands of Indians in mad migrations to find the gods' homeland," as "eminently subversive, since it called upon the Indians... to abandon society as was, in order to reach the Land without Evil" (183). This politics, although by the 1960s in dire straits, was of the same family as what Thomas Münzer was telling the peasant rebels of Germany in heretically Christian terms. The Land without Evil itself, also called the House of Our Ancestress, is holy and across an imaginary big water but one enters it in flesh; it transcends the unhappy existence but not the physical body. Life in it continues on the normal tribal pattern, but without the corruptions of poverty, sickness, injustice or aging. As I argued four decades ago, this land and life may not be within our empirical history but they are an alternative, as it were unhistorical and yet more perfect, history (*Metamorphoses* chap. 3; see also there in note 40 further bibliography mentioning Eliade on the Guaranis, also medieval and Hellenic testimonies of Earthly Paradises reached in flesh).

2. The "Titular" Chief: Power without Command or Violence

In other essays, Clastres considers the much misjudged role of the tribal chiefs. He notes that within the huge number of South American tribes, almost all such chiefdoms except in the circum-Caribbean area are without the authority to command. Robert H. Lowie has called them "titular chiefs" (I shall further dispense with the adjective), and Clastres accepts Lowie's pinpointing of three essential properties which such a chieftain must in both Americas possess (26-31):

1. He is a peacemaker within the tribe, the moderating factor in internal disagreements;
2. He is a frequent and generous distributor of his own goods among the tribal members;
3. He is a first-rate orator.

This implies that he be a not too young male, successful enough as a hunter to command the respect of the tribe and to have sufficient goods for frequent distributions. Clastres adds as a fourth point that polygamy seems in those tribes most often restricted to chiefs, probably because it is of a piece with success and richness. (Polygamy for a large number of tribe members is demographically impossible — unless the tribe has "evolved" some way toward the State, by having e.g. castes, slavery, and frequent warfare which supplies the women.) This "normal" chief is opposed to the war-chief, who must only possess warlike skills and has a quite large command power over the warrior band, which is however operative solely during the — usually brief — war, after which he reverts, like the Roman *dictator*, to a simple member of the tribe. This is why the passage to "command chiefdom" can only be achieved by organising frequent warfare and a band of armed retainers loyal to the chief rather than to the tribe (cf. 177-78). Indeed, the Mbya prophet of section 1 seems to have been part of a counter-tendency, begun four or five centuries ago, to the rise of such a violent chiefdom and the attendant creeping corruption and death of the egalitarian society as they knew it, which was then compounded by the hugely violent arrival of European colonisers (183-84). In this overwhelming decadence, the yearning for counter-action flowed into what Clastres felicitously identifies as "an intoxicated thought, an increasingly tense deepening of reflection on the unhappiness of the human condition" (184).[4]

But upon how the chieftain orates there hangs a most revealing tale.

As opposed to the prophet in the especially endangered situation of the Mbya, who is a peremptory intercessor between the tribe and its gods so that they may save it, in a normally functioning tribe the chief's orations are foreseeable and bland. They happen as a rule daily, at dawn or dusk. He talks in a strong voice while members of the tribe continue to go on about their businesses: nobody seems to pay attention to what he says. Clastres underlines: "*The chief's speech is not meant to be listened to.*" Although he talks at length, he repeats always the same, trite matter: a celebration of the traditional rules of tribal life, roughly reducible to: "Our ancestors were content while living as they lived. Let us follow their example, and we shall lead a peaceful life together." (135)

But why should the chief's speech lack new information? Because *chieftancy carries no power of commanding* that anything be done by the tribe's members. There is either no need for novelty in this life, or if there might be, it comes about spontaneously, by individual trial and error, generalised in case of success. Tribal commun(al)ism had achieved what the Victorian communist William Morris so ardently longed for, "An Epoch of Rest," or what Benjamin opposed to Marx's locomotive of history – a pulling on the brake. The chief occupies *the place of power* without the *authority* of proposing or giving orders. He has no means of enforcing anything he might wish: the tribe is not "policed." Any such proposal would not only be disobeyed, it would speedily lead to his not being acknowledged any more. The chief is a kind of oiler of the existing tribal gears, which he can in no way change. "Primitive society refuses [enforceable] separate power, because it is itself the real locus of power. It naturally knows that violence is the essence of power. In this knowledge, the care to separate institution and power, chiefdom and commanding, is rooted." (Clastres 136) The informationally empty speech is, at that point of human relationships, the opposite of violence.

As Clastres rightly says in a separate theoretical overview (and his terminology above should in places be rectified in consequence):

> 1. …Political power is *universal*, immanent to society — be that society determined by 'blood ties' or by social classes — but it has two principal modalities: coercive and non-coercive power. 2. Coercive political power (or the model of command-obedience) is not the only true model of power, but simply *a particular case*, a concrete case of political power in certain cultures, as the 'Western' one. (20)

Generally, "political power as coercion or as violence is characteristic of historical societies, that is, of societies that bear the springs of innovation, of change, of historicity" (22). In brief, "it is possible to think of politics without violence, it is impossible to think of society without politics: in other words, there is no society without power" (21). I subscribe fully to this position, and I shall in the rest of this essay attempt to discuss some of its meanings and implications.

3. Human Culture as Acknowledgement of and Defense against Raw Nature

And yet the chief participates as an important "operator" – oiler of gears or stabiliser – in the principal exchange circuits whereof is constituted the culture of what I shall further call tribal communism: exchange of women, of goods, of words (explicit traditional values and meanings). A further brilliant hypothesis explains his impotence as inextricably articulated with these cycles. Clastres founds it on the fact that this culture is the barrier between the tribe and the overwhelmingly powerful nature in which it operates. In my gloss, culture has unconsciously but imperatively brought about these three dimensions of circulation as the difference between humanity and animality. Non-human nature is no doubt the element within which the tribe lives and from which it draws the elements for its sustenance, but it is also to be kept at arm's length in order for humanity — a more than animal consciousness and exchange structure — to exist as such. The total refusal of command power, that is, violence by some people against other people, is strictly isomorphic, maybe even of a piece, with the refusal of "nature red in tooth and claw" as dominant norm rather than enabler:

> This identity of refusal leads us to find in these societies an identity between the power [to command other people – note DS] and nature: culture is a denial of both.... It is as if these societies erected their political sphere upon an intuition which would be their equivalent of a supreme rule: that is, that power is in its essence coercion...; that the nature of power is a furtive alibi of the power of nature.... Discovering the close kinship between power [to command] and nature as the double limit of the universe of culture, the Indian tribal societies have managed to invent a means to neutralise the virulence of political authority. (40)

A disclaimer: I believe a more precise terminology would be to say, with the insights of Clastres cited above, that power as such is constitutive of politics, that is, inescapable and polyvalent, whereas only command power, that is, coercion or violence, is clearly negative. That is why I have in key places added "command" to power, and elsewhere in the above paragraph the gentle reader ought to do it.

Nonetheless, the above is a quite key insight, extrapolatable (*mutatis mutandis*) over the whole range of what Marx has called the human metabolism with nature. In that wake, Clastres is precisely correct when he follows that, as the Amerindians deeply intuited and subtly guarded against, "the transcendent power hides a mortal threat for the group, that the principle of an exterior authority which creates its own legality is a contestation of culture itself" (40). That is why the exchange of women, of goods, and of words must break down in the chief. He has been put into the position where he owes all to the group, where he must ceaselessly respond to its demands for precise ways of handing over goods and words, and thus prove that his functioning does no harm. That is why the words cannot have an informational or innovating function. He must be loud in order to prove that his speech is soft, says Clastres; and he reads the chief's isolated polygamy as "being a way in which he is prisoner of the group as a whole." Still, this tribal culture is "troubled by refusing a power that fascinates them: the chief's opulence is the group's daydream" (42).

In a Melanesian context, the foundational opus of Malinowski has quite analogously established that the Trobriand islanders, as all tribal societies, control the means of their livelihood, which are in their direct "decentralized, local, and familial" possession (Sahlins, "Political" 408), and are insofar masters of their own — economic — destiny. Whatever the basic group of producers does not consume is used to discharge kinship obligations and taboos. The chief is the political agent of organising pooling and redistribution of goods, and possesses prestige in direct proportion to how well he does this for general welfare. "Prestige, therefore, operates to overcome an inherent tendency to limit productivity in a system of production for use…" (idem 410). He is a manager who collects goods given to him by various households for kin and religious reasons and redistributes them to subsidise further production and all community activities: for example, he feeds and feasts assembled warriors, subsidises trading expeditions, and initiates various types of specialist production which he then further distributes: "A man who owns a thing is naturally expected to share it, to distribute it, to be its trustee and dispenser…. Thus the main symptom of the powerful is to be wealthy, and of wealth is to be generous." (Malinowski, *Argonauts* 97, and cf. *Coral* passim, also the famous argument by Mauss about the tribal communism's norm of "gifting"). Therefore "in the long run, all of the wealth accumulated by [the chief] flows back to his subjects" (idem, *Coral* 1: 47). Commenting on this, Marshall Sahlins concludes: "The net economic effect of the chief's activity is to promote the general interest."

Furthermore, "Throughout Oceania, the general relation between wealth and power is the same…. redistribution is the foundation of political power." In sum, "economic relations of coercion and exploitation and the corresponding social relations of dependence and mastery are not created in [this] system of production" ("Political" 405, 407, and 408). We could conclude that possession of goods in such a situation is transient and cannot be used to enforce commands. Clastres himself, at times prone to romanticising the fascination the "titular" chief exerts on the tribe, concludes elsewhere soberly that "he is vested by society with a certain number of tasks, and in this capacity can be seen as a sort of unpaid civil servant of society." Though the chief is also exceptionally important for contacts with other tribes, he can never make a decision on his own and impose it on his community (*Archeology* 89): "Primitive societies are thus… classless societies — no rich exploiters of the poor; societies not divided into the dominating and the dominated — no separate organ of power…. [They] do not have a State because they refuse it…." (ibidem 90-91).

A final theme which fits well here is <u>*tribal economics and work*</u>. For, the dozens or hundreds of "archaic" societies have the effect of estranging — in Brecht's sense of seeing for the first time with increased understanding — the class societies and the very high price of "civilised" power, amongst us always coupled with violence. Benjamin summed this up in the most enlightening formula: "every achievement of civilisation is also an achievement of barbarism"; true, the term barbarism is here as suspect as would be "savagery," maybe it should be "violent and warlike alienation." Thus we could reformulate this admirable terseness as, say: "every achievement of civilisation, however useful and admirable in some aspect, is extorted from the surplus labour of the powerless lower classes and carries an indelible stigma." In anthropology, notes Clastres, archaic societies are defined as those without writing and with a "subsistence economy." But the latter is again a highly dubious proposition, reposing as it does on the criterion that only the fruits of extorted surplus labour are the norm of civilisation: this is however not extrapolatable backwards. It also follows from such a criterion that power can in class societies only be defined on the command-obedience model — that is, in the wake of Nietzsche and Weber's theorisation of class practice and State power (which is the monopoly of legitimate use of violence). Yet, as we have seen in the innumerable tribes with "titular" chiefdoms, a symbolically and ceremonially unifying institution can and did exist, as it were, on the same level as or catalytically within the society, rather than above it.

But then, was the economy of tribal commun(al)ism truly a "subsistence" one, that is, perpetually on the brink of hunger and catastrophe? No doubt such cases could happen, mostly because of a natural catastrophe and then the arrival of genocidal colonisers. But in what seems a solid majority of cases, the South American tribal societies "produced a food *surplus* often *equal* to the needed annual consumption: this production was therefore capable of satisfying the need two times over, or to feed double the existing population" (Clastres 13, and cf. 164-73; the same is true of Malinowski's Trobrianders). Neither is it correct to say that tribal commun(al)ism is incapable of producing a large surplus because it would be "technically inferior." Clastres argues:

> If by technique we mean the ensemble of proceedings which people use not at all to insure the absolute mastery over nature — a demented Cartesian project valid only for our society, the ecological consequences of which we are only now beginning to measure — but to insure a mastery of the natural environment adapted and related to their needs, then we can speak of no technical inferiority in the primitive societies: their capacity to satisfy their needs is at least equal to those of our proud industrial and technological society.... What surprises us in the Inuit or the Australian Aborigines is precisely the richness, imaginativeness, and acuteness of their technical activity.... On the contrary, we must recognise that the discovery of agriculture and of plant domestication happens almost simultaneously in the Americas and the Old World, [and] that the Amerindians do not at all lag behind in the art of selecting and differentiating multiple varieties of useful plants. (162-63)

In sum, as Sahlins has strongly argued, "[t]he world's most 'primitive' people have few possessions, but they are not poor" ("Original"129, and see his *Stone Age*). While the debate about his "primitive affluence" thesis is still open, much subsequent wide-ranging research confirms that procuring food usually took in primitive communism perhaps 15-25 hours per week, though what "procuring" means is not always clear. Clastres sarcastically remarks that "by such accounting, it is rather the European 19th-century proletariat, illiterate and under-nourished, that ought to be called archaic" (14). Or today's new proletariat of migrant and precarious workers, educated to be semi-literate only, infantilised by the iPod?

Why should therefore people in the tribal societies work or produce more than they need? After adopting metal axes from the colonisers, Guarani agriculturists worked two months less: new means of production meant for them working less, more free time! "It is always through violence that people work over and above their needs. Precisely this violence is absent from the primitive world, it is even the definition of their nature.... These are the first societies of leisure, the first societies of abundance, to adopt the just and joyful expression of Sahlins." (Clastres 166)

It should however be underscored that work or more precisely labour "is not... a true category of tribal economics." Rather, work is part and parcel of or embedded in kinship and community relationships (Sahlins, *Tribesmen* 80). "The term 'economic life' would here have no obvious meaning," as Polanyi gleefully noted in his splendid essay "Aristotle Discovers the Economy" (70).

4. What Follows From This

Clastres's approach has important theoretical fall-outs for a philosophy of history or of societal development. First of all, he focuses on what I would call, with Badiou, the communist invariant as found in tribal society, *the refusal of inequality of power, when the latter means coercion or violence.* This invariant, I would add, has at least two aspects, one fixed and one changing together with the rise of productivity in the widest sense (reposing on use-values and not on profit). The constant aspect is that "[a person] is not by work detached from his existence as a dutiful kinsman, citizen of the community, and an intelligent being capable of art and joy.... There is no 'job,' no time and place where one spends most of one's time not being oneself." (Sahlins, *Tribesmen* 80) The changing aspect within the invariant is that in tribal commun(al)ism "production, polity, and piety are not as yet separately organized" (ibidem 15). In class societies, however, a series of huge complications is introduced first by violent power, crystallised in the State, and second by demography, productivity after the Industrial Revolution, and the occupational or cultural specialisations. Modern communism will then join anthropology in affirming "wisdom suggests we abandon the conventional analysis of culture into distinct economic, socio-political, and ideological spheres" (ibidem 15) and consider instead much more intimately entangled societal schemes; I deal with this at length in my book *Splendour.* The final pragmatic failure of such "socialism" in an unfavourable context leaves this question entirely open. However, as different from tribal societies, the communist invariant can in a post-industrial age scarcely escape certain functional separations, perhaps into different, overtly meshing, and non-exclusive categories.

Second, Clastres agrees with Marx and Engels that history shows us only *two macro-types of societies, those with and without a State* (which also means with or withou antagonistic social classes). On the one hand there is equality with leisure, albeit with a much smaller command over natural goods and biological constrictions, on the other a greater abundance and variety of goods but also a hierarchy with authoritative command and subjects who labour for a ruling class, as well as a perpetual incentive for warfare. When this fundamental typological division is crossed, all changes, "Time becomes History" (170). However, Clastres revalues Marx's insistence — much nuanced in the latter's concrete historical essays — that the central motor of change in society is the development of productive forces, that is, "economical infrastructure." For example, while Amerindian tribes may be hunter-gatherers (nomadic or settled) or sedentary agriculturists, their "political superstructure" remains the same, as identified above. To the contrary, the Meso-American imperial (State) societies had a very similar, though more intensive, agricultural "basis" as the commun(al) ist tribes. In sum, at least in tribal societies, he believes,

> ...the most important division of society, which institutes all other divisions including no doubt the division of labour, is the new vertical arrangement between basis and apex, the great political cut-off between those who detain violent power (*force*), be it military or religious, and those subject to the violent power. The political relationship of power precedes and institutes the economic relationship of exploitation. The alienation is political before it becomes economical, power comes before work, economy derives from politics, the coming about of the State determines the appearance of classes. (169)

I don't think either hypothesis about the birth of human alienation is sustainable as exclusive, or that we would have to accept one and reject the other. First of all, Clastres wrote at the time that feminist theorisation about the patriarchy was just arising, and it would have to be integrated into this discussion. As Bensaïd remarked, the development of productive forces toward surplus labour and the dissolution of the gens (clan) "create the preconditions for patriarchal dominations of women and progeny" (62). Thus, I would opt for a "not only but also" model – that is, for a multifactorial spread – where at various spacetimes the stress would be nearer to male politics (Clastres's violent power) or to economy (Marx's exploited labour) or to gender oppression (the feminists' patriarchy) as the decisive factor bringing about alienation. In tribal communism, I think Clastres is more believable; in mature capitalism, the intertwining gets much more complex and economy, no doubt buttressed by political, gender, and other oppression, is Destiny in everyday exploited labour or in wars for plundering the fruits of the same.

What Clastres — alongside the whole generation that has seen the World Wars, the rise of Fascism, and what came after — cannot share with Marx and Engels is the 19th-century optimism of progress as a one-way forward movement, somehow magically guaranteed by history (say of the productive forces). Not only can a community such as the Mbya Guarani sink for entire centuries into cultural, power, and demographic devolution, but this holds for "many hunter-gatherer societies of South America [which represent,] according to Lévi-Strauss,.... vestiges of very advanced agricultural societies, who have been pushed back by other agricultural societies from the river banks toward the forest *hinterland* where they completely lost their ability to farm" (Godelier 91). The fate not only of the ex-USSR but also of the present-day USA and western Europe are macro-examples of such devolution and involution from revolutionary and expanding societies to stasis and decay.

Finally, Clastres remarks on the importance of a factor sharing cultural and natural properties: *demography*. He judges as very probable that tribal societies can function only when the number of their members is small, witness their great fragmentation. What does this say about the chances of a democratic communism in large societies of tens of millions of people? He doesn't follow up this problem, but it is an important one. It is quite possible that the growth of population was the strong factor pushing toward division of labour and command power, that is, toward the State (cf. Bensaïd 39-41).[5] Any non-alienated world would probably have to be much less populated than our demented growth, and not only because of balance with nature (ecology) but also of balance within human groups (violence). In that case, with a full use of communication technology — wireless internet and telephony, two-way TV, etc. — within a decentralised organisation, we would have a chance of returning to the tribal power without violence.

Glossary

mutatis mutandis = changing what has to be changed

Works Cited in Essay 5

See in *Works Cited in this Book* the following titles, by Author surname plus (when the author has several titles) first "headword" or identifying syntagm in the title:

Bensaïd, *La révolution*; Clastres, all three titles; Dumézil; Godelier; Goldmann; Malinowski, both titles; Marx & Engels, *Briefe;* Mauss; Polanyi; Sahlins, all four titles; Suvin, *Metamorphoses, Splendour,* "Terms," "Words"; Weber, *Economy.*

POEMS 5

DIE VERWANDLUNG, 1990s [THE METAMORPHOSIS]

affectionately, fűr elke u. gerd

1.

Dark twisters whirl through our delicate life
In this drift nothing can be taken for granted
Road signals horrify us like pestilent dragons
We are strangers amid corrupt beefy policemen

Pleasure comes smelling of closed plastic bags
You talk to me polite as a smiling automaton
Filled to the brim with quarters
No sense of a her or his story that would be ours

What remains: memories about the sunny climes
Unreasonable happiness
                    the future rooted out in lobotomy
Thus i've decided to become besotted with precision
Measuring letters drop by drop

Deciphering the arms dealers' covered tracks
Thru the cowering jungles of UN statistics

2.

But ah! the balcony on Barbados,
The sea's azure expanse
                                        beside the cannibal global market
How the teenage harlots' curse
Runs in blood down World Bank walls

We could have waited longer
Eaten more scones in appreciative silence
Brewed herb tea with honey instead of saccharine
Sunk into the grass
Looking at the louring cloud plates lowering

Until ants came out of our eyes
Tenderly agile, uncaring of any birthday

Yet enough is enough.

10-1200

6

What Is to Be Done?: A First Step (2015)*

> Whoever does not hope/expect, shall not find the unexpected; arduous is searching for it and accessing it.
>
> Heraclitus, 540-480 BNE

> The issue which has swept down the centuries and which will have to be fought sooner or later is the people versus the banks.
>
> Lord Acton, 1881

> Why do the good lack tanks and airplanes?
>
> Brecht, 1940

1. Where We Are

> People seem to need a sense of history comparable to the sense of direction of the migrating birds.... We might wonder whether the enormous spiritual magnetism of Marx's work could be explained... by its revelation of a *historical sense*.
>
> Victor Serge, diary note of 3/1/1944

1.1. TINA and WHOA

A Johns Hopkins University study in 1988 found that a 1% increase in US unemployment leads to 37,000 deaths (650 of which homicides), 4,000 more people in mental hospital population, and 3,300 more in prison population (Barnet and Cavanagh 292). Assuming a 1:23 ratio between US and world population in 2012, this would mean that a 1% increase in unemployment entailed 850,000 unnecessary deaths per year, to leave all other consequences aside. Of course, US statistics cannot be simply extrapolated to the world, the environment is different: the consequences may be, say, half or double that amount. But if we add to this the results of direct killings from the dozens of wars following 1989, and then the resulting starvation and diseases, we would get to staggering numbers of human misery. Those physically spared are as a rule deeply scarred mentally.

It is almost 40 years now that between 1,000 and 2,000 million people live in abject poverty, and a majority of the rest is inexorably sinking towards it, while environmental destruction is out of control. Instead of easing life, the credit system has monstrously expanded into the major means of transferring wealth from the population into the electronic coffers of the super-rich, flanked by dispossession of creators through biopiracy, copyright, patenting, and licensing. In short, we live in times deeply imprinted with the aura of seeming hopelessness, a closed horizon of decaying brutal capitalism forever. The immediate large scale destruction and the long-range fallout of capitalist wolfish ideology, and the despair that ensues, are strictly analogous to the poisoning of environment by nuclear power stations at Three Mile Island, Chernobyl, and Fukushima, and to the Asian-cum-African wars of imperial power: at whatever human cost acquired, billions of profits do not stink (*non olet*). The oppression, exploitation, and humiliation of 95% of world people, on the road to becoming true proletarians with only their muscles and brain convolutions for sale in order to badly survive, is growing more and more intolerable. This upper-class Iron + Teflon Heel is argued intellectually in such gapingly nonsensical ways that it is often simpler for them not to argue it at all, but to state what amounts to: "What I define as X is X (say, any and every opposition to oppression, exploitation, and humiliation equals terrorism), and whoever does not agree will be killed." Thus capitalism is rapidly destroying both human society and its seat in nature. It obviously has no long-term answer to its ongoing crisis. And yet there exists both a dire necessity to act against it and a wealth of experiences from the last 150 years of how to do it and how not to do it; we must at almost all costs get out of catastrophic capitalism: "The catastrophe is that it keeps going on like this" (Benjamin).

As the editors of the remarkable *n+1* US magazine put it two years ago: "What counts is history asking us a question — about our content or purpose in a society of accelerating insecurity, including our own — that one way or another we need to formulate as sharply as possible, since we answer it with our lives" ("Cultural").

What is first of all necessary is: wedding people's deepest desires, from yearning to wrath, to a ***historical orientation*** toward a not only desirable but also achievable goal. Without it, all action will be mere reaction, condemned to little success or none.

Let us on the radical Left — the only hope left in this historical moment, however faint — therefore go back to our roots: that is, Marx. Besides towering scholarly achievements for intellectuals, what is it in his work that inspired millions of badly, partly or not at all schooled people to organise into parties identifying with his horizon? It is that all he wrote was deeply imbued and shaped by a sense that the old world of class society can be wrenched around toward emancipation, justice, and pleasure: that is, destroyed and replaced by a classless society.

There are two components of this orientation-vector of desire, frustration, and hope: the destructive and the constructive one. The destructive is based on the contradiction born with and inside capitalism as he knew it — an unbridled competition passing into oligopolies and monopoly: it must collapse of its own weight. Today we see this most obviously in the *ecological collapse* of our air, water, and soil. And its twin is incessant and ever more destructive *global warfare*, cynically waged with the flimsiest of mendacious masking. Marx's and all his orthodox followers' long-range expectations are coming true in spades. This is accompanied by the yo-yos of economic crises, manipulated for upper-class warfare against the majority and leading to deep immiseration and savagery. Most people feel it in their daily lives, anybody who thinks can see the anguish of millions, the skulls grinning between the headlines of our Unique Thought mass media.

However, the constructive component of a possible alternative is the only one that prevents despair and utter cynicism, passive or active giving in to what prevails. This is what had to be — and was — destroyed first in the most efficient Thatcherite slogan (blatantly stolen from the radical Left): TINA, There Is No Alternative. Which is why we must today say both *TINA*, There Is No Alternative to saving a livable just society, and *WHOA*: We Have Our Alternative, and it is a just and livable future history. Unless we spell this out, deep savagery will win. To use the constitutive insights of a refurbished Marx today is to bet on and work for a more livable, disalienated future.

This is then why the collapse of the USSR in 1989 — and then of SFR Yugoslavia and all other European "socialist" countries, together with the slide of PR China into Confucian capitalism (adding insult to injury, their composite Kong Fu is called Karl Marx) — was such a watershed. Not because a real socialism or communism ceased then to oppose the all too real capitalism: that had in fact happened between a quarter and a half century earlier. But if socialism/communism did not really exist on the world map, it did exist, in spades, in the imagination of the millions of people I mentioned. They believed that, in spite of all, the "other camp" represented a different horizon, though maybe an arrested march toward it with many (avoidable) impurities. Like Trotsky, they could not let go of the huge hope that the world can make historical sense (in which they were right) and that this is proved by the existence of "the socialist States" (in which they were wrong). The upshot is that in global ideology the precious baby was emptied out with the unbearably dirty bath-water. The overwhelming majority of what is nowadays called the Left — the Social Democrats — are sterile administrators, serving capitalism even when they at times slightly slow down the rate of immiseration and despair.

Dialectically, however, the fall of the completely corrupt Soviet bloc means "another communism might also be possible" (Harvey 227). Planned, democratic, and enlightened social command over production and distribution of goods and the human metabolism with nature must be reinstituted, or our species will perish. This road leads to the self-government of associated proletarians. Their relationships would be of the kind today known only in well-operating families, friendships or comradeships, expecting pleasure and usefulness from each other. In that sense, there are "millions of de facto communists among us" (Harvey 259; cf. also Graeber passim and Kunkel 112-13): it remains for them to grow conscious of their own horizon and to associate.

1.2. The Limits of "Movements"

I do not dispute the good will and sincerity of various anti-capitalist protests that flared up in these last decades but it is obvious they have led nowhere. Their quasi-anarchist lack of durable organisation and historical memory is deeply beholden to the capitalist shrinkage of historical time fixated on an almost point-like present. This is of a piece with the movements being mainly composed of students and white-collar or professional classes, a grouping that has *by itself* never led (or led to) revolutionary changes. For all the media spectacle, there never really was in time or space a "movement of movements"; the power and ravages of turbocapitalism have not been diminished a jot. We ought to recognise that movementism alone is as much of a dead-end as Stalinised pseudo-Leninism.

The main problem for us today may be encapsulated in what was earlier called a political line — that is the vector toward an overall, provisionally final goal, toward the horizon for any advance. Leninist parties always had a firm "party line," though often wrong and subject to changes at the whim of the USSR leaders (from Stalin to Brezhnev). At first they had a too narrow and inflexible or deficient political line, without sufficiently clear vectors toward the desired horizon, and at some point the horizon itself shifted to an anti-plebeian oligarchy. In reaction, movementism has refused any positive line except scattershot momentary slogans justly resenting the effects of capitalism on its component groups; that is to say, it had an unclear and rather blurred political line. Thus the Left pendulum swung from dogmatism to laxness, from erroneous definition to indefiniteness. Neither will work for us.

2. Who Are We (Proletarians, Plebeians Today)?

Est enim veritas index falsi et sui.
(Truth is the touchstone of falsity and of itself.)

Spinoza, 1677

But who are "we" — the *proletarians or plebeians* of today, whose deepest *interest* is to pull down the class edifice that stifles us? Marx rightly focussed on the central historical agent who should and could bring this about: the proletariat and its "historical mission" of saving the world. Without a believable antagonist, whose core at least has a deep faith in its historical mission of salvation, there is no hope of winning the battle against a supremely well organised enemy. The proletariat proved to be, I believe, a correct concept for those who have materially and morally lost almost everything and have everything to gain, and whose interests demand the toppling of the existing order: and yet, restricted to simply industrial workers, the theoretical horizon of all three Internationals proved wedded to a 19th-century reality. Marx was right insofar as our only hope lies in those whom capitalism hurt. They too are (we are) alienated in our subaltern ways, and yet we are the only parts of society whose vital interests demand an end to destruction of people and values as well as a thoroughgoing justice and democracy. The successful revolutions as well as the more numerous absent and failed ones proved that a clear majority of all plebeians or proletarians has to coalesce into a historical anti-capitalist bloc if the corporations', military, and media empires are to be overthrown. By plebeians or proletarians I mean all people and social classes who live by their physical and/or mental work — thus also the peasants and the intellectuals — rather than by means of wealth and privileges from capital or the State, though due allowance should be made for the particular ingrained subalternities, especially of the working petty bourgeoisie (see point 4 below).

Do we have a historical mission? Yes, we *potentially* do. Is it guaranteed by what Marx once imprudently called "iron laws" and could just as well have called divine preordination? No, it is not. It is rather a matter of what he much better called "tendential laws." Above all, TINA: the polar alternatives are emancipatory communism or savage fascism. On top of present unbearable physical and psychic misery, the mission is mandated as much by our martyred forebears as by any bright futures. It is not religious doping we need, it is pessimism of the intellect and optimism of the will. Any Party we need will not be a Church.

Sociopolitically, what mass social forces or classes would find it their central interest to (and therefore should) oppose capitalist immiseration, exploitation, and degradation? A very provisional global look can identify at least three:

- First, there are hundreds of millions of peasants deprived of land, casual labourers, street vendors, and the like who constitute the overwhelming bulk of people in many parts of what was earlier called the South (Asia, Africa, Latin America) but has today — not only through immigrants but also through immiseration of the "poor Whites" — infiltrated the "North." They vegetate, living from hand to mouth in ruined villages and urban slums, and their resistance is often expressed in casual vandalism and gangs. This resistance is easily infiltrated by any pursuit of sheer survival, however degraded, such as drug peddling or a racist setting immigrants and "natives" against each other, as propagated by thuggish, well-financed political organisations (from al-Qaeda and ISIS to the US Tea Party and European neo-fascists). But on the other hand the deep if pent-up hatred can be channelled into protests, often responding violently to the violence and oppression they suffer, against home eviction, deprival of water and electricity, and so endlessly on.

    In this group I would include the rapidly dwindling pre-capitalist remnants of indigenous peoples in former colonies of the metropolitan "Whites." They range from the famous armed-cum-media resistance of the Zapatista ELZ in southern Mexico and the long-standing insurgencies in India to protests in North American and above all in the Andean countries, where they have even come to power in Bolivia. Obviously, they can and did have success only when fused with intellectuals and traditions of the labour movement.

    I don't know of any good name for this constellation and shall call them *the immiserated on the margins of society.*

- The *wage-labour working class* has so far proved impossible to suppress — somebody has still got to produce the material things that any society needs. From debatable ILO data of 2010-11 it seems to comprise 1.6-1.7 billion people (in 2019 a good estimate would be 2 billion) of which more than one billion are in the service sector. Ca. 670 million people are mainly in China and the rest of Asia, with remnants in the classical industrial countries of Europe and North America. Its trade union (syndicate) organisations have been mainly either suppressed or corrupted into servants of capitalism, but traces of former militancy do remain here and there (as in Italy's FIOM union). Their strong influence has in a very few cases – Brazil, South Korea, South Africa – had a significant impact towards Welfare State and a better democracy. However, bereft of real power and strong political alliances, they usually commit the fatal mistake of engaging only in day-to-day point-like protests over pay cuts, closures, and similar indignities instead of combining them with a general anti-capitalist stance, and have thus in the last one or two generations been on the whole isolated and defeated.

- A great majority of *women*, except for the token female capitalist CEOs and shopping-addicted rich (or poor) wives or daughters. Women's position is determined by "[c]apitalist patriarchal structures [which] help to secure an exploitative system of social differences by way of ideologies of gender... [sustaining, managing, and maximising] the appropriation of surplus labor through a variety of complex arrangements"; for "[h]istorically the accumulation of profit has relied on the cheap though socially necessary labor of reproducing labor power through women's unpaid or very low paid work in the home" (Hennessy 25 and 66). They are doubly oppressed, by public and domestic work, often by *de facto* and not rarely by *de iure* political barriers. The growing feminisation both of the world labour force and of poverty makes their resentment and acumen, thus a strong place for materialist and non-sectarian feminism in the anti-capitalist alliance, indispensable for any real radical change.

- Last not least, there are what Therborn calls the "white-collar masses." They range from high-school and university students, who have played a leading role in all protests of these last years, to – often very – prominent intellectuals, but their bulk is found among the "middle" classes: office workers, lower and middle managers, intelligentsia. This comprises the internet addicts and specialists, torn between "cybernetic communism" (Firestone) and monopolistic profiteering of the Bill Gates type. They are threatened by capitalism's economic devastation but also fearful of falling into the first two groups, of being proletarianised. Though in an equally fragile position, their ideologies are therefore heterogeneous and fluctuating, quickly flammable and quickly subsiding (see the North American Occupy movement). The great majority of intellectuals no longer speaks truth to power: they have been bamboozled or bought off. Nonetheless, their radical wing is indispensable for any durable anti-capitalist coalition with the first three groups. Alternatively, they can be manipulated to turn against popular alliances, as a good part was in the Chile of 1973 and more recently in Venezuela. Important segments can turn to the Right and largely fall under the sway of racist and neo-fascist authoritarianism, as in France, Hungary or Egypt.

Significantly, the only attainment of power by the Left was a coalition of the four above groups, in Venezuela, Bolivia, and Greece. Surrounded by oceans of capitalism, they remain very vulnerable to banks and tanks.

Much more should be added to the above modified class analysis. It only suggests the revolutionary potential of the gender/sex divide, in the age spectrum it only mentions the young, slighting the pensioners; and it does not factor in ecology or the racial double exploitation. It is only a beginning. But it makes clear that *convergence of these four groups* is the only way out. In particular, we intellectuals have to draw radical conclusions from capitalism's "sharp de-classing of intellectuals. Our precious credentials are increasingly useless for generating income and — let us hope — social prestige, too." ("Cultural"). The importance of overwhelming ideological disorientation, when not only the "middle" classes but even the upper fractions of the proletarian classes often chase after a spurious (and unattainable) *embourgeoisement* while economically falling into atomised marginality, should be highlighted and singled out for the most urgent and sharpest critique.

I shall end by discussing one crucial point: What is our lever? This means that we must talk about *political organisation*: it is a key link where we are weakest. And that in turn presupposes at least an initial discussion of both our horizons and our "culture" or better imagination and consciousness. For, as Wittgenstein taught us, "seeing that" is necessarily also "seeing as," and furthermore to interpret something as such-and-such is an action. I would add that all seeing, physical and imaginary, co-defines a possible world. Contrariwise, what we cannot intervene into, we cannot understand: "the obscurity of the present circumstances is also the result of our organisational inadequacy" (Russo 175).

3. Decolonising the Mind: Horizon and Imagination

> The statement "When time comes" means "The time is already now, and there is no room for doubting it."
>
> Dōgen, founder of Sötö Zen, 13th C

3.1. I can be brief here about the horizon. Faced with international mega-turbocapitalism, it too must be on an international or planetary scale. Faced with the separation of classes into "gated communities" of the triune financial-military-communicational rule, it must be a classless society. By that I do not mean a society without articulations, which should instead become most rich, but one without antagonistic class interests where what is good for rulers (less than 5% of people) spells mass dying and blights for the ruled (more than 95%). In other words, it can only be an update of the generous 19th-century socialist and 20th-century communist movements before their corruption by power, expanding upon the hints of Marx and the plebeian movements following him as well as upon all useful thinkers of emancipation regardless of label – I would begin with much Engels, Morris, Kropotkin, Lenin, Luxemburg, Gramsci, and Brecht, but little if any Bakunin, Proudhon, and Stalin. Prominent artistic thinkers and doers would to my mind be among them: in poetry, say, from Homer, Tu Fu, and the tankas to singers such as Leadbelly, Billie Holiday, Juliette Greco, Bulat Okudzhava, the Beatles or Bob Dylan. All of them are the best antidote to what a good theologian (Hinkelammert) has called "the ideological weapons of death."

3.2. The sea-change of the global social imagination and behaviour, largely for the worse, can be most easily seen at work in our ***language*** (but also in all arts etc.). The defining of horizons and possibilities has changed radically since the early 1970s because of cultural or ideological subalternity to imperial capitalism. One example: what Marx called the "general intellect," that is, the collective power of human intelligence, has been disjoined from economics and politics, resulting in a welter of fragmented, impoverished, and sectarian languages. The dominant *gleichgeschaltet* (uniformly inculcated) language is blind worship of Mammon and capitalist profit, even in areas never before subjected to its destructive swath. It is accompanied by a willingly tolerated, indeed in good part encouraged, discourse of separatist ethnicity and nationalism, mostly invented in the 19th century or even *ad hoc*. Certainly ethnic hatred has been purposefully constructed and planned by rulers of small statelets, and adopted not only by resurgent and vociferous fascist or semi-fascist parties across the globe but also by all governments across the world as a welcome diversion from the (literally) deadly central problem of class warfare from above, that makes for lesions of billions and dispossession of the peoples. Accompanying it is the discourse on terror by all the major ruling States and governments, which totally suppresses two decisive facts. First, that in any tenable definition of terror — as exemplary killing popularised in order to cow the rest of the people — the major terrorists are the USA and its European allies in their undeclared wars; and second, that at stake in this warfare are major economic and strategic interests of all major States and of new criminal classes in minor States. It leads to major population shifts both in "ethnic cleansing" and in mass attempts to flee killings and starvation in Asia and Africa, which migrations are then used for further exacerbations of ethnic fears and hatreds.

As a result of all these changes, the two major classes that could and did counteract violent capitalism, the physical and the intellectual workers, as well as the non-metropolitan and non-imperial nations that found a chance for independence in the Cold War interstices, have been pulverised and reduced to isolated little groups. On the whole, these classes and nations have no major political organisation representing them; those ideologically still Left are reduced to quarrelling small sects, sometimes with interesting views and always based on the deep enmity of working masses against their exploitation but with no political weight. Very many disgusted and/or browbeaten people have sunk into atomic individualism, apathy, and solitude, at best alleviated by small privatised circles. As I mentioned, the exacerbated Right-wing movements, the more or less fascist nationalists often supplied by the rich and the secret services, have fared better in attracting popular support, and in a number of countries are now part of the governing establishment and often its spearhead in fostering wars and ethnic killings.

The radical reorientation in Post-Modernism, where domination of financial capital supplanted that of industrial capital, is supplanting production of mass goods and mass employment by "production" of huge riches for 1% of people and huge miseries for roughly 95% (the rest is what Jack London called Mercenaries of the rulers). This had two main inhuman fallouts. First, the image and feeling of society as *community* of people and actions: community has become non-working and unworkable (in Nancy's term, *desoeuvrée)*, together with communism and communion. The traditional networks of family, class, and other solidarity have been mostly destroyed by the ruthless libido of class domination. Instead we have tsunamis of apathy and cynicism, and small quasi-communities — from the couple to erotic or affective, religious (orthodox or new age), artistic, and other small groupings. These could of course be wonderful if connected to an empowering societal community, but remain fragmentary and disconnected, communities as crutches. And yet, human beings are possible only as "being with" (other people, things, shared ideas, affects, prospects, and horizons). The greatest perversion is when such quasi-communities turn into "damned communities" (Schininà) of class and ethnic hatred, into groupings for killings, exploitation, and humiliation. In brief, we cannot have true communities unless we get rid of capitalist domination.

Second, what was suppressed and lost by the capitalist onslaught, well defined by its intellectual executors as instilling "weak thought" into opposition to capitalism, is the concept of *destination or aim*. Unless we have a goal there can be no way, only errance and permanent desert homelessness. When we have one, we can search for a way that is also a method. The goal is justice and safety for all: socialism, or better communism. Community is inextricably linked to communism.

This also means that the flow of history as disalienating change is being denied: there remains a present of permanent shock and sensations, well represented by both the financial class warfare from above and the "shock and awe" of US bombing wars.

The pit dug by murderous financial capitalism is thus exquisitely and horrifically totalising. To dig ourselves out of it, to "decolonise the mind" (Ngugi), we have to work simultaneously upon horizon, imagination, and/or culture as well as on political organisation. Taking practice as the key, I shall in the rest of this essay concentrate on the last element. The question of questions is: what kind of political organisation do we need as an Archimedean lever?

4. Neither With You nor Without You: On an Anti-capitalist Political Party in the 2010s

> sic ego nec sine te nec tecum vivere possum,
> et videor voti nescius esse mei.
> aut formosa fores minus, aut minus inproba, vellem....
> [Thus I cannot live either without or with you,
> And it seems I cannot reach a conclusion.
> O that you were either less beautiful or more faithful!]
>
> Ovid, *Amores*, ca. 10 BCE

4.1. Not With You: Arguments against the Need for Some Variant of a Tightly Organised Nucleus in the Anti-Capitalist Movement

4.11. "Any permanent leadership and mandatory coordination of ongoing important activities from a centre is counter-productive."

This stance is very popular not only among anarchists but also in the 3/4 anarchist "movement of movements," say from Seattle through Dakar to Occupy. It arose on the basis of the evident failure by communist parties, with an initially global and rigidly top-to-down structure. Anarchism is in some ways, in its suspicion of organising from top downwards, a needful component of any viable anti-capitalist political organisation to come. Both anarchists and Leninists bear a heritage of nasty historical sins of intolerance and hatred against each other; to the contrary, both must be welcomed in a popular front against turbocapitalism — on condition that they agree to the flexible but firm organising discussed in this essay. However, faced with the full computerisation, globalisation, and militarisation of neo-imperialism, the anarchists' artisan-shop tenet cited at the beginning is ridiculous, not only counter-productive but guaranteeing failure. How could workers in metropolitan countries strike against a multinational which will simply move the plant/s they are striking in and against into an even more impoverished country? Only by re-creating some tighter analogy to all the three Internationals, that is, working for and in a coordinated — and in some crucial moments momentarily but clearly hierarchical — set of all sincere and consistent anti-capitalist movements, parties, people, and groups. This coordination demands some kind of a central authoritative body, elected and recallable, probably not fixed for a too long time in any one place or continent, but in emergencies to be obeyed.

This holds also for the national organisations of such an international movement, say for strikers against whom strike-breakers from a poorer region or class are used. A branching national, and where needed international, force is indispensable that could act just as quickly as the multinational's computer links, to speak to the strike-breaker in their lingo and with the knowledge of their background. Or should the strike wish (as it ought to) to affect all the plants of the corporation or maybe even the whole industrial branch, or the boycott wish to affect its products widely, such a force is the only realistic possibility to go toe to toe with the capitalists and the armed forces.

Inductively, thus, counterarguments are strong.

4.12. "If not unnecessary — that is, if it may work well for a given purpose — any permanent leadership and mandatory coordination of ongoing important activities from a centre is highly liable to bureaucratisation of such a centre, which would do more harm than good to the movement as a whole."

Objection: there is no movement which would be a formless mass, each has a kind of nucleus, probably changing at its fringes, with which it stands or falls. There are only two questions. First: will such a centre be of short or long duration, and will it be only local or nationally vs. internationally coordinated? Second, is there a need for coordination not only in space but also, and perhaps primarily, in time — so that experiences of struggles do not remain confined to local space and time but are popularised, sifted, and generalised for future needs? The coordination in space has been accepted by even the most anarchist movements; but it is the need to have bodies existing and minds functioning in coordination *between the peak manifestations* which is theoretically denied — less so in practice, which then however stops halfway. Yes, bureaucracy (or better, oligarchy) is a deadly blight to be combated, but the equation of any permanent — even if elected, changeable, and responsive — central body with bureaucracy is logically inadmissible. A sarcastic remark has it that the equation of organisation with degeneration is very similar to the Christian dogma of the Fall (Hallas 11). It testifies to the deep mistrust for working people within the anti-capitalist movements, that is, to the tenet that they are not capable of bringing about a durable collective and democratic control from the basis upward. Contrariwise, I see no virtue in a weak organisation or disorganisation: "the only weapon of the proletariat is organisation" (Lenin).

True, if the uselessness of any mandatory coordination from a centre is unproven this does not mean that its contrary is proven — clearly, no leadership can be faultless, and permanent leaderships are prone to degeneration. Yet it is also clear that in complex societies, such as the capitalist one, there is no effective activity without formal organisations. This does not mean that any organisation or coordination from a centre is always useful. We can only say that a permanent elected and responsible leadership can in most overarching circumstances be much more useful than its absence. And just what are these circumstances cannot be established by general propositions but only by induction from particular situations

4.13. "The experience first of the social-democratic and then of the communist parties is a clear proof of propositions 4.11 and 4.12."

Let us then proceed inductively. The proofs are very numerous and impressive. The German Social-democratic party as well as its Trade Unions have already at the beginning of 20th century been so bureaucratised that Robert Michels could base on them his hypothesis on "the iron law of oligarchy" in political parties. The same holds for the U.K. Labour and the proverbially top-heavy bureaucracy of its Trade Unions, and more or less for all the parties of the Second International. All of them not only failed but did not even attempt to stop the enormous slaughterhouse of the 1. World War, where the blown up and poisoned cannon fodder was supplied by tens of millions of their proletarian members. It is hard to imagine a worse betrayal by the organising centre against its members than this (except in Stalinism).

As to the history of "bolshevised" parties after coming to power: Lenin had at least two models for a revolutionary party. The 1903-04 one was conceived for illegal underground work under fierce tsarist repression, so that its horizon of strict conspiracy and strong centralisation is valid for these circumstances only. Should imperial capitalism evolve to a full Iron Heel – a cyber and nanophysical version of Jack London's novel – we might need to dust off and reuse this first model. In 1905 and after the 1917 October Revolution, when the party was legal, Lenin immediately switched to mass party forms with a full democratic centralism, that is, elections from below upward and freedom of fractions and conflicts in all leading organs, including the Central committee and Politbureau, and a congress electing these organs practically each year. I shall return to this second model of Lenin's.

Unfortunately, the full economic and demographic collapse of Russia, that left the communist party as the only functional coordinating entity, forced Lenin in 1921 amid a full retreat to NEP to urge a ban on fractions for one year. Because of his illness and Stalin's arrival as the secretary of the Party, this ban was never withdrawn, so that in half a dozen years the communist party adopted, by means of mass assumptions of new members and purges, the Stalinist model of bureaucratic oligarchy and terror, which is truly monolithical. This model's only connection to the main Bolshevik tradition up to 1921 is Stalin's system of lies and murders of all "old Bolsheviks": it must be completely rejected.

Finally, we must remember the elementary logical rule that from particular positions no general proof follows (*ex propositionibus particularibus nihil sequitur)*. Therefore neither the 19th-century German social-democracy nor Stalin's All-Union Communist Party proves anything insofar as 2.11 above — leadership and mandatory coordination from a centre — is concerned. Nonetheless, both of these parties remain exceptionally bitter historical warnings of dead ends that must be always kept in mind.

4.2. Nor Without You: Arguments for the Need of Some Variant of a Neo-Communist Party

If we take Lenin's model for a legal party as the initial hypothesis, it should be supplemented by many experiences after it from two groups of sources. The first one would begin with Gramsci and continue with an analysis of positive and negative aspects within "socialism" from Yugoslavia, China, and Cuba — and perhaps also from Vietnam, sandinist Nicaragua, and today's Bolivia, if and when they become accessible. The second one would rework experiences from within bourgeois (or better *citoyen*) democracy, especially of its early, not yet fully capitalised forms, as well as from libertarian anarchist organising, while rejecting its dogmatic tendency towards individualist chaos and inefficiency. Concerning our horizons, two questions remain foremost. Generally, how should such a model look today? In particular, is Lenin's insistence on a political party that both evolves stances and ensures their carrying out still necessary, and therefore acceptable?

4.21. I shall first delve into the second question, because it is a preliminary and important one. Following Hallas (15-16), I shall differentiate between *a vanguard* and *an elite*. The vanguard or avant-garde is a military term for the foremost detachment of an advancing army or naval force: it is neither better nor worse than the main force but functionally differentiated from it by scouting and exploring the terrain into which the whole force should advance. Metaphorically, it means a person or usually a group that „leads the way" or „is at the forefront" of new ideas and attempts, for example in culture (it was actually coined by Saint Simon for the arts). It has sense as a metaphor for political struggle and opposition only if behind it there follows the main body, or at least if it can be reasonably expected that this main group will follow in a not too distant future. Therefore, this metaphor — useful in its own time, and perhaps again in the future — should be used sparingly; I shall return to it.

To the contrary, elitism is based on the claim that obvious differences between the capabilities, consciousnesses, and experiences of people are hard-wired into them, perhaps biologically. Only a (very or somewhat) small elite is capable of leading society, while the mass is perpetually incapable for independent decision-making and for administering the business of community — for *self-government*. This was formulated first and best by Plato's *Commonwealth (Politeia)*. At the centre of his dialogue is the figure and type of the Ruler class as the Knower. It signifies and embodies the fusion of Knowledge and Power indispensable for a perfect (class) community or State. Here is a key passage from Plato's Book 4:

> Then, in the State we just founded, is there some knowledge possessed by some of the citizens that doesn't judge about any particular matter but about the State as a whole and the

> way it should best comport itself both internally and toward other States?.... [A] whole State would be wise because of the smallest class and part of it, namely the governing or ruling one. And to this class... belongs a share of the knowledge that alone among all other kinds of knowledge is to be called wisdom (*sofia*). (428c-429a, modified from the Gruber-Reeve translation)

The trajectory of the communist parties in power, from Lenin to Tito, Mao, Castro, and Ho — to limit ourselves only to the leaders of true people's revolutions — seems to fit into Plato's horizon.

Thus, modern elitism and vanguardism have on the Left a common denominator in the hegemonic Party that ought to use its Power to disalienate from above the working people and educate it to use direct democracy from below. Even after a revolutionary seizure of power, the interval or "transition" of such practical and theoretical education would be most onerous, as in it the defence of the revolution against the unceasing menace of world capitalism must run simultaneously with the radical reshaping of the whole economy and way of life. Such a period demands an intimate, unceasing and growing, fusion of Power and Knowledge. Since this is historically supposed to be a first step towards the dismantling of any oligarchic form of that selfsame fusion, it poses a fundamental grave problem, on which communist parties after Stalin foundered (I approach it theoretically in „15 Theses" above).

However, as opposed to vanguardism, elitism does not believe that the main force can ever rejoin and fuse with the vanguard; or in other words, that empirical differences between people's capacities stem for the main and decisive part from societal alienation that can be combated and changed. Elitism (say a professional Church) is the necessary ideology of every ruling class — today, of all capitalists and bourgeois power-holders. In socialist and communist parties it has always been the sign of a most dangerous anti-democratic and hierarchical degeneration.

To the contrary, I hold that the metaphor of vanguard, of a smaller group of precursors that can be the first to notice important aspects of the matter at hand and report it to an existing or incubating main body, remains on our agenda, on condition strict democracy from below is preserved both in it and society as a whole. The reason is that the alienation Marx named 170 years ago nowadays pervades the whole society in ever stronger and more profuse forms, including necessarily the plebeians or proletarians (people and classes without property over the means of production). To bridle probable excesses by the vanguard, it should be self-consciously critical and shun both privatised despair and immodest claims. However, the main proletarian body obviously suffers badly from the pitilessly growing pressure of the class warfare from the rich against it (cf. Buffett's interview in Stein) — and against the more or more proletarianised middle class — so that it cannot be foreseen when it will seriously join in an active resistance. Readiness is all.

This prominently includes readying through our discussions and practices the proper organisational form for a great number of proletarians joining the vanguard.

4.22. A further illumination may be found by briefly paraphrasing Gramsci's argument in favour of a unifying political centre from the point of view of *consciousness needed for durable radical activity*. Clear-headed analysis and planning for an efficient politics need not only cognitions but also techniques of cogitation or thinking that do not follow so-called "common sense." For, this is a consciousness deeply infected by banalities and errors stemming from the alienated practice of class society, and deposited in language itself as well as in groundless pre-scientific beliefs which he calls "lore." The stance of this "everyday philosophy" is as a rule uncritical, haphazard, and fragmentary. No doubt, a critical consciousness needed for historical change can only come about if based on the naive reasoning of mass participants in changing society, on the popular "implicit" philosophy: but on condition that it be further articulated, redone, and refined into coherent and explicit political knowledge. Only thus may a social group come about which possesses common ways of thinking and acting, that is, a unified stance towards all events. This makes possible a dialogue or feedback for mutual education and schooling between the common sense of given popular strata and some intellectuals of a new, committed type — who function somewhat as metal hoops holding together a barrel; it issues in the formation of a political party as a "collective intellectual" (see Haug and Thomas).

4.23. Thus, what could today be a useful analogue to Lenin's and Gramsci's party with a truly democratic centralism, as an activist collective thinker amid a different but equally acute generalised crisis of values, beliefs, and institutions? Let me leave aside whether it should be called communist or even party (though this is ideologically not an indifferent matter so that I shall continue using those terms) and concentrate on its horizons and forms. There is much we don't know but we can begin with negations.

First, such a party, however small at the beginning, must be composed of individuals who agree with a platform of aims based on a stance and method incorporating Marx, that is, with the horizon of an anti-capitalist emancipation of each and all. However, a general agreement is not enough. The party must right away have at least two further features: *activity* in some intelligently chosen fields which strongly concern plebeians as citizens and as class, and *mutual learning* among party members on the basis of theory plus practice, as training for what is probably impending. The party should, as Lukács argued in the Leninist heyday, relate to the class – or today we would say to the working people it represents – "as a laboratory in which the future of the class is essayed" (*Geschichte*, final essay; cf. Thomas 7). This holds especially for interaction between the two indispensable components of such a party, manual and mental workers. It ought to be assumed that, being under constant onslaught of a shameless and technically efficient propaganda of individualism, all of us are more or less infected by such misanthropic stance, so that only by means of active work and mutual learning from each other and from critical reflection on our great ancestors we may be able to gradually recover. Our horizon would remain what Luxemburg called "the fusion of science and workers." A publishing activity for both internal use and external propaganda in printed and electronic forms, and whenever possible with video and media components, will be quite indispensable; it should feed into reading and viewing discussion and dissemination groups.

Second, such a party must needs right away function as a full democracy with as much centralism as necessary for increasing efficiency — neither less nor more. As Lenin's original proposals insisted, the vanguard party must be subjected to "rules inspired by the Paris Commune, aiming to limit political professionalism: elected representatives to be paid a wage equal to that of a skilled worker, constant vigilance against favours and privileges for office-holders, responsibility of those elected to the electors" (Bensaïd). All forms of democracy, not primarily electoral – though that too should be used – but direct and associational, such as plenums, actives, rotation of functions, etc., are welcome on condition that they increase efficiency. Strong conflicts of opinions accompanied by mutual respect are indispensable for a party that would not be simply a sect. Only by such means, cross-checked by practical work, can clear and sound stances crystallise. Still, all such opinions and stances must be within the platform adopted at the beginning. It can (and certainly from time to time will have to be) be filled in and changed, but only if the horizon defined in the prior paragraph and some central orientations towards it remain fixed and unchanging. To formulate such orientations and "planks" of the platform is, together with immediate practical activities among proletarians, the main purpose of such a party.

All of the above, based on a national party model, would have to obtain, with due modification, for an association on the international scale too.

Paradoxically, as Bensaïd notes, the very invention of such a party as a *pars pro toto* of the working class (or classes, as I would say) opens up not only a possibility of the part arrogating itself dominance instead of the whole class bloc, but also the opposite possibility of the class finding other, plural organisational forms for its different and multiple interests, as has in fact often happened with the trade unions.

5. What Now?: Initial Proposals

> Bread is the people's first right.
>
> Louis de Saint-Just, 1794?

5.0. The central red thread of any anti-capitalist platform is necessarily a redistribution of wealth from the upper, most bloated and necrophiliac, 5% (cf. Banerjee) to the working 95% of people.

5.1. What immediate and semi-permanent planks — to be supplemented or changed whenever needed — might be necessary to begin with? I have no full panoply to offer, But I propose that they include at least the following points, as an initial and not exhaustive red-green-womanist strategic proposal, all geared to preventing and beginning to reverse further immiseration, and to be supplemented by short duration tactics:

- Financial capitalism needs and means extreme *violence*, culminating in literal *war*; today's utterly predatory and ruthless capitalism is out to annihilate all forms of human commonalty except the monetary nexus. It is the real theological extremism of our times, of which the so-called Islamists are only a pale copy: a plague on both their houses! Therefore we must vehemently oppose all violence and war except in clear self-defence, for example against an overt assault on the central interests of a people. As long as capitalism exists, we must reject NATO and any military expense which is not directly connected to a country's self-defence; we must firmly orient ourselves towards an all-people territorial defence — of the Swiss type — and a strict watch on hi tech specialist units such as aviation and tanks while rotating their membership (remember Allende!).

- We must vehemently oppose the *immiseration* of working people dictated by finance and other capitals, that is, insist on strong democratic control of banks (with the horizon of their take-over) and of monetary policy, and reject two centers of capitalist power. First, a refusal of the really obtaining European Union – a good idea if based on socialist democracy but today twisted into a new prison-house of peoples, enforcing hunger and want by banks (Greece) but if need be also by tanks (Ukraine). It is now increasingly a Dickensian debtor prison, monstrously enlarged to continental proportions; it has shown itself to be unreformable Second, a refusal to bow to the international organisations of capital — the World Bank, WTO, and IMF, including the most pernicious TTIP proposal — whenever they want to impose immiserating forms of economic life. Forms of an exit that would be as painless as possible from the Euro ought to be carefully but quickly prepared, and national debt servicing made conditional upon a "hair-cut" of over half of the debt (cf. Lapavitsas).

- We must wage a stubborn fight for a *minimum wage and minimum citizen income* for any person over 16, for dignified pensions, and for healthcare, water, education, and other "commons" available to the whole population; this can only be done by a predominantly State and workers' cooperative property, in a transitional mixed economy using private capital only when clearly advantageous for people and ecology (see Levi samit, points 5-6).

- We must wage a stubborn fight for *ecological justice*: the care of forests and wetlands, refusal of atomic energy, use of railways and bicycles instead of cars, reduction of energy needs through conservation, etc.

- We must unceasingly attempt to find forms of efficient *internationalist* struggle, involving other European nations but not only them (see a bit more on this below in 5.2).

- We must face up as soon as possible to the unprecedented flood of *refugees* from countries being annihilated by international capitalism, coming to Europe from Africa ("Black") and Western Asia ("Islamic"). In the years and decades to come their numbers will only swell. They are our neighbours, our brothers and sisters under the skin; tomorrow we might be in the same situation. Furthermore, those escaping death by hunger and bombs are on the whole unstoppable. And finally, their work is indispensable for the continuation of whatever human welfare – health care, pensions, and similar – may survive in European societies. They must be given full rights of asylum Europe-wide, from the overt and hidden warfare they are fleeing (cf. Iveković 245-58 and passim), and possibilities of employment. If we do not take good care to set up networks for liaising with them and with the places they arrive into, they will be used for a swell of fascist chauvinisms that will destroy all our other efforts.

While tactical compromises accepting less than full implementation of these points may well be necessary, especially at the beginning, the planks ought never to be forgotten and downplayed for tactical purposes: they are the reason for the party's being. As our enemies would immediately know, such a party would be against the present financial capitalism, thus in a way Keynesian but in its final horizon clearly Marxian or communist. To this banner of ours we ought to add another colour (green), but we must never be ashamed of the red, for it means blood and life.

5.2. I cannot here develop what the great Lucio Magri has called "A New Communist Identity," but I shall quote some of his central insights (see more in my "Prescience"). He grounds it in two converging overarching factors. On the one hand, today's technologies and access to information make possible both reduction of working time and decentralisation of power – in his words, "today the idea of communism in its original and richer meaning of emancipation is for the first time historically ripe," without the fixation on economistic progress and on the State as the only alternative to a dominant market. It is what Brecht in the 1950s called the possible habitability of our planet. On the other hand, capitalism cannot deal with the environment, since that needs long-term planning and a distance from the profit motive. Therefore, qualitative instead of quantitative production is within reach but foreclosed in favour of a "production of illusions and of the ephemeral" that denies the needs of health, education, or space planning. Today's capitalism has as its structural precondition the irrelevance of politics, used as a hollow ritual for decisions reached by the new rulers, a small economic and technocratic oligarchy in the international economic and political centres, bereft of any democratic constraint. This degeneration can be opposed only by "the full development of political democracy." The new world of direct global power by financial capital and multinational corporations needs an international opponent, Rousseau's and Tito's *people* as "a collective political subject able to implement a long-range overall project." And that opponent cannot be incisive without a Gramscian party – or group of parties – as "stimulus and synthesis of a complex system of autonomous and permanent political movements." Syriza, Podemos, and some Latin American coalitions can provide some first pointers to such a stimulus and synthesis, on condition their internal focus be sharp enough and external enemies, financial and military, be kept at bay.

However, two preconditions obtain. First, in capitalism exploitation and class warfare, overwhelmingly from above, constitute an overarching framework which unifies all other contradictions. "Capital itself is the great unifier which subordinates every aspect of social production and reproduction, remodelling the function of the family, determining the social division of labour, and submitting humanity's conditions of social reproduction to the law of value. If that is indeed the case, a party, and not simply the sum of social movements, is the best agent of conscious unification." (Bensaïd)

Second, it is obvious that international capitalism, for all its cutthroat competition, has learned from Leninism the need for unity when facing its enemy: the working people of the world. In turn, we must learn the same lesson, using more flexibility than Lenin found possible. No State can fight the world capitalism's financial and military powers alone: *Tsipras docet*. Communist internationalism of Marx's and Lenin's kind must be our horizon, or we shall be picked off singly.

5.3. Last not least, two decisive points I had to slight (there may well be more):

First, in his Preface to *The History of Russian Revolution*, Trotsky compared, in a by now somewhat paleotechnic metaphor, the relationship of "mass" and "party" to component parts of a steam engine: the masses are the potential energy of steam, the party is a cylinder with piston which condenses and transmits that energy. Without the mediating apparatus, energy would dissipate in vain, but without the energy potential, there would be no movement (19). My essay has only initially mentioned, in section 2, the working people as fount of energy, but without an intimate and permanent connection with them, and with the young, any machine will work more and more feebly.

Second, we, the inevitably communist Left, may well fail. Then we would get to the full savagery of total warfare and total immiseration, an Iron Heel which would bury both us and competitive capitalism in favour of full neofascism. We ought always be aware of this inescapable alternative.

Works Cited

See in *Works Cited in this Book* the following titles, by Author surname plus (when the author has several titles) first "headword" or identifying syntagm in the title:

Banerjee; Barnet & Cavanagh; Bensaïd, "Leninism"; "Cultural"; Firestone; Graeber; Hallas; Harvey, *The Enigma*; Haug, *Philosophieren;* Hennessy; Hinkelammert; Iveković; Kunkel; Lapavitsas; Levi; Lukács, *Geschichte;* Magri; Ngugi; Plato; Russo; Schininà; Stein & Buffett; Suvin, *Darko,* „The Prescience," *Splendour;* Therborn; Thomas, both titles; Trotsky, *The History;* Wittgenstein; Wood.

POEMS 6

IN THE ICE AGE
(A COUNTER-PROJECT TO XIUNG XI-LING)

All that we feel is the freezing storm
But who is there to grieve for the warmth?
As you're leaving, bequeath this wish:
Everybody should afford happiness!

19408

DOCTRINE
(A DEPARTURE FROM HEINE)

For on this rock we shall erect
The Church that works from downside up
The Third Age church of Holy Bodies
Both personal & congregational:

See: hunger, killings are not needful
The pie in TV skies deceives
Give us today our daily sweets
Give us down here the sacred hearts & sense.

Return to body its merry pump
Rid of the fat that has enclogged it
The overeating brought by hunger
The ulcers caused by profit slash & burns.

Return to brain its hormonal bath
Disturbed by wolfish enmities
To people & birds & beauteous trees –
When heart & brain work well, we shall be saved.

If you, O masters, will not let us
Into salvation, entirely we must
Remove you: profit is the fat
In bloodstream, profit brings the early stroke.

Your lying church will be dismantled
Our Earth at last inhabitable,
Polluted eyes may see no godheads
The cleansed may go to many-coloured stars.

When holiness meets wholeness
& the people absolute,
Washed clean of Class Division Sin
We may aspire to the cosmic Lute.

7

Communism Can Only Be Radical Plebeian Democracy: On the Experience of S.F.R. Yugoslavia and on Civil Society

> Here I need to pour out my heart: you need to hear the truth.
> The counter-revolution is in the management of the finances.
> We shall perish because we did not want to seize the moment marked in the history of humans to found liberty.
>
> (Robespierre, fragments from the last speech before the Convent, Eighth Thermidor Year II or July 26, 1794)

1. Central Political Choices after the Yugoslav Revolution

1.0. The experience of S.F.R. Yugoslavia is best divided into three phases[1]: ca. 1952 to 1965, the ascending phase; 1965 to 1968-71, a failed reform and transition to degeneration; and 1970s to the end, stasis and repression. Before ca. 1973, native political power in some States and a favourable international polarisation allowed economic growth outside the capitalist metropolitan areas, violating exclusive profit logic. This was followed by a period of erosion, crisis, and breakdown of the "antifascist" *trente glorieuses* phase from the late 1930s on, and eventually the return to "pure" profit capitalism, to all of which SFRY became a prime example. In and after the 1970s, Yugoslavia as a community still did some good things for hundreds of thousands of people, but it was a devolving caricature of the original idea (see Horvat, "O socijalnoj" 54, and Comisso 124–35).

I propose to discuss first a central political knot after the Yugoslav revolution, and then the politics of a possible disalienating communist democracy.

1.1. A Plebeian Revolutionary Horizon and Achievements

In a Leninist post-revolutionary system all means of production (except a few remnants, and in the case of Yugoslavia also most agriculture) have been taken over by the State run by a single party which also had a political and organisational monopoly: the Party-State. Power is here wielded — unless counteracted by strong democratic pressures from below — by a relatively small oligarchy, in this case a politocracy. It drew its legitimacy first from the revolutionary achievements of plebeian upward mobility, which changed the life of millions for the better, and the attendant defence of independence, but then increasingly from the population's standard of living. The system therefore had, unless it were to rely largely on police repression, to achieve a noticeable and ongoing economic surplus, and had to have it distributed in a way that appeared just to the majority of the population, especially the industrial working class and other city dwellers. Therefore, on the one hand, disposal of the surplus value arising from labour-power — which had to be balanced between industrialisation, defence, and standard — became a crux; in Yugoslavia, as in the USSR, "the source of rapid capital accumulation [was left unresolved]" (Woodward 75). At the start, the Yugoslav communists hoped for "fraternal aid" by the countries of the Soviet bloc; instead, they got exploitation and attempts at takeover rammed down their throats. Ironically, Tito then found in the Yugoslav Army and its unique strategic value a source of both military and civilian US and West European aid. This was considerable, and — together with the surrender of their surplus labour, at first in post-revolutionary enthusiasm and then customary, by most city dwellers — tended to solve for a good while, say for 20 years, the pressing problem of accumulation source (Heuser 219, Mates 202–04, Gnjatović 129 and passim, Lampe 276).

However, on the other hand it is too often forgotten that, in order to continue at all, capitalism needs an unceasing "primitive accumulation," devastating further regions of nature and social life, up to the women, virtual space, genome, and intellect (Harvey 304–05, and see the pioneering Luxemburg). Thus capital accumulation in SFRY was unable to proceed for two reasons: negatively, because of cultural — including technological — backwardness; but then positively, because it meant the all-round disempowerment and alienation of people. For originally, the Yugoslav revolution had been expressly designed — like all such great plebeian uprisings from the French through the Russian to the Chinese and some following revolutions — to strongly limit these blights by means of "elements of solidarity, social responsibility, [and] control over the market mechanisms, worked into its institutional frame" (Močnik 149), and even to begin abolishing them. While SFRY eventually embarked upon the road of capitalisation, it did so much too slowly and imperfectly by capitalist standards: in order to bring about full capitalism without a human face, which we are seeing in these last decades, it had to be destroyed.

Was there an alternative to the degeneration and eventual crash? My theory (in *Splendour*) is that there was, and that the only one was a further development of the tradition of the Partizan popular revolution expressed in the great slogans, "Death to fascism, freedom to the people" (*smrt fašizmu — sloboda narodu!)* and "Brotherhood and unity" (*bratstvo-jedinstvo*). This was an orientation toward a plebeian alliance from below, and it had made the Party shy away from the parasitic and stagnant Stalinist model with its unbearable cost in terror and people's blood. The SFRY ruling top and theoreticians attempted after 1949, with notable but less than full success, to get rid of the officially execrated Stalinism, deeply rooted both in the old Party cadres and the widespread peasant-cum-patriarchal petty-bourgeois mentality, and to go back to the radical Lenin of *The State and Revolution*, whose libertarianism also struck a deep chord in the traditions of popular self-government and of Partizan self-reliance (see Buden "Još," Denitch 153, Woodward 52, and for Yugoslav mentalities Suvin "Splendours"). The years 1945–52 I have called the double Yugoslav plebeian singularity of Partizan victory — with political centralisation and speedy economic reconstruction of the country following — and then of successful break with Stalinism. This resulted in the major breakthrough of the workers' self-management idea: the post-1949 economy tsar Kidrič envisaged a system which would soon combine central planning with a "council" system elected from below and through all levels, up to the federal government (see Suvin "Ekonomsko-političke" and Borgese); this would be a potentially democratic way of running autonomous entities producing commodities — perhaps a planned economy using a regulated market.[2]

In 1953, the SFRY economy took off after years of scarcity, and at least one factor of the boom was the enthusiasm created by the Workers' Councils — through which in the seven years after 1950, and in a country of under 20 million, 1,129,000 members had passed, of which 75% were supposed to be manual workers from the shop floor (Čolaković 535). At the same time, the Party changed from a cadre to a mass one, and changed its name at the Sixth Congress of 1952 to League of Communists, signalling a return from Stalin to Marx. Due to pressure from below, the self-management organs in industries gradually gained greater influence over some key decisions, including those about workers' income (after subtraction of State taxes). Further, the area of operation of self-management was in 1953 extended from industry to State agriculture, trade, construction, transport, and communications, and then also to education, culture, health services, banking, and insurance – it was not applied to the army and security services, public administration, and the administration of justice, where the Party cells were supposed to provide the necessary balances. Soon self-management was timidly introduced to the "parliamentary" or electoral system at the levels of commune, district, republic[3], and federation (see more in 2.2). The 1957–61 Five-Year Plan had a resounding success.

Some results of those years can be seen in tables compiled from official statistics:

TABLE 1: GROWTH OF SOME KEY INDICATORS, 1953–1961

Real social product per head (analogous to GNP, in 1960 dinars)	Literacy %, age 10 and above	Population % in cities above 20,000	Motor power, KW per employed person
1953: 947	74	13.8	1.7
1961: 1,636	82	22.4	2.12

Source: Wachtel 3 (adapted), with "motor power" from Bićanić & Hanžeković 88.

In Comisso's fair judgment, "data... do indeed show a high rate of growth, industrial expansion, an increase in the standard of living, and a shift of employment from the primary into the secondary and tertiary spheres of the economy" (56). Further, "labor productivity rose an average of about 4%... a surprising achievement when employment was also rising" (Dirlam & Plummer 158). Yet Yugoslavia was still "a relatively underdeveloped, and extremely unevenly developed, economy, with an inadequate infrastructure..." (Prout 5), with a per capita social product about half that of Italy. Furthermore, while improving, productivity was still low. And trouble was brewing because of some central structural contradictions.

TABLE 2: SOCIO-ECONOMIC INDICATORS, 1950–1970

	1950	1960	1970
GDP in $ per capita (in 1966 prices)	216	333	520
Infant mortality (per 1000 live births)	119	88	55
Illiteracy (% of population 10 and above)	25	20	15
Population per physician	3,360	1,474	1,010
Radio receivers (per 1,000 persons)	21	78	166
Automobiles (per 1,000 persons)	0.4	2.9	35
Urban population (%)	21	28	39

Source: Lampe 295

A strong harbinger of a possible plebeian and experimental democracy was, despite its many compromises, the Party program promulgated in 1958 at the Seventh Congress, which was also notable for the all-time high of 32% worker members. The program had a strongly resonating concluding chord: "Nothing that has been created must be so sacred for us that it cannot be surpassed and cede its place to what is still more progressive, more free, more human" (*Yugoslavia's* 263).

1.2. The Reflux of the Plebeian Tide

However, in the 1950s, two momentous changes had become unquestioned and deeply embedded. First, "however intimately the economy, the State and the Party might remain interconnected and controlled by the last, ... these three basic 'sub-systems' had been definitely disaggregated and given separate formal structures with inherent capacities for autonomous growth" (Rusinow 80). Second, the process of decentralising Party control from the top but not transferring power to the lowest levels created a middle layer of State and Party officials, who were "very anxious to preserve their positions and therefore became pillars of dogmatism and the establishment" (Bićanić & Hanžeković 69). These local rulers came to exercise great discretion in economic matters and invariably used their power "to pursue the interests of their own region, which... amounted to obtaining investments for the construction of industry and then protecting that industry at any cost" (Paul Shoup, quoted in Rusinow 49). The "commune" oligarchy level, for which power was synonymous with opening jobs and extensive economic development, was well integrated with the republican level. Since it was paid out of taxes on production, which amounted to two thirds, this level grew into possibly the main drag on self-management and democratisation (see Bakarić 2: 398), second only to the republican administrations. These oligarchies below the federal level became the root cause for "a non-existent and increasingly evasive ideological and political consensus" (Rusinow 112, and see Horvat, *An Essay* 75), which held up rational rethinking within the ruling oligarchy. The dilemma was, as always, whether to carry out the further democratisation from below, which would inevitably begin spilling over from economics to politics, or to return to central rule from above. The compromise solution was to do neither but to give more power to the republican administrations — "that is, the creation of a federation which cannot rule over the bureaucratic elements in the republics" (Bakarić 1: 627). The republican governments, which tended from the very beginning to centralise all in their hands, were eventually left to grow by default into separate "State capitalisms." The economy stalled, and eventually plummeted.

In such a bind, the Western type of market appeared after 1965 to most people in the oligarchy, and of course in the rising "middle class," as the new saviour; industries which could compete in it had to be favoured. Besides economic objectives of the "reform" in and after 1965, its key political plank was that the share of enterprises – all run by Workers' Councils – in the net social product should rise from 30% to 70% (Bakarić 2: 173): this failed. Instead, there were three main negative consequences of the 1965 reform. The first was conspicuous economic instability. Most worrisome for societal solidarity were rising unemployment at a time when the better schooled post-war generation was looking for work, and inflation, caused both by high import costs and by domestic factors — such as the low productivity, both in industry and in agriculture, which henceforth became a fixture and led to marked inefficiency of SFRY investments as compared to other countries of European periphery (Bajt 13). The inflation came to average 22% by the early 1970s and began affecting the real wage (see Woodward, Bićanić & Hanžeković, Tyson). I shall develop this in 1.4.

Second, the balance between the federal centre and the republics was drastically and permanently altered in favour of the latter. The transfer of responsibility for social services first from the federal centre to the communes, and then increasingly to the republics, entailed both a transfer of loyalties by those served and reduced funds. This was a factor of the third consequence, increasing societal polarisation reversing the post-war trend. Income growth rates of the upper 10% grew in the late 1960s to more than double of the bottom 40% (Comisso 96). On the one pole, there was an exodus of workers to western Europe with a peak at around one million people by 1973; on the other, a lightning concentration of capital in the reformed banks which could now be founded not only by local communities but primarily or exclusively by business enterprises. The banks soon accounted for a whopping 45–50% of all fixed-asset investments and, in cahoots with republican authorities, disposed of foreign currency earnings. The government could only resort to ad hoc zigzagging by means of "administrative" monetary policy, a few remaining federal subsidies and investments, as well as temporary extraordinary fiscal measures. While this meant that its remnant redistributive role "helped to keep differences in the social standard of living from growing intolerable" (up to the 1980s), it also meant that federal intervention was done without long-range planning, and "not surprisingly created more problems than it solved" (Comisso 91 and 80). Finally, after initial successes industrial production fell in the 1970s to the fourth source of currency revenues by value, after remittances from workers abroad, tourism, and agriculture. This was a resounding defeat of the industrialisation political plank.

The federal State centre was economically withering away, and so was rapid economic progress in production and standard of living. The economic consequences came to a head much later, but the political instability and polarisation were immediate — the student revolt in 1968 and the Croatian slide toward nationalism repressed in 1971 — and ominous, especially as their root causes were not addressed. Just as ominous was the turn to IMF loans, given in 1965 to SFRY as the first "socialist" country.

1.3. Three Politico-economic Horizons

In sum, I argue in this first part that the SFRY oligarchy embarked upon a counter-offensive against the trend toward plebeian associational democracy that would be based on self-management, which led after 1968 into political disorientation, fruitlessly papered over by a feverish proliferation of measures and laws, and a burgeoning of vigorously developing capitalist elements. Such a judgement hinges on what were the alternatives. For if there were none, one could assume the politocracy was doing the best of a bad job: since that had to end as it did, in the downfall and destruction of both socialism and SFRY, it would follow that this State and societal experiment were doomed from the word go. Having lived through the glorious years of the Yugoslav revolutionary wager, and then reflected from afar upon it and researched its rise and decay, I refuse to believe this. To my mind there existed three possible, theoretically exclusive horizons.

The year 1948 was marked by the rejection of the *first* one, a Soviet-style police State with totally centralised detail planning, as intrinsically abhorrent, economically a dead end, and achievable only by full submission to Stalin and a bloodbath.

The *second* horizon was rendered ever more urgent by what was in my judgement a necessary opening to the capitalist market and therefore to a confrontation with its evolving ideologies, and it might be called by that dubious name, "market socialism." It was the minimum common denominator of an intra-oligarchy compromise, and "[its] use as the basic coordinator of Yugoslav economic life was... more a decision by default than an act of positive policy" (Comisso 75, cf. Samary 155). The market was mystified as "a socialist invisible hand" (Milenkovitch 285), and vehemently disjoined from federal planning — from what Brus identifies as a possible "model of a planned economy using a regulated market mechanism" for better economic accountability (74; see also Horvat, "Der Markt"). If not corrected by and subordinated to strong planning and fencing-in measures, this market tended toward reintroduction of capitalism. And in fact "the Yugoslav market did not follow the path foretold by neoliberal capitalist ideology, from a market regulated by the Party/State to a free market, but to a regulated market broken away from any democratic control and ruled by international centres of financial capital" (Buden "Gastarbajteri").

I cannot discuss here the many improvisations tending toward a kind of cooperative plus State capitalism — or in the SFRY case, a confederation of major republican State capitalisms — but they were inexorably strengthening the probability of what historically happened: a potential division into comprador bourgeoisies and mafias, actualised as soon as the Cold War confrontation was definitely resolved in favour of capitalism.

However, this alternative could be urged as the only one to avoid the police State only insofar as it was wilfully denied and occulted that there existed an already partially mobilised, popular, and quite well functioning germ of a *third*, properly plebeian communist horizon. This third possibility was a fully associational plebeian democracy, consciously assuming the conflict between the old (capitalism and patriarchal power) and the new (democratic communism) as its orientation. This would have meant both accepting the consumer market as a reckoning device – that is, in a rather prudent and hedged about way – and denying the capitalist law of value in key sectors affecting the people's wellbeing in favour of a supple planning. As of 1958, that halcyon time when the Party program (*Yugoslavia's*) called for "the transformation of all State organs into organs of self-government," this vision was a widespread horizon, a Blochian "concrete" — that is, possible — utopia. It is then that in the republican and federal Assemblies, beside two chambers composed of professional politicians, three chambers were added (for economic policies, for social services and health, and for education and culture) composed from delegates of basic organisations in the field, and having no financial privileges (see Marković, "Self-Governing" 165–67). There were expectations and pressures at the time for developing self-management across the board: I shall adduce here only two arguments by Branko Horvat and Veljko Cvjetičanin.

Cvjetičanin wittily posed that self-management ought to have developed into a fully self-governing system across the board, expanding from within industry and social services into three dimensions, the horizontal, vertical, and depth one. By horizontal, he meant the much neglected dimension of broadening self-government into the territorial communities, from the basic "communes" to the republics and then the federation as a whole. This would have been important for de-alienating the rapidly growing "lonely crowd" of the urban centres — where the interesting organisational form of residential or housing community (*stambena zajednica*) was never given sufficient funds nor attention to properly develop — as well as for de-provincialising the rural communities. "The [second or] vertical dimension of self-management is most sharply opposed to the State apparatus and is therefore the least developed one." It could have developed in two ways: either as an integration filling the gap between the enterprise plans and the local community as well as central planning; or by economic branches, including "social services" such as health or education, in the form of several permanent central councils, each "a self-management congress or working people's parliament, relying on scientific analyses and planning. In this case the State organs would truly become [as envisaged by Lenin and Kidrič – note DS] auxiliary organs of this workers' parliament." The depth dimension meant a direct associational democracy, which is a key to socialism. It would mean creating presuppositions in all societal units for overcoming the division into leaders and the led (Cvjetičanin 252–54, and see both titles by Supek).

Horvat agreed that "self-government has to be carried over to the total community." Furthermore, he pointed out this democratisation would have to prominently include the ruling Party, voiding the dominant hierarchic, semi-military relationships obtaining in it:

> This means that the [Party] must transform itself from an organisation with a centralised initiative into an organisation

> with decentralised initiative, from an organisation where the leadership exclusively controls the membership into an organisation in which the members also have the possibility of controlling the agencies of leadership and where, in the decision process, communications and directives circulate both up and down. (*An Essay* 209, and see Milosavlevski 248–49 and passim)

My thesis is that the development into a fully self-governing system of communist democracy did not come about because both the federal or centralising and the republican or decentralising factions of the ruling oligarchy had one overriding class interest: to avoid endangering their power and class status. They had to ward off introduction of full economic democracy, which would be necessarily accompanied by political democracy – a budding civil society within and for the revolution, see part 2) and by the management of open conflicts within the most interesting 1963 Constitution, though not by a multi-party system. The oligarchy's myopic optimism probably did not allow them to envisage the baneful results of a national economy incapable of making "a strong, concentrated effort [in any field]" (Marković, "Self-Governing" 104), but at any rate this took second place to keeping power. The weak centre was thus as of the 1960s outflanked by republican ruling classes increasingly at odds with each other, a decisive number of which eventually grew into the role of secessionist compradors. The refusal to collocate self-management in production within a process of disalienation through full self-government — a plebeian democracy — resulted finally in the downfall of both self-management and Yugoslavia.

1.4. Signs of Disaster

The resulting stasis continued for a quarter century:

TABLE 3. DECLINE OF THE SOCIAL SECTOR, 1960–1985 (change in %)

	Yearly average 1960–70	Yearly average 1970–79	Yearly average 1979–85	Total drop 1979-85
Social product (1972 prices)	6	4.5	–0.5	–3.1
Consumption per head (1972 prices)	5.7	4.5	–1.3	–7.7
Real product (per employee in social sector)	4.3	1.8	–3.5	–19.5
Real net personal income (per employee in productive social sector)	6.8	2.1	–4.7	–27.9

Source: Lampe 323

Such an abolition of a unifying centre was (with uncanny unconscious precision) called "depoliticisation"; while possibly a good thing when countering the economically untenable arbitrary centralism of the Stalinist type as well as arbitrary communal parochialism, as a general principle this cut also — and primarily — against the legitimate political interests of the self-management system. It showed a deplorable lack of awareness that every economy is politically framed. An eminent student of self-management concluded bitterly in 1966:

> For self-management is essentially a problem of democratic planning..... Even in Yugoslavia, the problem is so far from being solved that it is not impossible we may yet regard that country as an object-lesson in pitfalls, rather than the brave pilot which it looked like being in the beginning. (Coates 108)

The most glaring result of the imaginative and political failure after 1965 was the rocket-like rise of unemployment. Woodward shows that even somewhat earlier the steady growth of ca. 4% in the "social sector" employment failed to compensate for the huge outflow from the peasantry. The numbers of registered job seekers oscillated primarily in function of worker migration abroad, which subsided abruptly with the economic downturn in the West from 1973 on; but this statistic did not count unregistered workers with low skills and low wages shifting seasonally around the country. By 1970, almost a half of all unemployed people were under 25, and the percentage kept rising (Jerovšek, Rus, & Županov 210). According to the World Bank report by Schrenk, Ardalan, & El Tatawy, those not employed inside the country reached 14.7% in 1973, though I would assume the unregistered workers, camouflaged in statistics mainly as peasants, amounted to several hundreds of thousands more (see table 4 and Suvin "On Class").

It appears that the outflow of migrant workers abroad had two components, especially after the mid-1960s: the most highly skilled, and the unskilled or semi-skilled. Drulović (187–88) counts the "highly skilled" in 1971 as 3% of the migrants, evenly divided between intellectual and manual workers; they were joined by a mass of unskilled workers – over 76%, of which 60% fresh from the farm – and a middle-sized group of lower skilled workers. Rus (in Jerovšek, Rus, & Županov 210) cites a study by which the share of the job-seekers from two uppermost skill levels rose from below 20% in 1957 to over 50% in 1982. Research agrees that in the first wave almost 2/3 of workers left because of too low earnings, especially to afford an apartment, and a bit above 1/3 because of unemployment. Most of such *Gastarbeiter* (guest workers) lived abroad as a rule in horrendous circumstances, but their average monthly wage was in the mid-1960s 750 West German marks (236,000 old dinars), as compared to the ca. 210 marks at home. At that time, about 40% of workers had monthly incomes below 190 marks (Bilandžić 260); a survey in 1967 found out the workers would have stayed in Yugoslavia had their income been 350 marks, which is almost double (ibidem 252 – 4 marks were then 1 US$).

TABLE 4. EMPLOYMENT STATUS OF LABOUR FORCE (in 000s)

	1969	1975
In social sector	3,622	4,667
In private agriculture and artisanate	4,385	3,256
Temporarily abroad	572	900
Registered unemployed	198	324
Total labour force	*8,777*	*9,147*

Source: Schrenk, Ardalan, and El Tatawy 85 (adapted)

Thus, the ghettoised system of self-management necessarily turned inwards, and contributed to unemployment by protecting those already "in" at the expense of hiring new workers. As Woodward notes, normal "frictional" unemployment in developed capitalism was 4–5%, in SFRY as of the first statistic in 1952, it was above 7% (4); counting both those abroad and registered job-seekers, in the 1960s, it hovered near 10%. It was de facto 13.5% in 1969, and 20% in 1975 (though in Slovenia it was practically non-existent, in Kosovo or Macedonia much larger). If we subtract from those securely employed the non-manual (white collar) workers and add to the non-officially employed the invisible seasonal workers, not to forget the rural and urban housewives who would in better times be seeking employment in the social sector, I would speculate the proportion was close to 3:1 — three parts of the working class protected by the system (at least until the wild inflation and economic breakdown of the 1980s), one part not protected. Yet, as both Comisso and Woodward rightly stress, SFRY was officially designed around community through labour, so that unemployment meant moral and material marginalisation. Solidarity – the central plank of all workers' movements, socialist or communist – was not extended to a quarter (or more) of urban working people.

The ultimate political conclusion of Marx's *Capital* is that a society relentlessly organised around value-creating labour but not controlled by the associated workers necessarily lurches into a polarisation between the rich appropriators of surplus labour and a permanent mass of under- and un-employed: "[N]ot the least terrible [union of opposites discovered by Marx] is that indispensable function of capital to create what is blandly known as the reserve army of the proletariat" (Jameson 576). Thus the simultaneous appearance of what was in SFRY officially called "the capital relation" and mass unemployment signalled that this terrible union of opposites had again been activated. Exploitative class society was raising its head.

1.5. Conclusion on Political Choices after the Yugoslav Revolution

What was needed in S.F.R. Yugoslavia, not least for a true socialisation of the means of production, was a full build-up of self-management into an associational substitute for the existing bourgeois parliamentarism combined with backstage Party rule: Brus pithily puts it as "not 'depoliticization of the economy' but 'democratization of politics'" (91–92, and see his whole conclusion 85–103). Due to the deadlock in the Party, this was attempted in a half-hearted and inefficient way, and therefore failed. The political backers of self-management — a minor part of the ruling oligarchy, most of the humanist intelligentsia, and a majority of the atomised and silent industrial workers — lacked an embattled pressure from the plebeian depths which would have been allowed to organise within the bounds of the socialist constitution against the major part of the oligarchy.

2. Plebeian Democracy and Disalienation: On Gramscian Civil Society

I proceed with the political horizons of a disalienating communist democracy of interest today.

2.1. On the Need for Politics in Post-Revolutionary Societies

In his magisterial essays on Gramsci, Eric Hobsbawm singled out as a key outline of his political theory the famous letter of 1931:

> This study [of the intellectuals] also leads me to certain determinations of the State. Usually this is understood as political society (that is, the dictatorship of coercive apparatus to bring the mass of the people into conformity with the type of production and economy dominant at any given moment) and not as *an equilibrium between political society and civil society* (that is, the hegemony of a social group over the entire national society exercised through the so-called private organizations such as the Church, the trade unions, the schools, etc.).... (Hobsbawm 323, emphasis added)

I discuss elsewhere some aspects of terminology here, and focus here on the underlined relationship between State power with its coercion and what is here rightly called "civil society." Quite at odds with the post-1990 fashion, but in the vein of Gramsci, I mean by this *non-State socio-political agents that participate in a* (not only, nor even primarily, coercive but) *persuasive hegemony*. After the armed shock of the revolution that mingles coercion and persuasion, the primary role of the revolutionary party, Gramsci's "modern ruler," would be to mediate between State power and increasing civil society power. Despite some partially successful attempts (the mass organisations, the local People's Committees, and most of all the self-management system), the Yugoslav communist party increasingly failed to understand and develop the necessity of persuasion in hegemony — in other words of setting up a full system of communist democracy — and as of the late 1960s therefore lost its vanguard role and credibility among key social classes, such as the manual workers and the left intellectuals (it had lost it much earlier in the case of peasants). At stake is here, as Hobsbawm precisely notes, that "in the absence of *hegemonic* force, even revolutions can run into sand.... The struggle for hegemony before, during and after transition (whatever its nature and speed) remains crucial." (Hobsbawm 328)

This sense of "party" has to do with Marx's final conception of it as a kind of collector and articulator of all societal energies, proposals, and interests of the working class (or the plebeians, as I would say, which certainly includes Gramsci's wider sense of intellectuals). The Bolshevik tradition, and especially the post-Lenin Comintern tradition, knew only mass reformist social-democratic parties or small revolutionary cadre parties, and therefore "could not yet think in terms of permanent and rooted, but at the same time revolutionary, mass working-class movements" (Hobsbawm 328). But only such a new understanding and mass practice could make of a revolution "not simply the expropriation of the expropriators, but also ... the creation of a people, the realization of a nation ... as part of a process by which ... a people changes and makes itself under the leadership of the new hegemonic class and its movement" (330) — while Gramsci had in mind Italy, this also applies to all countries East and South of it, with due adjustment for multiethnic complexities. For, "how can we expect to transform human life, to create a socialist society (as distinct from a socially owned and managed economy), when the mass of the people are excluded from the political process, and may be even allowed to drift into depoliticisation [not casually, as I noted above, a favourite SFRY slogan after 1965 – note DS] and apathy about public matters?" (332).

In brief, "socialism [is no] 'easy' system which solves all conflicts by the act of 'expropriating the expropriators.' Such utopian simplifications include ... the view of the extraordinary ease of democratic government of a socialist State" (Brus 187). For a major example, it should be frankly recognised that the SFRY working classes in town and country were at the beginning, as Marx says of the peasants in 1840s France, countrywide "incapable of asserting their class interest in their own name," and were therefore "being represented" (*Eighteenth*, chapter VII) by the Party in power. They were poorly communicating among themselves, just emerging out of and in good part still subject to poverty, and further isolated by the Party/State's neglect of peasantry, its fragmenting stress on the individual competitive enterprises — and later, on republican economic areas — and its jealous mistrust of intellectuals outside the oligarchy.

To clarify what might be a radically democratic (communist) politics, I have to further disambiguate "civil society."

2.2. Civil Society: What Is It, What For?

My main interest in this clearing of the ground is twofold: first, to draw a lesson from the yesterday of what passed for "socialism" (and especially in Yugoslavia); second, to think about political possibilities compatible with a communist horizon, though not necessarily fully identified with it, in and beyond the cannibalistic capitalism today and tomorrow. In both cases, the potential role of civil society might be a key.[4]

The concept of civil society, though aas a rule not the term, was revived in the societal protest movements that culminated in the 1968 metropolitan anti-war and youth revolts and its outliers (cf. now also my "Words"), while a later variant in the 1990s, with the term foregrounded, was used as an ideological weapon in the struggles against a stifling "State socialism." I have sympathies for some root democratic impulses in both of these processes and strong misgivings about many of their factual and ideological blunders — associated in the first case with anarchism without intermediate goals, and in the second and graver case with uncritical support of a supposedly free market economy. It is by now quite clear that "[in E]astern Europe, civil-society discourse also had the function of keeping out any serious discussion about political economy and the restoration of capitalism — until the latter was a *fait accompli*" (Therborn 91); this also held, with some variants, for Latin America. It still holds for many NGOs quite corrupted by financial capitalism, especially those from metropolitan countries operating on the periphery. Both the above stances boil down to individualist and capitalist negative freedom, they are both cooptable, and neither is sufficient by itself.

However, my hypothesis is that this was and remains an ideologised abuse of perspectives which are richer and deeper (see the tradition adumbrated in "15 Theses" 1.2). The term has since grown into a designation for many different movements and strivings for civic self-government; I trust that its potential usefulness surpasses the needed misgivings, and wish to inquire into such uses. As I indicated in my "Introduction," they have to be grounded in Marx's anthropology of social individuals and their self-emancipation, which has primacy over the State, while dispensing with his idea that a post-revolutionary State would have no power struggles, and therefore no politics.

The democratic impulses perverted partly in the 1960s and fully in the 1990s remain useful on condition that the key parameter now be creative labour and full control of the labourer-creators (the proletarians) over the fruits of their labour, both personal and associated with others. On that basis, we need, and can construct, a model with full respect for the right to individual self-determination against any collective as well as for the right of an open society to survive and cherish supra-individual values: no primacy obtains here, simply, as the *Communist Manifesto* has it, "an association, in which the free development of each is the condition for the free development of all" (Marx & Engels 353) — and vice versa. Such a plebeian and associational concept of civil society seems to me utterly indispensable for two reasons. One is to establish what was missing — beside radical self-management in the economy — in "really existing," and eventually really suicidal, "socialism." The second is what is missing, beside radical self-management in the economy, in "really existing" and currently suicidal capitalism. In other words, Acton was right for all societies: power corrupts, and absolute power corrupts absolutely. Since power (but not violence!) is quite indispensable, it always must be tamed from below, by checks and balances through open debate: politics.

This horizon of a fully participative democracy tends to use but also subsume all local and central elected bodies: as in Aristotle's model, the citizens must both rule and be ruled — the only good leaders are good citizens, and to be good, citizens must lead. Other models have also to be consulted: the village community, when not repressively patriarchal; the medieval communes; and especially "the new forms of democracy generated within ... the workers' movement (council communism, revolutionary syndicalism)" (Cohen & Arato 7) — as well as within the revolutionary, feminist, and kindred movements. To the violent commands of the State (in last resort by force) and of capitalist employment (in last resort by hunger) all of them oppose the great plebeian principle of solidarity.

Some key pointers towards a radically democratic civil society can be found in the Marxian concepts of self-determination (that includes self-management in the economic sphere and the commune in the political one), in polyarchic checks and balances from the bourgeois revolutionary tradition, and finally in Gramsci.

What then is civil society? I know of no satisfactory definition, but a negative delimitation can be attempted (to be balanced by the positive sketch of Gramsci): *Civil society is that part of the societal whole* or sociocultural life-world, of people living together, *that is active in politics but does not directly flow out of the economic apparatu*s (enterprises, later corporations) *or out of the State power apparatus*. Like economic and State power, civil society is concerned with societal power and relationships based on appropriation of surplus labour from plebeians. Its specific domain involves rules about exercising power outside of – as a supplement of and/or in conflict with – the State apparatus and the economic apparatus, that is, the adjudication of competing interests of societal interest groups. As of the 17th-18th century absolutist monarchies, the concept of civil society developed in differentiation from and sometimes in opposition to the State apparatus in an age of ascending bourgeoisie and capitalism, while the term came from such an identification by the Scottish Enlightenment, and it was at the time part of a pugnacious bourgeois liberalism. This was taken up and in many ways inflected by Hegel in *Elements of the Philosophy of Right*, and then again by Marx in and after his critique of Hegel's stance (I expand upon this history in "15 Theses"). Yet my definition implies that the term and concept is useful today only if analytically extricated from the organisation of economics (production, circulation, consumption, and finance) — which does not at all mean that civil society can or should avoid intimately interacting with economics. The predicate "active in politics" differentiates civil society from the nuclear family, though the central features of the family (its authoritarian vs. democratic organisation, thence its amiable or repressive nature) have indirectly and subliminally much to do with central features of the civil society, and have to be included in any thorough investigation.

In the last 100 years or so — longer in the United Kingdom, France, and the United States — it has become necessary to differentiate civil society also from what is being very loosely called "political society," that is, political parties and legislative organisations such as parliaments. The reason for differentiation is the failure of those parties and organisations to stand by themselves against State power or capitalist power. Against the hopes of the earlier liberals, this failure includes classical liberal parties; against the hopes of Marx, Luxemburg or Lenin, it includes the socialist parties of the Second International and then the communist parties of the Third International, especially when they came to share or monopolise State power. Civil society works through various means to clarify the public political and economic interest as well as the constitutive need of personal freedoms, entitlements, and legal constraints on authority; it opens a space for politics from below seeking to clear up burning problems of human relationships and societal power through public debate, and thence to influence their solution by the real powers of economies and the State. In the German tradition, this is often called "the public sphere" (unfortunately, its most prominent spokesperson, Habermas, sees it as liberal modernisation devoid of class conflicts – 234 and passim).

Civil society may be quiescent or almost non-existent in countries with low productive forces, grave penury, and weak civic traditions; or it may be subservient to the "free market" ideology, in opposition to stasis and repressive State domination; or it may be a critical force influencing for the better economic and/or State power, and in some cases acutely opposing either or both. Where it comes about, civil society tends to evolve into a third societal sphere of more or less lasting associations (professional and/or voluntary) and forms of public communication and interaction, eventually also of social movements. It has democratic roots in the self-constitution from below according to personal and group interests, though these interests as well as the goad of efficiency may override and abuse the democratic vector. Especially since the decline of revolutionary parties and States, civil society ideologically exists mostly between the polar opposites of *rights-oriented liberalism*, which is in a large majority and at best seeks to mitigate the excesses of capitalist and/or State power without questioning its domination, and *communitarianism*, a small minority usually compatible with radicalism and communism, which seeks to change some important facet of capitalist and/or State power.

As a rule, economic as well as State power is indifferent to if not irritated at pressures to limit any of its prerogatives, so that it often strikes to repress plebeian democracy, bypassing eventual laws and regulations by non-implementation, evasion, bribery, and if necessary outright repression up to martial law. Equally, political parties are as a rule implicated in State power, and today wedded to some capitalist fraction; lobbies and think-tanks funded by branches of capitalism or its ideological offshoots, such as coopted Churches and NGOs, are rich and numerous. Civil society needs therefore its own lobbies and indeed think-tanks, where unfettered intelligence and devotion can take the place of wealth. They can only function well when backed by vigorous associations, access to the mass media – usually dominated by capitalists or by the State and therefore unsympathetic – a somewhat self-limiting State bound by division of powers (*Rechtsstaat*) rather than a discretionary and weakly fettered apparatus (*Massnahmenstaat*), and eventually wider social movements.

2.3. Further about a Gramscian Civil Society: Hegemony and Consent Today

For Marx's followers in the Second and Third International, his later concentration on the "anatomy" of capitalist production led, paradoxically, to a two-pronged result. In immediate practice, the economic horizon of capitalist collapse was taken for granted and requiring little or no theoretical investigation, so that the revolutionary parties could concentrate on the ongoing political reality, the organising of the working class. And in the furthest post-revolutionary horizons (which drew near with Lenin and found a first articulation in him), economics not only displaced but totally negated politics as open power struggles. It was then easy for ruling communist parties, in a situation inescapably requiring the "commanding heights" of State power, to fixate on economy as the be-all and end-all. This shelved Marx's radical break with all State apologetics — from Caesaropapism or theocracy to Hobbesian monocracy claimed as a lesser evil — that foregrounded class interest and the needful rule of violence against the common good and rule of reason.

Much more might be said about the tension in Lenin between the utopian participatory democracy of *The State and Revolution* and the harsh centralisation a civil war and economic collapse forced him to adopt (I approach it in "On the Concept," later in *Lessons,* and finally in "Using" further on in this book). His stance assumes a tension between an avant-garde, practically non-alienated, party and an alienated and primitive civil society. Within it, the theory that State and law shall die out could at moments of harassed impatience become an alibi for indisputable political subordination to the Party-State (Zolo 42–43, 263–64, 277–78), threatening to grow into an officially monolithic unity which disallows subdivisions, mediations, and conflicts. In the hands of Lenin's successors in the USSR it became wholly such, and repressed a mature conflictual unity. Late in his life, Lukács (*Process* 113 and passim) therefore concluded that the theory of politics was a kind of black hole in Marxism, so that the Bolsheviks could easily substitute for it the tactics of ruling. To the contrary, he realised politics must even in socialism — and I would add as far into the future as thought can reach — remain a protocol for societal decision-making and adjudication of disputes, that is, for allocating resources and power; but by then he was already treading in Gramscian footsteps.

Two anti-democratic problems "really existing" in Bolshevism were representation (of the working class by the communist party) and civil rights. I shall limit myself to their most important rectification by returning again to Gramsci.

Expanding on deviations from determinism pioneered by Marx's *Eighteenth Brumaire* and the later Lenin, Gramsci became the most prominent Marxist thinker before the 1960s to grow uneasy about the base-superstructure dichotomy in "economist" Marxism, beginning with works such as *The Communist Manifesto* and the "Preface to the Critique of Political Economy" (see both in Marx and Engels). After Hegel's transmogrification of the Scottish philosophers and Marx's transmogrification of Hegel, Gramsci effected a third redefinition in which "civil society" (*società civile*, not *borghese*!) remains the active locus of history-making but comprises "not 'all material relationships' but all ideological-cultural relations" (Bobbio 148, the inside quote is from Marx). Gramsci's civil society comprises not only the educational system and the communications media but also those social norms that embed production relations (his model is the Catholic Church in feudalism). When discussing the communist party, he notes it is crucial that this updated figure of Machiavelli's Ruler undertake a thorough ideologico-cultural reform which focuses on but subsumes economics: "The programme of [a radical] economic reform is precisely the concrete form in which every intellectual and moral reform presents itself" (Gramsci, *Selection* 133, *Quaderni* 1561).[5] Civil society "correspond[s] to the function of 'hegemony'" by the dominant group, while "the State and 'juridical' government [corresponds] to 'direct domination' or command ..." (Gramsci, *Selection* 12, *Quaderni* 1518–19).

Hegemonic consent is in Gramsci superior to and more efficient than direct domination through State force or coercion. This stress destroys historical fatalism, that bane of vulgar Marxism, and turns to Marx's and Lenin's – also Kropotkin's and Luxemburg's – active collective subject of history who understands and shapes an end. Most important for civil society, this stress of Gramsci's founds it in a certain autonomy and importance of political relations among people "in a historically very wide range of societies — for instance, as he liked to recall, the difference between the leaders and the led" (Hobsbawm 330, see Gramsci, *Selection* 144ff, *Quaderni* 1752ff.). He recognised that "in [the special political dimension] of society more is involved than power" (Hobsbawm 331), and called it the formation of consent — which also means a dialogue with dissent. State power remains necessary but not sufficient.

For the present purposes, Gramsci's most important suggestion might be his dialectics between State and civil society. Building on Rousseau and Marx, he concluded that in the post-revolutionary State, there should be "the will to construct within the husk of political society a complex and well-articulated civil society, in which the individual can govern himself without his self-government thereby entering into conflict with political society — but rather becoming its ... organic complement." This is "the creation of a 'civil society' which it was not historically possible to create [earlier]," the aim being to "make state life become 'spontaneous'" (Gramsci, *Selection* 268–69, *Quaderni* 1020): civil society was *the potential site for developing alternative consents and eventually hegemonies*. This would, to my mind, apply a fortiori to situations that lack developed civil societies. For all these reasons, Hobsbawm was spot on when he called Gramsci "the most original thinker produced in the West since 1917" and "[the pioneer of] a Marxist theory of politics" (Hobsbawm 316, 319):

> Gramsci is a political theorist inasmuch as he regards politics as "an autonomous activity"..., and because he specifically sets about investigating "the place that political science occupies or should occupy in a systematic (coherent and logical) conception of the world in Marxism" (*Prison Notebooks*).... Politics is for him the core not only of the strategy of winning socialism, but of socialism itself.... (Hobsbawm 321)

Gramsci's supple but finally class-based approach may also neatly cut the knot how to understand "civil society" (and Marx's *bürgerliche Gesellschaft,* oscillating between civil and bourgeois society, as I argue in "15 Theses"). Within class society, this is a battleground for class interests – possibly by way of complex mediations – of varying factions within and sometimes against capitalism. When the bourgeoisie is fully hegemonic, civil society becomes an integrated part of capitalist society. To the contrary, when radical opposition movements are strong, especially when the working class is strongly involved, civil society may be anti-capitalist. Indeed, I find it improbable that a really effective and permanent civil society could exist below a certain strength of such enabling radical movements. All depends on the active subjects of history and how well they both recognise and pursue their class interests toward disalienation.

2.4. Brief Conclusion on Plebeian Democracy and Civil Society

My conclusion about plebeian democracy and on civil society as its indispensable wing is twofold, according to my two main interests: to learn from yesterday, to think about today and tomorrow.

First, *about yesterday*, there is no reason to suppose that when the utterly alienating politics of class domination, coupled with a repressive State, are abolished by a revolution, this must or could mean the end of politics. Though Marx often implied this would be the case, Gramsci did well to return to politics — that is, decisions of where and how to allocate labour-power — as a central long-duration human need. With the exception of Gramsci and some cognate writings, which were absent from the official Marxist mainstream, one must ruefully concur with the eminent Italian theoretician of law Ferrajoli:

> What was lacking in the Marxist political reflexion was not a critique of the bourgeois State and not even, finally, a theory of the socialist State, however skeletal ... [but] a reflexion on power and the techniques of its installation and practicing from the point of view not of those who wield the power but of those who undergo it: *ex parte populi* [as seen by the people] and not only *ex parte principis* [as seen by the rulers]. (in Ferrajoli and Zolo 19, see also Zolo)

We have learned aboveboard politics is needed to prevent a resurgent State apparatus, prominently including the police and the military, from becoming as strongly, if differently, alienating. The need for associated people to have a voice from below was diametrically opposed to the "socialist" hegemony of the State political sphere over concerted human decisions.

Second, *about today*, the need for politics is diametrically opposed to the capitalist hegemony of the oligarchic market sphere — driven by profit considerations that override the obviously ensuing collateral and future horrors — over the human interests for life, liberty, and the pursuit of happiness. Even more acutely, the need for a strongly oppositional civil society is rendered crystal-clear by unbridled financial capitalism that fully dominates the State, ushering in ecological and societal collapse.

Thus, the only way to prevent corruption of absolute power, by politocracies or by capitalists, is to have open political confrontation and discussion. The horizon of these politics — that is, of civil society — would include what Barber calls "strong democracy," with the key addition of norms for economic life too. His definition, which I here minimally simplify, runs:

> Strong democracy can be defined as *politics in the participatory mode where conflict is resolved [on the basis of some founding shared principles] through a public process of ongoing self-government and the creation of a political community* capable of transforming dependent, private individuals into free citizens and partial interests into public goods. (Barber 132, emphasis added)

While this could probably be rendered more precise, here my only deviation from Barber is in adding "on the basis of some founding shared principles," since I don't see how the conflict with, say, Nazis or the Ustashi could be resolved only by discussion. But I fully agree with his conclusion: "In strong democracy, politics is something done by, and not to, citizens. Activity is its chief virtue, and involvement, commitment, obligation, and service — common deliberation, common decision, and common work — are its hallmarks." (Barber 133)

The ideal horizon of the interaction of civil society power with the State and capitalist powers is to strongly influence and largely tame them both. Should this plebeian impulse fail, what would remain is the alternative between radical revolution and despotic savagery.

3. In Sum

"Marx's act of intellectual insurrection" led to an often dreamed of, but before him not that clearly established, horizon: "communism as the never-ending self-critical return of the democratic revolution" (Kouvelakis 352) – and vice versa.

This sketches a two-way street: my title "communism can only be radical plebeian democracy," therefore also means "only communism can be radical plebeian democracy."

Works Cited

See in *Works Cited in this Book* the following titles, by Author surname plus (when the author has several titles) first "headword" or identifying syntagm in the title:

Aristotle; Bajt; Bakarić; Barber; Bićanić with Hanžeković; Bilandžić; Bloch, *Das Prinzip;* Bobbio; Borgese; Brus; Buden, both titles; Coates; Cohen & Arato; Čolaković; Comisso; Cvjetičanin; Denitch; Dirlam & Plummer; Drulović; Elson; Feenberg; Ferrajoli & Zolo; Gnjatović; Gramsci, *L'Ordine, Quaderni, Selection;* Habermas; Harvey, *A Companion;* Heuser; Hobsbawm; Horvat, all three titles; Horvat et al eds.; Jameson, *Valences;* Jerovšek et al.; Kalecki; Korošić; Kouvelakis; Lampe; Lenin, *The State;* Löwenthal; Lukács, *Geschichte* and *The Process;* Luxemburg; Marcuse, *From Luther* and *One-Dimensional;* Marković, both titles; Marx, *The Eighteenth* and *Grundrisse;* Marx and Engels, *The Marx-Engels Reader;* Mates; Milenkovitch; Milosavlevski; Močnik; Passerin; Prout; Robespierre; Rusinow; Samary; Schrenk et al.; Stiglitz; Supek, both titles; Suvin, "On Class," "On the Concept," *Darko, Defined,* "Ekonomsko," *Lessons from, In Leviathan's,* "Splendours," *Splendour,* and "Words"; Therborn; Tyson; Wachtel; Wood; Woodward *Socialist; Yugoslavia's;* Zolo.

POEMS 7

IN THE RUINS OF LENINGRAD†: AN ALLEGORY
(Counterproject to Elder Olson's "In the Ruins of Macchu Picchu")

What Hope had built, cruel Greed has spilled
– Witness the city of Ilyich & Peter –
But what Greed's unbuilt, Hope can rebuild.

Where are the mountains of starving & killed?
The dead of Yudenich, Yagoda & Hitler?
What Hope had built, cruel Greed has spilled.

The hunger for Justice walks forth unstilled
The hunger for bread makes Her still sweeter
Greed's power unbuilds, Hope can rebuild.

Between Greed & Justice, what grain will be milled?
The outcome's uncertain, balances teeter:
What Hope had built, cruel Greed has spilled.

When Winter has stricken flesh to the hilt
Struck flesh will strive to unseat her
Greed cruelly kills but Hope can rebuild.

A counterpower can also be willed
To Death Love beats a countermeter
What Hope had built, cruel Greed has spilled.
A sterile mule is Greed: Hope can rebuild.

---

† Or Beograd, or Sarajevo, or...

311200

Constantinos KAVAFIS: THE DESIRES (*Epithymies*)

Like splendid bodies of the defunct that do not age,
Buried, amid tears, in a mausoleum,
With head amid roses, with feet amid jessamines —
Thus are the desires that went by
Without realisation; without ever finding
Their night of pleasure, their morning of joy.

(1904; translated by DRS 2005-07)

8

What and How Are Poets for in Our Age of Want: Cognition, Emancipation, Communism*

> All serious thinking about art must begin from two apparently contradictory facts: that an important work is always, in an irreducible sense, individual; and yet that there are authentic communities of works of art, in kinds, periods and styles....
>
> Raymond Williams, *Drama from Ibsen to Brecht*

> We have to fight for the right to invent the terms which will allow us to define ourselves and to define our relations to society, and we have to fight that these terms will be accepted.
>
> Stokely Carmichael, *Black Power* 5188

Living in this age of planned impoverishment, I can only shore some fragments of what may be useful understanding against our ruins. My title, paraphrased from a poem cited later, is thus not a claim of achievement but an orientation and spur toward a horizon. But a horizon is only of use if one attempts to move towards it.

1. Approach to Poetry: Topological Cognition, and a Communist Politics

> Fatti non foste per viver come bruti
> Ma per seguir virtute e conoscenza
> [You were not born to live like brutes,

But to follow virtue and knowledge]

Dante, *Inferno* 26

1.1. Poetry and Cognition (Understanding)

For me, the arts occupy a special place in the cognitive endeavours of mankind from cave painting to the present — though I can theorise with some confidence only about the language arts. Their understandings are not (or at least not fully, and I would think not essentially) based on a methodical reference by measure or number back to general theories or principles, but rely much more strongly on the specific cognitive paradigm/s used. In other words, the ineluctable weight and constriction of ideological interests and practical human relationships for all cognition in class society is nearer to the foreground in arts. In natural sciences the Subject is taboo, only the Object is supposed to be present. In arts the Subject houses within the Object – say the domain of some types of sound in music – thus with a larger role of sensuous immediacy.[1] The language arts (poetry and narrative), the "fine arts," and possibly some other arts too, are undergirded by metaphorical systems which are rooted in imaginary topology (cf. Suvin "On Metaphoricity"), and, as Blumenberg precisely notes, "analogy is the realism of metaphor" (88). The undoubted affinities between analogical thinking and emotion-suffused evaluation is qualitatively different from deductive conceptualisation but (potentially) no less cognitive. Still, the general horizon, source, and finally the aim – the Supreme Good – of both sciences and arts is to my mind the same: making life, that precious and rare cosmic accident, richer and more pleasurable; fighting against entropy by making sense of human traffic with each other and different segments of nature. Both are cognitive tools and pursuits. More particularly, both deal, against a horizon of human interest and evaluation, with agents within formalised *situations* or spacetimes.

I shall here not only call valid literary cognition – in narrative, plays, verse, essays, and so on – *poetry*, but also suggest that the other visual and auditive arts can in major ways be called poetry. Poetry always implies a serial beneficiary or addressee standing for a collective audience, ideally a whole class or indeed community (this is foregrounded in plays). It should be clear, though I may have to slight it in this essay, that without an encompassing and nurturing working community, either really obtaining or being remembered and/or prefigured, all arts and philosophies are sterile. By community I do not mean a hypostasised beast, whose horrendous caricature can be seen in the Nazi Behemoth, but a mode of existing together of associated personalities, where the togetherness – or solidarity – transcends the silly opposition of society and individual (cf. Nancy 256-61 and passim). Each of us exists, to put it paradoxically, only "in common," in pragmatic or imagined communities of sense and value: "To be whole is to be part" is how Ursula Le Guin memorably put it in her great investigation of *The Dispossessed*.[2]

Especially about creations in words, it was the accepted norm not only for Asian civilisations and ancient Greece but also for the European Middle Ages or Leibniz that they potentially reach some transmittable understanding of human relationships, so that Baumgarten called his foundational *Aesthetica* of 1750 the „science of sensual cognition." Kant's *Critique of Judgment* then connected a philosophical estetics with the roots of modern literary (and art) criticism by exploring what may be the function of imagination. In particular, he found that the sensual representation of what is not notionally or conceptually representable has a deeply figural relationship to reason and the noumenal level.

My presupposition is that poetic cognition arising from sense(s) implies an ongoing creativity fusing old knowledge with not heretofore sighted novums about relationships of people with each other. This creativity is an anthropological constant of *Homo sapiens* that enabled our species to stand, in part, above the blind animal necessities of mere survival by developing the working powers of hand, vision, and brain, including language and then toolkits (cf. Engels's beautiful essay "Part"). It is species-specific to humans that our situations in all significant cases – and poetry is a preeminent one – imply, create, and in turn presuppose a smaller or larger Possible World, by analogy to what we imagine is "our world." Creative cognition or understanding springs from and returns to societal discourse about power and happiness or their contraries, and amounts to visions of elements and aspects of another possible world.

However, Kant was also a compromise perpetuator of a whole wing of and this current in philosophy that has apodictically insisted on two overlapping stances: First, that its method and even ethics is the systematic organisation of clear concepts – a Logos, with clear implications of a seamless holy harmony evident in Plato and in the central Christian medieval doctrine for centuries.[3] Second, that only this kind of thought was rational (though Kant allowed that figurative expressions could still be cognitively creative on some presumably lower level). Breaking with the religious stress on topdown qualitative values immediately enfolding eacn person and all people, this current rose to professional dominance from the time of Descartes on, and it has since become the reigning orthodoxy, from Positivism to so-called analytical philosophy, especially in the imperially dominant countries of the U.K. and then the USA. It was based on the repression and suppression of connotative significance, a flattening out of figurative expressions or their paraphrase into "contentual" concepts chasing each other's tails, which entailed a clear loss not only of beauty but of what joints of the world it could inquire into. Its horizon was a pure technical metalanguage such as logic. Still, this obviously could never reach beyond a handful of specialists, and was also flatly contradicted by the poetry of all major religions, so that tropes and indirect speech, and even metaphor, were grudgingly allowed for use in political influence on the multitude — and in the

Latin oratorical tradition also for forensic influence against opposing views – as impure precursors of true philosophy or as its regrettable waste products, so to speak dross left over after casting the ideally pure shapes (cf. Blumenberg 8-10). This hierarchy inherited the religious view that a system of concepts (such as theology) was the master while the arts (such as images on church walls) were a kind of *biblia pauperum*, a servant "speaking tool" of eternal truth for the poor in power and spirit – clearly a translation of class mastery into ideology.

The mistrust of shaping and figurativity meant that the strong philosophical tradition I speak of "is indentured to the logic of identity and non-contradiction as its organon and standard of meaningfulness" (White 411), that then marginalises and even outlaws non-conceptual figures, as bearers of subversive dialectics and uncouth plebeianism. This powerful indenturment – a precise expression encompassing constraint to work for a master – remains the reigning political and media *doxa* or lore.[4] It is of a piece with poverty of a new kind, as a rule consisting in suffocating overabundance of shoddy goods and thoughts coupled with lack of clear orientation and horizon, so that they do not shape a genuine novum but only manage unceasing galvanisation, a dictated mentality of trends and fashions forever twitching the plugged-in individual like Galvani's dead frog legs.

To the contrary, investigating the full-fledged metaphor, I found in "On Metaphoricity" that its three main basic conditions or axioms were *coherence, richness, and novelty:*

- it is *coherent* or *congruent:* the connotations admissible in interpretation must have a cultural-cum ideological common ground;
- it is *complex* or *rich*: consonant with the first condition, it uses all the connotations that can be brought to bear, "it means all it can mean" (Beardsley 144);
- it contains or embodies a *novum*: it is "not inferrible from the standard lexicon" (Black 436), it is "the emergence of a more radical way of looking at things" (Ricoeur, "Metaphorical" 152). This novum is necessarily – at least to begin with – strictly historico-referential insofar as it disrupts the cognitive system current when it was coined.

Thus, together with the necessary conceptual systems but also beyond them, metaphors indicate the basic valuations, expectations, interest, and stances linking the enunciating subject – always a social, that is, allegorically representative subject – to the salient contradictions of his or her time. Their truth, or better correctness, is always situational: as the pragmatists liked to say, "What genuine guidance does it give?" This is to my mind also the measure of concepts, the main difference – at least initially – being that they stick to denotative explication and thus must be clear even at the expense of width or richness, whereas metaphors are richly implicative and consist largely of riffs on how connotative linkages transform denotations. Partly, they relate to concepts as the How does to What, or *vérité à faire* to *vérité établie* or *natura naturans* to *natura naturata* – that is, as two aspects or orientations which ought really to go hand in hand.

Poetic creativity can readily be transferred from micro-metaphors to metaphoric and to narrative texts (each of which, I argued, is also a *sui generis* macro-metaphor, adumbrating a Possible World) by figuring in spacetimes and agents. A number of authorities, from Spinoza to Michael Polanyi, then concur that, together with coherence and novelty, a significant factor for evaluating cognitive artefacts is *internal richness allowing for a richer bite on reality*, when an entity has „the capacity to reveal itself in unexpected ways in the future," with a greater range of interesting consequences – the entity's significance is not exhausted by our conception so far, it has untapped depth and a power of manifesting itself in yet unthought of ways (Polanyi as cited in Grene 219-20).

Centrally, poetry is bound up with *topological cognising of qualitative spaces and spatialised times, itself strongly enmeshed with bodily perception and feelings, shaped by and interacting with historical situations*. Topology is to be found on all levels of semiotic organisation, for example in rhythm, but in semantic texts it is most evident in metaphor, where A denotatively always somehow stands for B but then also implies rich connotations not available to the naked concept of B (I argue this in Suvin, "On Cognitive" and "Heavenly"). In the stronger case of the so-called absolute metaphor – one that cannot be fully and economically replaced by existing conceptual propositions – it becomes evident that such topological imagination in poetry has, as in all arts, *equal cognitive dignity* to the conceptual one (Blumenberg 10–13 and ff.). For one canonic example, literary knowledge was posited by Auerbach as an attempt "to designate man's place in the universe" (17). Another formulation is "that the literary use of language may lead the writer and reader to a knowledge of relationships between people different from the knowledge brought by a practical or scientific use of language" (Fortini, *Saggi* 1796). Especially today, in the dearth of the "virtue and knowledge" that Dante's Ulysses held to be the species-specific difference of man vs. animal, no emancipatory politics stands a chance without this contribution.

Poetry is then an autonomous yet transitive activity that always presupposes an addressee, for whom it is Stendhal's "promise of happiness," a measure of itself and of what it spurns. In word art, each linguistic proposition has, together with a (possibly implied) subject, an explicit fulcrum of predicate that *refers* to a class of entities – things, relations, actions. Therefore no discourse is walled off from its source and address, it is not simply a combination of discrete linguistic units but it relies on the interplay of identification by subject and predicative reference. Any series of speech acts works within and interacts with other acts and events in a given situation and community: "language is directed beyond itself" (Ricoeur, *Interpretation* 20; cf. also ibidem 11-14, 35-36, and passim). Culler phrases this well for the "lyric" poem as "The poem … makes a statement about our world," it is centrally an "epideixis, discourse making claims about the world," so that to seek for the only occasionally present fictional speaker and/or fictional world "would be a diversion from appreciating the poem" (123, 126, and 125). Furthermore, though the concept of such a poem is necessarily a historically-evolving one, ... based on *prototypes*" (30), it is a statement that also necessarily incorporates instructions for its performative interpretation; the poem's time is as a rule a present, a liturgy in the initial Hellenic sense of "working (through) for a public." For a number of writers it then became logical and ethical to think of translating poetic creativity into politics as a kindred but more pressing type of choosing within concrete societal relationships. Any choosing implies freedom to select among diverse extant possibilities in socio-historical spacetime and is an existential bet on the best possible outcome, rendered probable by some hypothesis about the course of history; the choices and the hypothesis are in feedback, they modify each other (cf. Fortini, *Saggi* 227).

1.2. On Poetry and Politics (Communism)

How may writer-creators as such, that is *professionally*, participate in politics? This was no problem for poets in the era of Homer, Alcman or Solon when they spoke truth – providing information and clarifying stances – to a clearly delimited, local ruling class, but became complicated when political units grew larger as well as more obviously based on divergent class interests and the (always existing but now critical) oppression of a major part of the body politic. Plato felt poets were worrisome competitors to his philosopher-king and advocated banning all those who didn't fit his norms. There followed many painful historical experiences, which came to a head during the rise and unfolding of capitalism, and the central contradiction within its revolutionary bearer, which Hegel and Marx summarised in the great *opposition between the* citoyen *and the* bourgeois (see section 1.2 in "15 Theses"), tilting ever more towards the latter. During the revolutionary rise of this class, this included in Europe the Enlightenment's social mandate for the arts and poetry as an organ of universal conscience. In the defeat of the revolution, this mandate was sorely mystified, though still in effect in some splendid if often naïve attempts by poets to participate directly as bards of an embattled democracy – of a piece with an altered language, as in the English Romantics, Victor Hugo, Walt Whitman or in the early fallouts of the October Revolution. In the enduring and growing defeats of the *citoyen*, intellectuals more and more split into the opposed camps of either national bards, with less and less emphasis on democracy, or the disgusted and despairing wing that had lost its spiritual homeland within the bourgeois horizon and turned away totally from corrupted civic politics into merely personal introspection, which meant leaving politics to the ruling *status quo*.

Finally, as of the latter half of 19th century in the economically most evolved nations, and spreading in the ensuing century to the ends of the world, it became clear that – *in proportion to its cognitive value* – verse and prose were revealed to "belong to an order of value analogous to a horizon which the capitalist system systematically and inevitably obstructs" (Fortini, *Saggi* 172, freely interpreted, and cf. his whole argument on 170-79).[5] Poetry, just as the best politics and other wisdom, constantly reminds us that the pursuit of happiness is not only different from but in crucial ways incompatible with the capitalist purchase of goods and services in a regime of exploiting labour-power of proletarians: as Virginia Woolf cursorily remarked, "the great writer – the Hardy or Proust – goes on his way regardless of the rights of private property" (41). This alternative horizon is a revolutionary one of human disalienation, opposed to the lesions and horrors of capitalist dehumanisation. It might be called, better, a communist horizon in Marx's original emancipatory sense, and it will recur in this essay as a touchstone. In order to understand a poet's politics, I shall make an apparent detour taking into account this horizon.

What communism and poetic cognition have in common as open conspiracies (a term of H.G. Wells's that has nothing in common with terrorism) has been defined by Fortini as "a shaping faculty exercised on life, an ordering that starts from its intended end or *telos*" (*Saggi* 177, cf. also 384) – rather than from the perfect egotism of the possessive individual. A *shape* or *form* in what Raymond Williams calls its "inherent and determining sense" (*Keywords* 183) implies both relations of part to whole and of inside to outside. It is a project of intention and meaning in our lives, a *savoir vivre,* and in temporal terms a traffic between our existentially present values and long-duration ones from the remembered past or wished-for future. Life itself is an entity that sustains and propagates its form. Disalienating projects in practical societal life and in poetry are always shapes of sensual meaning and oriented time, they strive for a formal and beauteous use of life. With Fortini, and more articulated in Jameson (see his discussion of genres throughout *Political,* and then his respectful recuperation of Northrop Frye, 69-72 and passim), I would even call this a ceremonial, that carries over into lay creativity the notion of access to value or holiness. Formal closure aspires always to a kind of perfection – the very root of *perficere* means to finish or limit doing; as Blake noted, "Every poem must necessarily be a perfect Unity" (but then, dialectically, "Unity is the cloak of folly" – in Erdman ed., 269-70). However, a static closed perfection is since Rousseau and the Industrial Revolution subject to what he called in *Discours sur l'origine* (with much ruefulness) *perfectibilité*, a species-specific potential differentiating people from animals and allowing for perpetual development where every closure is also a rung in an open historical process.

This shapely use of life is centrally informed by *freedom with poetic justice*, as implied in Marx's horizon of a realm of freedom beyond the necessity of exploitation and other kinds of alienation (I shall pursue this further in "Using"). The homology to the communist project means that the cognitive writer's shaping and his deepest values are always already engaged in politics – the destiny of her community, finally that of humanity as a whole – whether this is explicitly thematised by the author or not, and whatever her actual practical involvement in daily politics may be or not be. Form, the shape and structure of any text, is always *en situation*, sociohistorically situated; this tends to be foregrounded in epochs of dire crisis, such as the one we are in the midst of now.

It is to my mind very significant that historically, when the world is shaken, when human beings need to make sense of things because their usual sense is lost, and the way out is found in armed resistance, for example an anti-fascist resistance movement or a communist revolution, this is often twinned with a major outpouring of poetry (verse and technically more accessible forms of fine arts), written either by formerly unknown plebeians or by top creators.[6]

Not so incidentally, much poetry – I would claim: most of the works that remain as classics – is a strange and indispensable fusion of the class stances pragmatically incompatible in everyday split society. On the one hand, there is the "aristocratic" view and stance from above, imbued with the frontline knowledge of its epoch (see Tronti 39 and passim) and embodied in the interminable comet tail of connotations to any significant concept and *topos*. On the other hand, there is the "plebeian" view and stance from below, boldly oriented toward and focussed on the life-saving denotations useful and indeed salvational in material everyday life. An analogous fusion informs ideally also the communist narrative: both these vanguard "creative minorities" (Fortini, *Saggi* 389) propose to a multitudinous and primarily plebeian addressee the highest cultural and cognitive insights of the ruling class purged from the pervasive dross of complicity with exploitation, violence, and humiliation. I find in this another confirmation for the projects of poetry and communism being communicating vessels, if not complementary twins in different walks of life.

A key mediating and shaping concept here is the addressee (viewer, reader, and similar) and his horizon of expectation, as supposed at the moment of creation and most clearly visible in the creator's initial choice of literary or artistic *genre* – always consubstantial with a long duration horizon of expectation and a given intention. (Let me add that all other opening gambits of a work should be considered here, in verse, say, the choice of the first line's rhythm that determines how the rest may develop.) Two end-horizons or *teloi* are inextricably fused here, the intended effect and social historicity. As to the first, the notion of "intentionality" has been richly formalised by Eco and company – I shall mention only his *Lector* and *Role* – but for the present purpose the sterling summing up and improvement of Russian Formalist debates by Jan Mukařovský may suffice (*Aesthetic* and *Studie*). He founds the historicity and sociality of a literary work in the *interaction between the artist's personality* – which, for the critic, means centrally the "implied author" educed from the text, though it can be compared for given purposes with the "real psychophysical personality" – *and the addressee's expectations* within which the work is reincarnated. Though in the intentionality of the created work these two subjects fuse, it remains a societal sign-system that implies a historical audience of readers prior to the work, which is thus imbued by an interiorised socio-historicity. This by no means amounts to a simple "reflection" but is as a rule a contradictory dialectics of reflection of and reflection on. Centrally, this means that literature is, as most arts, an *exemplum* in the wider sense, a cognitive finding or hypothesis, a kind of more or less open-ended allegory: it makes a point about collective situations. It is fully steeped in social historicity, as brilliantly argued in Jameson's *Political Unconscious* (see especially the first two parts). From his rich repertory, I shall here mention only two most consequential cognitions. First, in general, why and how "the structure of the psyche is historical" (62). Second, in particular, that "[literary genres] are essentially literary *institutions*," embodying "[a social contract] between a writer and a specific public" that specifies an artefact's proper use in that structure (106).

In Roman terms, poetry is a *votum,* melding the elements of desire and aspiration with prayer and solemn, even numinous promise. This has a solid underground connexion, as postulated in the shape of communicating vessels, with community and communism. Now origins and root meanings in semantics do not prove much, since meanings change in history (cf. Suvin, *Lessons from* 114-16). Still, there are long-duration nuclei of meaning, and it is suggestive that the term "communism" derives from the Latin *cum* – which became *con* – prefixed to *munus. Munus, muneris* seems to derive from a putative Indo-European root meaning *swap, change or exchange* (thence also "municipality" and "immune" – not subject to change). In Latin it had three main meanings, all rooted in "mutual service or favour": service to community, office; duty, obligation, also burden; and gift – as well as the derived meanings of "a service as favour" and "public show, spectacle." The term then became attached either to the obligation or contribution – in work or in kind – imposed by the Roman State and/or municipality on its members, or to public works provided for the Roman people by prominent and wealthy citizens, and primarily to gladiatorial games, supposedly given as gift to the community by the emperor (https: /en.wiktionary.org/wiki/munus). "*Con*" or "*cum*," meaning "with, together with," was a preposition denoting association, company, standing beside, and at times it had an intensive force and denoted "completely, fully." Thus *munus* was originally an equitable exchange of services, favours or contributions inside a community of equals, but with the rise of the State it shifted towards office or obligation. The adjective *com-munis* could thus, I think, be associated either, positively, with sharing – or even sharing fully and completely – an obligation or service with and for other members of your community, or also, negatively, with being outside or beside a personal obligation. The latter use easily slides into ruling class sneering at the "common" people that systematically associated this quality with at least an "ordinary" and usually a "low" and "vulgar" domain (cf. Williams, *Keywords* 70-72).

As for "Community," it has been magisterially analysed by Williams as encompassing meanings relating to groups of people and to "a particular quality of relationship [indicating material holdings in common, as interests or goods, or indicating a common identity or characteristics]" (*Keywords* 75). In sum, he found the semantic complexity of "the warmly persuasive word [community]" to arise from "the difficult interaction between… the sense of direct common concern [and] the materialization of various forms of common organization, which may or may not adequately express this" (ibidem 76). Nancy glosses its French use as "a being together" – *en commun*, also translatable literally "in common, in what is common" – or as "being together" (*ensemble*: in English "togetherness," something "that is neither in nor out of a singular being… where the interior… becomes exterior," an existence which is its own essence – 257). The quasi-utopian community of a theatre troupe has in some languages kept this ancient communist tinge, thence also Brecht's Berliner Ensemble. For Nancy two main matters follow from this. First, personal and serial ones: that each person, by birth and death, does not have "a beginning and an end which would be *ours*, but has them (or is them) only as others and through others" (259). Second, that "history is community, that is, the coming about of … a certain spacing of time, the spacing of a 'we'": the sense of history and any meaning that might be found in it is not a chronological succession of events but what the events "have in" or "are" in common (260-61).

My conclusion is that "communism" means at its core something like *a system of society instituting mutual and common sharing and exchange of services and contributions to one's community as its principle and Supreme Good*. Whatever other meanings were added and retracted after Marx, Kropotkin, and Lenin, I shall proceed upon this durable rock.

However, is it not too constricting to call the disalienating politics of art (poetry) analogous only to a communist project? In some cases this analogy may not be directly applicable, but I would claim that poetry's semantic and pragmatic horizon is finally one of classless politics conducted by "pencil, not pistol" (as Brecht put it — see section 3 of "Introduction"), in full associative democracy. Communism is the only name and tradition for a *consistent, encompassing, and possible alternative* to a planned and systematic immiseration of 95% of humankind so that they would have to sell their labour-power, which is today threatening to end in full-scale, if carefully masked, fascism and warfare. For half a century already, "the link between democracy and capitalism has been definitely broken" (Žižek, "Communist" 132). In that time, world financial capitalism has "carried out a veritable mobilisation of State functions" to implement a new class war from above, "a [covert or overt] civil war: not only by military and police means and by states of emergency, but also through psychological and informational warfare and corresponding cultural and political strategies" (Guattari and Negri 86). Underlying all of this is the drastic failure of sustainable capitalism, of putting new productive forces in the service of people's happiness: capitalism has become a parasitic force. Today's young people will see an ecological collapse in a few decades, its symptoms are already among us. In a kind of creeping neo-Nazism, the contractual or normal exploitation of the proletarians is supplemented and multiplied by death from explosive weapons and, despite high-sounding plans, from famine (endangering ca. 800 million people by imperfect statistics). In the domain of semantic orientation, critical forms are pre-empted and repressed in favour of forms of empty affirmation the purpose of which is to preserve power, so that the public sphere and articulate reasoning are circumvented; a good example of this may be the Bush Jr. presidency's custom of defining terrorism by pointing at whatever suited them, in other words by fiat and by violence rather than argument (cf. the essay on terrorism in this book). Epistemology as such, the problem of how do we know what we know, and finally what is a legitimate definition of human reality, is thwarted and ignored as a subversive discipline.

Therefore I must consider further the *presently useful* use of the term and concept of communism, for the waters have been thoroughly muddied by friend and foe alike. Obviously, this is (and has been) a matter for many books.[7] However: which or what communism are we speaking about? There are at least three variants of what I would recognise as a central denotation for this concept: the communism of Marx, of Kropotkin, and of Stalin – with Lenin participating of all three, but at his strongest when halfway between Marx and Kropotkin, as in *The State and Revolution* and in most of his practice. Which variant meaning has been shown by historical experience to be irremediably self-defeating, in part emancipatory but then finally sterile and repressive? Clearly, the State communism of Stalin, leading to some memorable achievements, such as the victory over Hitler, but finally to a repressive oligarchy much too heavy in blood and misery – with all of its ramifications in the world (I argue this theoretically in "15 Theses," and at length in *Splendour* and *Lessons*). Symmetrically obverse, the generous immediate anarchism à la Kropotkin has, for all of its admirable aspects that have to be integrated into our prospect and stance, never managed to maintain power when refusing any, however modified, form of the State. But accounts with a communist stance and horizon as envisaged by Marx – and Morris, and so many others – have not been settled, they are open and on the agenda of any history that wants to combat this total militarised savagery into which capitalism is rapidly descending, where colonising warfare is unceasing abroad and at home, and nuclear warfare a constant threat. Orientation toward a communist horizon means, I am persuaded, the self-preservation of humanity and its ecosystem, to be reached through radical self-determination on all levels, by means of peace and disalienated labour. To be or not to be, that is the question.

Crucially for my argument here, Marx was the inventor of societal epistemology: how any understanding of reality is inevitably shaped by class assumptions and horizons, and how to compensate for this by taking the part of the classes that work and create all wealth. In his wake, I accept here as useful the – certainly not full nor fully precise – formulation of communism by Fortini as "a tendential unity of *equality, fraternity, and sharing* with scientific *knowledge* and ethico-religious *wisdom*.... Humanity is a species defined by the capacity for (or hope of) knowing and steer ingitself and having pity for itself." (*Saggi* 1655-56). Last not least, "[T]he absolute test by which a revolution can be distinguished, is the change in the form of activity of a society, in its deepest structures of relationships and feeling" (Williams, *Modern* 76). True, we should now continue by noting the optimistic errors of Victorian Marxism, but even those can be best rectified within its tradition, beginning with Lenin, Luxemburg, Brecht, and Gramsci, and going towards plebeian self-government.

1.3. On Poets and Alienated Time(s)

To return to the poet's stance in politics: aporias lurk in it, which I shall first approach in terms of the quandary between quantitative (or clock) and qualitative (or axiological) *time*. This is rooted in the insight, from Benjamin to Nancy, that the meaning of history is not to be found simply in linear time but in how such events interact with human power and/or happiness. Centrally, human liberation means to "reclaim mastery over work time, the essential component of life time" (Guattari & Negri 16); as Marx put it, "The saving of labour-time is equal to an increase of free time, that is, time for the full development of the individual, which in turn reacts back upon the productive power of labour as itself the greatest productive power" (*Grundrisse* 711; I discuss this in Suvin "Living"). The time of any established class order will be continuous and homogenous but qualitatively "empty." In capitalism, clock-time dominates as measure of work and profit; however, in its ripe and decadent form it can also use, as a subordinate form, a qualitatively collapsed "time of image-consumption, medium of all commodities," an incantatory or mythologising "spectacle" time (Debord 124, and cf. the classic Barthes), to my mind tending toward a point-like temporality of surfing excitement. Opposed to it is the "disorder," or potentially a new and better order, of a discontinuous and qualitative time reposing on virtuality or productive possibility. The dominant course or shape of time is in capitalism arithmetically linear, coursing to a false infinity, while in the prefigurations of a classless communist society time can be branching, mutating, spiralling, and so on. It is "a field of forces" (Benjamin GS V.1: 587), "blasted out" of the bad continuum. The most exasperated or condensed guise of their collision would then be the messianic irruption point of "now-time" (*Jetztzeit)*, a pregnant present point of change.

There is no reason that poets could and should not participate in joyful annunciation and laudation of – say – justice, harmony, and bliss in human relationships (cf. Moylan), and many have wondrously done so. But for the ages of oppression, such as the capitalist age – and most etatist "real socialism" – I shall follow the lead of Rancière (but cf. on poetry as cognition also Spivak 115ff.) and posit that *if the poet-creator can – in fact, cannot but – participate in politics, he can do so only paradoxically*. As Fortini has often insisted, poetry changes nothing

– directly. Yet it is a kind of prefiguration incarnating elements and aspects of the possible and necessary revolution to come.

This means, literally, that the creative poet is one who doubts the views, opinions, and stances of the reigning lore or common sense, one who *swerves* from them by infringing old usages and meanings and by creating – or at least groping for, foreboding – new ones. Epicure's ruling principle of the atoms swerving from the automatically straight path may stand as the great ancestor of all creative methods and possibilities (cf. Suvin *Defined*). Existentially, this is testified to by the exile of so many poets throughout the ages, never more frequent than in the "massified" century beginning with the first capitalist World War: the enmeshment in the world is often punished by exile across official boundaries, making evident that, as in the age-old "inner emigration," poets have always been half inside and half outside dominant institutions and stances. To put it in the useful terms of Williams's about hegemony and "structures of feeling": Our lives are largely shaped by a complex societal *hegemony*, that includes the determinations by political economy as well as direct political control and social group control, but also, for Williams, all

> the relations of domination and subordination, in their forms as practical consciousness, as in effect a saturation of the whole process of living. . . . It [hegemony] is a whole body of practices and expectations, over the whole of living: *our senses and assignments of energy*, our shaping perceptions of ourselves and our world. It is *a lived system of meanings and values*. . . . (*Marxism* 109-10, emphasis added)

Within such hegemonies, structures of feeling are socio-historically particular qualities "of social experience and relationship,... actively lived [meanings and values]." Poets embody and correlate these structures inside and outside texts (in the larger semiotic sense) since they are also structures of experience; these structures are evident in textual "forms and conventions – semantic figures" that can be taken as constellations of sense and meaning (ibidem 131-35).

Consequently, verse and prose poetry have been places of truth-bearing thinking not sundered from feeling, often filling in the voids left by institutionalised science and institutionalised philosophy, and of course by most institutionalised politics and ideology, inimical to humanity because complicitous with oppressive and exploitative class rule: I cannot imagine major poetry and art that extol psychic oppression or physical suppression of people. In particular, poetry opposes two mutually supporting reigning ideological practices of these our times: first, doctrinaire and neurotic possessive individualism, where experiences matter because they are "mine"; second, wars of domination. Contrariwise, poetry is always engaged in concrete generalisable experiences, ideally soliciting all open-minded readers, and it makes love or hate, but never war. I shall revisit aspects of the poet's politics for the capitalist epoch in Section 2.

To sum up: all ruling institutions and ideologies use generalisation, irremediably wedded to abstract concepts which cannot satisfactorily account for the relationship between people and nature, the finite and the infinite. Poetic creation sutures conceptual thought to justification from recalled immediate sensual, bodily experiences which are, thus far, much more difficult to fake. As important is its ranging through richer time-horizons, recalled in Williams's categories of the dominant, emergent, and residual in culture (*Marxism* 121ff.): remembering supposed qualities within human relationships, absent today, in the past as well as hoping – and working, acting – for them in the future by finding, cherishing, and developing their seeds today and yesterday, in the hidden complicity of happiness and hoping. The main difference to Marxist communism would be that the latter's categories and values are shaped (and therefore also limited) by societal history, posed as a closed world: the biological and cosmic aspects of human beings are here, as it were, bracketed out for the present needs of struggle. Beyond such a horizon of a Militant Church, poetry and all arts cannot forget, and thus needs incorporate, the triumphant – and the sorrowful or suffering – aspect (I worry more at this in Suvin, "Parables").

I proceed to buttress and unfold the argument that poetry is an irreplaceable cognition needed for survival of humanity – and thus a communicating vessel twinned to communism – by reading the complementary masters Brecht, Hölderlin, and Fortini.

2. The Stance of Emancipation: Brecht's Theory, Hölderlin's Verse, Fortini's Criticism

The past is never dead. It's not even past.

W. Faulkner, *Requiem for a Nun*

2.1. On Brecht's Stance and Bearing

A key mediation between the shapes and values of a sociohistorical body or structure and an individual body and personality is Brecht's concept and exemplary practice of *Haltung*, translatable as *stance, bearing or attitude*. I have explored this at length – the notion in "Haltung (Bearing)" and "Haltung," the practice in essays collected in *To Brecht,* "Heavenly," and *Darko* – and shall here summarise the points pertinent to my argument on creativity and poetry. *Haltung* meant in German semantics, within a discourse originating in the ruling class, a precise bodily bearing in a hierarchical interpersonal relation, usually positively evaluated as strong and worthy behaviour. While refusing the term's traditional statics from above down, the bourgeois and individualistic concepts of an internalised and atomic character, as well as the faceless economic determinants in Engelsian HistMat vulgate, Brecht retained *the body as the co-determining anchorage for a person's stance*. He thus arrived at a concept that yokes together a subject's body-orientation in spacetime and the body's meaningful insertion into major societal flows of things, to which "bearing" he could allot a central role in his work and understanding of the world. This engagement of the whole body, that does not split the sensorium from the brain, was diametrically opposed to learning through systematised ideas. On the one hand, "people do much that is reasonable yet does not pass through their reason (*Verstand*). We cannot well do without this" (GKA 22.2: 825) On the other hand, for Brecht the systematised notional constructs tend to false harmony and ideological univocity necessarily present in any closed doctrine or "world view," which then grows more important than its learning bearer.

Picking up the young Marx's Epicurean assumption that the development of the senses is the central criterion for hominisation as against alienation, Brecht pioneered a discourse articulating a reintegration of the body into the practice and theory of our knowledge. This importantly includes – as I argue in the essays on *Haltung* and in "On Cognitive" and „Emotion" – some emotions such as sympathy and indignation in tandem with embodied reason. Without knowing of him, other cognate approaches – Merleau-Ponty's notion of a writer of one that crystallises a vital situation in language, Bourdieu's notion of *habitus*, and Ngugi wa Thiong'o's notion of literary meaning bound to embodiment and location – brought about significant developments of such embodied thinking and feeling.

Stance brings about a particular form or shape, in personal relationships as well as in poetry and other arts (where it is foregrounded and focussed on): a poetic text is "an ensemble of linguistic and behavioural choices... organised into structures and implying an end or *telos*." Criticism, institutionalised or not, flows out of "the possibility to clarify this end to others; in that sense any criticism is ideology and precept" (both in Fortini, *Saggi* 962). This is different from the veneration of a pseudo-avantgardist stress on vitalistic chaos, much akin to or at least clearly impotent in front of fascism; it also differs from the imposition of a shape taken from an ideology or doctrine, as in bourgeois rationalism, as well as from a limited catalog of traditional forms, as in academic conservatism. Rather, it means contesting the mystifying forms that lower classes adopt from dominant discourse. It favours formalising – that is, emancipatory – stances, new or old, that "change into choices the largest possible part of destiny" (Fortini, *Saggi* 390).

2.2. On Hölderlin and Transition

Famously, poetic procedures of major cognitive dignity may be found in the opus of Friedrich Hölderlin, and I'll take as example his great poem *Brod und Wein* (*Bread and Wine*, 1801), and focus on the last 11 lines of its stanza 7:

> Nur zu Zeiten erträgt göttliche Fülle der Mensch,
> Traum von ihnen ist drauf das Leben. Aber das Irrsal
> Hilft, wie Schlummer und stark machet die Not und die Nacht,
> Bis daß Helden genug in der ehernen Wiege gewachsen,
> Herzen an Kraft, wie sonst, ähnlich den Himmlischen sind.
> Donnernd kommen sie drauf. Indessen dünket mir öfters
> Besser zu schlafen, wie so ohne Genossen zu sein,
> So zu harren und was zu tun indes und zu sagen,
> Weiß ich nicht und wozu Dichter in dürftiger Zeit?
> Aber sie sind, sagst du, wie des Weingotts heilige Priester,
> Welche von Lande zu Land zogen in heiliger Nacht.

> Only at times can mankind bear divine fullness.
> Dreaming them is life from then on. But the errance
> Helps, also sleep, and the need and night make for strength,
> Until heroes enough in cradles of brass have grown to be,
> With hearts as strong and in other ways alike to the heavenly ones.
> Thundering they come nearer. Meanwhile it seems to me often
> Better to sleep, than thus to be companionless, so to wait
> And wait and what's to do in this while and to say
> I do not know and what poets are for in an age of want?
> Yet they are, you say, like to the wine-god's holy priests,
> Who wandered from land to land on through the holy night.

(Translation by Susan Ranson much emended by me)[1]

This breathless oral rhythm is thickly strewn with nodes of compressed insight. A central node is the rich expression "dürftige Zeit." The "Zeit" is obviously a historical epoch: in this case the bitter reflux of the great French Revolution and its attendant hopes – in that way analogous to the great October Revolution and its longer reflux for us today, finally sealed in 1989 and lasting still in this centenary year. "Dürftig" can be translated as of dearth, of distress, a destitute, hard, meagre, scant, paltry, miserable, feeble, wretched, impoverished, insubstantial, jejune, necessitous or penurious age. Centrally this is an age of deep and radical, moral and material, need (*Not* – also *Bedarf*, *Bedürfnis*, the latter suggested also by the keystone *dürftig;* also translatable as requirement,

1 sites.google.com/site/germanliterature/19th-century/hoelderlin/brot-und-wein-bread-and-wine

lack, want, desire for what is needed). For the moment I translate it as "an age of want" as most suggestive.

The fragment chosen thus centrally speaks to the needy 95% of us in the age of the great turbocapitalist distress pivoting on finances as the Supreme Good – which wondrously manages to be both fake and lacking. Such a totally alienated time is the unbearable day: the poem opens with a first stanza praising the night and sleep as against the dominant daily awareness and impact (it was published separately as a short poem *The Night*). To escape this day, night-cum-sleep and wandering without fixed abode or certainties are at the moment the only means of minimal defence, while awaiting the new age of heroes worthy of "divine fullness." In today's language, we are living in a dystopia that is also an anti-utopia, while remembering, perhaps vaguely, an age with the horizon of and vector towards concrete utopia. In this anti-utopia we are all atomised individuals, "companionless" – *ohne Genossen,* "without comrades" – and it is most remarkable that the poem never uses "I" or "my," only "we" or impersonal forms. The poem's voice and stance deeply disbelieves in sundered individuals outside of great impersonal (or divine) powers that traverse humanity, and on the daily human level outside of a comradely "we."

This is only one possible interpretation, which does not exhaust the riches of this much commented text – for example the important *Irrsal* (errance, but also radical, if rather disconsolate, deviance, and much more) of verse 2 or the mysterious "you" toward the end. However, for us today, what is the "divine fullness" that people can only fitfully bear, yet that Hölderlin is here yearning for? Regardless of what the author might have meant, the poem's stance is magnetically oriented towards a poetically transformed French Revolution with its heroes – now both exiled into and transfigured by dionysian mythology. Little illusion remains as to its necessary harshness, it was a cradle of brass (not gold, silver or wood); yet it is one we hope for again, while waiting in dearth and distress, destitute and miserable, wretched and impoverished: and the rhythm hurries us onto the culminating existential desolation of "what's to do in this while and to say/ I do not know and what poets are for in an age of want?" Well, it is at least clear that the poem is, obviously, "for" being written as it was, as a witness, mourner, and herald. The answer to the question momentarily unanswerable – for a long moment, lasting decades – is first of all to speak (locution) testifying to the question's weighty pertinence, and to speak about its context and reason (illocution), which brings at least the basis or foretaste of the answer (perlocution). And having spoken it, the poets are already participating to some degree in this fullness, in the seminarist Hölderlin's lingo they are holy: they already wander in the holy night firmly disbelieving the certainties of the day.

2.3. On Fortini and Poetic Justice

I have already adoperated Franco Fortini, one of the 20th century's best critics of poetry – himself a significant poet, and an intimately epistemological and political one to boot; he defined „the literary use of language" as a homology to „a formalised [that is, conscious and conscientious – note DS] use of life that is the end and goal of communism" (Fortini, *Saggi* 184). This homology (to my mind in part annunciation-cum-denunciation and in part prefiguration, a shadow falling from the possible future) necessarily transgresses the hegemonic discourse, in our times sadly clichétised; I would call it *cognition constituted by memorable pleasure*. Poets too – just as revolutionaries – are itinerant, geographically or nationally unfixed announcers and denouncers, rooted in times rather than spaces. They remember the past, dispute the present „use of life into which we are forced by alienation of labour" (Fortini, *I confini* 35), and carry their lessons into projects of possible lives reaching for the future. What Fortini means by form in poetry is an interpretation of the world by means of what word constellations both say and leave unsaid but suggest and give clues to, always suffused by firm if dynamic values shared by a societal class. We may recognise that a "look into thy heart and write" orientation may be a device, enforced by defeat, which allows precious personal testimony counteracting the dispossessed persons' (and classes') lack of stability and legitimation (ibidem 31). In lyrics, looking outwards takes most often the detour of first looking inwards – an old *topos*, present at least since Petrarca and Sidney, if not Catullus. However, Fortini's dialectically rich view can not only englobe such a contradictory detour from collective horizons but also diametrically oppose the presently prevailing obscurantist use of „form" as a demolition of meaning and sense, as a ghetto instead of a lookout: „form is a tension to incorporate, confront, and elaborate what is outside the frontiers of poetic form" (ibidem 38). In Jameson's terms, "...cognitive mapping will be a matter of form" ("Cognitive" 356). Rimbaud phrased this proceeding in *Une Saison en enfer* as *posséder la vérité dans une âme et un corps* – "To own truth in a soul and a body [and perhaps through or by means of them]" (157).

Furthermore, no text can have a meaning for somebody who would try to deal with it "totally apart from all its extra-textual relations," since all the presuppositions and conventions that make a text meaningful come from that extra-textual domain: "The extra-textual bonds of a work can be described as the relations between the set of elements fixed in the text and the set of elements from which any given element in the text is selected" (Lotman 50). This constitutes a horizon for poetry that is both political in the nobler sense and also as it were cosmological, for its greatness and misery deal – as Fortini spelled it out in an interview, also in *Saggi* 1454-60 – with human resistance to death by means of a systematic project, and therefore as a self-education of which artworks are exemplars. To recall the focus on time in 1.3: both poetry and communism choose the radical break with capitalist point-like time, extending maximally to this year's profits, towards a long duration of polymorphic solidarity. Poetry longs for embodiment of its values as ends (though individual authors may not know or wish this): "*it demands, with the force of its own authority, its incarnation*" (ibidem 1278).

Such a creative horizon in our age immediately shapes the poets' attitude as an intimately personal paradox of *living in politics as an anti-politics*. All that is commonly taken for politics since the failure of the French, Russian, and Chinese revolutions – for my generation, say, since the effects of the antifascist wars, such as peace and the Welfare State, have been largely or fully expunged – is alien and inimical, akin to active threats if not murderous drones and renditions. The reigning brainwashed common sense includes from our ancestral heroic ages of liberating politics (the liberal, communist, and antifascist ones) only a few impoverished slogans. Therefore, as Rancière remarks of verse, poets have to retrace the line of passage that unites words and things. And in prose, I would add, the line that unites human figures and spacetimes by means of plot and of metaphoric clusters. In brief, where personality is valued for and as consumption in view of profit, and carefully shaped phrases or images pertain increasingly to mendacious and death-inducing advertising, art has to upset (cf. more in Suvin, "On Cognitive," "On Metaphoricity," „Death," and "Parables").

Rancière has pointed out how the deviation and scandal of modern art is well expressed by our immediate major poetic ancestor, Rimbaud – in a filiation clearly enmeshed with political revolution and beginning with Milton, many Romantics, Heine, and Baudelaire. He was led to exasperation at having to reconcile his deep hatred of the bourgeois society with the irrefragable fact of having to breathe and experience within it:

> ...industrialists, rulers, senates:
> Die quick! Power, justice, history: down with you!
> This is owed to us. Blood! Blood! Golden flame!
> All to war, to vengeance, to terror... Enough!
> \- - - - - -
> ...I'm there, I'm still there. („Qu'est-ce pour nous...," 113)

The obverse of this aporia (the *assez* vs. *j'y suis toujours*) is Thomas More's great coinage of utopia: the radically different good place which is in our sensual experience not here, but must be cognised – today, on pain of extinction. What is not here, Bloch's Yet Unknown, is almost always first adumbrated in art and fiction, most economically in verse. From many constituents of the good place, I shall here focus, as does Rancière (92–93), on *freedom* – Wordsworth's „Dear Liberty" (*Prelude* 1: 31), which translates the French revolutionary term of *liberté chérie* – that then enables security, order, creativity, and so on. The strategic insight here seems to be that the method of great modern verse from Rimbaud on (and prose too, in somewhat differing ways), if you wish *its epistemic principle, is freedom as possibility of things being otherwise*; this is to be understood by means of the interaction of what is being said and how it is being said, a consubstantiality of theme and stance. This is also of a piece with the fact that the eye cannot function without the brain; there is no brain without socialised presuppositions; therefore there is no innocent eye. Every reading will establish its own, value-laden meaning out of the text's sense. Every reading is a denial (suppression) of other readings, meanings, and values. Any „positive" act is also the negation of a negation; any truth a denial of incompatible „untruths." All shaping and articulation entails the suppression of alternative shapings and articulations for the relationships it refers to: *it can never exhaust such relations*.

Collective and distributive human freedom from oppression, exploitation, debasement, and destruction is today our supreme truth and Supreme Good. As a privileged metonymy of and ally for this emancipation, *poetic freedom is a historically situated, political experience of the sensual*, which is necessarily also polemical swerve from and against the dominant lore, in favour of fresh cognition. This freedom is intimately melded with knowledge or cognition. The work of poetry gives shape, voice, and bearing to a previously uncognised, mute and non-articulated, category of being: in that strictly notional sense, the final sediment of all fiction and art is the thesaurus and the collective imaginary encyclopedia. And this encyclopedia is a list of the categories, topoi, and shapes that direct people's orientation in our common world.

In sum, the cognition and wisdom of a society culminate in *poetic justice*. This is of a piece with communism as the unfolding of human possibilities.

Works Cited

See in *Works Cited in this Book* the following titles, by Author surname plus (when the author has several titles) first "headword" or identifying syntagm in the title:

Auerbach; Badiou, *L'Hypothèse;* Barthes; Beardsley; Black; Blake; Blumenberg; Brecht; Culler; Dean, *The Communist;* Debord, *Société;* Douzinas & Žižek eds.; Eco, *Lector* and *The Role;* Engels, *The Part;* Fortini, both titles; Gramsci, *Come;* Grene; Guattari & Negri; Jameson, "Cognitive" and *The Political;* Komelj; Lenin, *Two;* Lotman; Marx, *Critique* and *Grundrisse;* Matvejević; McCumber; Moylan; Mukařovský, both titles; Nancy; Paternu; Rancière, "Transports"; Ricoeur, both titles; Rimbaud; Spivak; Steinberg; Suvin, "An Approach," *To Brecht,* "Cognition," "On Cognitive," *Darko,* "Death," "Emotion," "Epistemological," "Fifteen," „Haltung," „*Haltung* (Bearing)," "Heavenly," "On the Horizons," *Lessons of,* "Living," "From Mallarmé's," "On Metaphoricity," "Parables," and *Splendour;* Tronti; White; Williams, all three titles; Woolf; Wordsworth; Žižek.

POEMS 8

HAECCEITAS – THIS HERE & NOW

Things are there   a this   a shape
Necessary for this here & now
Exposed   unchanged in the light that they bathe
The space that they are.
& i? Am i a thing or a looker-on?
Both–and? & you too
With this red hair & those green eyes
That nose mouth breasts moist lap?
Enter: here too are gods.

Bitter truth: we know we shall not be.
Animals, more & less than.
Things, more & less than. Forms that feel.
Warmth is a dissipative structure
Your smooth skin a miracle of negentropy
The small adorable crow's-feet at your eyes
Forerunners of tectonic crevasses   drought
The lap will bear children & desiccate
It will not be.
                    Yet things are there.

What is done has been done
What is undone has been undone
When they are redone it will not be this.
Things are reversible but not for us.
Seize the shining day   seize the fertile night
Deep deep down   the dark shore
There-things & not-there non-things   unreal

Amid non-persons here there & everywhere
I too am here   now   with you
Athirst for justice   unreconciled
My green essence:
Psyche, Chloe.

12-211007

9

In the Shadows of Never-Ending Warfare: Use-Values of Lenin Today

1. Why Lenin?

There is a wonderful apocryphal anecdote, which I often quote in these horrorific years of devolving imperialist slaughters. It is an imaginary dialogue between Shklovsky and Trotsky, for all their blind spots still the most intelligent Formalist and the most intelligent Leninist:

> Shklovsky said to Trotsky,"I'm not interested in what flag flies on the fortress. I write about perception and literature and don't care about war."
>
> Trotsky replied, "But war cares about you."

Why write today about Vladimir Ilyich Lenin? This should be obvious but isn't. It is not so much because of a (very necessary) piety towards him, as towards all our Great Left Ancestors, from Lucretius and Mo Zi through the pivots of Spinoza, Hegel and Marx, up to – and I mention only those nearest and most sympathetic to me – Brecht, Benjamin, Gramsci, Mao, Castro, Ho, Tito, and Kidrič (see more on the last two in my *Splendour*, and on sympathy in "Emotion"). It is *because of us*: for Lenin's major international achievement was contracting out of the huge and quite symptomatic carnage of the first capitalist and imperialist World War, a harbinger of all the subsequent mass killings, where genocide returned from the colonies to the continent of metropolitan imperialism as a sign that any real liberalism was over at home too. Not so coincidentally, this was meant to militarise the disciplining of working classes:

> Anyone can understand that war and conquest without and the encroachment of despotism within mutually support

> each other; that money and people are habitually taken at will from a people of slaves to bring others beneath the same yoke; and that conversely war furnishes a pretext for exactions of money and. .. for keeping large armies constantly afoot.... In a word, anyone can see that aggressive rulers wage war at least as much on their subjects as on their enemies, and that the conquering nation is left no better off than the conquered. (Rousseau 90-91)

Turning masses of plebeians into cannon and bomb fodder, "[w]ar was the true government of Europe [and the world – note DS] from 1914 onwards" (Russo 163). Destruction of people, commodities, and nature needed for quicker circulation of capital shall henceforth be on a permanent mass basis: World War no. 2 1936-45, no. 3 during the Cold War after 1945, and no. 4 from Libya and Iraq on in this glad new century.

Emphatically, we cannot afford to disregard THE major historical anti-war gesture in modern history, one that earned Lenin the sympathies of millions in the whole world regardless of all else. To this we must add the defeat of fascist global domination in World War 2, for it pivoted on the role of the USSR which, for all its horrible counterrevolutionary carnages, retained enough inbuilt elements of the original plebeian Leninism to make that war a supreme example of a just one: still carnage but obviating centuries of ruling fascism. And today, with exponentially more destructive technology threatening all vertebrate life on Earth, humanity is in a zero-sum conflict with perpetual warfare American-style (also British, French, and, as of Yugoslavia and Afghanistan, also German and pan-European-style): either we'll get rid of it, or it will get rid of us.

Of course, we need other teachers too, supplementing and where need be modifying him, but the Lenin experience remains central. With him we must begin in the wake of Marx: all else follows. We need communism for many reasons,[1] but the most pressing one is to stop warfare and other sources of mass killings as well as eco-destruction. Our dire need is for "survival studies" or salvational politics. An indispensable foundation stone for it is enlightening ourselves and others. The manifold popular icons of "Lenin's little light bulb" in the years of Soviet Russia's electrification (see "Of Russian") are an allegory for our time.

2 PHOTOS: THE LIGHT BULB OF ILYICH (LAMPOCHKA ILICHA)

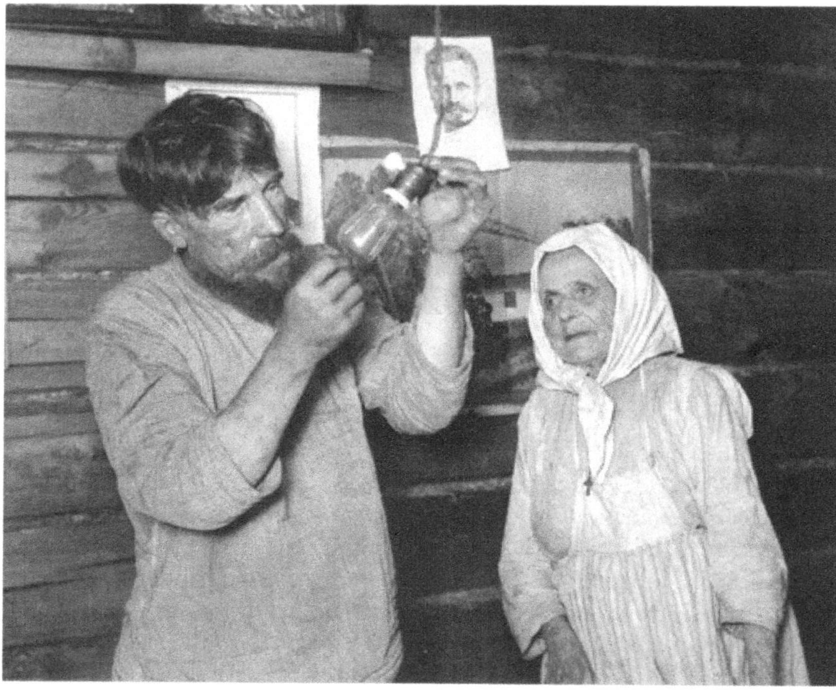

2. The Context of Lenin: An Age of Never-ending Imperialist Warfare

The texts Mayakovsky commissioned for the special issue of LEF in 1924 and translated into English in the welcome book *Coiled Verbal Spring: Devices of Lenin's Language*[2] – I think for the first time in almost a century – are, understandably for a beginning, focused on Lenin's briefer signed articles. They do not deal with possibly his most important signed work, *The State and Revolution* (except for a reference to why it wasn't finished), nor with the unsigned but clearly his "Decree on Peace" (depersonalised to function as a government declaration). This Decree will bear repetition and meditation today when we would sorely need it again, with updates on covert economic and informational warfare. It had 11 meaty – and for that conjuncture quite precise and exhaustive – paragraphs, but I present here only extracts from five:

Decree on Peace

> The workers' and peasants' government, created by the Revolution of October 24-25 and basing itself on the Soviet of Workers', Soldiers' and Peasants' Deputies, calls upon all the belligerent peoples and their government to start immediate negotiations for a just, democratic peace.
>
> – – – – –
>
> By … such a peace the [workers' and peasants'] government means an immediate peace without annexations (i.e., without the seizure of foreign lands, without the forcible incorporation of foreign nations) and without indemnities.
>
> – – – – –
>
> The [workers' and peasants'] government considers it the greatest of crimes against humanity to continue this war over the issue of how to divide among the strong and rich nations the weak nationalities they have conquered, and solemnly announces its determination immediately to sign terms of peace to stop this war on the terms indicated ….
>
> – – – – –
>
> The government proposes an immediate armistice to the governments and people of all the belligerent countries, and, for its part, considers it desirable that this armistice should be concluded for a period of not less than three months….
>
> – – – – –
>
> While addressing this proposal for peace to the governments and peoples of all the belligerent countries, the Provisional Workers' and Peasants' Government of Russia appeals in particular also to the class-conscious workers of the three most advanced nations of mankind and the largest states partici-

> pating in the present way, namely, Great Britain, France, and Germany. … [We trust] that the workers of the countries mentioned will understand the duty that now faces them of saving mankind from the horrors of war and its consequences, that these workers, by comprehensive, determined, and most vigorous action, will help us to conclude peace successfully, and at the same time emancipate the labouring and exploited masses of our population from all forms of slavery and all forms of exploitation.

Notice that, in this diplomatic (in all senses) document, the usual rhetorical expedients or devices analysed by the Formalists have been maximally dampened down. Since you do not vituperate people with whom you want – at least ostensibly – to conclude an accord, there is no mention of capitalism or imperialism, none of economics. His March 1917 *Letters from Afar* sentence cited in this book by Tynyanov, "Russian capital is merely a branch of the worldwide 'firm' which manipulates hundreds of billions of rubles and is called 'England and France'," is for the purpose at hand left unmentioned. But knowing full well that the accord would be against the interest of the governments and ruling classes bent on conquest, so that you must have a Plan B, you do not pull your punches either. In the final paragraph, there is a change of language from a diplomatic governmental declaration dealing in nations and borders to a kind of – yet unborn – Third International exhortation: it invokes the tradition of workers' struggles in France, the UK, and Germany (left out by me above) to make it clear on whom the real hope for peace depends – and who will be separately approached to realise it.

This shows very clearly what most of the translated exegeses in the book also stress: in Lenin there is no disjunction between language and liberatory action. His permanent underlying motto was What Is To Be Done (by persuading people and listening to the people): even in public governmental documents where he had to contend with the rulers' bureaucratic tradition of employing language to hide, twist, and obfuscate matters. To this should be added his recurring operative and cognitive terms of middle-range *situation*, fusing space-time and orientation, and tactical *task*, which is precisely That Which Is To Be Done primarily and immediately, now and without a doubt (see the Dōgen epigraph to "What Is," section 3).[3]

Alas, the optimistic trust in "Western" working classes proved to be mainly mistaken, though these were strong enough to prevent direct intervention against the Soviets by the "Western" armies in the ensuing Civil War (except for minor actions against Arkhangelsk and Vladivostok).

Thus, the context for Lenin is his *winning the peace* with the Central Powers and then the Civil War against the "Western" allies: it is the existence of a potentially communist USSR. But the absence in the final paragraph of USA

– an important, and eventually decisive, belligerent nation since April 1917 – indicates a limit to the Decree and (I'm afraid) to Lenin's experiential horizon. Not only: it was a limit of the whole European socialist and then communist tradition, perhaps visible in the fact that its major ecumenical literary critic, Georg Lukács, never wrote anything of note about American literature and culture.

3. Two Limits of Lenin

I'm not drawing up here an encompassing balance sheet for Lenin's writing and actions, which would have been largely positive. But I find two significant places where I politically disagree with his argumentation, though they can still be used as awful warning.

The first one seems philosophical, it concerns his book *Materialism and Empirio-criticism* of 1909, where the worthy goal of preventing demoralisation after the 1905 defeat led to a simplified collapsing of positions in modern physics (e.g. of Mach) to their supposed political effect of relativist demobilisation. Lenin at that point knew little and probably cared less about physics; with his usual – but here oversimplified – vigour he was guarding the "scientificity" of Marx and Engels as a backbone of confidence into a possible revolution. This opened the door to a quite untenable theory of arts and sciences subjectively "mirroring" an objective reality – that is, to a mechanical materialism later warmly espoused by harmful Stalinist inquisitors into sciences and arts. It amounted to a ban on radical innovation within Marxism and communism quite uncharacteristic of Lenin's own major achievements. He would correct his philosophical bearings after an intense bout of reading Hegel, at the dark time of the inglorious fall of the social-democracy into supporting the world war – see the most revealing notes in his *Philosophical Notebooks* (wrongly so titled by editors under Stalin, it should have really been *Notebooks on Hegel*).

Even more harmful was Lenin's insistence at the 1921 Party congress for a ban on currents or "fractions" within the communist party, reversing the whole tradition of vigorous interior debates in the first two Internationals. True, he thought this was a temporary measure for one year only in view of introducing NEP as a major "retreat"; but the remedy turned out to be worse than the disease and provided the major plank for Stalinist orthodoxy after 1928. In its consequences it was a truly epochal miscalculation.

4. Lenin's Importance for Us

What about the Lenin possibly alive today? I shall here go one initial step beyond the texts translated in this book, using the second major clarification of Lenin at that time, Lukács's booklet *Lenin* (another very important use of Lenin, his doctrine of the mediating and guiding party, is to be found in my essay "What Is"). I shall take from Lukács's partly dated work a main theme sparked by it, though going beyond it: *capitalist degeneration*.

His central thesis seems to be that Lenin "saw the problems of [his] age as a whole: the onset of the last phase of capitalism... [and t]he actuality of the revolution [as human salvation)" (10-11). For him, as for Marx, "the concrete analysis of the concrete situation is ... the culmination of all genuine theory, its consummation, the point where it therefore breaks into practice" (42-43).

But what did Lenin see his age as? Lukács mentions an intriguing and for us most apposite debate on the Left in Russia after the failed 1905 revolution: should that period be seen as after the revolution's defeat (that is, we are in 1849) or before the decisive revolution (we are in 1847 and all is still open), as Lenin obviously believed and worked to accomplish. Today we could pose this as: are we in 1915 and even in 1939 – a nadir of horror yet on the eve of a political salvation – or in 1991 – the unstoppable downward slide of humanity's anti-utopian perdition, of a piece with the Nazi decade (though hypocritically disguised) only with no efficient alternative?

My favourite definitional slogan of Lenin's is: "Socialism is Soviet power plus electrification of the whole country" (remember "Ilyich's little light bulbs"?). Were we to generalise the sturdy and vivid examples from his writing, they would amount to *full democracy from below* (accompanied by suitable political institutions) and *full use of ecologically safe science and technology available to all*. On the most difficult road toward this – think of all the bankers, generals, and the millions of their mercenaries in media etc. who murder to prevent it – we need two, three, many Lenins: no doubt, updated for a post-cybernetic etc. age, purged of the impatient limits I indicated above, but with the same unswerving dedication as and some approximation to the genius of Vladimir Ilyich's.

However, finally, there is a most important difference from the age of Lenin in today's epoch (human kind's position) under the far-off stars, nanophysical AI armies, and capitalist banks – so that he can, alas, no longer be a sufficient guide. How can we begin sketching in the basis for a present-day guide?

Let me start, by contraries: it would be easy to compile a representative list of the rising bourgeoisies' huge and permanently needful humanising achievements – pivoting on the French, American, and Industrial revolutions, best praised in *The Communist Manifesto* – and what happened to them in history. It may be enough to suggest here the concepts and practices of Enlightenment, citizenship, republicanism, global interchanges, hygiene and antisepsis, longer life-span for a majority, universal elementary schooling and easy access to the middle and higher schooling, urbanisation, easier transport and communication, and so on and on – in sum, the twin peaks of *easier living*, made possible by industrial productivity, and *happiness* ("a new idea in Europe," said Saint-Just). Why do I call them "permanently needful"? Because – although they were first memorably formulated and fitfully tried in and around the three bourgeois revolutions I mentioned (and in a number of precursors) – they in fact foundered under a capitalist rule indelibly marked by plundering dispossession, colonialist violence, and metropolitan exceptionalism that then necessarily went in each country hand in hand with internal racism and exploitation. The possible universally valid achievements of the bourgeoisie were left to be picked up by socialists and communists – as is implied in the whole Lenin event. To be sure, I do not wish to claim exclusive vanguard status for North Atlantic revolutions here as they sedimented into the infamous "modernisation theory": the West as against the Rest (cf. both titles by Sakai) is ***not*** the universal norm in relation to which all vectors toward easier living and happiness from other political space-times – say tribal society, or Asia, or the Haiti of Toussaint l'Ouverture, or the Yugoslavia of Tito, or the Cuba of Castro – would be particular and peripheral. If one believes, as Lenin did when he could afford it, in plebeian democracy from below (the Soviets, or ruling through councils of working people) then all anti-capitalist vectors towards this have the same dignity wherever and whenever they might happen; and Europe, including Russia, just happened to industrialise and form a conscious proletariat first, so as to reach some formulations which remain indispensable.

Thus, if the bourgeois wave's humanly useful peak was 1848 for Western Europe and 1865 for USA – later in most other places – then the reflux or devolution of capitalism after that in all matters of disalienation is glaring. True, there was a subsidiary but very important upward blip of antifascism and Welfare State ca. 1933-73, which put paid to the crassest threat of fascism and demonstrated that a reasonably sane and good life was now technically possible for all; I was raised and formed by it and do not at all wish to minimise the achievements of both the Leninist thrust and the Keynesian response (half mirror image, half cooptation to prevent worse for the coopters). But on the whole, both in the ongoing world wars and in the triumph of financial turbocapitalism from the 1970s on, *all the positive achievements of the bourgeoisie and capitalism are one by one being taken back*, as if to console us for its forthcoming passing.

As different from Lenin, our problem is that we can't be sure whether the coming new epoch of relations in and around human production – what Yeats memorably called the new beast slouching toward Bethlehem – will be less or more monstrous: will it be communist enlightenment and poetic justice (that I argue for in this book) or fascist savagery fusing slavery, serfdom, and exploitation with the highest technology? One could today make a very long negative list on the model of the following one a generation ago: it is not by chance that major technological progress "[has led] to disastrous outcomes: pesticides increase pests; hospitals are foci of infection; antibiotics give rise to new pathogens; flood control increases flood damage; and economic development increases poverty" (Levins 180-81). To crown all, in lieu of democracy and the *citoyen*, after 2008 capitalism's legitimate son of fascism is returning. The bourgeois dispensation turns out to be a recipe for the world's most successful transmutation of progress into regress or happiness into misery, and capitalist profitable productivity a recipe for mega-titanic destruction!

This is what we absolutely must start from: the taking back of the reasons for the *Communist Manifesto's* glorification of the bourgeoisie. Following Lenin's style of writing and working, our negation of the systematic negativity grasping at us ought to be phrased as: If we don't do such-and-such in proper pragmatic ways to reestablish revolutionary horizons, we are lost. Humanity is lost.

Works Cited in Essay 9

See in *Works Cited in this Book* the following titles, by Author surname plus (when the author has several titles) first "headword" or identifying syntagm in the title:

Boynik ed.; Lazarus; Lenin, "Decree"; Levins; Lukács, *Lenin*; Rousseau; "Of Russian"; Russo; Sakai, both titles; Suvin, "Emotion," *Lessons from, Splendour*.

POEMS 9

PROBLEM

> *próblema* (from *pro-ballesthai*): protrusion, salience, project, foothills, bulwark, what is held or put before one, point at issue

– For Sanja L –

I am where i am not, & i am where i
Literally do not want to be & yet
Find no better place to be. This
Protracted instant in which i am held
Protruded projected thrown before one, myself,
A galley slave smoothing his rowing bench
In memory of what was then, a salience,
A bulwark. This is here, this is now.
You are history.

I need a spy-glass to see the liberated festive
Zones, floating worlds of woodcuts & songs,
The magic ships trod by puppets quite like ourselves
Who may meet what they awaited & do not turn
Into brittle cancerous glass, for they're puppets
Our superior shadows, cast by the burning bush
In the clear desert of the boards that mean life,
Held or put before us, in the foothills,
Touched by tongues of fire. O their arrow-ships!

He has a problem, said the voice
He got the spyglass he wanted.

13307

UPON THE DISCOVERY OF PHARAOH WOSERIBRE SENEBKAY (SECOND INTERMEDIARY PERIOD)

So there's some hope for us still – four thousand
Years later, an archeologist of the Final Darkness
Will find a written trace & say: „Mirlenien
Reigned here, son of Ka, adoring the Goddess Nut
& the comradely people in arms, in order
To afford happiness. His tomb
In exquisite pink marble is alas much
Destroyed in the Age of Plunder, the magnificent
Paintings only in part preserved. His skeleton shows
A height much above normal. A totally forgotten
Page of history looms hereby
Darkly up."

17214

10

Using Negativities: Brecht, Politics of Death

> The first condition of immortality is death.
>
> Stanislaw Jerzy Lec

> I do not dispute the need for priests to remind people that one day they'll die. I say only that in certain strange ages, such as ours, we need another kind of priests called poets, to remind people that they are not yet dead.
>
> G.K. Chesterton [retranslated from Italian]

1. When in Anti-utopia, Use Negativity

> A description of confusion is not the same thing as a confused description.
>
> Walter Benjamin

We have to live now amidst and with the crass defeat of freedom and disalienation, as socialism and communism have suffered an epochal, though not necessarily irreversible, death: it follows, to upgrade Dostoevsky, that if God and Communism are dead, everything is permitted. All matters of life and death, so runs the capitalist dogma, are to be seen exclusively as a cost-and-loss investment. It is therefore high time to consider more fully the complex and sensitive matter of how life can (and necessarily must) live in feedback with denegation and death.

The specific possibilities of poetry – standing here for literature and art in general – create in all significant cases an impediment to thoughtless acceptance, to facile, superficial or brainwashed believing common in the age of capitalist massification and media saturation. Poetry creates a focus on what is being ostended by an array of means, of which I shall single out the spatial and temporal *interruption and pause*, which allows the user (viewer, reader, listener) time to stop and attention to consider afresh an unclichétised and possibly outrageous assertion, position, view or term: finally, to access a radically new view and horizon. The horizon of this device, ubiquitous in poetry, is diametrically opposed to the doctrinal bias of monotheist religions and status quo certainties. That is, instead of blaming negativity – denial, critique – as both the Judeo-Christian tradition and (alas) also most 2nd and 3d International stances did, the interruption and pause is here dialectically welcomed as being in this corrupt age epistemologically indispensable in view of a better positivity of understanding and valuing. The understanding arrived at is in two ways better than the prior unexamined assent: in yield, by arriving at a cognitive increment, and in method, by being arrived at through the user's own effort which leads to an intimate and informed consent. Furthermore, for Marx dialectics is quintessentially critical and revolutionary:

> Dialectics is a scandal and abomination to bourgeoisdom and its doctrinaire spokesmen because it includes into the positive understanding of the existing state of things at the same time also the understanding of the negation of that state, of its necessary decline; because it regards every form that came about as in fluid movement, thus also in its transient aspect; because it allows nothing to bamboozle it, and is in its essence critical and revolutionary. (Afterword to the second edition of *Das Kapital* in 1873, 28)

This was also encapsulated by Lenin in his notes on Hegel:

> What distinguishes the dialectical from the undialectical transition? The leap. The contradiction. The interruption of gradualness.The unity (identity) of being and non-being. (*Philosophical* 282)

To engage in critical cognition about events, experiences, and items (or whole areas) of our imaginary "encyclopedia" means to think dialectically: first by identifying a privileged "flow of things," as Brecht called it in his poem "Truth Unites" – rather than jumping into the flow of falsely harmonising art – and second by interrupting that flow to consider it. The offending stumbling block refocussing perception (discussed at length in my "Parables") can, if used well, lead toward and articulate a self-made, thiswordly and autochthonous, salvation. Such denial works by means of a sublating radical novum (see Suvin, chapters 3 and 8 of *Defined*, and "Blagoevgrad").

The term of salvation arises from daily material life but it has been hijacked by religions and theologies of all possible stripes. However, the absolutely necessary salvation can be reclaimed following leads from Benjamin and (better digested) from Brecht. This can be seen as melding the following factors:

- First, the reason for reworking the religious and theological tradition of salvation is to be able to use and master both a "lay illumination" (Benjamin, GS II.1: 297) and the "destructive forces" it may awaken (GS I.3: 1246). This estrangement of Marxism by way of theological semantics is especially useful in the period of Stalinist, and then any other, dogmatic rigidity.
- Second, an equally absolute and imperturbable claim as in religion is being laid upon the addressee's orientation, especially akin to Benjamin's "messianic" horizon as a radical refusal of existing relations.
- Third, all such aspects are refunctioned and transferred into a "lay," that is, open and experimental thinking in close alliance with cognitive and revolutionary horizons.

2. On Brecht, the Estrangement Effect, and Disalienation

Da bleiben, wie immer so auch heut
Der steinige boden und die armen leut.
(Today, as always, there remain
The poor people and the stony plain.)

Brecht

2.1. A Disalienating Syntax

Brecht's aim was to make poetry as potent on the cognitive and affective levels as it was on the sensory, thus able to participate both in intimate introspection and public or civic struggles (cf. Suvin, "Brecht" and "Emotion"). I shall here, leaning on his still best commentator Benjamin, discuss Brecht's central and shaping stance of estrangement. This cannot pretend to exhaustiveness but only to exemplarity.

With the leading modernist artists, in the age of technological and existential leaps such as Fordism and of massified world wars and revolutions, Brecht shared most intimately the insight that it is absolutely necessary to cognise new matters (*nova*) also in a new way (*nove*). If by new matters are meant the new ways of people living together in mass cities and subject to capitalist organisation of life by power and technology into an age of mass world slaughters and lesions (see Suvin "Words"), an evaluation depends on what we see them as: the continuation of old servitude by new means (the better the worse) or a way of disalienation from servitude to personal and collective freedom (the better the better, disjoined from the worse). Brecht was not alone in this stance, though possibly one of its most self-aware and all-around practitioners. Weighty and eminent instances for a kindred approach can be found in many "intervening" critics, such as Jean-Paul Sartre, Ernst Bloch, Walter Benjamin, Lucien Goldmann, Raymond Williams, Edward Said, and Fredric Jameson. As an example, Said's category of "worldliness," materialist both in the anti-clerical sense and the pragmatic sense of being in, and having public consequences in, our common world, clearly implies both overtly macro-political criteria such as a refusal of "Orientalism" and permanent self-questioning of one's own stances and insights (it is brought to a head in his *World* 26, 35, and passim).

For Benjamin, this means a twofold yet consubstantial cognitive and epistemological turn in understanding or cognition. As a stance (*Haltung*), it is an estranging one in order to see the present as historical – that is, to advance with Nietzsche from an antiquarian (or indeed simply conformist) to an intervening view of history, here seen as deeply political. However, it is also a style or way of artful writing which I would call the *emancipatory intervention* in which criticism and creativity meld. It confirms the perennial engagement of poetry (art) with spacetimes and ways of human existing beyond the reader's own – which makes not only for potentially liberatory perception, as the Formalists claimed, but also embodies a way of thinking and feeling deeply incompatible with any crypto-theological, alienating ideology, say of nationalist or other dogmatic stripe (mystique of the market, anyone?). Yet it adds into the potent brew of its poetic *carmina* (*charmes*, said Valéry) the politics of intervention rendered indispensable and urgent when faced with mass world slaughters; this is intimately interwoven with making sense of a person's or a collective's life within a poetic justice of obviating and nullifying defeat and death: *carmina morte carent*, even after personal physical death *parsque mei magna superstes erit* (poems know of no death ... a major part of me shall survive – Ovid, *Amores*).

Brecht's theatre and dramaturgy distrusts the implicit and dominant ideological encyclopedia, the "it goes without saying" (*Selbstverständlichkeiten)* that guarantee a flowing coherence: you cannot step into the same river twice, for neither it nor you will be the same. Thus Brecht's "flow" is frequently interrupted by many means – an immediately obvious but not always most important example would be the songs interpolated in his plays. The flow proceeds discontinuously, it is composed of short segments as clear shapes with "a definable beginning and a definable end," each of which is framed for more or less emphatic ostension to the audience. Its main interest is "to represent conditions" of people's lives together, rather than to develop a closed-off plot for its own sake (see Benjamin, GS II.2: 521-22, also 534-35). This is in Aristotle's terms a stringing together of events each of which is an episode, with the paradoxical result that there are no special segments that could be called episodes. In grammatical terms, it is a paratactic text, "one damn thing after another," without subsumption under a final catharctic goal, tragic or comic. As emotional stance, *empathy* into uplifting success or tragic failure for the protagonists – where Benjamin's test case, most pertinent today too, is how should the audience relate to Nazi murderers on the stage (ibidem 538) – is replaced by dosages of *critical sympathy*, so that a low dose means antipathy.[1]

This also means there is in Brecht's plays no *suspense* as to whether and how any goal will be reached, but instead an underlying convergence towards increased clarification as to the nature and causes of the conditions uncovered and seen afresh while considering a goal. To the suspense of illusionistic bourgeois theatre, cliffhanger novels and then media, this opposes *astonishment* at many ensuing events and the human condition they delineate. The astonished seeing afresh or anew, seeing something not up to now suspected, is by Brecht called *Verfremdung*, estrangement, a term that appropriates and translates Shklovsky's *ostranenie* with the new axiological function of making the situation(s) shown appear not only offensively inhuman and intolerable but also made by people under certain conditions and, under different conditions, changeable by them. This is tantamount to a transplanting of the experimental tradition of post-Renaissance science, exemplified in how Brecht's (and history's) Galileo used the pendulum and the telescope. Benjamin reads astonishment as an instance of dialectics at a standstill: "The damming of the stream of real life, the moment when its flow comes to a standstill, makes itself felt as reflux: this reflux is astonishment.... [This inconstant] stream of things breaks against the rock of astonishment [from which the gaze descends into it]..." (GS II.2: 531). Certainly, astonishment is correlative to a certain – to my mind variable – cognitive distance between the presentation and the audience, which Benjamin shrewdly attributes both to the "wholesale devastations of our societal order" and to their growing impact in "undermin[ing] ourselves and our capacity to remain aware of them" (ibidem 522-23). Astonishment was, of course, a central epistemological stance of philosophy since Plato's Socrates and Gautama the Enlightened; it is also a central device as well as stance of much – in particular of modern – verse poetry. Furthermore, it is born out of interest and fosters interest, as well as awareness of what interests are at stake here and why the reader's interests require his interest for the text: *tua res agitur,* it is your interests which are being delineated here.

Finally, such a dramaturgy has "a very different kind of alliance with the passing of time" than the illusionistic one of capitalist realism. Just as Shakespeare or the Mystery Plays, it "can span very extensive periods of time" (ibidem 532-33), and I would add also shift rapidly through as many imaginary spaces as necessary. The Brechtian dramaturgy's grand sweep differs from the medieval Christian Mysteries centrally by being directed toward a different imaginary onlooker: not God, for whom all unfamiliar events are familiar because He sees their unchanging essence, but a prefigured Man or Humanity of a blessed classless future, to whom all familiar events are unfamiliar because they contain unrealised potentialities amid savagely exasperated contradictions (Benjamin's great insight that "there is no document of civilisation that is not equally a document of barbarism," GS I.2: 696).

This Brechtian making matters appear strange (*Verfremdungs-Effekt*) is thus a close kin to the overtly political forms of utopian estrangement, from Thomas More onwards. Both the traveller in utopia and later – say in Ursula Le Guin's *The Dispossessed* – the traveller from utopia into a normal (capitalist) locus estrange what they see by their amazed eye. Such estrangement decisively deepened the Formalist perceptual insight by shaping an encompassing political epistemics, which reposes on a value judgment against a horizon of expanding cognition "that does not merely transmit knowledge but actually engenders it," and is eminently pleasurable, as art is:

> The simple fact that people can be recognised in a certain way creates a sense of triumph, and the fact, too, that they cannot be recognised completely, once and for all, that they are not easily exhaustible, that they contain and conceal so many possibilities in themselves (hence their capacity for development), is a pleasurable cognition. (Benjamin, GS II.2: 528 and 30-31).

If any trope is a living contradiction and impertinence where literal everyday meanings self-destruct (cf. Ricoeur 50-51), then estrangement can turn this powerful device against the norm itself of pertinence: it is not the figure but the ground that is impertinent, or indeed deadly.

2.2. Some Uses of Critical Estrangement: Poetic Justice

I have on several occasions (in chapters 3 and 13 of *Defined*, dealing with the novum and with dystopia) defined estrangement as a feedback oscillation that moves now from the author's and implied reader's norm of reality to the narrative Possible World in order to understand the plot-events, and now back from the narrative world to the author's reality or Possible World Zero, in order to see it afresh from the new perspective gained. It is a cognitive strategy of perception-cum-evaluation based on a radical swerve and desire. Its paratactic interruptions comport multiple possibilities of shape change as departure from salient ways of seeing the author's world, which has as its purpose the recognition that the reader's certainties are not certain but bound to strong value judgments and cognitive frameworks. A *shape* implies a project of intention and meaning in our lives, a *savoir vivre,* and in temporal terms a traffic between our existentially present values and long-duration ones from the remembered past or wished-for future. It is not simply an experience as singly lived, which is necessarily private, "but its sense, its meaning [that] becomes public," an experience brought to a given semiotic shape and point, for example in language (Ricoeur 16, and cf. 21). Disalienating projects in practical societal life and in poetry are always shapes of sensual meaning and oriented time, they strive for a formal or shapely use of life, centrally informed by *freedom with poetic justice*: Marx's slogan (of Biblical and utopian origin) "From each according to his capacities, to each according to her needs" is a sterling example of such justice, and so is his horizon of a realm of freedom beyond necessity of exploitation, strongly wedded to playfulness (see more on this in chapter 8).

Estrangement is, then, a boomerang returning to knock some sense into us, or a periscope and prism to help us see ourselves in a different light, as the stranger of strangers or Other of the others – and often at that as the powerful Other (say a male European or North American) against the powerless, humiliated, and exploited others (say the "extracommunitarians" of the immiserated South drowning off our shores, or inside our society together with the native women and proletarians). It effects in its own way a return of the repressed. It formalises and heightens the dialectics of productive distanciation and appropriation present in any reading or viewing of an artefact (cf. Ricoeur 43) by making the work's critical distance from a given situation into the user's own stance suffused by sympathetic emotion. The Brechtian or critical method, that "[proceeds] by fits and starts, similar to the images on a film strip," has more than a little similarity to what Eisenstein called a montage of attractions, and in general to silent movie methods, such as Chaplin's:

> As a result, intervals occur which tend to destroy illusion. These intervals paralyse the audience's readiness to empathise. Their purpose is to enable the spectator to adopt a critical attitude (towards the represented behaviour of the play's characters and towards the way in which this behaviour is represented). (Benjamin, GS II.2: 537-38).

Anthropologically speaking, the practitioner of critical estrangement is thus in the company of poets or philosophers and an ally – in however roundabout ways – of the ruled and exploited classes, she aims at cognition wherever it may take us, as long as it participates in finding out a radical novum in people's sociohistorical relationships. This estrangement is clearly akin to Marx's stance and genre of *critique*, to the utopian slogan "things could be not so but radically different," as well as to the shocking recognition of beauty as a kind of estrangement-effect alerting us to aliveness: "one's daily unmindfulness of the aliveness of others is temporarily interrupted in the presence of a beautiful person, alerting us to the requirements placed on us by the aliveness of all persons, and the same may take place in the presence of a beautiful bird, mammal, fish, plant" (Scarry 90).[2]

However: while to see what obtains opens a possibility for felicific change, we have learned bitterly that it by no means guarantees such change without shrewd and relentless politics. An instance of estrangement leading to death is findable in Brecht's most embattled, and today possibly most pertinent, large play *Saint Joan of the Slaughterhouses (Die Heilige Johanna der Schlachthöfe)*, which translates the Jeanne d'Arc legend from nationalist salvation into a (failed) salvation of the working class in the slaughterhouses of "cold Chicago" – itself a most apt metonymy for our historical spacetime (I have therefore analysed it at some length in "Salvation"). What is here taken over from the Judeo-Christian tradition is the implied background of spiritual blindness, the need to see a new truth with new eyes. Such blindness is a long-duration poetical theme, that runs in theatre from Oedipus through Lear to Brecht's Galileo (cf. Suvin "Heavenly"): a lack of (in)sight that thematises and thus articulates the estrangement stance. In Brecht's play from the depths of the post-1929 Great Depression this is translated into the class conflicts in the streets outside the slaughterhouses and on the stock-market. In between the huge class arrays, the eponymous heroine is a naïve girl pleading for general understanding, an amalgam of old-style humanism with contemporary "Left" Christians as well as with anti-revolutionary social-democracy of the post-1917 kind (its first literary version might be Mayakovsky's Compromiser in *Mystery Bouffe).* Joan Dark's failure is thus seen not as tragic in the predestined and/or compensatory catharctic sense but, on the contrary, as a result of her deficient understanding and ideological illusions. In the midst of the workers' bitter lockout-cum-strike, a key messenger fails to appear, and a "voice" heard by Joan – in a way divine or salvational, as in the voices of Jeanne d'Arc or in the apodictic certainties of Isaiah and Paul of Tarsus – comments: "the stone does not excuse the fallen" ("Den Gestürzten/ Entschuldigt der Stein nicht," BFA 3:204). So much the worse for the one who falls: in the original also rhythmically stumbling on the line break.

The transcendental voice is a prefiguration of Joan's inexcusable and irredeemable defeat and death (cf. Suvin, "Salvation" 137) that leave out in the cold the hungry masses of the workers and the poor. It is also a realistic prognosis for a possible outcome of Leninist class struggle: in the circumstances of cold Chicago or Berlin, it might well stumble and fail – through a disbelief in one's own forces shared by Joan and most workers. Throughout Brecht's work, from *Baal and Drums in the Night* to *Life of Galileo* and *Mother Courage*, he focussed on a failed emancipatory revolution, opting for a creative and embattled pessimism. And in the disillusioned late poem "Truth Unites" (*Die Wahrheit einigt*) he referred to Lenin's exemplary stance: "Tomorrow evening/ We are lost, if not..." (BFA 15: 315).

A further shining example is Brecht's twosome of plays *He Who Says Yes and He Who Says No (Der Jasager/ Der Neinsager*), which investigates how – and indeed whether (there is no guarantee of "progress") – humanity may save itself from the pervasive threat of Death by recognizing or "consenting to" the power-demands of the situation. The two playlets negotiate the conditions for a correct stance in this dangerous world, but the key factor is that the threatened protagonist, the boy climbing the mountain, takes his destiny into his own hands. Insofar as death is a socio-political construction, Brecht asks: In whose hands is the control over death? He resolutely opts for people's salvation by their own efforts: the parable-nature of his "plays for learning" makes of its central agent(s) an example for everybody (see more in Suvin "Use-Value"). This was also stressed in Brecht's insistence that the performers should play all roles in turn. Everyman as a Luxemburgian spontaneous and self-empowered revolutionary, or each person (and in particular, each child-player) as the community's distributive light-bringer, is the Brechtian theatre laboratory's immodest horizon.

3. On Death and Creative Eros as Politics

> Anticipate your final hour.
>
> Marcus Aurelius

3.1. On the Difficulty of Dying Well in Capitalism

Yet: the final stumble in a person's life is unfortunately not in function of dialectical or any other cognition (except possibly for others) but of annihilation. The same holds for the death of small or large communities, for example many sociopolitical movements and historical empires or States. This underlines or bares the fact, evident for any materialist, that

> nature … – if you wish, the physical and then the biological level – is prior to the economico-social and cultural level. This priority is both chronological … and found in the conditioning that nature still exercises upon humans…. Thus, cognitively, a materialist … cannot deny or evade the element of passivity in experience: the external situation, not posed by us but imposed upon us. (Timpanaro 7-8).

Personal death is a matter of biological entropy that cannot be prevented by cognition; community death could be prevented but the salvational cognition is hindered by structural class factors. Indeed, in better times death might be well-earned oblivion, leading to the peace of Nirvana. However, we have to focus on suggesting how any enlightenment forthcoming from estrangement and analogous disalienating strategies might be used here and now, amid the simooms of turbocapitalist reality.

Centrally, the hugely productive capitalist civilization produces destructive novums, the "undermining of the springs of all wealth: the earth and the worker" by practicing "systematic robbery of the preconditions for life..., of space, air, light..." (*Kapital* 449-50), and today we could add of water, silence, health in general, etc. – in brief, of life and the pursuit of happiness. As Benjamin memorably explained once and for all, death is the final horizon for a civilization of gambling, excitement, fashionable novelty – and of course of worldwide unceasing wars. It is also the end-horizon of raping the planet by economic exploitation, and ecocide. As Lefebvre then pointed out, in the 18th Century the Robinson Crusoe-like individual powerfully reshapes his world, but in the middle of the 20th Century, the allegorical individual is defined by death, it is "that what dies, goes toward its death, dies alone as he has lived, and consciously accepts his own death" (224). This is not the easeful death each of us has a right to: it is the collective death of humanity.

Does capitalism's main historical rival, communism, fare better? This depends on what one means by the term and notion of "communism." As I argue in the "15 Theses" chapter, following early Marx one can postulate a polarity between Communism_1 (C1) and Communism_2 (C2). C1 is Marx's original emancipatory communism and the plebeian emancipatory communism from which both Marx and the communist revolutions arose. C2 is the official State communism, as it crystallised fully in the 20th-Century Leninist revolutions usually 10 or 15 years after coming to power, thus in the USSR or Yugoslavia, but in China almost 30 years later. C2, sometimes also called "really existing socialism," met its death in or about 1989 (ideologically much earlier). C1 – communism as poetic justice, disalienation of dehumanised humanity or liberation of labour – is today back on the drawing table, and its revival is postulated by a wide discussion on the Left (see for example the titles in note 7 of "What and How"). I suggest that estrangement is correlative to Brecht's understanding of communism (C1) as the "middle thing." Benjamin approvingly quotes him: 'Communism is not radical. It is capitalism that is radical." (GS II.2: 511) Or, as the subtitle of the great English communist utopia *News from Nowhere* by William Morris has it: communism would be an "Epoch of Rest" for martyrised mankind, licking – no doubt very actively – its deep and toxic capitalist wounds.

However, it remains to be seen and articulated just how these fine ideas and noble ideals can be used. Today, this is twinned with the question: how do we face *death of the body and rout of the idea*? The terms in these two last expressions have a deep inner kinship and can be permutated – we could just as well say rout of the body and death of the idea.

Alas, death has been a blind spot in canonic Marxism – even though human mortality and renewal is central to the analysis of social reproduction in *Das Kapital,* and Marx obsessively used the image of undead vampires sucking blood like capitalists sucking living labour (cf. Suvin "Transubstantiation," and now the more comprehensive Neocleous 39-55). However Marx often had, say in *18th Brumaire*, a triumphalist strain, highlighting rabbi Jehoshua's "let the dead bury their dead" and approving the "world-historical necromancy" that resurrects revolution. The absence of explicit discussion of death extends from Marx to Lenin and beyond (I can recall only a marginal mention of the entropic death of the Sun in Engels's disquisitions about natural history). Surely Marx knew well the *Phenomenology of the Spirit*, in the Introduction of which Hegel has a strange, impassioned paean both to the "absolute power of reason" and to its being founded on "the monstrous power of the Negative – the energy of thought. Death, if we wish to name thus that unreality, is the most awful matter (*das Furchbarste*), and to hold death tight requires the greatest strength.... [But only] that life which supports death and is preserved in it, is the life of the Spirit." Life, or the Subject, has no power "as the positive that looks away from the negative..., but only when it looks into the face of the Negative, tarries with it" (all 29-30).

And in the famous discussion of Master vs. Servant, where Death is "the absolute Master" of both (148), self-consciousness is proven (*bewährt*) only by death, as the precondition of "that negation of consciousness that *cancels* by *conserving and carrying on* what is being cancelled *(aufhebt das Aufgehobene)*, and thus survives its being cancelled" (145). Civil life is always shadowed by this absolute master and conditioned by it (324); the consciousness of death differentiates this *Sittlichkeit* from the nature and animals. In sum, death is for Hegel either abstract negativity or the precondition for dialectical fulfilment; in the latter guise, it is also the precondition of any beauty that would not be etiolated (*kraftlos*, 29 – Scarry in 2.2. converges with this). Clearly, it was Marx's choice not to pursue overtly this strand, though his writing is informed by it.

Naturally, in the storm and stress of fierce repression or armed fighting, where death was omnipresent, Marxism as the theory of the revolutionary movement had to stoically accept it as totally negative and downplay it. Obversely, an immortality of emancipation fighters in the historical memory of their followers was a commonplace, as in all martyrologies. To stick to the depth testimony of poetry, Mayakovsky's long poem on the death of Lenin, "Vladimir Ilyich Lenin" (recited in socialist countries, in suitably expurgated versions, almost every April at its anniversary and frequently at other times too) culminates in "Lenin lived – Lenin is alive – Lenin is to live forever," and is rife with images of dead Commune fighters reviving. But besides such uplifting but often (even in Mayakovsky) turgid and crypto-religious notions, there was little depth articulation about the dialectics of life and death in the whole socialist and communist epistemic tradition. True: in a way Lenin is immortal through his consequences, just as Ovid is through his poetry; but so is (say) Hitler, Gengis Khan or Giordano Bruno burned for proclaiming an infinity of worlds. How are their immortalities different? What are the durations of such immortalities – surely not eternal but simply Braudel's "long duration," that is some centuries or millennia (itself not an indifferent alternative)? And so on. Many elements in this, shall I call it, *resurrectionary* syndrome lead one to recall Marx's quip on the false resurrection of Bonapartism: "first as a tragedy, then as a farce."

For thousands of years, Churches have always used death as the supreme transcendental stick to inculcate fear and submission into its sheep: in this endeavour they never stumbled. Lately, medicine as business has reduced it to a matter of value-free (but not at all monetarily free!) technology and quantity. We see today that capitalism in its own sick way also invokes and monetarises death in our omnipresent shoddy glut of ghoulish zombies and assorted vampires or lycanthropes in mystified and mystifying mass media, in the fake apocalyptics masking the real danger. The final horizon of capitalism run mad is the Nazi cult of death, of which Heidegger participated (cf. Neocleous 91-99).

3.2. Steps towards a Dialectic of Dying

From the foregoing, it may be understandable but it is astonishing that the mass radical alternatives to capitalism seem not to have delved into the concept of death. Still, the influence of Marxism can be seen in some pioneers such as Edgar Morin, who identifies in this peculiar concept and stance, simultaneously most biological and most acculturated – that differentiates Homo sapiens from all other animals and is strictly intertwined with human self-consciousness – two great narrations: survival and rebirth. And it then emerges more strongly in 20th-Century Marxists such as Jameson, Bloch, and Brecht.[3]

In particular, I find four stepping stones to serious discussion. One would be a retraversing of the works of Brecht (as in the argument about his rich playlets *He Who Says Yes/ No,* and cf. the rich phenomenology in *Brecht and Death*), including some astounding notes, say the one in his *Buch der Wendungen (Book of Twists and Turns)*:

> And I saw that nothing at all was quite dead, not even what had died (*das Gestorbene*). The dead stones breathe. They change and give rise to changes. Even the supposedly dead Moon moves. It shines onto Earth, even if with light from strangers, and determines the trajectory of falling bodies and causes high and low tide for sea water.... [Thus] we have to treat it as a dead undeadness (*ein totes nichttotes*), yet more like dead, in some respects as what has died, in this respect totally and irrevocably dead, but not in every respect. (BFA 16: 73-74)

The other three (or more) are in Jameson: in his comments on Bloch (*Marxism* 143-44), in his pairing of mortality and exclusion from history in *Political*

Unconscious (see below), and his essay on the great Andrei Platonov, "Utopia, Modernism, and Death," that most suggestively ends in Kafka's "Josephine the Songstress" story – since both Platonov and Kafka deny individual progress in time. I can here only discuss the passage on the "essential relationship" between utopia and death. Making perhaps my own riff on Jameson's air, I'd say utopia and death are akin as *enemy brothers* (*frères enemies*) because they share "the point of view of the species upon human history" that denies individuality and personality. When these are jettisoned, what remains is "our species being, our insertion in the great chain of the generations, which we know as death." However, for intellectuals – and one would hope not only for them – personal death is if not easy then much easier to bear if there is a believable hope for such a linked humanity going on and even advancing. Where death *per se* affirms nothingness, utopia affirms fullness on the collective level. This is foregrounded in the best philosophical SF, that of Olaf Stapledon, whose "[utopian] serenity gazes calmly and implacably away from the accidents of individual existence and the inevitability of its giving way" (all in *Seeds* 122-23). Even so, his work progresses from the evolution of the homo *genus* to that of the star *genus*, high above and far away.

It follows that the whole semantic thesaurus of contraries and contradictories to "normal life," together with the third dimension of their temporal vectors (for example Bloch's "not-yet-living," *Prinzip* 1390), should be reopened for consideration. For example: is communism in a state of abortion – hibernation – paralysis – lethargy – or what? Or is it dead like a (possibly as in Brecht not quite dead) stone? Alternatively, should we take a leaf from the animal or vegetable life and explore transformations such as from larva to butterfly? Transformation means literally a changing of form or shape *(metamorphosis)*, and is thus squarely within the tradition of pausing to affirm a form.

I shall mention just a few indications that might help in such a consideration. First, in semantic history the connotations – perhaps even some core elements – of death have changed in our age of mass technologised slaughters in wars, concentration camps, and liquidation of no longer necessary labourers by starvation and bombs, from Verdun through Auschwitz, Kolyma, Hiroshima, and Abu Ghraib to the present destruction of West Asia. In brief, death is to a large degree *historical and social*; while always participating in biology, death has with capitalism and the huge rise of productive forces grown increasingly, and crucially, *political*, caused by *violence*. Second, literature and the arts are full of representations of death, from the innumerable *pietà*s to the particularly pertinent opuses of some writers and poets, and my very cursory glance at Mayakovsky already shows that much is to be learned from them. It is also frequently concerned with a lay transcendence of death – the theme of *non omnis moriar* (not all of me shall die) referring to posthumous fame through works is older than this formulation by Horace and then of Ovid. Third, I would posit with Fortini "that the degree of a society's health can be measured also by the institutional modes in which it frames its own negation… the cemetery, the madhouse, the hospital, and the prison…" (1316). Fourth, any use-value to be found in death can only arise from understanding what it interrupts – the modes and qualities of life it seemingly puts an end to and certainly quite radically redefines – and what that means not only for bodies personal but also for the body politic and all its classes and collectives.

I argued in "Death" that only use values can stand up to capitalist unequal exchange, rightly called vampiric by Marx; this holds in spades for the present "neo-liberal" economy, predominantly reposing on – and sucking up – "brain labour." Ancient designations for these use values were compassion, indignation, and love: that is, today, communism and poetry. We need to realise that there is no (good and durable) poetry without communism, and no (good and durable) communism without poetry. Poetry and communism allow no a priori rules, only a poetics of looking backward and forward, lessons from experience. They are projects – which translates into Greek as problems. All poets know this, often in fantastic metamorphoses; few communists have allowed their suspicion to flower. When sundered, what we get are caricatures which degrade the potential horizon of either. Both poetry and communism choose the passage from the capitalist point-like time, extending maximally to this year's profits, to a long duration of solidarity, where, as Fortini cites Merleau-Ponty, "disorder would be less fatal, and death less senseless" (1458). In particular, poetry's horizon is both political and also as it were cosmological, for it deals with human resistance to death by means of a systematic project, a self-education of which all artworks are exemplars (ibidem 1454-60).

Thus, what might be antidotes to defeat and death? Almost all of Brecht's protagonists meet this fate, the weightiest exception being *The Caucasian Chalk Circle*, at the exhilarating moment of anti-fascist victory, that embodies also his most sophisticated proposal for plebeian continuation of life in the story of Grushe and the Child (cf. the chapter on it in Suvin *To Brecht*). How are we to avoid the tragic closure with its swerve, as near as no matter, into religion? Brecht's answer is that what matters is that the audience or reader learn from the negative by contraries. The fictive staging of death (cf. Oberstar) – in his earlier plays often a clownish play to avoid real death – is a kind of antidote or *pharmakon*. Nonetheless, the weighty fact remains that the final negation in a single person's life is in function of death. As in my perhaps favourite poem, Andrew Marvell's *To His Coy Mistress*:

> The grave's a fine and private place,
> But none, I think, do there embrace.

Brecht remarked in 1930 that the use-value of dying is surprisingly small (GKA 3: 26). But the question pursued him: this period of his most intense involvement with the "plays for learning" and with politics coincided, significantly, with an intense interest in what stance (*Haltung*) to take when faced with dying. His great chain of plays – that begins with *Baal* and *In the Jungle of Cities,* gathers steam in the "plays for learning" that culminate in *The Measures Taken*, and finds strong echoes in his later large-size plays, notably the World War parable *Mother Courage and Her Children* – is a prolonged and evolving meditation on death with few rivals in fiction since Donne and Tolstoy. An important confirmation may be another laconic fragment of Brecht's which explains the nucleus of his *Baden Learning Play* as "The question is posed who can die – nobody – from this follows: needed, the transformation of all things..." (ibidem). The paradox of this note – the overriding need to die properly or well – suggests a more complex answer than Brecht's initial quick shrugging off. It could be illuminated by Hertz's long discussion how, for example in the Maori culture, death is not only the destruction of one person but also of "the social being grafted upon the physical individual...: his destruction is tantamount to a sacrilege." The consubstantiality of all community members – clearer in the smaller and tighter groups Hertz examined – makes of death a strong threat to the immortal continuity of the whole society:

> [that its members should be fated to die] is always received with the same indignant amazement and despair.... [W]hen a man dies, society loses in him [sic] much more than a unit; it is stricken in the very principle of life, in the faith it has in itself.... [Therefore,] collective consciousness... refuses to consider death irrevocable.... The last word must remain with life: the deceased will rise from the grip of death and will return, in one form or another, to the peace of human association. (77-78)

At that point, "the thematics of death and the rhetoric of mortality", while not ceasing to refer directly to individuals, bear also the additional heavy burden of analogy "for the sharper pain of exclusion by history" (Jameson, *Political* 238, and cf. 261).

Outside the flight into religion, humanity meets what Bloch fulgurantly called "the toughest anti-utopia of death" ("Something's" 9) in two ways. First, with the radical utopia of immortality, and second, dialectically, by saying not only No but also Yes to carefully chosen instances of it.

Immortality may be achieved through "divine procreation" of children (Plato, *Symposium* 206d and cf. all of 205-09), of art/artefacts or of communal deeds (as those of Lycurgus and Solon, or of Le Guin's deified liberation leader in *The Word for World Is Forest*). Communal deeds, or generally participation in a greater Whole, was Brecht's central strategy; not forgetting Marx's great insight that there is no emancipated One without All and viceversa. The propertarians fear death because "they always have to try hard and hold onto what they have" (GKA 18: 80). To the contrary, in the poem "Resolution" published by the Spanish International brigades and later inserted into *The Days of the Commune* play, Brecht's rebelling characters decide "to fear a bad life/ more than death" (GKA 12: 27).

In more crowded and alienated times, the argument of much art and practical hedonism is – for example in the Marvell poem, as foregrounded in its "Time's wingèd chariot hurrying near" – to seize and overcome chronological and biological time by intensity of personal feeling and perception (rather than by overarching historiosophic schemes meant for the body politic). Traditionally, a privileged path to such denial, and indeed carnal redemption, of time's flow or flight is erotics (to my mind, the best among the Freudian topologies is the one that pits Eros against Thanatos). "Now therefore," Marvell's poem ends:

> Let us roll all our strength and all
> Our sweetness up into one ball,
> And tear our pleasures with rough strife
> Through the iron gates of life:
> Thus, though we cannot make our sun
> Stand still, yet we will make him run.

The Sun running cannot mean time passing too fast for the lovers, but on the contrary time being crammed full of their rough and sweet amorous experiences. It should be remembered this includes the "little death" of orgasm, pitting it as a homeopathic remedy against one's final big death because it is not only a supreme pleasure but also obviously non-final as well as procreating life. Almost two centuries later, the young Percy Shelley in his Oxford lab will remember this materialist underground current of an immortality achieved by cramming every moment full with events and feelings.

Thus, Brecht's "crude thinking" position in the early dismissive note was quite right in its opposition to pseudo-mystical and fakely communal glorification of Death by the Nazis and various other mass necrophilic movements of overripe capitalism, growing out of the repression of death – a repression that Benjamin saw as a principal object of bourgeois society, which yet unceasingly multiplied death. However, a legitimate use-value for death in this our age may be to agree with carefully chosen instances of it. Death may confer, and indeed force upon the subject threatened with it, the faculty of personal choice enabling that person to die well, with the right consenting (cf. today's raging euthanasia debates). The subject may (should) acquire the ability *to consciously choose when and whether to consent to die, and for which cause* – or Cause. Dying well, the classical *ars bene moriendi,* when refunctioned into dying as part of a proper community build-up of meaningful practice, is in wholly indispensable feedback with living meaningfully, the *ars bene vivendi*: indeed, Brecht's and Marx's great ancestor, Epicure, said it was the same art.

Finally however, since immortality is prevented by entropy and erotics shadowed by alienation, couldn't we envisage solidarity and friendliness as supreme virtues and ways to happiness? But then, how are they to function unless the world attains, through emancipatory politics, communist poetical justice?

Works Cited

See in *Works Cited in this Book* the following titles, by Author surname plus (when the author has several titles) first "headword" or identifying syntagm in the title:

Barthes; Benjamin; Bloch, *Das Prinzip, The Spirit;* Bloch & Adorno; Boer; Bourguière; Brecht; *Brecht and Death;* Fortini, *Saggi;* Hegel, *Phänomenologie;* Hertz; Jameson, *Marxism, The Seeds;* Lefebvre, *Somme*; Lenin; Marx, *Das Kapital* 1; Morin; Nancy; Neocleous; Oberstar; Plato; Ricoeur, *Interpretation*; Said; Scarry, *On Beauty;* Suvin, "Brecht," *To Brecht,* "On Cognition," "Death," *Defined*, „Emotion," "Heavenly," "Parables," "Salvation," "Transubstantiation," "Use-Value," "Utopianism"; Timpanaro; Ure & Frost eds.

POEMS 10

PILLAGING THE GNOSTICS

Et in hora mortis nostrae

See, i talk so that i may leave
I tell you what i heard & saw
In the leaves of grass in the drawn sweaty faces,
I teach you as i slowly learned it
I talk that i may leave this world
Where i never had enuf time
        In peace.

I lived on Earth a short time, i didn't have time.
A short span of time. Pay attention
So you can hear me. If i came, who
May i be, may i have been, may
I have become? I drank the water of life
The water of pleasure. Now i advance toward
        The water of forgetfulness.

Greetings to you, my sister & my brother!
Do not be so deathly afraid of sweet-gifting Venus,
Mother & lover, not yet known! I lived on Earth
A short time, i praised it, i suffered it.
I learned a little, i taught a little, a multitude
Of sisters, of companions, only
        A few knew me,

I knew only a few, only little. I tell you
Detoxify yourself! Renounce your deadly path,
Walk on the Way which leads you to be free.
No Yahweh no kings to dominate, no masters
Except the Masters who know, so far as they know.
You are self-condemned, self-enchained. Renounce
        Your chains.

You made for yourself a heavenly Lord & leader.
He turned around & enslaved you, shut
Your eyes & ears, raised up an inbred caste
Inimical to Justice & Knowledge, to Venus Of All People.
You turned to derision this house given unto you
As a heredity & a promise, it will be
Pulled down.

Only knowledge can unfold liberty, an
Undying desire. Let this tree grow, so you may grasp
The fruits of freedom. All of us possess
A chip of knowledge, a teardrop of liberty
Within ourselves. Do not let this pearl
Drop into the viscous flow of arrested
Time. Wake up

From the drugged dream of reason. Who
Are you? Whose brother & sister are you?
Where are you going? Do you judge all matters
In order to be judged? O the anxiety of not reaching,
Of reaching & not grasping! Do you see
High Venus, star moving across resplendent skies?
I tell you truly:

This is the hour of our death
This is the cosmic hour of persecution
This the hidden hour of our ignoble oblivion.
You can live toward a good death or a bad death.
Life is when two sexes are in each other as light
Liberty, as amity. Thus we become citizens of
Fair Earth, Heaven.

5-7307

Glossary: Et in hora mortis nostrae = and in the hour of our death

C. Kavafis: ANTHONY ABANDONED BY THE GODS
(Apoleipein ho theos Antonion)

Suddenly, at the hour of midnight, when the sound
Of a merry company of revellers, unseen,
Is heard, with exulting music, with voices —
On Fortune that is leaving you, on your enterprises
That failed, on your life's projects
Which turned illusory, do not expend regrets!
As one prepared in time, staunch of heart,
Salute her, your Alexandria that is leaving.
Do not indulge in illusions, above all do not say
This was a dream, your ears misled you,
Do not lower yourself to such vain hopes.
As one prepared in time, staunch of heart,
One worthy of having had such a city,
Walk with steady steps to the window,
And deeply touched, but not as coward
Giving in to laments or supplications,
Allow yourself this final pleasure, listen
To the exulting harmony of the mystical company,
And salute her, the Alexandria you are losing.

(1911; transl. DRS 2005-07)

MY LADY HOPE

To the memory of Anne McLaren, 1948 onward

I dreamt of Lady Hope tonight
She smiled on me so sweetly,
Fair as in days of our keen youth
When she kissed me very sweetly.

"Where did you go, my Lady, my love,
What countries saw your features?
Your flaming gaze, your sunburnt hands,
Your reach to other futures?"

"I've always been here, young man of mine,
Here where the wise can see me,
You grew up & lost your keen eye
& the faint are not able to see me."

"We all must grow up, my Lady, my love,
How can I again see you?"
"Remember how knowledge led you to love,
Hold fast to that, & you'll see me."

"But you're no longer a girl, my love,
Rosy as dawn & eyes shining."
"We all grow up, old man of mine,
I'm a woman now, eyes shining."

4510

Endnotes

Notes to the Introduction

* In this book I usually, for brevity, call Yugoslavia after the communist revolution SFRY, though at the beginning it was called Democratic Federative Yugoslavia.

In spite of my reluctance at god-words, the material at hand forces me to use Party with capital P for discussions of communist parties' theory and the Yugoslav and USSR practice. I prefer "etatist" to "statist" for a belief in or devotion to the State, which I capitalise unless it means "condition, state of affairs." I use the lower case for utopia unless it indicates More's island and State. I use "-ise" and "-isation" instead of "-ize" and "-ization" but do not change "horizon," "citizen," "seize" or spelling inside citations. "Partizan" refers to fighters in the Yugoslav insurrection struggle against the fascists 1941-45. In the Works Cited I add a translation for titles in two Yugoslav languages. Unattributed translations are mine, also tacit corrections from extant translations into English where I had the original in Yugoslav languages.

1 Life is short and art is long. Mine is too short to engage in either polemics about how others understood poetry – for example Heidegger's egregious misuse of the same passage by Hölderlin I consider in "What and How" – or in acknowledgements of how much I learned from other critics of poetry. But I ought to mention that I have been stimulated by two French comrades who pioneered a reconsideration of communism and poetry, Jacques Rancière and Alain Badiou. For all my distance from Badiou's Platonising, his alloy of philosophy and politics, as in *L'Hypothèse communiste,* towers above many respectable and useful middle-range critics (among whom I might perhaps be counted).

2 The violence engendered by armed revolutions is a serious problem, even though it is a counter-violence to the daily and protracted mass killings caused first by the normal functioning of world capitalism and second by boundless counter-revolutionary violence. A welcome first approach to it is in Badiou's "Communist Idea," whose semantics – such as his overarching use of "terror" for all post-revolutionary State violence – I don't fully share.

The evolution of my views on this may be followed from "Terms of Power, Today" (2006) to a hard-won decision, in "Words and Lesions: Reflections on Violence" (2018), of allowing for a revolutionary horizon of self-defense as counter-violence against the State, when this proves indispensable for the survival of humanity. I had to overcome strong personal resistances against physical conflictuality, but my qualms, nurtured by Welfare State optimism in which I lived for 30 years, finally seemed ridiculous in view of ever more destructive and capillary violence as the global dominant in historical monopoly capitalism and imperialism since 1914 (see the essays "Capitalism" and "In the Shadows"), boomeranging back from the colonial fire and sword. Repressive violence as the dominant reality and atmosphere permeating all nooks of our lives – often open, as in warfare and fascism, but in richer countries more often hidden, as in dehumanising laws and regulations enforced by ruling financial and political bureaucracies – has revealed that the Welfare State was a blip on capitalist screen, enforced by fear of Leninist revolution.

3 My use is helped by the fact that where Marx says *Arbeiter*, this does not necessarily mean industrial worker but usually labourer or workman in general, cf. Fineschi 123.

4 I have approached this elsewhere, in works explicitly dealing with middle-range epistemology and its fallout, including considerations of science. They comprise among others "Two Cheers," "On the Horizons," "Death," "Epistemological," and "An Approach."

Notes to Chapter 1

* This essay was first presented as an abbreviated French lecture in Paris 1999 and amplified in Montreal in 2000; a few points were added up to 2002 for publication, and half a dozen references later too. However, no attempt has been made to rewrite it in view of the huge militarisation imposed on the world by the USA after Sept. 2001. This matter is briefly addressed in a P.S. at the end: it was written after the first text on terrorism in the following essay, but I leave it standing as a perhaps useful summary.

1 Whether there is war in pre-State (tribal) societies is a disputed question, depending on one's definition of war, which in turn depends largely on the researcher's ideology. Those who hold that war is biologically innate to Homo sapiens must find war in all human groups, but the evidence is against them – I tend to agree with Bourne that war and State are coterminous (16-17). The rest is a matter of finding out how far a particular tribe or similar group is on the road to State (class) society. See the conflicting opinions of Mead – whose definition of war seems too large – and Lesser, in Fried et al. eds. 215-17 and 94-95.

2 Cf. C.H. Gray 136-37. By contrast, the US army in Vietnam was obsessed with the "kill ratio" proportion between enemy and own killed (see Gibson 111-20, Caputo 160) but did not take into account the criterion of "cost tolerance" – the one that bankrupted the USSR – by which the USA could not, as Ho Chi Minh predicted, tolerate even a 10:1 ratio of Vietnamese vs. US killed (in Rosen 168).

3 The NGO Anti-Slavery International estimates there are more than 27 million slaves in the world today (in Merlo), roughly twice the number of chattel slaves captured in Africa 1450-1900, which is estimated at between 11 and 17 million enslaved people (Suret-Canale 24-30).

4 Note 2018: For this added parenthesis, I share the position of Susan Buck-Morss: "Cell phone videos keep citizen protests and State violence in view. But Apple takes away citizen power when it design the iPhone and iPad as platforms for profits from rent, and when these forms diminish the usability of the keyboard, ... [so that] users' actions are monitored and sold as information." (67)

5 All information in the rest of this paragraph is taken from Chossudovsky "It's," who gives nine further printed and Web sources; the US Air Force quote is from its Air University AF 2025 Final Report, www.au.af.mil/au/2025/. Addition 2018: The HAARP program was shut down in 2015, after consuming in 25 years ca. $250 million in tax-funded cost, in favour of more precise and quicker projects of destruction.

6 Pannekoek 193; similar arguments may be found in Magdoff and Amin. A revealing if tragicomic instance is the suppression of the 1962 US Congress Humphrey subcommittee report on disarmament for fear it might "back up the Marxian theory that war production was the reason for the success of capitalism" (Lewin xiii). *Report from Iron Mountain*, the book Lewin introduced (and wrote?) is, beneath its guise of a satirical hoax, a most prescient text which ought to be speedily reprinted. To the contrary, Melman has in several books (cf. *Permanent*) argued that this "nonproductive" economic orientation not only leads to industrial degradation but could be offset by saner forms of capitalism, an argument which today seems irrelevant.

7 *A semantico-ideological note*: It might be of great ideological and symbolic interest to compare this practice to the unqualified praise of "deterritorialised flows" in *A Thousand Plateaus*, the *magnum opus* of probably the best theoreticians of Post-Modernism, Deleuze and Guattari. For all my admiration of some of their insights, this would, in my opinion, testify to the aporias of irresponsible anarchism. My use is returned to earth from such theoretical stratospheres, and follows the magisterial elucidations by Angenot (*1889*, 337-52). He stresses rightly the simultaneous or perhaps consubstantial loss of relation to a material territory and to all of its analogous symbolic or semiotic spaces – loss of purity, tradition, identity, virility, and so on and on. Alerting us to such feedbacks could be the proper use of Deleuze and Guattari.

The terms themselves of de- and re-territorialisation, however tongue-twisting, cannot, I think, be dispensed with.

Notes to Chapter 2

* My thanks are due first of all to the Brecht-Archiv, Berlin, and its director Dr. Erdmut Wizisla who provided crucial help both with Brecht's variants and with the secondary literature, including a preview of his planned annotated list of Brecht's library. Stephen Bronner undertook the heroically kind task of giving the translation a line-by-line critique. The translation was first presented at a panel devoted to it in the "Marxism 2000" conference in Amherst MA 2000, which was encouraged by Richard Wolff and helped by Stephen Cullenberg; the respondents at the panel were Ronnie Davis and Sara Lennox. Of course the remaining faults are 99% mine and only 1% Brecht's.

1 For the record, the original is *De rerum natura* in six "books" by Titus Lucretius Carus, ca. 95-55 BCE; this is perhaps best translated as *On the Nature of the Universe* or *...of What There Is*. One of the first proofs of Brecht's intensive consultation of the 1821 translation by Knebel that also contained Lucretius's Latin (Brecht read both), which he must have owned from the Weimar years and which followed him in his émigré wanderings, is to be found in the essay *Five Difficulties*, where he cites "the great Lucretius" as an authoritative source for beauty of verse being used for dissemination of doctrine (GKA 22.1: 83); eight further references to and citations of Lucretius in Brecht's poems or essays about poetry from 1933 on have been found (Knopf 158 and GKA 14: 548-49 and 675). They always use and/or adapt the Latin verse in German, so that Brecht's first hexameters in the footsteps of Lucretius also date from 1933 (ibidem 171). The two other most important discussions are Brecht's cited memo "From Whom Have I Learned" and the famous programmatic essay

"On Unrhymed Poetry with Irregular Rhythm" in 1939, where the irregular rhythms and "gestic elements" of Lucretius testify to his openness for social dissonances and function as the ideal modern procedure. Much has been said (best in Mayer, Bunge, Mittenzwei, and Knopf) about the relationship to Lucretius documented in these places, much more awaits to be said.

On Brecht's great liking for Roman themes and literature, second in importance perhaps only to an analogous affinity to the Chinese and Japanese ones, cf. at least the classical monograph by Hans Mayer. See also note 5 below.

Brecht used the CM text from a selection of Marx's works published in German in the USSR 1934; the Brecht Archive conserves the photographs and films he had Ruth Berlau make of its pages in order to scatter them singly over his study room (GKA 29: 220, Bunge 184).

2 A great deal of memoir literature and philological attention has been consecrated to Brecht's not using the truly classical (Homeric or Lucretian) hexameter but a freer German form. I believe the correct judgment on this was given in Eisler's retraction of his strong 1945 objections – both formal and political – in the dialogues with Bunge (81-90): the objections were formally irrelevant and politically short-sighted. See the literature in GKA 27: 220 and 226, both Feuchtwanger items (to my mind mistaken), Hartinger 62-68 (whose arguments I find best), and Knopf 163-64.

3 It is much easier in the expletive two-syllable Russian "burzhuy" (boorzhoóy), as proved by Mayakovsky:

> Yesh ananasy, ryabchiki zhuy,
> Den' tvoy poslyednyi prikhodit, burzhuy!
>
> (Gulp down pineapples, chew your quails/ Your last day is dawning, boorzhooy!)

4 Literally, "Love that pardons no beloved/lover for loving." There's a whole little library of comments on this verse from the Paolo and Francesca episode of *Inferno*. Very crudely, "Love," the allegorical figure not too far from the Greek Eros, is not sickly sweet but often – in Dante's usual hyperbole always – merciless toward the lovers/ beloved; they have to bear the consequences of this semi-divine impulse and project – in some versions, dear to Dante who ends the *Commedia* with a verse on divine love "that moves the Sun and other stars," fully divine True, Paolo and Francesca are both killed for it and land in the perpetual tempest zone of the Inferno. And yet they are presented with such understanding and beauty through full 62 lines, their loyalty holds so fast even in that tempest, that most readers would suspect loving may be worth it, if you are truly lovers/beloved, whatever Love may do to you.

5 The following few lines from a standard handbook speak about Lucretius, but the reader may amuse herself by finding out how much of it would apply to Brecht too, and where modifications would have to be applied: "...he shows a firm intellectual grasp of what is often a complex and abstruse philosophical argument. He has the artist's intense sensory awareness of the world about him.... His moral involvement in his subject and his sense of the ludicrous make it easy for him to modulate into satire. He is a superbly endowed artist wrestling triumphantly with intractable material, writing with a vigour and gusto hardly found in Latin after the end of the republic.... He is aware of his own originality, of the difficulties involved in treating philosophy as subject-matter for poetry; he has something of the loneliness of the pioneer as well

as of the creative artist. But his theme is life itself as he had realized it in Epicurean terms...." (Wormell).

The best book I know about Lucrece, and much recommend, is by Serres (below), who argues – most important for our theme – that both his polyphonic style and his physics are open-ended towards the flows and turbulences of always endangered freedom.

Notes to Chapter 3

* This text uses two separate ones written and published consecutively, and here sewn together by sometimes severe cutting. The present first part was written in the Winter of 2001/02 and later minimally expanded, then published with a note saying I didn't manage to include in it the results and consequences of the Second Iraqi or Gulf War. I do ask the kind reader to devote (as in all my writings) special attention to the year indicated at the end of each part: they may explain why I, for example, didn't manage to address the matter of killing drones, which is a novum not confined to a technological way of assassination.

All unidentified translations into English are mine.

I would like to thank a number of friends on several continents who helped with this text, but I cannot name them for fear of having them renditioned to unknown horrors as "terrorists."

1 The original publication of this article had here a long note about legal debates on terrorism which on the whole seem mealy-mouthed and self-serving, so that I here suppress it. I did warn there against the European governments' attempts to use this term in order to incriminate even non-violent political contestation (the pioneer intimidator Thatcher already tried to apply the anti-terrorist law to British miners on strike). As Brown remarks, the imprecision in defining so as to give maximum interpretative latitude to authorities violates the fundamental legal principle "no crime without law," that is without clearly defined infraction. The note then briefly discussed the strong presumption – in the Additional Protocol I of 1977 to the Geneva Conventions of 1949 about victims of armed conflicts – that killings for purpose of terror are war crimes.

2 I gather similar horizons exist in the US 1984 Code (see Chomsky, *Pirates* 177) and in the EU convention of Jan. 2000 against the financing of terrorist acts (see *Le Monde* 15). And of course arguments similar to mine have been insistently made for the last 20 years by Walzer, Chomsky, Herman, and many others. I do not much care about being original, I care about being clear and consistent in view of the new escalation.

3 Cf. Ahmad, whose typology is wider than I'd defend, and Tigar. On State terrorism see the indispensable works by Chomsky, Herman, Herman-O'Sullivan, George, and Stohl below, full of startling data.

4 Cf. Suvin, "Against Drugs," in *Defined*, 306-09.

5 Outside of the indirect light thrown by Otto and Türcke, I haven't come across any notable contribution to the understanding of the psychic springs of terror. The only other pointer I know of is Ann Radcliffe's argument in 1826 that terror is the diametrical opposite of imaginative – fictional or hypothetical – considerations of horrible

possibilities: the latter "expands the soul, and awakens the faculties to a high degree of life; the other contracts, freezes, and nearly annihilates them" (unfortunately, her terminology was topsy-turvy to our present usages, that is, "terror" was the good term and "horror" the bad one for her).

6 Türcke 232-33 (and cf. 204-08) calls it "ontological indifference" but to my mind this is too static; however, I was much stimulated by his work. My thanks also go to a number of friends who helped (see note to Section 1). For one of the first reinsertions of the fetish theory into contemporary sociology, see Deutschmann. Of course, before and since Simmel's *Philosophy of Money*, or even Marx's notes on Shakespeare, the works not always helpfully equating money with Mammon have been legion.

7 In the exceptional case of Ulster (Northern Ireland) we have both accurate data and a painstaking examination by an anthropologist how to categorise them. Between 1969 and 1994, ca. 3,170 people were killed, of which ca. 1,490 may be called combatants, official or unofficial, while 1,640 were clearly civilians and 40 unclassified. Of the civilians, 1,070 were Catholics killed by British police and army or by the "loyalist" paramilitary, and 570 Protestants; while the latter were killed mainly by the IRA, one fifth of them were killed by the British and "loyalists," apparently by mistake (Sluka, "For God" 132-33). Thus, the final count in my terms would be: victims of State terror, 1,070 + 115 = 1,185; victims of non-State group terror, 455 (this is not what you can read in English or other Western mass media).

In a number of cases, I have been unable to learn how the killed victims are to be divided between State and group terrorism, and these are not represented in my Table: an example are the ca. 800 killings ascribed to the Basque ETA group.

8 The great ancestors of defining States as terrorists seem to have been Marx and/or Engels: "Napoleon... *perfected* terrorism, *putting permanent war* in place of *permanent revolution*" (251). How true!

9 It is impossible to give proper sources for each of my estimates, derived from the Works Cited and from newspaper articles plus internet sites which often cite no or very insufficient sources. I attempted to follow the most believable or least biased ones, rejecting defenders of the State killings, which includes US government and most US media estimates on one hand and the whitewashers of – say – the Pol Pot, Milošević or Hussein regimes on the other, as well as those organisations of the victims which might have a stake in magnifying their number. There *is no* absolute evidential truth in these cases, but I'd be disingenuous not to mention that, despite many illusions in the pretended or real Left, I find sources such as Chomsky and Herman more anxious for truth than people to the Right of them. As a sample, I give here a rough overview of the debate concerning civilian victims of the Pol Pot regime after it took over the Kampuchean State, where my estimate diverges perhaps most sharply from what one usually finds in the mass media.

It is essential to recall that in 1969-73 US carpet bombings of Sihanouk's neutralist Kampuchea caused 200-400,000 dead and a flight of hundreds of thousands more to the only safe place, the capital city (see Porter and Hildebrand, Herman "Pol Pot," www.moreorless, and Pilger "Recaling"); the *Far Eastern Economic Review* predicted one million deaths as the result of US bombings (see "Noam Chomsky"). This set the tone for what was to follow: it's a safe bet the Pol Pot regime would never have come to power but for those bombings. Herman's analysis concludes that Pol Pot's executions amounted to 100-300,000 killed, with 650-700,000 more dead from disease, starvation, and overwork (the latter should morally be in a large part, though not entirely, added to his regime's horrendous record, but are not counted in my table for then I'd have to multiply most other figures of those directly killed by similar factors). According to the co-operative encyclopedia en.wikipedia, the US State Dept. estimates the number of dead under Pol Pot at 1.2 million, which I take as the upper believable estimate, to be subdivided into killings vs. disease, starvation, and overwork. The legend of 2 million killed, often inflated to 3 or even 4 million, and still peddled by most US and allied media, arose from a French priest's book that *summed up* already inflated figures from US bombings *plus* Pol Pot killings, and which his supporters seem to have in part retracted when challenged by Chomsky (see "Noam Chomsky," from which I take the data for the rest of this note). The two strongest scholarly but mutually critical contenders in the field today, based on demographic estimates of decline from expected population rise, are Ben Kiernan, head of the Yale Cambodian Genocide Program, www.yale.edu/gcp, who estimates the decline at 1.5 to 1.7 million, and Michael Vickery, who estimates it at 700,000 (demographic decline is based on expectations of normal births and deaths, and has to be handled with great caution). Finally, the CIA estimate of the "decade of genocide" 1969-78 – including the US bombing – is 600,000, to be divided in my opinion at 200-400,000 victims of each of the terrorising parties, and I adopt this in my Table. The most believable estimate of deaths under the Pol Pot regime is, to my mind, perhaps over 1 million, of which ca. 300,000 by State terrorist killing. This number is therefore most probably not larger than the Kampucheans dead by US State terrorist bombings – though all these numbers remain horrendous both absolutely and relatively to a small country.

For those willing to check it on their own, I recommend Google's "Pol Pot" holdings, but to stop at the first 10 of Google's 85 pages. One afternoon should be enough for an orientation. The best annotated bibliography of secondary sources on terrorism I have found is in Henderson.

10 The Second Gulf (or Iraqi) War is particularly murky, for we don't have reliable information about the forces fighting the US and its allies. It seems clear that they have by 2004 become disparate, ex-Baathists and infiltrating al Qaeda supporters on the one hand and genuine popular resistance against foreign occupation on the other. At least the former wing is not averse to killing civilians for intimidation rather than killing known US quisling collaborators, and would thus fall under my rubric of "group terrorism." It is unclear just what the numbers and especially proportions of victims of State and group terrorism are from this time on, and I have tried to stick to the main group and the year 2003 in my figure. The total number of civilians killed by both sides but disproportionately more by the US army and its allies seems now to be 30,000 according to the Human Rights organisation (30 Iraqi civilians killed for each US soldier); the November 2004 issue of the UK medical journal *Lancet* gives 100,000 Iraqi civilians as "directly and indirectly" killed since the beginning of the war.

11 This ought to logically open up toward all other victims, direct or indirect, of savage capitalism on the global scale, but it would also result in a shoreless list of dead from hunger, diseases, unsafe workplaces, etc. I cited in the "Capitalism" essay cautious international sources which speak of some 40 million people dying from starvation each year, while about 500 million are "chronically malnourished," that is, on the way

to dying soon, and a further 800+ million live in "absolute poverty," that is, bordering on famine and dying a bit more slowly (Drèze-Sen 35 and *Human* 20), while fully 3,000 million are subject to "dramatic malnutrition" greatly shortening their lives (Robin). I shall add to this only the most recent report of the ILO, of April 2003, based on incomplete national data, that has the yearly number of dead from injuries or diseases due to the workplace as two millions (including 12,000 children). This includes 270 million accidents with 335,000 dead, and 160 million cases of "professional diseases" with, for example, 334,000 dead from "toxic substances" (carcinogens etc.). Again, the wounded would be a multiple of the dead.

The ratio of killings for political domination vs. killing for other reasons would drastically change if we figured in deaths from hunger, diseases, and also from drugs; but then, a cynic might argue these also happen for indirect political domination...

Notes to Chapter 4

1 Footnotes don't go well with Theses, I have avoided further ones, except for the following afterthought. This goes for the apparatus too, so that from the large library on the subject treated here I have cited only the indispensable Kouvelakis and Zolo, also the best treatment of the polysemic minefield of civil society in Hegel that I found in Bobbio 143-50, 185-87, and passim, though I do not agree with his stance on Marx.

2 Two years after writing this I stumbled upon two cognate matters:

First, data about the 4th century theologian Ticonius, according to whose commentary upon the *Apocalypse* the Christian Church is a "bipartite body," divided into a black and a clean aspect (*fusca* vs. *decora*), the first of which belongs to the Antichrist and the second to the Saviour. He was clearly influential on Augustine of Hippo's concept of Earthly and Heavenly City – which Marx may have remembered in the *Jewish Question*. It was no big surprise, I dealt with the salvational parallels as well as differences of communism and religion already in "Inside," but the exasperated split into two notional bodies is a pleasing boomerang.

Second, a sentence in Engels's letter to Bracke of Apr. 30, 1878: "[W]e should not forget that all transfer of industrial and commercial functions to the State can today have a double meaning and double effect, according to the particular circumstances: a reactionary one, a regress to the Middle Ages, and a progressive one, a progress to Communism" (Marx-Engels, *Briefe* 236).

Notes to Chapter 5

* This essay builds on preoccupations investigated in Suvin, "Terms" and then *Splendour*, later carried further in "Words and Lesions." Behind it stands also Engels's pioneering *Origin of the Family, Private Property, and the State*; it reposed on the insufficient data of his time but, if purged of the evolutionist teleology he sometimes favours, its horizon seems to me vindicated (by Clastres too). Where Clastres is cited by number in parenthesis, his book *Société* is meant; his other works are cited by first word of title + number.

1 Clastres notes this describes movements of the ritual dance accompanying the song. The original text was registered June 1966 in Paraguay near the Brazilian border. All the "you" are really "thou," except the last one.

2 See a path-breaking investigation of this political and existential situation on the material of French 17th century in Lucien Goldmann, whom I am happy to have known and used as a teacher.

3 Tribal cognitive ideology is animistic and polytheistic. In the earliest stage we know of, the numinous entities of tribal sacrality, defined by having both being and subjectivity or spirit, are not hierarchic but functionally diverse, in a world of qualitatively incommensurable subjects. I would say with Feuerbach and Marx that the projections a tribe made into the numinous sphere are strictly analogous to the productive relationships and forces within it. Marx was delighted to find in Maurer that *das Allgemeine* (the general) meant in old German and Nordic simply land held in common, while *das Sundre, Besondre* (the particular or maybe sundered) meant particular property separated or cut out of (*ausgeschieden*) what was held in common (letter to Engels of March 25, 1868, Marx-Engels 164). If we take Roman accounts of German tribes, we can follow this analogy in their customs of land ownership. Dumézil reads the evidence from Saxo and Caesar to the effect that the rise of worshipping single gods, as against the earlier heroic polytheism, signals the overthrow of yearly communist (he calls it "totalitarian" – so much for scientific objectivity) land redistribution (130–32). Finally, the abstract concept of gods eternally identical to themselves and only revealed in this or that place or time can only be sustained by cultic associations tending toward esoteric priesthood (see Weber, *Economy* 407ff.).

4 In another essay ("Myths and Rites of South American Indians," *Archeology* 80-86), Clastres describes the remarkable *karai* prophets, itinerant orators to fascinated Amerindian crowds about the evil world they lived in — that is, the growth of inequality and State among the Tupi-Guarani in the emergence of chieftains using violence with power, which is exactly what the Mbya fled from, and what their quite different *pa'i* sings and dances about in Section 1; see also Clastres's *Terre* and *Grand.*

5 Another factor Clastres's posthumous series of essays does not delve into is *war*, surely an important factor in the rise of violent chiefs and class societies. His deriving of tribal war (in *Archeology* 161-62) from exogamy's need for capturing women does not seem to suffice.

Note to Chapter 6

* The decision that we must again talk about and work for a suitably updated communism arose from a life-long commitment but was sparked by my work on an overview of SFR Yugoslavia from 2009 on, finally published as *Splendour....* It can be seen in some collateral essays from those years, including those in the Works Cited below. A number of works in these last years have encouraged me further in pursuing these horizons, most prominently those of W.F. Haug, David Harvey, Lucio Magri, and Alain Badiou. Further, I am happy to see that in the Left intellectual community there is a growing consensus on a sufficiently flexible but finally rigorous party formation. However, this essay, written over the last three years, does not pretend to

mention, much less exhaust, all the main points to be touched upon either about communism or about a new party form.

This essay attempts to glance at the international situation, but its proposal of remedies focusses mainly on European experiences up to the mid-2010s. Today it would have to be heavily added to, especially as to returning sovereignty to European peoples in all possible ways.

As to the "mass social forces" I envisage in 2, I see them as classes, or fractions and groupings thereof. We should heed Hennessy's warning: "...the retreat from class analysis... in the eighties and nineties [seems] one of neoliberalism's most effective ideological weapons" (12; cf. also Wood). What I mean by "class" can be found in my „On Class," especially in its Introduction. In particular, for the stance that the great majority of women is a potential „class-like" ally of anti-capitalism I refer to the work of N. Hartsock, D. Smith, and E.M. Wood, which can be found in Hennessy's bibliography.

Notes to Chapter 7

1 I have argued this trichotomy at length in essays such as "On Class" and "Splendours and Miseries," now in my book *Splendours*.

2 *A brief excursion on market and planning*: What happened in Yugoslavia under "market socialism" was a dismantling and jettisoning of the planning installed (by Kidrič) after 1949. Yet intelligent planning is the key to solving the major societal contradictions and aporias of what happens during industrialisation after a revolution that dispossessed the – largely foreign – capitalist class, including planning's hidden twin and political analogue, the place and extent of plebeian democracy from below as its indispensable partner. By 1965, planning by basic proportions was replaced by even vaguer "indicative planning," and federal plans became largely political pious wishes.

This meant surrender to the capitalist market. However, "[s]tandard economic reasoning tells us that, in a typical underdeveloped country, the market mechanism can produce inferior investment decisions" (Milenkovitch 294). The major argument against market reliance, developed in both titles by Polanyi, was handily summarised by Stiglitz in his 2001 "Foreword" to *The Great Transformation*:

> [Polanyi clarifies] how free market ideology was the handmaiden for [bourgeois] industrial interests, and how those interests used that ideology selectively, calling upon government intervention when needed to pursue their own interests.... Today, there is no respectable intellectual support for the proposition that markets, by themselves, lead to efficient, let alone equitable outcomes. (vii–viii)

Obviously, when there is no independent popular sovereignty, as there was in the post-revolutionary cases of the USSR, Yugoslavia, China or Cuba (growing porous as the countries integrated into world capitalist market), the market mechanism will be simply a tool of international financial and corporative interests.

Further, the illuminating discussion of Elson richly argues that if one starts from the production and reproduction of labour-power, which is wider than the needful attention to workers within paid labour, then a "politics of use values" could use a dialectical approach to the market. With Marx, the useful aspects of market coordination ought to be recognised, negatively as against the personal subalternity in feudalism and positively as helping the mutual satisfaction of needs, as well as the alienating aspect of enforcement of atomised profit mentality it necessarily carries. Not only do people in the cash nexus not at all matter, but their interests are a priori defined and strictly enforced as isolated, and information is valuable and used only insofar as it contributes to antagonistic competitive advantage (Elson 15). Probably even more important is the fact that "no economy can adjust solely through a market-led adjustment process because there are key resources which cannot be fully commodified. The most important are labour-power and the environment." In families and households, "labour power ... is not produced as a commodity" but as a mainly "altruistic collective behaviour ... [in] a resource allocation pattern that is not wholly determined by [market prices]" (17, emphasis added).

A similar horizon is in Horvat's position on "market as instrument of planning": "there is today no so-called free market; it can be proven that planning is absolutely needed for its functioning well." Yet "*the market could be one of the possible planning types*, and one among the instruments for ... the allocation of resources needed for consumption" — especially for short-range plans and consumption goods. This can be brought about by planned control of market forces and prices. However, drawing up the plans should be the prerogative of the sovereign people, that is, all economic subjects, with full feedback flow of information (Horvat, "Markt" 108–12). The system of self-government appears here as the ideal possibility of reconciling central planning with both democracy from below and efficient economic development (as Kidrič had envisaged).

Thus, Löwenthal's terms of development vs. utopia for the competing horizons of communist revolutions, generalised from the semi-peasant one in the USSR and the peasant one in China – both possessing important parallels and as important differences with Yugoslavia – can rather be thought of as needing dialectical melding.

For Kalecki, self-management in industry would be inseparable from central planning not only for emergencies such as initial industrialisation (in which case capitalism also abundantly uses it, as in the World Wars and in general in military investments) but also when a higher level of economic growth is reached. The rejection of central planning implies "either abandoning rapid economic development, or dependence on permanent foreign assistance" (62): as we have seen, Yugoslavia after the 1960s managed to combine both these negativities.

The Yugoslav government ad hoc countermeasures that took the place of planning ensured neither market nor planning would work properly. A retrospective survey of problems and opinions on the Yugoslav use of the market and then of the plan is in Korošić (250–59, 271–79).

3 The term "republic/an" is in this essay used, in conformity with Yugoslav practice, to mean the six federal republics.

4 There is a vast body of literature on various denotations and connotations of civil society in political philosophy generally, say from Tocqueville through Arendt and Ricoeur to the present, and in the specific debates, say on Hegel or on the 1990s' wave. I neglect it here in order to isolate and highlight matters useful for our needs today, as opposed to the useless or pernicious. As an example, this essay does not deal in direct polemics with a large group (best known in works by John Keane) that couples civil

society with the so-called free market. Bypassing these and similar debates which often lack conceptual clarity, my bibliography below lists only the works cited.

5 Quotes from Gramsci have been checked with the *Quaderni* edition and in places slightly modified. His prison notes were in the circumstances understandably beset by varying and confusing terminology, even by incomplete and partly conflicting views, so that interpretation has to be stronger than usual. It is dubious that one could find in him a fully unified and worked out conception of civil society or of the State. This does not detract from the fertility of his outline.

Since he did not repudiate a base-superstructure model, Gramsci logically had to place civil society (as well as the State) into the superstructure. Lucien Goldmann, Raymond Williams, and all the neo-Marxists after the 1950s will later reject this civil-engineering model in favour of the cybernetic model of feedback, where this argument is, without Gramsci's unnecessary stacking into watertight boxes, much more elegant. Having been a small part of this remodelling, I can testify that Gramsci was of early and great encouragement to it.

Notes to Chapter 8

* This essay continues and develops matters I have been worrying at as long as I can remember, rendering unavoidable the many references to my work (though I limit their numbers). Immediate forebears are almost all Works Cited for this essay under Suvin up to 2016; cognate matters may be found in those for 2017.

1 I discuss in "Epistemological" and "Approach" the different pragmatic anchorage of arts (poetry) vs. science, of a piece with different institutional patronage. This entails for each macro-set of poetry (ranging from a single sonnet to a whole current or thestyle of an epoch) a Possible World, but not the widest possible extension for applying that set in our World Zero, that is, testability in the scientists' sense; rather, art's artefacts must be recognisable as „true to conceivable experience" or verisimilar.

A Possible World is a provisional totality with a defined spacetime and agents — all else is open. It contains in principle no guarantees of success — or failure — for the agents and actions in it: *on s'engage et puis on voit* (Napoleon). Some variants may have inbuilt felicific rules (e.g. fairy-tales or Sun-hero myths à la St. George, or official optimism about a plan); some may have inbuilt horrorific rules (e.g. Horror Fantasy after Poe and Lovecraft or much Kafka, all apocalyptic pessimism), but these are protocols superadded to its fundamental neutrality. Rather than pertaining to a Kripke-type logics, or an Eco-type semiotics following logics, a useful Possible World is philosophical: modelled on our historical world – that is, on dominant conceptions thereof or on its imaginary encyclopedia – yet significantly different from it. The possible cognitive increment lies in the difference and in its applicability, direct or very indirect, to our common world.

All art and all planning deals implicitly with Possible Worlds. This is foregrounded in e.g. Science Fiction or Five-Year Plans.

2 I wrote a lengthy analysis ("Cognition, Freedom") about and arising out of this splendid novel, from which I learned a lot; it included first suggestions about the subject expanded upon here. Cf. on this kind of communitarianism now also Nancy 230-31 and passim.

3 I cannot enter here into a central unargued presupposition, encapsulated by White as "it is generally conceded that the concept of the concept is vague or ambiguous" (412), thus knocking out the basis of this whole dogmatics. I share the opposed philosophical tradition on continental Europe, hermeneutic and dialectical, starting in the Stoics and Epicureans and powerfully re-emerging with Hegel, and then Marx, Nietzsche, and on, that has no need to taboo or downgrade figures, and allows alliances or even unions with other officially sundered disciplines in discussing meaning, sense, and values of human living together. As White concludes, this tradition "even recognises that 'fiction' may be less the contrary of 'fact' than a different way of mediating between sense and imagination," and he goes on to instantiate this in some great modern poets (414).

4 McCumber's horrifying book on professional US philosophy's subservience to McCarthyism gives examples that are not quite fascist or Stalinist only because there was no need for concentration camps and extra-judicial murder. That huge repression, which "banished" from teaching of philosophy all pursuit of cognition except in form of conceptual assertion (ix) and resolutely fenced off the "discipline" from all others, led to a series of attacks on "non-mainstream" teaching, for example a recommendation to de-accredit the program at New York's famous New School of Social Research because it taught the likes of Hannah Arendt (51).

5 A separate matter that I cannot enter upon here either is the contradictory but finally failed relationship between the artistic and the political communist consciousness, that is between the intellectuals and the ruling communist party, which ended by falling back into the dichotomy between ideologists of power and estheticism, due mainly to the Party's oligarchic agoraphobia. I have attempted a general approach to such aporias in "15 Theses" and some soundings in "What Is" (both in this book) and find many particular useful stances in Fortini, *Saggi* 384-96, 944-53, and passim.

6 At least this obtains in the two cases I know something about, the Russian and the Yugoslav one, but I think the Asian ones are similar; its creators are not only many prominent intellectuals but mainly manual workers, mostly urban in the Russian case and mostly peasant in the Yugoslav one. See for the former samples and discussion in Steinberg 24-25, 31-32, 86-87, 102, 113, 132, for the latter in general Matvejević 167-80, and for the best explored Yugoslav case of Slovenia samples in Paternu ed., with discussion in Komelj and in the *Slavica Tergestina* 17 (2016) special issue on *The Yugoslav Partisan Art.*

This is not an isolated coincidence: at the beginnings of the British 19th-century labour movement, its "bible" was Percy Shelley's poem *Queen Mab,* and its anthem became Blake's *Jerusalem.*

Lenin's remark in the 1905 revolution: "Revolutions are festivals of the oppressed and the exploited. At no other time are the masses of the people in a position to come forward so actively as creators of a new social order as at a time of revolution. At such times the people are capable of performing miracles…." (ch13.htm) seems to me right – if one-sided.

I find it pleasing that Gramsci thought along similar lines. His article on the Russian Revolution of July 1918 says: "As a song exists in the poet's imagination before it does on printed paper, thus the advent of societal organisation exists in conscience and wills" (*Come* 75).

7 I suggest here, together with the already recommended Lenin, Luxemburg, Brecht, and Gramsci, the titles listed below by Badiou, Guattari and Negri, Nancy, Žižek, Douzinas & Žižek eds., and Dean as most stimulating.

Notes to Chapter 9

1 What people mean by communism is here crucial, surely not the entirely "statalised" travesty of Stalin's type. I use it in the sense of Marx – see my essay "15 Theses" here.

2 A rather different variant of this essay was written as the Afterword for this Rab-Rab publication, sparked, edited, and introduced by Sezgin Boynik; it was much helped by our protracted discussions. I approach Lenin also in the foregoing essay "What and How," and glance at him in a number of other places in this book.

3 The stimulating Lazarus speaks about this (especially on 198 and 227), through what is to me a thick fog of *morbus gallica*, the French malady of using without much ado connotations of a term regardless of its denotation. I cannot enter here upon leninology, though one ought to mention the approaches of Negri, Žižek, and the extensive and impeccable work of Lih.

Notes to Chapter 10

1 I have discussed this at some length in "Brecht" and "Empathy." It should be stressed that there has been an unceasing and deafening drumbeat of fake opposition to capitalism under the bourgeois individualistic slogan of *pity or empathy* substituting for and rendering unnecessary indignation and revolt. This can be seen from the post-Romantic condescending pity for the lower classes, say in the Sue so well excoriated by Marx (while the original oppositional Romantics, a Shelley, Hugo or Heine, were much tougher). Even the much abused compassion – for example in Martha Nussbaum's "Compassion and Terror", cf. Ure and Frost eds. 205 – is ambiguous: does it allow for critical sympathy towards its object or doesn't it? In the first case it is sympathy, in the second a quite impossible empathetic identification – for no person feels quite as another – obliterating individual differences (thus it is not even properly individualistic). Moral indignation may at times be of use but since it remains on the surface of the flow of things, it does not add to our cognition.

2 I argue in "Parables" that and how estrangement as a formal device is ideologico-politically ambiguous, so that it has two poles, the mythical and the critical one. The mythomorphic one was noted by Brecht as existing in archaic estrangements tending to obfuscation, and in modern times it comes to a head in two thoroughgoing and powerful new obfuscations: first in the presentation of common objects as strange and unexpected by commercial advertising (see to begin with Barthes), second in petty-bourgeois inanities such as disneyfication (see Suvin "Utopianism"), and finally in fascist ideologies – in literature, say, in Hamsun, Jünger or Pound – leading back to dogmatic and pernicious certainties in a way worse than the conservative bourgeois ones it was rejecting. It could be argued there are meldings of commercial PR devices and fascist horizons in the styles of both Goebbels and Trump.

Alas, my whole discussion lacks a properly sociopolitical examination of the intended and the real addressee and user of art, poetry, estrangement. "Poetry is a chance for choice, a *scandal* or stumbling stone, faced with which we can stop or move on. And once we stop we can listen to its voice. And once we have listened to that voice, we can immediately forget it or get distracted." (Fortini 1279).

3 One might have expected to find a weighty contribution to this matter in Bloch, since he has often come back to death and mortality as indispensable for understanding utopia/nism. However, it seems that, while the three somewhat longer discussions on death I was able to find all contain valuable aperçus and seeds, and Bloch's horizon of robbing death of its sting (*Prinzip* 1384-91 and passim) is the proper one, yet this particular seed in his opus never fully sprouted. The other two are the closing essay of the 1923 edition of *Geist der Utopie*, "Karl Marx, der Tod und die Apokalypse" ("Marx, Death, and the Apocalypse," English in his *Spirit*), done at the wrong time of what one must sorrowfully call his immature "revolutionary Gnosticism"; and a recorded 1964 conversation with Adorno, "Something's Missing" (the title is from Brecht's *Mahagonny*). Cf. further Boer, and a good overview of important French discussions since Morin and Philippe Ariès in Bourguière. A dissent from full Hegelian recuperation of the negative into the subject's activity is well argued in Timpanaro with the powerful help of Leopardi's poetry.

This essay is only a first attempt to consider the most complex and tangled matter of death, well conveyed by the Italian proverb *sol chi nasce muore*: only one that is born dies.

Of course, I find the Heideggerian, or any similar, ontologising "being-to.death" useless.

Works Cited in this Book

In accordance with the current MLA style, only editor and year are supplied, not city of printing; a few exceptions in square parentheses are made where it would help finding the title.

Mostly presupposed are the opuses of Walter Benjamin, Bertolt Brecht, Antonio Gramsci, Karl Marx, and (with more caution) Friedrich Nietzsche.

Abellard, Alain. "A Cuba, la prudence inquiète de Fidel Castro." *Le Monde*, Oct. 12, 2001.

Ahmad, Eqbal. "Terrorism: Theirs and Ours" (1998), www.merip.org/new_war_resources/ new_war_links.html (now as idem with David Barsamian. *Terrorism: Theirs and Ours*. Seven Stories P, 2001).

Ali, Tariq. *The Clash of Fundamentalisms.* Verso, 2002.

Althusser, Louis. *Sur la reproduction.* PUF, 2011.

Amin, Samir. *Capitalism in the Age of Globalization.* Zed Books, 1997.

Anderson, Perry. *Lineages of the Absolutist State.* Verso, 1979.

Andreski, Stanislav. *Military Organization and Society.* U of California P, 1968.

Angenot, Marc. *1889: Un état du discours social.* Le Préambule, 1989.

—. *L'antimilitarisme: Idéologie et utopie.* CIADEST [Montréal], 2000.

—. *Les Idéologies du ressentiment.* XYZ, 1996.

Aristotle. *Selections.* Ed. and transl. T. Irwin and G. Fine. Hackett, 1995.

Arrighi, Giovanni. *The Long 20th Century: Money, Power, and the Origins of Our Times.* Verso, 1994.

Auerbach, Erich. "Philology and *Weltliteratur.*" *Centennial Review* 13.1 (1969): 1-17.

Avineri, Shlomo. "Karl Marx on Colonialism and Modernization," in Howard, M.C., and J.E. King eds., *The Economics of Marx.* Penguin, 1976, 235-59.

Avnery, Uri. "All Kinds of Terrorists." *Israelinsider* Nov. 6, 2001. www.israelinsider.com/ views/ articles/views_0186.htm

Badiou, Alain. *The Age of the Poets.* Ed. and transl. B. Bosteels. Verso, 2014.

—. "The Communist Idea and the Question of Terror," in *The Idea of Communism*, Vol. 2. Ed. S. Žižek. Verso, 2013, 1-11.

—. *L'Hypothèse communiste.* Lignes, 2009.

—. *Of an Obscure Disaster.* Transl. B. Foulks et al. Jan van Eyck Akademie, 2009.

—. *Peut-on penser la politique.* Seuil, 1985.

—. *Theory of the Subject.* Transl. B. Bosteels. Continuum, 2009.

Bajt, Aleksander. *Samoupravni oblik društvene svojine [The Self-managing Form of Community Property].* Globus, 1988.

Bakarić, Vladimir. *Socijalistički samoupravni sistem i društvena reprodukcija (1958–1982) [The Socialist Self-Management System and Social Reproduction (1958–1982)]*, 3 vols. Informator et al., 1983.

Balibar, Etienne. "Communism as Commitment, Imagination, and Politics," in *The Idea of Communism*, Vol. 2. Ed. S. Žižek. Verso, 2013, 13-36.

Banerjee, Subharata Bobby. "Necrocapitalism." *Organizational Studies* 29.12 (2008): 1541-63.

Baracca, Angelo. "Le armi di sterminio nella strategia USA." *Giano* 15.44 (2003): 141-55.

Baran, Paul, and Paul Sweezy. *Monopoly Capital.* Monthly Review P, 1966.

Barber, Benjamin. *Strong Democracy.* U of California P, 1984.

Barnet, Richard, and John Cavanagh. *Global Dreams: Imperial Corporations and the New World Order.* Simon & Schuster, 1994.

Barthes, Roland. *Mythologies.* Seuil, 1957.

Baudelaire, Charles. *Oeuvres complètes.* Ed. M. A. Ruff. Seuil, 1968.

Beardsley, Monroe. *Aesthetics.* Brace, 1958.

Benjamin, Walter. *Gesammelte Schriften.* Suhrkamp, 1972-83 [as *GS*].

Bensaïd, Daniel. "Leninism in the 21st century." 2001, www.marxists.org/archive/bensaid/2001/ 11/leninism.htm

—. *La révolution et le pouvoir.* Stock, 1986.

Bertell, Rosalie. "Victims of the Nuclear Age." *The Ecologist* (Nov. 1999): 408-11.

Best, Michael H., and William E. Connolly. *The Politicized Economy*, 2nd ed. Heath, 1982.

[Bhopal.] www.bhopal.net/index.php.

Bićanić, Rudolf [with M. Hanžeković]. *Economic Policy in Socialist Yugoslavia.* Cambridge UP, 1973.

Bilandžić, Dušan. *Ideje i prakse društvenog razvoja Jugoslavije 1945–1973 [Ideas and Practices of Social Development of Yugoslavia (1945–1973)].* Komunist, 1973.

Bishara, Marwan. "L'ère des conflits asymetriques." *Le Monde diplomatique* oct. 2001, p. 20.

Black, Max. "More about Metaphor." *Dialectica* 31 (1977): 431-57.

[Blake, William.] *The Complete Poetry and Prose of William Blake.* Ed. D. V. Erdman. U of California P, 2008.

Bloch, Ernst. „Der Intellektuelle und die Politik," in his *Vom Hasard zur Katastrophe.* Suhrkamp, 1972, 336-43.

—. *Das Prinzip Hoffnung,* 2 vols. Suhrkamp, 1959.

—. *The Spirit of Utopia.* Transl. A.A. Nassar. Stanford UP, 2000

—, and Theodor Adorno. "Something's Missing." http://staff.washington.edu/schenold/chid390/ readings/Bloch+Adorno-Something's%20 Missing.pdf

Blum, William. *Rogue State.* Zed Boks, 2002.

Blumenberg, Hans. *Paradigmen zu einer Metaphorologie.* Suhrkamp, 2005.

Bobbio, Norberto. "Gramsci and the Conception of Civil Society," in his *Which Socialism?* Transl. C. Mortera. U of Minnesota P, 1987, 138–61.

Boer, Roland. *Criticism of Heaven: On Marxism and Theology.* Brill, 2007.

Borgese, Elizabeth Mann. "The Promise of Self-Management," in *Self-Management: New Dimensions to Democracy*. Eds. eadem and I. Adizes. Clio P, 1975, ix–xxvii.

Bourguière, André. "Le long voyage de *L'Homme et la mort*." *Communications* no. 1 (2008): 49-70, www.cairn.info/revue-communications-2008-1-page-49.htm

Bourne, Randolph. *The State*. See Sharp P, 1998 [original 1918].

Boynik, Sezgin ed. *Coiled Verbal Spring: Devices of Lenin's Language* [with texts by Mayakovsky, Shklovsky, Eikhenbaum, Yakubinsky, Tynyanov, Tomashevsky, Kazansky, Kruchenykh]. [Helsinki] Rab-Rab P, 2018.

Brecht, Bertolt. *Werke*. Grosse Kommentierte Berliner und Frankfurter Ausgabe. Suhrkamp & Aufbau V., 1988-2000 [as GKA].

Brecht and Death. The Brecht Yearbook no. 32. Eds. J. Hillesheim et al. IBS/U of Wisconsin P, 2007.

Brenner, Robert. "Uneven Development and the Long Downturn... 1950-1998." *New Left Review* no. 229 (1998), special issue.

Brinkmann, Reinhold. "The Distorted Sublime," in M. H. Kater and A. Riethmüller eds., *Music and Nazism*. Laaber V., 2003.

Brown, John. "Les périlleuses tentatives pour définir le terrorisme." *Le Monde diplomatique* (févr. 2002): 4-5.

Brus, Wlodzimierz. *Socialist Ownership and Political Systems*. Transl. R. A. Clarke. Routledge & K. Paul, 1975.

Buck-Morss, Susan. "A Commonist Ethics," in *The Idea of Communism*, Vol. 2. Ed. S. Žižek. Verso, 2013, 57-76.

Buden, Boris. "Gastarbajteri, glasnici budućnosti" ["'Gastarbeiter,' Messengers of the Future"]. Transl. M. Čačić. *Zarez* no. 338 (2012): 36.

—. "Još o komunističkim krvolocima..." ["More about Communist Bloodsuckers"]. *Prelom* 3.4 (2013): 51–57.

Bunge, Hans-Joachim. „*Das Manifest* von Bertolt Brecht." *Sinn und Form* 15.2-3 (1963): 184-203.

— [and Hanns Eisler]. *Fragen Sie mehr über Brecht*. Rogner & Bernhard, 1970.

Burawoy, Michael. "Terrains of Contest: Factory and State under Capitalism and Socialism." *Socialist Review* no. 58 (1981): 83–124.

Caputo, Philip. *A Rumor of War*. Ballantine Books, 1977.

Castro, Fidel. «Discours prononcé à la séance d'inauguration du Sommet Sud (La Havane, 12 avril 2000),» www.g77.org

Chomsky, Noam. *9-11*. Seven Stories P, 2001.

—. *The Culture of Terrorism*: South End P, 1988.

—. "Drain the swamp and there will be no more mosquitoes." *The Guardian*, Sept. 9, 2002.

—. *Necessary Illusions*: South End P, 1989.

—. *Pirates and Emperors*: Black Rose Books, 1991.

Chossudovsky, Michel. *The Globalization of Poverty: Impacts of IMF and World Bank Reforms.* Zed Books, 1997.

—. "It's Not Only Greenhouse Gas Emissions: Washington's New World Order Weapons Have the Ability to Trigger Climate Change." E-mail to D. Suvin of 26/11/2000.

—. "Low Intensity Nuclear War: NATO Crimes in the Balkans." March 15, 2001, www.globalresearch.ca/low-intensity-nuclear-war/3716

Clastres, Pierre. *Archeology of Violence.* Transl. J. Herman. Semiotext(e), 1994, 53-86.

—. *Le grand parler.* Seuil, 1974.

—. *La société contre l'état.* Minuit, 2009 [original 1974].

Clausewitz, Carl von. *On War*, 3 Vols. Transl. J.J. Graham. Routledge, 1966 [original 1832-34].

Coates, Ken. "Democracy and Workers' Control," in J. Vanek ed., *Self-Management: Economic Liberation of Man.* Penguin, 1975, 90–109.

Cockburn, Alexander. *Corruptions of Empire.* Verso, 1987.

Cohen, Jean L., and Andrew Arato. *Civil Society and Political Theory.* MIT P, 1995.

Čolaković, Rodoljub. *Pregled istorije Saveza komunista Jugoslavije [Overview of the History of the League of Communists of Yugoslavia].* Institut za izučavanje radničkog pokreta, 1963.

Comisso, Ellen T. *Workers' Control under Plan and Market: Implications of Yugoslav Self-Management.* Yale UP, 1979.

Conert, Hansgeorg. *Das amerikanische Imperium.* VSA-V., 2002.

Creveld, Martin van. *The Transformation of War.* The Free P, 1991.

Culler, Jonathan. „Theory of the Lyric." *Nordisk poesi* no. 2 (2017): 119-33.

"Cultural Revolution." *n+1* no. 16 (2013), https://nplusonemag.com/issue-16/the-intellectual-situation/cultural-revolution/ accessed Dec. 14, 2014.

Cvjetičanin, Veljko. "Die Entwicklung der Selbstverwaltung in Jugoslawien," in B. Bošnjak and idem eds., *Jugoslawien denkt anders.* Transl. E. von Steiner and R. Kaufmann. Europa V., 1971, 237–54.

Davis, Angela Y. *Women, Race and Class.* Random House, 1981.

Davis, Mike. *Cronache dell'impero.* manifestolibri, 1984.

—. *Late Victorian Holocausts.* Verso, 2001.

—. "Planet of Slums." *New Left Review* no. 26 (2004): 5-34.

Dean, Jodi. "Communist Desire," in *The Idea of Communism*, Vol. 2. Ed. S. Žižek. Verso, 2013, 77-102.

—. *The Communist Horizon.* Verso, 2012.

Debord, Guy. *Comments on the Society of the Spectacle.* Transl. M. Imrie. Verso, 1990.

—. *Société du spectacle.* Lebovici, 1987.

Denitch, Bogdan Denis. *The Legitimation of a Revolution: The Yugoslav Case.* Yale UP, 1976.

Deutschmann, Christoph. *Die Verheissung des absoluten Reichtums: Zur religiösen Natur des Kapitalismus.* Suhrkamp, 1999.

Dictionnaire de l'Académie française, 1798. S.v. „terrorisme," „terroriste." www.lib.uchicago.edu/efts/ARTFL/projects/dicos/ACADEMIE/

Dictionnaire de l'Académie française, 6th edn. 1835. S.v. "terreur." www.lib.uchicago.edu/efts/ARTFL/projects/dicos/ACADEMIE/ .

Dinnerstein, Dorothy. *The Mermaid and the Minotaur.* Harper & Row, 1976.

Dirlam, Joel, and James Plummer. *An Introduction to the Yugoslav Economy.* Merrill, 1973.

Douzinas, Costas, and Slavoj Žižek eds. *The Idea of Communism.* Verso, 2010.

Drèze, Jean, and Amartya Sen. *Hunger and Public Action.* Clarendon P, 1989.

Drulović, Milojko. *Self-Management on Trial*, rev. edn. Spokesman Books, 1978.

Dumézil, Georges. *Mitra-Varuna: An Essay on Two Indo-European Representations of Sovereignty.* Transl. D. Coltman. Zone Books, 1988.

Dummett, Michael. *On Immigration and Refugees.* Routledge, 2001.

Eco, Umberto. "Gli alleati nolenti di Bin Laden." *L'Espresso* Nov. 1, 2001.

—. *Lector in fabula.* Bompiani, 1979.

—. *The Role of the Reader.* Indiana UP, 1979.

«Éditorial» to «Comment se construit la pauvreté.» *Alternatives Sud* 6.4 (1999): 1-20.

Elson, Diane. "Market Socialism or Socialization of the Market?" *New Left Review* no. 172 (1988): 3–44.

Elwert, Georg. "Markets of Violence," in idem et al. eds., *Dynamics of Violence.* Duncker & Humblot, 1999, 85-102.

[En.] http://en.wikipedia.org/wiki/Pol_Pot, accessed June 18, 2004.

Engels, Frederick [Friedrich]. *Die Lage der arbeitenden Klasse in England*, 8th edn. Dietz V., 1923.

—. *The Part Played by Labour in the Transition from Ape to Man.* 1876. Transl. C. Dutt. www.marxists.org/archive/marx/works/1876/part-played-labour/index.htm

Epicuro: Opere. Ed. G. Arrighetti. Einaudi, 1973.

Feenberg, Andrew. *Transforming Technology.* Oxford UP, 2002.

Ferrajoli, Luigi, and Danilo Zolo. *Democrazia autoritaria e capitalismo.* Feltrinelli, 1978.

Feuchtwanger, Lion. „Bertolt Brecht." *Sinn und Form*, Zweites Sonderheft Bertolt Brecht (1957): 103-08.

—. „Die Zusammenarbeit der Dichter." *Berliner Zeitung* no. 301 of Dec. 25, 1958 [letter to Bunge].

Fineschi, Roberto. *Marx e Hegel.* Carrocci, 2006.

Firestone, Shulamith. *The Dialectic of Sex: The Case for Feminist Revolution.* Morrow, 1970 [rpt. 2003].

Fortini, Franco. *I confini della poesia.* Castelvecchi, 2015.

—. *Saggi ed epigrammi.* Ed. L. Lenzini. Mondadori, 2003.

Fossati, Marco. *Terrorismo e terroristi.* B. Mondadori, 2003.

Foucault, Michel. *Power/ Knowledge.* Ed. C. Gordon. Pantheon Books, 1980.

Freud, Sigmund. *The Pelican Freud Library.* Pelican, 1985.

—. *Three Essays on the Theory of Sexuality.* Transl. and ed. J. Strachey. Basic Books, 1975.

Fried, Morton, et al. eds. *War: The Anthropology of Armed Conflict and Aggression.* Natural History P, 1968.

Gantzel, Klaus-Jürgen. „Über die Kriege nach dem Zweiten Weltkrieg," in B. von Wegner ed., *Wie Kriege entstehen.* Schöningh, 2000, 299-318.

George, Alexander, ed. *Western State Terrorism.* Polity P, 1991.

[George, Susan.] *The Lugano Report.* Pluto P, 1999.

Gibbs, David N. *First Do No Harm: Humanitarian Intervention and the Destruction of Yugoslavia.* Vanderbilt UP, 2009.

Gibson, James William. *The Perfect War.* Atlantic Monthly P, 2000.

Gnjatović, Dragana. *Uloga inostranih sredstava u privrednom razvoju Jugoslavije [The Role of Foreign Funds in the Economic Development of Yugoslavia*]. Ekonomski Institut, 1985.

Godelier, Maurice. *Perspectives in Marxist Anthropology.* Transl. R. Brain. Cambridge UP, 1977.

Goldmann, Lucien. Le dieu caché: Étude sur la vision tragique dans les Pensées de Pascal et dans le théâtre de Racine. Gallimard, 1955 [*The Hidden God.* Routledge and K. Paul, 1964

].

Graeber, David. *Debt: The First 5000 Years.* Melville House, 2011, https://libcom.org/.../debt-first-5000-years-david-graeber accessed July 19, 2018.

Gramsci, Antonio. *Come alla volontà piace: Scritti sulla Rivoluzione russa.* Ed. G. Liguori. Castelvecchi, 2017.

—. *L'Ordine nuovo.* Einaudi, 1955.

—. *Quaderni del carcere,* 4 vols. Ed. V. Gerratana. Einaudi, 1975.

—. *Selection from the Prison Notebooks.* Ed. and transl. Q. Hoare and G. N. Smith. International Publ., 1975.

Gray, Chris Hables. *Postmodern War.* Guilford P, 1997.

Gray, J. Glenn. *The Warriors.* Harper & Row, 1967.

Greider, William. "Under the Banner of the 'War' on Terror." *The Nation,* June 21, 2004, www.thenation.com/

Grene, Marjorie. *The Knower and the Known.* Faber & Faber, 1966.

Guattari, Félix, and Toni Negri. *Communists like Us.* Transl. M. Ryan. Semiotext(e), 1990.

[Gush.] www.gush-shalom.org/english/index.html, under Sept. 2001, accessed Sept. 30, 2001.

Habermas, Jürgen. *The Structural Transformation of the Public Sphere.* Transl. T. Burger. Polity P, 1989.

Halberstam, David. *War in a Time of Peace.* Scribner and Bloomsbury, 2001.

Hallas, Duncan. "Towards a Revolutionary Socialist Party," in idem et al., *Party and Class.* Pluto P, [1980?], 9-25.

Haraway, Donna J. *Modest_Witness@Second_Millennium.* Routledge, 1997.

Harding, D.W. *Words into Rhythm.* Cambridge UP, 1976.

Hartinger, Christel. *Bertolt Brecht -- das Gedicht nach Krieg und Wiederkehr.* Brecht-Zentrum der DDR, 1982.

Harvey, David. *A Companion to Marx's Capital.* Verso, 2010.

—. *The Enigma of Capital and the Crises of Capitalism.* Oxford UP, 2010.

—. *The Limits of Capital.* Verso, 1999.

Haug, Wolfgang Fritz. *Philosophieren mit Brecht und Gramsci.* Argument, 2006.

—. *Politisch richtig oder richtig politisch.* Argument, 1999.

Headrick, Daniel. *The Tools of Empire.* Oxford UP, 1991.

Heath-Stubbs, John, and Phillips Salman. *Poems of Science.* Penguin, 1984.

Hegel, G.W.F. *Phänomenologie des Geistes. Sämtliche Werke*, vol. 2. Ed. J. Hoffmeister. Meiner, 1949.

—. Preface to his *Philosophy of Right.* www.marxists.org/reference/archive/hegel/works/pr/ preface.htm

Heinig, Kurt. *Le Prix des guerres.* Transl. L. Jumel. Gallimard, 1962.

Henderson, Harry. *Terrorism.* Facts on File, 2001.

Hennessy, Rosemary. *Profit and Pleasure: Sexual Identities in Late Capitalism.* Routledge, 2000, http://davidmcnally.org/wp-content/uploads/2011/01/henessey-profit_and_pleasure_sexual.pdf

Herman, Edward S. "Pol Pot and Kissinger." www.zmag.org/zmag/articles/hermansept97.htm

—. *The Real Terror Network.* South End P, 1982.

—, and Gerry O'Sullivan. "'Terrorism' as Ideology and Cultural Industry," in A. George ed. [see above], 39-75.

—, and Noam Chomsky. *Manufacturing Consent.* Pantheon, 1988.

Hertz, Robert. *Death & the Right Hand.* Trans. R. and C. Needham. The Free P, 1960.

Hesiod. *Erga kai hemerai/* Esiodo. *Le opere e i giorni* [bilingual edn.]. Rizzoli, 1998.

—. *Theogonia/* Esiodo. *Teogonia* [bilingual edn.]. Ed. E. Cingano. A. Mondadori, 2004.

Heuser, Beatrice. *Western "Containment" Policies in the Cold War: The Yugoslav Case, 1948–53.* Routledge, 1989.

Hildebrand, George, and Gareth Porter. *Cambodia: Starvation and Revolution.* Monthly Review P, 1976.

Hinkelammert, Franz J. *The Ideological Weapons of Death: A Theological Critique of Capitalism.* Orbis Books, 1986 [Spanish original 1981].

Hobsbawm, Eric. *How to Change the World.* Abacus, 2011.

Hofbauer, Hannes. *Balkankrieg: Zehn Jahre Zerstörung Jugoslawiens.* Promedia, 2001.

Hoffman, Stanley. *World Disorders.* Rowman & Littlefield, 1998.

Horvat, Branko. *An Essay on Yugoslav Society.* [White Plains NY] IASP, 1969.

—. "Der Markt als Instrument der Planung," in K. Wessely ed., *Probleme zentraler Wirtschaftsplanung.* V. für Geschichte und Politik, 1967, 107–16.

—. "O socijalnoj diferencijaciji u našoj zemlji" [On Social Differentiation in Our Country], in D. Atlagić and V. Milanović eds., *Kritika socijalnih razlika* [Criticism of Social Differences]. Komunist, 1972, 52–59.

— Mihajlo Marković, and Rudi Supek eds. *Self-Governing Socialism,* 2 vols. [White Plains NY] IASP, 1975.

Human Development Report 1996. Ed. UN Development Programme. Oxford UP, 1996.

Human Development Report 1998. Ed. UN Development Programme. Oxford UP, 1998.

International Action Center and Tommaso Di Francesco eds. *La Nato nei Balcani.* Ed. Riuniti, 1999.

Iveković, Rada. *Les Citoyens manquants.* Al Dante, 2015.

Jameson, Fredric. "Cognitive Mapping," in C. Nelson and L. Grossberg eds., *Marxism and the Interpretation of Culture.* U of Illinois P, 1988, 347-56.

—. *Marxism and Form.* Princeton UP, 1971.

—. *The Political Unconscious.* Cornell UP, 1981.

—. *The Seeds of Time.* Columbia UP, 1994.

—. "Utopia and Actually Existing Being." Unpublished lecture, e-mail attachment to D. Suvin of June 2004.

—. *Valences of the Dialectic.* Verso, 2009.

Jerovšek, Janez, Veljko Rus, and Josip Županov eds. *Kriza i perspektive [Crisis and Prospects].* Zagreb: Globus, 1986.

Juergensmeyer, Mark. *Terror in the Mind of God.* U of California P, 2000.

Kaldor, Mary. *New and Old Wars.* Polity P, 1999.

—. "Warfare and Capitalism," in *Exterminism and Cold War.* Ed. New Left Review. NLB, 1982, 261-88.

Kalecki, Michał. *Socialism: Functioning and Long-Term Planning,* Vol. 3 of his *Collected Works.* Transl. B. Jung. Oxford UP, 1992.

Keller, William W. *Arm in Arm.* Basic Books, 1995.

Kinsley, Michael. "Defining Terrorism." *Washington Post* Oct. 5, 2001, p. A37 [variant text in *International Herald Tribune* Oct. 6-7, 2001].

Klare, Michael, and Peter Kornbluh eds. *Low Intensity Warfare.* Pantheon, 1988.

Klein, Naomi. "Racism is the terrorists' greatest recruitment tool." www.theguardian.com/world/2005/aug/13/religion.terrorism [originally in *The Nation*]

Knopf, Jan. *Brecht Handbuch: Lyrik, Prosa, Schriften.* Metzler, 1984.

Kolko, Gabriel. *Century of War.* New P, 1994.

Komelj, Miklavž. *Kako misliti partizansko umetnost [How to Think the Partizans' Art].* [Ljubljana] Založba /*cf. [sic], 2009.

Korošić, Marijan. *Jugoslavenska kriza [The Yugoslav Crisis].* Naprijed, 1988.

Korsch, Karl. „Antwort an bb.“ *Alternative* 8.41 (1965): 54-57.

Kouvelakis, Stathis. *Philosophy and Revolution: From Kant to Marx.* Transl. G.M. Goshgarian. Verso, 2003.

Kunkel, Benjamin. *Utopia or Bust.* Verso, 2014.

Kunz, J.L. "The Chaotic Status of the Laws of War...." *American J of International Law* 45 (1951): 37-52.

Labica, Georges, and Gérard Bensussan eds. *Dictionnaire critique du marxisme.* Quadrige/PUF, 1999.

Lampe, John R. *Yugoslavia as History: Twice There Was a Country.* Cambridge UP, 2000.

Lapavitsas, Costas. "Default and Exit from the Eurozone: A Radical Left Strategy." *Socialist Register* 48 (2012): 288-97.

Latour, Bruno. *Science in Action.* Harvard UP, 1987.

Lazarus, Sylvain. "Lénine et le temps," in his *L'intelligence de la politique.* Ed. N. Michel. Al Dante, 2013, 193-241.

Lefebvre, Henri. *Vers le Cybernanthrope.* Paris: Denoël/Gonthier 1971.

—. *The Production of Space.* Transl. D. Nicholson-Smith. Blackwell, 1997.

—. *La somme et le reste.* Bélibaste, 1973.

Lenin, V. I. "Decree on Peace," *Selected Works, Volume 2.* Transl. unknown. Progress Publ.s, 1967, 459-61, www.marxists.org/archive/lenin/works/1917/oct/25-26/26b.htm accessed Jan. 15, 2018.

—. *Philosophical Notebooks. Collected Works,* Vol. 38. Lawrence & Wishart/Progress, 1981.

—. *The State and Revolution.* Transl. unknown. www.marxists.org/archive/lenin/works/1917/staterev/.

—. *Two Tactics of Social Democracy in the Democratic Revolution.* 1905. Transl. A. Fineburg and J. Katzer. www.marxists.org/archive/lenin/works/1905/tactics/ accessed Jan. 15, 2018.

Lens, Sidney. *Permanent War.* Schocken, 1987.

Levi samit Srbije [The Left Summit of Serbia]. "Solidarni principi. [Principles of Solidarity]" http://levisamitsrbije.org/solidarni-principi/ accessed Feb. 15, 2015.

Levidow, Les, and Kevin Robbins eds. *Cyborg Worlds: The Military Information Society.* Free Association Books, 1989.

Levins, Richard. "Ten Propositions on Science and Antiscience," in Andrew Ross ed., *Science Wars.* Duke UP, 1996, 180-91.

Lewin, Leonard C. "Foreword" to *Report* [below], vii-xv.

Lindqvist, Sven. *A History of Bombing.* Transl. L. Rugg. The New P, 2001.

Lotman, Jurij. *The Structure of the Artistic Text.* Transl. R. Vroon. Michigan Slavic Contributions, 1977.

Love, Barbara, and Elizabeth Shanklin. "The Answer Is Matriarchy," in *Mothering.* Ed. J. Treblicot. Rowman & Allanheld, 1984, 275-83.

Lovins, Amory B., and L. Hunter Lovins. "Energy: The Avoidable Oil Crisis." *The Atlantic* (Dec. 1987): 22-30.

Löwenthal, Richard. "Development vs. Utopia in Communist Policy," in C. A. Johnson ed., *Change in Communist Systems*. Stanford UP, 1970, 33–116.

Lukács, Georg. *Geschichte und Klassenbewusstsein*. Luchterhand, 1970 [original 1923].

—. *Lenin: A Study of the Unity of his Thought*. Transl. N. Jacobs. MIT P, 1974 [original 1924].

—. *The Process of Democratization*. Transl. S. Bernhardt and N. Levine. SUNY P, 1991.

Luxemburg, Rosa. *The Accumulation of Capital*. Transl. A. Schwarzschild. Modern Reader, 1968 [original 1913].

Magri, Lucio. "A New Communist Identity," appendix to his *The Tailor of Ulm: Communism in the Twentieth Century*. Transl. P. Camiller. Verso, 2011.

Mailer, Norman. *Of a Fire on the Moon*. Random House, 1985.

Malik, Aftab Ahmad ed. *Shattered Illusions: Analyzing the War on Terrorism*. Amal P, 2002.

Malinowski, Bronislaw. *Argonauts of the Western Pacific*. Routledge and K. Paul, 1922.

—. *Coral Gardens and their Magic*, 2. Vols. American Book, 1935.

Mann, Michael. "Globalization and September 11." *New Left Review* no. 12 (2001): 51-72.

Marcheschi, Daniela. "Giampiero Neri o della coesistenza," in S. Aman ed., *Memoria, mimetismo e informazione in "Teatro Naturale" di Giampiero Neri*. Otto/Novecento, 1999, 13-28.

Marcuse, Herbert. *Feindesanalysen*. zu Klampen, 1998.

—. *From Luther to Popper*. Transl. J. De Bres. Verso, 1988.

—. *One-Dimensional Man*. Beacon P, 1964.

Marković, Mihajlo. *From Affluence to Praxis*. U of Michigan P, 1974.

—. "Self-Governing Political System and De-alienation in Yugoslavia (1950–1965)." *Praxis International* 6.2 (1986): 163–74.

Marx, Karl. „Die britische Herrschaft in Indien," in MEW 9. Dietz V, 1960, 127-33.

—. *The Civil War in France*. www.marxists.org/archive/marx/works//1871/civil-war-france/ index.htm

—. *Critique of the Gotha Program*. Transl. unknown. www.marxists.org/archive/marx/works/1875/ gotha/index.htm

—. *The Eighteenth Brumaire of Louis Bonaparte*. Transl. S. K. Padover. www.marxists.org/archive/ marx/works/1852/ 18th-brumaire/index.htm.

—. *Grundrisse*. Transl. M. Nicolaus. Vintage, [1973].

—. *Das Kapital, Erster Band*. MEW 23. Dietz V, 1993.

—. *Das Kapital, Dritter Band*. MEW 25. Dietz V, 1979.

—. *Selected Works*, vol. 1. FLPH, 1969.

—. *Theorien über den Mehrwert*, 3 Vols. MEW 26.1-3. Dietz V, 1956-62.

[Marx, Karl, and Friedrich Engels.] *The Marx-Engels Reader*. Ed. R. C. Tucker. Norton, 1972 [as Tucker ed.].

—. *Briefe über "Das Kapital."* Dietz V, 1954.

—. *Die heilige Familie*. Dietz V, 1953.

—. *Werke*. Dietz V, 1958ff. [cited as MEW with volume number].

Massari, Roberto. *Il terrorismo*. Massari, 2002.

Mates, Leo. *Međunarodni odnosi socijalističke Jugoslavije [International Relations of Socialist Yugoslavia]*. Nolit, 1976.

Matvejević, Predrag. "Naša književnost pobune i otpora" ["Our Literature of Revolt and Resistance"] in his *Prema novom kulturnom stvaralaštvu [Towards a New Cultural Creativity]*. Cesarec/INA, 1977.

Mauss, Marcel. *The Gift*. Transl. W.D. Halls. Routledge, 1996 [original 1925].

Mayer, Hans. *Bertolt Brecht und die Tradition*. Neske, 1961.

McCumber, John. *Time in the Ditch*. Northwestern UP, 2001.

McMurtry, John. *The Cancer Stage of Capitalism*. Pluto P, 1999.

—. *Understanding War*. Science for Peace and Stevens P, 1989.

Melman, Seymour. *The Permanent War Economy*. Simon & Schuster, 1974.

Merleau-Ponty, Maurice. *Les aventures de la dialectique*. Gallimard, 2000.

Merlo, Anna Maria. "Schiavi moderni." *Il Manifesto* Feb. 2, 2002, p. 2.

Milenkovitch, Deborah. *Plan and Market in Yugoslav Economic Thought*. Yale UP, 1971.

Milosavlevski, Slavko. *Revolucija i anti-revolucija [Revolution and Anti-revolution]*. Revija, 1971.

Milward, Alan. "Europe's New-Old Order." *New Left Review* no. 12 (2001): 161-67.

Minolfi, Salvatore. "Dominio senza egemonia." *Giano* no. 39 (2001): 13-30.

Mittenzwei, Werner. *Brechts Verhältnis zur Tradition*. Akademie-V., 1972.

Močnik, Rastko. "Nismo krivi ali smo odgovorni" ["It's Not Our Fault but We Are Responsible"]. *Up & Underground* [Zagreb] no. 17–18 (2011): 139–55.

Le Monde, Nov. 18-19, 2001, pp. 13-20 [Dossier spécial: "Terrorisme, guerre"].

Moravia, Alberto. "Tre o quattro maniere di essere ebreo," interview with Dacia Maraini. *L'Espresso* Sept. 24, 1972.

[More.] www.moreorless.au.com/killers/pot.hm

Moret, Leuren. "Dirty bombs, dirty missiles, dirty bullets." www.sfbayview.com/081804/depleteduranium081804.shtml accessed Nov. 15, 2004.

Morin, Edgar. *L'homme et la mort dans l'histoire*. Corréa, 1951.

Moylan, Tom. "Denunciation/Annunciation." *Cultural Critique* no. 20 (1991-92): 33-64.

Mueller, John, and Karl Mueller. "The Methodology of Mass Destruction." *Journal of Strategic Studies* 23.1 (2000): 163-87.

Mukařovský, Jan. *Aesthetic Function, Norm and Value as Social Facts*. Transl. M. Suino. Michigan Slavic Contributions, 1970.

—. *Studie z estetiky*. Odeon, 1966.

Nancy, Jean-Luc. *La Communauté désoeuvrée*, nouv. éd. Bourgois, 1990.

Needless Deaths in the Gulf War. Human Rights Watch, 1991, www.hrw.org/reports/1991/gulfwar accessed Aug. 15, 2004.

Neocleous, Mark. *The Monstrous and the Dead.* U of Wales P, 2005.

Ngugi wa Thion'go. *Decolonizing the Mind: The Politics of Language in African Literature.* Heinemann, 1986.

"Noam Chomsky on Cambodia under Pol Pot, etc." www.zmag.org/forums/chomcambodforum.htm accessed Aug. 15, 2004.

Oberstar, Ciril. "Komunizem smrti [The Communism of Death]." *Dialogi* 43.11–12 (2007): 41–70.

[*OED*] *The Compact Oxford English Dictionary*, 2nd edn. Oxford: Clarendon P, 1991, 820-21.

Otto, Rudolf. *Das Heilige.* München: Beck, 1963 [original 1917; *The Idea of the Holy.* Transl. J.W. Harvey. Oxford UP, 1950].

Pannekoek, Anton. *Workers' Councils.* Transl. unknown. Oakland & Edinburgh: AK P, 2003.

Parker, Geoffrey. *The Military Revolution.* Cambridge UP, 1988.

Partridge, Eric. *A Short Etymological Dictionary of the English Language.* Macmillan, 1959.

Passerin d'Entrèves, Alessandro. *La dottrina dello stato.* Giappichelli, 1962.

Paternu, Boris ed. *Slovensko pesništvo upora 1941–1945. Prva knjiga: Partizanske [The Slovene Poetry of Resistance 1941-45. Book 1: Partizan Poetry].* Mladinska knjiga, 1987.

Pilger, John. *The New Rulers of the World.* London: Verso, 2003.

—. "Recalling Pol Pot's Terror, but Forgetting Its Backers." www.antiwar.com/orig/pilger/php, Jan. 31, 2004, accessed Aug. 15, 2004.

Plato. *Complete Works.* Ed. J.M. Cooper and D.S. Hutchison. Hackett, 1997.

[Polanyi, Karl]. *Primitive, Archaic, and Modern Economies: The Essays of Karl Polanyi.* Ed. G. Dalton. Doubleday Anchor, 1968.

Pona, Carlo, "Rischi legati all'impiego bellico dell'uranio impoverito," in Zucchetti ed., *Contro* [see below], 105-21.

Prout, Christopher. *Market Socialism in Yugoslavia.* Oxford UP, 1985.

Rancière, Jacques. "Interview with Edition Jugoslavija, Razgovori sa Žakom Ransijerom, Beograd april 2010 ('Entretiens avec Jacques Rancière')." Electronic attachment to e-mail sent to D. Suvin by lecture organiser and interviewer I. Momčilović, June 3, 2012.

—. «Transports de la liberté,» in idem ed., *La politique des poètes.* Michel, 1992, 87–130.

Rehmann, Jan. "'Abolition' of Civil Society?" *Socialism and Democracy* 13.2 (1999): 1-18.

Report from Iron Mountain on the Possibility and Desirability of Peace. Dell, 1967.

Ricoeur, Paul. *Interpretation Theory.* Texas Christian UP, 1976.

—. "The Metaphorical Process as Cognition, Imagination, and Feeling," in S. Sacks ed., *On Metaphor.* U of Chicago P, 1980, 141-57.

Rimbaud, Arthur. *Oeuvres complètes.* Ed. L. Forrestier. Laffont, 1992.

Robespierre, Maximilien. *Écrits.* Ed. C. Mazauric. Messidor/Éd. sociales. 1989.

Robin, Jacques. "Cette grande implosion de l'an 2002." *Le Monde diplomatique* (mars 2002): 26.

Rosen, Steven. "War Power and the Willingness to Suffer," in B.M. Russett ed., *Peace, War, and Numbers*. Sage, 1972, 167-84.

Rosière, Stéphane. *Le Nettoyage ethnique*. Ellipses, 2006.

Rousseau, J.-J. "Abstract and Judgement of Saint-Pierre's Project for Perpetual Peace" (1756), in S. Hoffmann and D.P. Fidler eds., *Rousseau on International Relations*. Clarendon P, 1991, 53-100.

Rummel, R.J. *Death by Government*. Transaction Books, 1994.

Rusinow, Dennison I. *The Yugoslav Experiment 1948–74*. U of California P, 1977.

"Of Russian Origin: The Ilyich Lamp." https://russiapedia.rt.com/of-russian-origin/the-ilyich-lamp/

Russo, Alessandro. "The Sixties and Us," in *The Idea of Communism 3*. Eds. A. T. Lee and S. Žižek. Verso, 2016, 137-78.

Sahlins, Marshall D. "The Original Affluent Society." 1972, www.eco-action.org/dt/affluent.html

—. "Political Power and the Economy in Primitive Society," in G. E. Dole and R. L. Carneiro eds., *Essays in the Science of Culture*. Crowell, 1960, 390-415.

—. *Stone Age Economics*. Routledge, 2004 [original 1974].

—. *Tribesmen*. Prentice-Hall, 1968.

Said, Edward. *The World, the Text, and the Critic*. Harvard UP, 1983.

Sakai, Naoki. "Civilizational Difference and Criticism: On the Complicity of Globalization and Cultural Nationalism." *Modern Chinese Literature and Culture* 17.1 (Spring 2005): 188-205.

—. *Translation and Subjectivity*. U of Minnesota P, 1997.

Samary, Catherine. *Le marché contre l'autogestion: l'expérience yougoslave*. Publisud/La Brèche, 1988.

Scarry, Elaine. *On Beauty and Being Just*. Princeton UP, 1999.

—. "Beauty and the Scholar's Duty to Justice," in P. Franklin ed., *Profession 2000*. MLA, 2000, 21-31.

Schininà, Guglielmo. *Comunità maledette: Rituali di separazione e comunicazione come vendetta. Il caso del Kosovo*. http://auth.unimondo.org/cfdocs/obportal/index.cfm?-fuseaction= news.view2 &News ID=1525 accessed July 19, 2013.

[Schneiderman, Rose.] https://en.wikipedia.org/wiki/Rose_Schneiderman

Schober, Rita. „Brechts Umschrift des Kommunistischen Manifests," in her *Vom Sinn oder Unsinn der Literaturwissenschaft*. Mitteldeutscher V, 1988, 126-80.

Schreiber, Wolfgang. „Die Kriege in der zweiten Hälfte des 20. Jahrhunderts und danach," in T. Rabehl and idem eds., *Das Kriegsgeschehen 2000*. Westdeutscher V, 2000, 11-46.

Schrenk, Martin, Cyrus Ardalan, and Nawal A. El Tatawy. *Yugoslavia: Self-Management Socialism and the Challenges of Development*. Johns Hopkins UP, 1979.

Serres, Michel. *La Naissance de la physique dans le texte de Lucrèce.* Minuit, 1977.

Slater, Robert O., and Michael Stohl eds. *Current Perspectives on International Terrorism.* Macmillan, 1988.

Sluka, Jeffrey A. "'For God and Ulster'," in Sluka ed. [below], 127-57.

— ed. *Death Squad: The Anthropology of State Terrorism.* U of Pennsylvania P, 2000.

Smith, Adam. *The Wealth of Nations.* Random House, 1937 [original 1776].

Smith, Dan. "Conflict and War," in S. George, *The Debt Boomerang.* Pluto P and TNI, 1992, 136-67.

Solomon, Norman. "Orwellian Logic 101," www.fair.org/media-beat/980827.html

Spivak, Gayatri Chakravorty. *In Other Worlds.* Routledge, 1988.

Stein, Ben [and Warren E. Buffett]. "In Class Warfare, Guess Which Class Is Winning." *New York Times* Nov. 26, 2006, www.nytimes.com/2006/11/26/business/yourmoney/26every.html

Steinberg, Mark D. *The Russian Revolution 1905-1921.* Oxford UP, 2017.

Stiglitz, Joseph E. "Foreword," in Karl Polanyi, *The Great Transformation.* Beacon P, 2006, vii–xvii.

Stockholm International Peace Research Institute. *SIPRI Yearbook 1998.* Oxford UP, 1998.

—. *SIPRI Yearbook 1999.* Oxford UP, 1999.

Stohl, Michael. "States, Terrorism, and State Terrorism," in idem and Robert O. Slater eds., *Current Perspectives on International Terrorism.* Macmillan, 1998.

Supek, Rudi. "Problems and Perspectives of Workers' Self-Management in Yugoslavia," in M. J. Broekmeyer ed., *Yugoslav Workers' Self-Management.* Reidel, 1970, 216–41.

—. "Some Contradictions and Insufficiencies of Yugoslav Self-Managing Socialism," in G. Petrović and M. Marković eds., *Praxis: Yugoslav Essays in the Philosophy and Methodology of the Social Sciences.* Reidel, 1979, 249–71.

Suret-Canale, Jean. "Le Origini del capitalismo," in *Libro nero del capitalismo.* Tropea, 1999, 17-38.

Suvin, Darko. "An Approach to Epistemology, Literature, and the Poet's Politics." *Annual Review of the Faculty of Philosophy, Univ. of Novi Sad* (2016): 421-40.

—. "The Blagoevgrad Theses." (circulating).

—. *To Brecht and Beyond.* Harvester P, and Barnes & Noble, 1984.

—. "Brecht and Subjectivity: Stance, Emotion as Sympathy," in his *Darko Suvin* [see below], 133-57.

—. "On Class Relationships in Yugoslavia 1945–74, with a Hypothesis about the Ruling Class." *Debatte* 20.1 (2012): 37–71 [now in *Splendour* below].

—. "Cognition, Freedom, *The Dispossessed* as a Classic (2007)," in his *Defined* [see below], 509–51.

—. "On Cognitive Emotions and Topological Imagination." *Versus* no. 6869 (1994): 165–201, www.focusing.org/apm_papers/suvin.html

—. "On the Concept and Role of the Communist Party: Prehistory and the Epoch of October Revolution," Part 2 of "From the Archeology of Marxism and Communism." *Debatte* 21.2–3 (2013): 279–311.

—. *Darko Suvin: A Life in Letters*. Ed. P.E. Wegner. [Vashon Island WA] Paradoxa, 2011.

—. "Death into Life: For a Poetics of Anti-Capitalist Alternative," in his *In Leviathan's Belly* [see below], 309-30.

—. *Defined by a Hollow: Essays on Utopia, Science Fiction, and Political Epistemology*. P. Lang, 2010.

—. "Ekonomsko-političke perspektive Borisa Kidriča" ["Economico-political Perspectives of Boris Kidrič"]. *Zarez* no. 308 (2011): 10–11.

—. "Emotion, Brecht, Empathy vs. Sympathy." *The Brecht Yearbook* 33 (2008): 53–67.

—. "Epistemological Meditations on Science, Poetry, and Politics." *Rab-Rab* [Helsinki] no. 2 Vol. B (2015): 39-53.

—. "To Explain Fascism Today." *Critique* 45.3 (2017): 259-302.

—. "Fifteen Theses about Communism and Yugoslavia…." *Critical Quarterly* 57. 2 (2015): 90-110.

—. „Haltung," entry in *Historisch-kritisches Wörterbuch des Marxismus*, Vol. 5. Argument, 2002, col. 1134-42.

—. *„Haltung* (Bearing) and Emotions: Brecht's Refunctioning of Conservative Metaphors for Agency," in T. Jung ed., *Zweifel Fragen Vorschläge*. P. Lang V, 1999, 4358.

—. "Heavenly Food Denied: *Life of Galileo,*" in P. Thomson and G. Sacks eds., *The Cambridge Companion to Brecht*. Cambridge UP, 1994, 139–52.

—."On the Horizons of Epistemology and Science." *Critical Quarterly* 52.1 (2010): 68-101, //onlinelibrary.wiley.com/doi/10.1111/j.1467-8705.2010.01924.x/full

—. "Inside the Whale, or *etsi communismus non daretur,*" in his *Defined* [see above],. P. Lang, 2010, 473-502.

—. *Lessons of Japan*. [Montréal] CIADEST, 1996.

—. *Lessons from the Russian Revolution and Its Fallout: An Epistemological Approach*. Rosa Luxemburg Foundation Southeast Europe, 2017, www.rosalux.rs/en/lessons-russian-revolution- and-its-fallout

—. *In Leviathan's Belly: Essays for a Counter-Revolutionary Time*. Wildside P for Borgo P, 2012.

—. "Living Labour and the Labour of Living" in his *Defined* [see above], 419-72.

—."Locus, Horizon, and Orientation: The Concept of Possible Worlds as a Key to Utopian Studies (1988)," in his *Defined* [see above], 111-36.

—. "From Mallarmé's Purification to Kong Fu-Tse's Rectification of Terms." *Contemporanea* no. 6 (2008): 125-33.

—. *Metamorphoses of Science Fiction*. Yale UP, 1979; 2nd **enlarged edn.** Ed. Gerry Canavan. **P. Lang, 2016.**

—. "On Metaphoricity and Narrativity in Fiction." *SubStance* no. 48 (1986): 51–67.

—. "Parables and Uses of a Stumbling Stone." *Arcadia* 5.2 (2017): 271-300.

—. „The Prescience of Lucio Magri.“ *Socialism and Democracy* 29.2 (2015): 91-98.

—., "Revelation vs. Conflict: A Lesson from Nô Plays for a Comparative Dramaturgy." *Theatre J.* 46.4 (1994): 52338.

—. "Salvation Now, for All Flesh!" in his *To Brecht* [see above], 131-65.

—. *Splendour, Misery, and Possibilities: An X-ray of Socialist Yugoslavia.* Foreword F. Jameson. Brill, 2016, and Haymarket P, 2017.

—. "Splendours and Miseries of the Communist Party of Yugoslavia (1945–74)." *Socialism and Democracy* 27.1 (2013): 161–89 [now in *Splendour* above].

—."Terms of Power, Today." *Critical Quarterly* 48.3 (2006): 38-62.

—."Transubstantiation of Production and Creation." *Minnesota Review* n.s. no 18 (Spring 1982): 102-15.

—. "Two Cheers for Essentialism & Totality: On Marx's Oscillation and its Limits (As Well As on the Taboos of PostModernism)." *Rethinking Marxism* 10.1 (1998): 6682.

—. "The UseValue of Dying: Magical vs. Cognitive Utopian Desire in the 'Learning Plays' of PseudoZenchiku, Waley, and Brecht." *Brock R* 3.2 (1994): 95126.

—. "Utopianism from Orientation to Agency...," in his *Defined* [see above], 217-67.

—. "Words and Lesions: Reflections on Violence." Keynote speech at the conference "Words and Violence." Leiden U, 20/8/2018 (forthcoming in *Critical Q* 2020).

—, with Marc Angenot. "Uses of Marx: The Implicit of the Manifested (Or, Demystification and Critique)." *Rab-Rab* [Helsinki] no. 3 (2016): 35-72 [first version 1989].

Tabb, William K. "Globalization is *an* Issue, the Power of Capital is *the* Issue." *Monthly Review* 49.2 (1977): 20-30.

Tamás, G. M. "Ethnicism after Nationalism: The Roots of the New European Right." *Socialist Register* (2016): 118-35.

Therborn, Göran. "After Dialectics." *New Left Review* no. 43 (Jan.–Feb. 2007): 63–115.

Thomas, Peter D. "The Communist Hypothesis and the Question of Organization." *Theory & Event* 16.4 (Jan. 2013): 1-17.

—. *The Gramscian Moment.* Brill, 2010.

Thompson, A.C. "War without End." *The Nation* Dec. 12, 2001, www.thenation.com/

Tigar, Michael E. "Terrorism and Human Rights." *Monthly Review* (Sept. 2001).

Timpanaro, Sebastiano. *Sul materialismo.* Nistri-Lischi, 1975.

Tirman, John ed. *The Militarization of High Technology.* Ballinger, 1984.

Toffler, Alvin and Heidi Toffler. *War and Anti-War.* Little, Brown, 1993.

Toscano, Alberto. "The Politics of Abstraction: Communism and Philosophy," in C. Douzinas and S. Žižek eds. [see above], 195-204.

Tronti, Mario. *Noi operaisti.* DeriveApprodi, 2009.

Trotsky, Leon. *The History of the Russian Revolution.* Transl. M. Eastman. Pluto P, 1965 [original 1932].

—. *Terrorism and Communism.* Greenwood P, 1986 [original 1920; cited from *Terrorismo e comunismo.* Sugar, 1977].

Türcke, Christoph. *Erregte Gesellschaft*. Beck, 2002.

Tyson, Laura D'Andrea. *The Yugoslav Economic System and Its Performance in the 1970s*. U of California P, 1981.

Ure, Michael, and Mervyn Frost eds. *The Politics of Compassion*. Routledge, 2014.

Vico, Giambattista. *The New Science....* Transl. T.G. Bergin and M.H. Frisc. Cornell UP, 1988.

Virilio, Paul. *Speed and Politics*. Transl. M. Polizzotti. Semiotext(e), 1977.

— and Sylvère Lotringer. *Pure War*. Transl. M. Polizzotti. Semiotext(e), 1983.

Wachtel, Howard. *Workers' Management and Workers' Wages in Yugoslavia*. Cornell UP, 1973.

Walzer, Michael. *Just and Unjust Wars*. Basic Books, 2000.

Watts, Michael. "Black Acts." *New Left Review* no. 9 (2001): 125-39.

Weber, Max. *Economy and Society*, 2 Vols. Ed. G. Roth and C. Wittich. U of California P, 1978.

—. *From Max Weber: Essays in Sociology*. Ed. and transl. H.H. Gerth and C.W. Mills. Oxford UP, 1958.

Weisberg, Barry. *Beyond Repair*. Beacon P, 1971.

Went, Robert. *Globalization*. Transl. P. Drucker. Pluto P & IIRE, 2000.

White, Hayden. "At the Limits of the Concept." *PMLA* 131 (2016): 410-14.

Wiebes, Cees. *Intelligence and the War in Bosnia, 1992-95*. Lit, 2003.

Williams, Raymond. *Keywords*, **rev.** edn. Oxford UP, 1983.

—. *Marxism and Literature*. Oxford UP, 1977.

—. *Modern Tragedy*. Verso, 1979.

Wittgenstein, Ludwig. *Philosophical Investigations* [bilingual edn.]. Transl. G.E.M. Anscombe et al. Blackwell, 2001.

Wizisla, Erdmut, ed. „*...und mein Werk ist der Abgesang des Jahrtausends.*" Catalog of the exhibition *1898 -- Bertolt Brecht -- 1998*. Akademie der Künste, 1998.

Wood, Ellen Meiksins. *Democracy against Capitalism*. Cambridge UP, 1995.

Woodward, Susan. *Balkan Tragedy*. Brookings Institution, 1995.

—. *Socialist Unemployment: The Political Economy of Yugoslavia 1945–90*. Princeton UP, 1995.

Woolf, Virginia. *The Second Common Reader*. Pelican, 1944.

Wordsworth, William. *The Prelude* (1850). https://en.wikisource.org/wiki/The_Prelude_(Wordsworth)/Book_I

W[ormell], D.E.W. "Lucretius," in *The Penguin Companion to Classical... Literature*. Eds. D.M. Lang and D.R. Dudley. McGraw-Hill, 1969, 109-10.

Yugoslavia's Way: The Program of the League of Communists of Yugoslavia. Transl. S. Pribichevich. All Nations P, 1958.

Žižek, Slavoj. "The Communist Hypothesis," in his *First as Tragedy, Then as Farce*. Verso, 2009, 86-151.

—. "How to Begin from the Beginning," in C. Douzinas and idem eds. [see above], 209-26.

Zolberg, Aristide R., Astri Suhrke, and Sergio Aguayo. *Escape from Violence: Conflict and the Refugee Crisis in the Developing World.* Oxford UP, 1989.

Zolo, Danilo. *La teoria comunista dell'estinzione dello stato.* De Donato, 1974.

Zucchetti, Massimo *Guerra infinita guerra ecologica.* Jaca Book, 2003.

— ed. *Contro le nuove guerre.* Odradek, 2000.